Coming of Age

Coming of Age

*The Life and Times of Chelmsford
Cathedral 1914-2014*

Tony Tuckwell

To order additional copies of this book, contact:
Xlibris Corporation
0-800-644-6988
www.xlibrispublishing.co.uk
Orders@xlibrispublishing.co.uk
305530

CONTENTS

By the same author:

"Managing Teaching and Learning" in *School Leadership for the 21st century; a competency and knowledge approach*: Routledge (London and New York) 1997

"Teacher participation in decision-making" in *Living Headship: Voices, Values, Vision*: Paul Chapman: 1999

"That honourable and gentlemanlike house"; the history of King Edward VI Grammar School, Chelmsford 1551-2001, first edition, The Printing Place, 2001; second edition, Free Range Publications, 2008

New Hall and its School; "a true school of virtuous demeanour"; Free Range Publications, 2006

FOREWORD

I am so glad I asked Tony Tuckwell to write the book about the Centenary of the Cathedral in 2014. I knew it would be a good book, and that Tony would have done his research. I also knew that he would put it together well and that it would be a good read. In fact what has happened is that Tony has surpassed himself. He has left no stone unturned, researching at the Essex Records Office, *Hansard*, newspapers local and national. He has combed through church records, and interviewed numerous people. Despite all this information Tony never loses the plot; he always sees the bigger picture, and he has a journalist's eye for a good story and a roguish character. If someone were to say to me; "To be honest I'm not interested in a book about a cathedral" I could honestly reply; "you will find this riveting, because although it is the story of a cathedral, it is also a story about our time and our recent history; it is a story about politics and social attitudes; it is a story about the politicians and public figures who profoundly influenced these decades." In short it is a brilliant read and you will be fascinated by it. I am so grateful to Tony for this wonderful book.

Peter Judd
Dean of Chelmsford Cathedral

ACKNOWLEDGEMENTS

Back in 2009 the Dean, Peter Judd, asked me if I would be interested in writing a history of Chelmsford Cathedral ready for its centenary in 2014. Having already written the histories of King Edward VI Grammar School and New Hall, which seem to have been well-received, I was delighted to have the opportunity to tell the story of Chelmsford's third ancient institution. It has been a fascinating journey which I have enjoyed hugely.

I owe thanks to a number of people. Ann Cowper-Coles, the Cathedral Archivist, helped me find my way round the sources; Ralph Meloy gathered together cardboard boxes of diocesan publications from the depths of the Diocesan Offices; Mervyn Marshall made available some of his compendious collection of pictures of the Cathedral and its life; David Lloyd digitalised them and also computerised the index to the cathedral archive so that searching became a little less random; Amanda Wright in the Cathedral Office helped with the provision of the cover picture and special software to transmit photographic images to our online publisher; Ann Lloyd's many interesting historical vignettes in *Cathedral News* pointed me down productive alleyways; Rex Broad, historian of St. John the Evangelist Church, Moulsham, shared his sources, swapped books and introduced me to the invaluable online British Newspaper Archive; Christopher Barlow read early drafts and pointed out infelicities and inconsistencies in his own tactful way; and the vergers patiently tolerated my frequent requests for the key to the Knightbridge Library often when they were in the midst of some other urgent task.

Special thanks are due to those who spared time to meet me and respond to my questions. John Brown and I were university contemporaries but we more or less avoided nostalgia and managed to stick to the subject in hand; Nick Alston's association with the Cathedral as boy and man enabled us both to take the long view; Geoffrey Ireland was immensely helpful on buildings and personnel issues; and Dennis and Eileen Hance shared sharp memories of Luftwaffe raids and cathedral micropolitics.

Musicians are always good talkers. The sessions with Peter Cross, David Sparrow, Peter Nardone and the late John Jordan were not without their laughs and occasional indiscretions which I enjoyed but have not used. I am grateful to the late Sir Philip Ledger for responding to my email requests for information and to Graham Elliott who treated me to lunch in London in between his time in Scotland and the United States and was exceptionally helpful in subsequent email exchanges. Martyn Vann was also kind enough to provide me with information on his father's time on the cathedral organ stool.

I met up with Bishop John Perry in London and Bishop John Waine kindly invited me up to Suffolk. Both of them had been first-class school Prize-Giving speakers in my previous professional existence and were willing to let me pump them with questions. The conversations were so enjoyable it seemed a shame to bring them to an end.

The 1980s proved to be complex times at the Cathedral. I am grateful to Natalie and Wesley Carr for their hospitality in Romsey and for discussing issues surrounding the Centre for Research and Training; to Michael Yorke for inviting me up to Norfolk so that I could get his take on events during his years in Chelmsford; to Susan and John Moses for their hospitality and to John in particular for providing access to some private papers, helping correct errors of fact or omission in the text concerning his years at the Cathedral (although all the judgements remain mine) and giving me a delightful tour of Southwell Minster; to Barry Thompson for helping me understand the experiment with the Centre for Theology at the University of Essex; and to Judy and Martin Connop Price for their hospitality in Ross-on-Wye where Martin, the son of former provost, Hilary Connop Price, kindly gave me access to some of his father's private papers, while my wife Kathleen and Judy, who were at school together in Manchester, relived old times.

And here, I must return to current and recent Cathedral staff. Andrew Knowles and Simon Pothen helped me understand the functions of Canon Theologian and Canon Precentor and the delicate dual function that parish church cathedrals perform. But above all I am indebted to the Dean, Peter Judd. He has been constantly supportive, enthusiastic about the various drafts as they have come into his hands and willing to give me editorial control over what I write. Not least, he has shared his insights on the Cathedral which have been invaluable.

Loving thanks go to my wife, Kathleen, who has read the final draft and pointed out where explanation or syntax need to be clearer; she has been ever encouraging, tolerant of piles of books and papers and the hours spent glued to my laptop. I also fondly remember my parents whose church youth work back in my Wiltshire days inspired me to teach. Belated thanks go to the many family churchwardens, notably my father (who loved to challenge bishops of Bristol at Diocesan Conferences), father-in-law, uncles, brother, sister-in-law and various cousins. Their conversations, always interesting, immersed me in church politics. Like them, I enjoy lifting the lids off organisations to see how they work or, indeed, to wonder how they work at all.

At this point I should apologise to those with whom I did not speak who may have had some valuable insight to add. The omission was never intended to be personal. Partly time was the dictator; partly I could not think of any more pressing questions to ask.

Finally I must pay tribute to the unjustly maligned County of Essex with whose villages, market towns and mysterious coastline I became enamoured many years ago. A retirement enthusiasm for walking has led me along the full winding length of Essex's coast and its great estuaries, down the Lea Valley on the western border of the County and along the Essex Way which cuts diagonally across it. So, while researching the origins of Essex's cathedral I seem to have beaten most of its diocese's bounds and developed an empathy with the bishops and clergy who ploughed a lonely furrow before the luxury of modern transport.

I have been sparing in using formal terms of address. The Church can be as confusing to the layman as the armed services as it ranges from Reverend to His Grace, passing through all ranks in between. For simplicity I have confined myself just to the title e.g. bishop but without the Rt. Rev.. It seems to fit the spirit of the age and will save a page or two.

In the introduction to his book, *English Cathedrals*, the historian, Professor Stanford Lehmberg, complained that cathedral histories were largely of two sorts. One consisted of glossy photographs with bland text. The other confined itself to the special interests of its local community without relating its experience to that of cathedrals elsewhere. I would add a third, histories written by clergy who know which cupboards contain skeletons but still keep the doors locked.

I hope I have avoided all three pitfalls.

From *The Mystery of Edwin Drood* by Charles Dickens

"You may offer bad grammar to the laity, or to the humbler clergy, not to the Dean."

"You are evidently to write a book about us . . . Well! We are very ancient and we ought to make a good book. We are not so richly endowed with possessions as in age; but perhaps you will put *that* in your book, among other things, and call attention to our wrongs."

CHAPTER 1

The Parish Church

By the start of the 20th century St. Mary's Parish Church had been guarding the northern end of Chelmsford's High Street for nigh on 800 years. The earliest recorded rector, Richard de Gorges in 1242, led worship in a simple Early English structure of aisled nave, chancel and west tower. It was rebuilt in the 15th century on its existing foundations[1] in the fashionable perpendicular style with a more imposing tower, a higher nave and clerestory, battlemented parapets and magnificent south porch and could accommodate 2,000 people standing.[2] It was a long drawn out project. Work started at some time after 1406 but it was not until 1489 that nave and clerestory were finished. The tower was completed in the early 1500s.[3] The de Vere five-pointed star and chained blue boar and the Bourchier reef knot on the west front indicate that these Essex grandees financed it.

According to the Domesday Book, the de Vere estates in East Anglia, half of them in north Essex, included a large family estate at Great Bentley near Colchester and the motte and bailey castle at Hedingham. It is reasonable to assume that they were a reward for military service to William the Conqueror in 1066. De Veres fought in the first of their many crusades from 1096-99 when a five-pointed star allegedly illuminated their standard as a presage of victory and was subsequently incorporated in their coat of arms.[3] Their support for the Empress Matilda, daughter of Henry I, against her cousin Stephen of Blois during a protracted struggle for the crown earned Aubrey de Vere the Earldom of Oxford in 1141. Subsequent earls helped extract the concessions of *Magna Carta* from King John in 1215, supported Simon de Montfort's baronial rebellion against Henry III's foreign favourites in 1265 and participated in Edward I's subjection of Wales in the 1280s. As a reward they held high office as royal justices and hereditary master chamberlains of England but remained distant from court politics. They probably could not afford it as a series of modest marriages meant that the growth of their estates had been slow until John, the 7th Earl, married a wealthy heiress and accumulated spoils of war in France in the service of Edward III, notably at the extraordinary victories of Crécy in 1346 and Poitiers in 1356.[4] Even then a succession of long-lived dowager countesses, who retained a third of their late husbands' estates, imposed financial restraints on the ambitions of late 14th and early 15th century earls.[5]

The Bourchiers were relative latecomers but made a meteoric rise. Robert Bourchier's military service alongside the 7th Earl of Oxford earned him appointment as the first lay Chancellor of England in 1340 supported by a peerage and a large estate at Halstead in north Essex to add to the family seat at Little Easton. He went on to command a substantial force at Crécy before succumbing to the Black Death. His grandson, William, acquired additional Essex manors stretching from Maldon eastwards through the Dengie Peninsula where there was a Bourchier's Hall at Tollesbury to match the one at Halstead and two others at Messing, near Tiptree, and Moreton, near Ongar, where he had smaller manorial holdings. He also had a territorial interest in Chelmsford owning the Patching Hall manor to the west of the town to which his son would add the contiguous manors of Widford and Woodhall.[6]

In his youth William Bourchier may well have been at Pleshey Castle in the household of Edward III's youngest son, Thomas Woodstock, Duke of Gloucester, who led the Lords Appellant in opposition to the vicious autocratic rule of his nephew, Richard II. In 1387 they forced Richard's overweening favourite, Robert de Vere, 9th Earl of Oxford, to flee abroad after the Battle of Radcot Bridge and sentenced him to death in his absence. Ten years later Gloucester himself was dragged out of bed at Pleshey by Richard II with his men-at-arms and subsequently murdered in prison.[7] After Richard's deposition by his cousin, Henry of Lancaster, who had himself crowned Henry IV, de Vere royal connections were restored when Richard de Vere, the 11th Earl, married Alice Holland, the new king's niece. William Bourchier kept pace, marrying Gloucester's daughter, Anne Plantagenet, whose huge wealth catapulted the Bourchier family into the big league.

The de Veres might have resented the Bourchiers' rise—their family seats at Hedingham and Halstead were only five miles apart—but admirably cooperated with them so that Essex remained a well-ordered and peaceful county.[8] The commencement of the church building project at St. Mary's around 1406 symbolised this partnership and, with Alice (who had died a few years earlier) and Anne claiming direct descent from Edward III, may well have been intended to celebrate the eminent status of both families in this world as much as to ensure their speedy passage through purgatory in the next.

Under Henry V both the 11th Earl of Oxford and William Bourchier fought at Agincourt in 1415. William was rewarded with the confiscated French title of Count of Eu. His son, Henry, cemented the family's power base by marrying Isabel of Cambridge, yet another direct descendant of Edward III, and, after his father's death, was elevated to an English viscountcy by Henry VI as a reward for his continuing military service.[9] William's brother, Thomas Bourchier, also rose rapidly in the Church through the bishoprics of Worcester and Ely to the Archbishopric of Canterbury and, like his great-grandfather before him, the Chancellorship of England. He was to navigate his way through the political storms, completing 32 years as Primate of All England (only two Saxon archbishops have ever served longer), in the process anointing and crowning three usurpers: Edward IV, Richard III and Henry VII.

The dynastic armed conflict that erupted in 1455 as Henry VI's mental health collapsed, and lasted until 1485, saw two kings murdered and a third slain in battle. The great landed magnates were forced to make a choice in this War of the Roses. The de Veres and Bourchiers took different sides. Inevitably, therefore, work on St. Mary's Church appears to have ground to a halt.

Henry Bourchier fought for the Yorkist cause in 1461 at the battles at St. Albans and Towton that unseated Henry VI. He was rewarded by the triumphant Edward IV with the post of Lord High Treasurer and the title of 1st Earl of Essex (a re-creation of one of his posthumous father-in-law's titles that had gone into abeyance after his murder).

By contrast, John de Vere, the 12th Earl of Oxford, had desperately tried to stay neutral in the clash between Lancaster and York and distanced himself from the growing tensions by only spasmodically attending court.[10] Bearing in mind the fate of Robert, the 9th Earl, in 1387, he may have decided that involvement in the cut-throat rivalries of court politics was not worth the risk to life and land. Events vindicated his initial judgement. Having delayed his involvement until late 1461, after the crucial battles of that year, he and his eldest son, Aubrey, the more enthusiastic Lancastrian of the two,[11] were, within a few months, arrested at Hedingham and executed at the Tower in 1462 for allegedly scheming with Henry VI's queen, Margaret of Anjou, to overthrow and kill Edward IV. Nonetheless, Edward was conscious of the de Veres' power base in East Anglia which had been vastly augmented by the 12th Earl's marriage to a daughter of the Mowbrays who were Dukes of Norfolk.[12] He therefore sought to buy off John, the 13th Earl, by allowing him to retain his lands and marrying him off to the equally land-rich Margaret Neville, sister of Richard, the Earl of Warwick, whose desertion of Henry VI for Edward had tipped the military balance and earned him the title of "the Kingmaker." At much the same time Viscount William Bourchier, eldest son of the 1st Earl of Essex, married the 13th Earl of Oxford's sister, Isabel, probably encouraged by the King as yet another peace-making move. However Isabel died within a couple of years.

Old fractures quickly reappeared. In 1464 Edward IV married a commoner, Elizabeth Woodville. Favours bestowed on her family angered many aristocratic grandees, not least the earls of Warwick and Oxford. The new queen's sister, Anne, had, at much the same time and with almost undue haste, become William Bourchier's second wife as the King probably wanted to secure an ally in the eastern counties, a sign, perhaps, that he had begun to doubt the de Veres' continuing support. De Vere and Warwick bided their time but in 1470 marched to London to rescue Henry VI from the Tower and restore him to the throne. However, Warwick was killed at the Battle of Barnet as was one of his Yorkist opponents, Humphrey Bourchier, a second son of the 1st Earl of Essex: the previous year, Edward, a third son, had been killed at the Battle of Wakefield. Henry VI was re-imprisoned and soon died, probably murdered. De Vere fled to France, returned in 1473 to attempt a landing at St. Osyth in Essex but rapidly re-embarked when he heard that the 1st Earl of Essex's men were closing in on him. He moved west to take St. Michael's Mount in Cornwall where he surrendered to Edward IV after a long siege and was imprisoned at Calais for 12 years.

It took the excesses of Richard III to reconcile the two families. John de Vere, the 13th Earl of Oxford, escaped from Calais to command the archers for Henry Tudor at the Battle of Bosworth Field in 1485. Henry Bourchier, 2nd Earl of Essex (his father Viscount William Bourchier had died in 1480 and his grandfather, the 1st Earl in 1483), was another enthusiastic Tudor supporter. With peace restored, work on St. Mary's was immediately resumed and brought to a satisfactory conclusion.

Other major families with local estates, yet their main power bases elsewhere, had their arms adorning the east window or the bosses on the nave roof. So one may have glimpsed the escutcheons of the Nevilles who owned the manors of Sandon and Hanningfield; the Beauchamps into whose hands those same manors passed through marriage; the Mowbrays who, when the St.

Mary's project began, owned manors in Romford, Prittlewell and Rochford, which, by the time it finished, had passed by marriage to the Howards as also, soon after, their dukedom of Norfolk. Maybe even the Mounteneys of Mountnessing (from whose chantry chapel in St. Mary's churchyard Chelmsford's grammar school sprang) and the Warners of Great Waltham[13] might have been represented, although they were comparatively minor gentry and would not normally have been talked about in the same breath.

There were no further major developments to St. Mary's until 1800 when a second rebuilding was required after workmen digging to open a vault undermined the piers of the south arcade bringing the roof, south aisle and part of the north aisle crashing down. John Johnson, County Surveyor for Essex, carried out the restoration. The neighbouring Shire Hall, which he had built ten years earlier, housed services until St. Mary's re-opened in 1803. The Act for Repairing Chelmsford Parish Church permitted £5,000 (about £300,000 in today's money) to be borrowed to restore the building and its organ and provide a salary for the organist.[14] The opportunity was taken to enhance as well as repair. Having made good the west gallery, which was erected in 1772 to house the new organ (the earliest record of an organ in St. Mary's is in 1558),[15] north and south galleries were added in 1812 and 1818 respectively.[16]

1800 collapse looking west from the front row of box pews to the tower and organ: Chelmsford Cathedral Knightbridge Library

The advowson of St. Mary's with the right to appoint the rector had been seized at the Reformation by Henry VIII from the bishops of London who had held it since the first church was built. In 1563 Elizabeth I sold the manor of Bishop's Hall together with St. Mary's advowson to local man Thomas Mildmay,[17] the family name aptly deriving from Mild Mary to whom Chelmsford's church was dedicated.[18] Thomas had been a major figure in the Tudor civil service since his appointment by Henry VIII in 1536 as an auditor of the Court of Augmentations which drew up an inventory of the confiscated monastic lands and administered their transfer to the Crown. Thomas the Auditor, as he was known, enjoyed his new status as manorial lord for only three years, dying in 1566: his multi-coloured tomb depicting his wife and fifteen children still adorns the entrance to the North or Mildmay Chapel.

The advowson stayed with the Mildmay family for over 300 years save for a 30 year interruption from 1644 when Parliament installed its own nominee to replace the royalist Rector, John Michaelson.[19] Although Charles II restored Michaelson in 1660 the Mildmays would have been livid as the family had never forgiven him for securing the benefice in the first place in 1617 by appealing over their heads to James I when they had left it vacant for a year.[20] On Michaelson's death in 1674 Charles II returned the advowson to the Mildmays who enjoyed two more centuries of patronage until they surrendered it in 1878 to Thomas Claughton, Bishop of St. Albans, on the death of Archdeacon Mildmay. He was the only rector to bear the family name and had served St. Mary's for 52 years. An ageing incumbent would have been increasingly dependent on his curates. In his last four years one of them was Frederick Binyon whose son, Lawrence, a pupil at Chelmsford's grammar school,[21] was later to achieve immortality for his poem, *For the Fallen*.

Unusually there were three churchwardens. Until the Reformation the bishops of London held the manor of Chelmsford and the abbots of Westminster the manor of Moulsham, a hamlet to the south of the town on the far bank of the River Can. The manors were linked from about 1100 by a bridge which was probably financed by Bishop Maurice. Bishop and abbot had each appointed a churchwarden to represent their interests in addition to the warden nominated by the Rector.

Like many a small market town Chelmsford was unremarkable. On a brief visit in 1835 Charles Dickens described it as "the dullest and most stupid spot on the face of the earth."[22]

But that opinion was not shared by the local burghers who had a high opinion of their town and, in some cases, of themselves.

CHAPTER 2

The Pew Rent War

The long incumbency of Rector Carew Anthony St. John Mildmay (1826-78) saw a sequence of improvements that modernised and beautified St. Mary's. Interestingly, most of them came after 1858 when he divested himself of the additional livings he enjoyed at Shorwell, on the Isle of Wight, and Burnham-on-Crouch. A mocking exposé in *Punch* on September 19th 1857 had revealed that the three livings, all in the gift of the Mildmay family—so nepotism as well as pluralism was the charge—provided him with an aggregate annual income of £1,900 (£140,000 in today's money) which was particularly handsome even allowing for the expense of paying curates. That he immediately dropped the two surplus parishes paved the way for his bishop to appoint him Archdeacon of Essex in 1862 with pastoral responsibility for parishes in the southern half of the county.

Archdeacon Carew Anthony St. John Mildmay:
Chelmsford Cathedral Knightbridge Library

21

The first improvements to St. Mary's came in 1842 when the bulky Georgian box pews began to be replaced by open oak benches thereby ensuring a clear view of the chancel and the communion table: their sheer height had also precluded sidesmen of shorter stature from peering over the sides to ascertain whether there were empty seats and, according to the Rector, had encouraged graffiti and immoral behaviour,[1] the latter, presumably, visible only from the pulpit. In 1858 the stone mouldings of the east window were altered to a three-light perpendicular style consonant with the rest of the building and decorated with Clayton and Bell stained glass, an early example from this workshop whose prolific output was soon to fill Victorian churches; the window was a memorial to the Rector's mother, Lady Jane Mildmay, and replaced the 1825 evangelists' window that itself had superseded the plain glass installed after the Puritan iconoclasm of the 1640s. Clayton and Bell windows were also installed at the eastern end of the north and south aisles,[2] one of them a memorial to the son of local solicitor, Thomas Gepp, who had been killed in action during the conflict that followed the Indian Mutiny.[3] In 1867 the west gallery was demolished and the organ was relocated to the downstairs south-west corner thereby opening up the internal view of the west window.[4] In 1869 a marble font was donated by the Archdeacon's daughter, Evelyn, superseding one in terracotta[5] that had replaced the medieval original crushed in 1800.

The pace really picked up in 1873, no doubt spurred on by the improvements at Coggeshall, High Easter, Great Dunmow and Ulting which were leaving the county town's Parish Church in their wake. The north and south galleries were taken down and a northward extension built, comprising a transept and additional outer aisle which partly compensated for the lost gallery seats and was designed to accommodate the organ; the outer north wall was faced in stone rather than brick so that it matched the south frontage[6]; the south aisle was restored and its walls decorated with biblical scenes and arts and crafts foliage that were to horrify later mid-20th century taste; and the final oak benches were installed to complete the process started in 1842.[7] All of this cost £1,800 (£840,000 in today's money) which was raised by public subscription. At the same time a marble pulpit, the panels depicting the life of Rachel, was donated by R.W. Hanbury, Conservative M.P. for Tamworth, in memory of his late wife, the daughter of Thomas Gepp who was by now the Rector's Warden.[8] In 1875 the organ was uprooted for the second time in eight years to the opposite corner of the church in its bespoke space under the new north transept arch: it was powered by larger hand bellows, encased in a new wooden frame and the arrangement of the organ pipes, with the largest at either end diminishing to the smallest in the centre, ensured a clear view of the window behind;[9] soon after the marble font was relocated from its position at the west end of the church to the space vacated by the organ in the south-west corner. In 1878 the chancel roof was raised and new clerestory windows added which significantly improved the source of natural light and the east window was enlarged to five lights, a gift from Archdeacon Mildmay and his daughters[10] in memory of the Archdeacon's wife though, with the chancel closed for a year, the restrictions placed on Christmas decorations provoked criticism.[11]

The Archdeacon generally trod carefully at each step, assiduously consulting his churchwardens about congregational feelings. Any departure from Puritan whitewash and plain furnishing might be construed as a shift towards popish practice and raise parochial hackles. Charles Stuart, the Catholic French-sponsored Jacobite Pretender, may have been routed at Culloden in 1746 and the proven loyalty of England's old aristocratic Catholic families, who wanted nothing to do with such extremism, may have led to the repeal of the anti-Catholic penal laws in 1778 and 1791, but Victorian suspicion of Rome still remained deeply ingrained. For many, membership of the established Anglican Church was as much a statement of national identity as a declaration of belief.

Anti-Catholicism erupted again in 1850. Catholic numbers in England, swollen by Irish immigrants, many with separatist Republican sympathies, encouraged Pope Pius IX to restore the full panoply of English Catholic bishops while reasserting the illegitimacy of their Anglican counterparts. The triumphant creation of a Catholic Archdiocese of Westminster—the very seat of Parliament and coronations—was considered so provocative that in 1851 Parliament barred Catholic dioceses from using English place-names. This had the forceful backing of the then Archdeacon of Essex, Hugh Jones, who, in an address to his clergy, laid into the Roman Catholic Church, describing it as "one great and mighty confederacy devoted and directed by the most conservative artifice and subtlety to enslave man and obtain worldly power."[12] His bishop, George Murray of Rochester, into whose diocese Essex had recently been delivered, called more temperately for the Catholics "to recede from the pretensions and titles they have recently assumed."[13] They did not, but their new dioceses wisely eschewed city names already attached to Anglican dioceses. The civility was not reciprocated when Catholics got in first with naming rights, hence the later duplication of diocesan titles in Birmingham, Liverpool and Portsmouth. But this parliamentary and ecclesiastical bluster proved to be embarrassingly over the top. No one could be bothered to take Catholic infringements of such a pointless law to court and the act was repealed in 1871.

In 1879 those who perused St. Mary's first *Parish Magazine* would still have regarded the Roman Church as an alien enemy of liberty and free thought but far from obtaining worldly power, as Archdeacon Jones had feared, the papacy had, in 1870, been reduced to the few acres of the Vatican as a result of Italy's unification under a liberal constitutional monarchy. The Victorian Church and state could therefore stop looking over its shoulder and seek out new challenges. In the century since Bonnie Prince Charlie had died and the papacy had withdrawn its support from the Catholic Stuarts, Britain had industrialised, expanded its Empire to cover a quarter of the globe and come to dominate the world stage. Confident in her God-given strength (for surely it must be a sign of divine grace) colonial administrators and missionaries were despatched to take the English Protestant version of Christian civilisation to the indigenous peoples in the outposts of Empire. At home a parallel domestic mission in the squalid industrial slums sought to rescue the godless destitute from ignorance and immorality which were seen as a threat to social order and an offence to God, probably in that order of importance. As the *Parish Magazine* of June 1887 warned:

> "It is a dangerous and even fearful thing to gather great multitudes together in these days of agitation and discontent without providing for them that steadying and hope-giving power which true religion alone can give."

The gentry, newspaper editors, bankers, architects, solicitors and businessmen of St. Mary's congregation, each with their privately rented pew, who also dominated the governance of local charities and societies, were prepared to support missions to working-class areas into which they themselves were unlikely to wander but wanted the lower orders to know their place, especially in Chelmsford. Archdeacon Mildmay seemed to confirm this comfortable conservatism when, at the parish celebrations of his golden jubilee as incumbent, he mused:

> "We have gone on you and I, your fathers, your grandfathers and your grandmothers, pretty well holding the same opinions and following the same ways of conduct as we did in 1826."[14]

In January 1878 the Archdeacon's wife, Caroline, died from burns after falling on an open fire;[15] he never recovered from the shock and followed her to the grave six months later. Ill-health then cut short the incumbency of his successor, Sir John Caesar Hawkins.

In 1880 Frank Johnson, Vicar of High Wych near Sawbridgeworth in Hertfordshire, was installed as Rector. St. Mary's congregation was about to feel the wind of change for Frank Johnson was in sympathy with the more inclusive thinking that was influencing the bishops' bench. The old Victorian view of poverty as a natural state ordained by God, to be borne nobly by those who endured it—"the rich man in his castle, the poor man at the gate"—may have been that of John Sumner, Archbishop of Canterbury, who died in 1862[16] but not his successor, Archibald Tait, who, as Bishop of London, had taken the gospel to the street corners and markets and set up afternoon services in church where the shabby poor could attend without offending their social superiors.[17] Frank Johnson was in tune with him and those Christian social thinkers who advocated much greater emphasis on the gospel-orientated ideals of brotherhood and service in a quest to moderate the social consequences of wealth-creation.[18] They were to organise themselves into the Christian Social Union in 1889. Their inspiration, Brook Westcott, later Bishop of Durham, wrote: "we need, in fact, far more to reform the unwritten rules of social intercourse than to alter the statute book."[19] Frank Johnson concurred: pew rents were his target.

The *Essex Chronicle* of October 29th 1880 hinted at the difficulties that were to come: "his parishioners are a quiet folk who dislike changes." That was not quite true: it was just the wealthier ones who would be the problem. The Bishop wanted the Rector to evangelise the poor, who had not had much of a look in at their parish church, but hoped that this could be achieved "without disturbing the equanimity and settled habits of the older parishioners."[20] Some hopes!

In the May 1881 *Parish Magazine* the new Rector called for an end to pew rents whereby, for an annual payment, the wealthy appropriated pews for exclusive family use. Although in 1851 45.6% of Anglican churches operated this system[21] by the 1880s only 15.6% retained the practice[22] which provided a guaranteed source of income but left limited free seats for the poor, usually at the back, so that the actual seating arrangements reflected the social pecking order.

Frank Johnson asked the churchwardens who organised the pews to leave a greater proportion of seats free; they prevaricated. They had been used to a much more deferential approach from Archdeacon Mildmay who would have asked their opinion first and then probably followed it, as, on one of his archidiaconal visitations, he had advised his clergy they should do with their own churchwardens.[23] On March 27th 1882, Thomas Gepp, the Rector's Warden, wrote a letter of protest to the Rector. Describing himself as "an old man habituated to a certain groove" he dug his heels in: "the churchwardens are to seat the parishioners with some regard to their station."[24] As far as he was concerned seats were appropriated for life and could only be reallocated if a family ceased to attend or became so reduced in numbers that they could be merged on a pew elsewhere with another depleted tribe. His practice was to keep "strangers" at bay outside the church until five minutes after the service began, only then admitting them to fill unclaimed spaces. As Matins was not as well-attended as early morning Holy Communion or Evensong he suggested that Frank Johnson make it more attractive, "so as to bring to it those who have no seat."

The Rector targeted Lenten Evensong instead. In the December 1882 *Parish Magazine* he wrote an open letter:

> "More direct efforts to evangelise the masses ought to be made.
> Is it too much to ask of the seat-holders that on Sunday evenings
> during Lent they should give up their claim to a particular place
> in the church and allow every seat to be declared free to all alike
> on those occasions?"

His congregation may have been prepared to make some nominal sacrifice for Lent—maybe a cigar or that extra glass of port—but never their seats. They ignored him and further imprecations failed so eventually he sought a wider view at a public meeting held on June 4th 1884. This was the established parish church; it did not belong to a sect; all had the right of access. Frank Johnson wanted to hear parish, not just congregational, opinion. He stated his case:

> "It is not surprising that those families who have occupied the
> same seats for years should be unwilling to be displaced . . . but
> the poor are very ill provided for and whole families are lost to the
> Church partly because they cannot get convenient seats, partly
> because they have been treated rudely by some seat holders . . .
> The law is clear, that every parishioner has an equal right to a
> place in the parish church . . . One great argument used in favour
> of appropriation is that it enables whole families to sit together

but this is only done at the cost of wasting a seat when a member is absent . . . With free seats . . . whole families, if the members all enter the church together . . . can occupy any vacant bench which will accommodate them all . . . The only just and equitable course is to declare the church free . . . Better provision ought to be made for the poor and for those slow of hearing or understanding and cushions and other marks of exclusive possession should be removed."

The meeting overwhelmingly supported the free seat agenda but the churchwardens refused to act: they had received a counter-protest from 135 families representing 350 members of the congregation whose vested interests they sought to defend.

Antagonistic correspondence followed, all published in the *Parish Magazine*. The Rector took the recalcitrant churchwardens to task. He excluded Frederick Veley who represented less well-heeled Moulsham—he was for change—but targeted the two die-hards, Frederic Chancellor, representing Chelmsford, and his own warden, Thomas Gepp. Chancellor, like Veley, had been elected at the annual Easter Parish Vestry by the town's major property owners who included non-Anglicans. As the churchwardens exercised additional secular responsibilities such as the administration of charities, voters did not have to be Anglicans and were not always swayed by exclusively church matters.

Unsurprisingly the Rector refused to accept the pew renters' protests. Thomas Gepp and Frederic Chancellor wrote peremptorily on July 18th:

"No amount of pressure or persuasion will induce us to do that which . . . we very strongly feel would be the means of prolonging the irritation which has been caused in the minds of our regular churchgoers."

These big men in a small town demanded that the Rector "let the matter rest." He would not and on July 29th wrote a vehement reply:

"You make no attempt at all to help us to meet a growing and well-founded grievance. You will not have the church free even for one service on Sunday: neither will you allow *one half* of the church to be made free . . . so as to give the poor the same consideration as the rich. At present there is nothing to show what seats are free or that there are any free seats at all and you do not seem to realise, nor will you take any steps to ascertain, that there are many parishioners (of whom equally with the seat holders you are representative) who *by this state of things* are repelled from their parish church . . . The question is either solved or is pressing for solution in the towns of the Diocese, conspicuously in St. Albans, Romford, Brentwood and Chelmsford. The fact too that it is chosen for discussion at Diocesan Conference and at the Church Congress itself, proves that it cannot be ignored. Is it possible that a movement of this sort can be successfully resisted . . . with many of the bishops—our own diocesan being among the number—being patrons? How can we clergy 'let it rest'? . . . I cannot allow myself to be the pastor of only one portion of the flock . . . and, therefore, I feel bound . . . to join with others in forming a Free Church Association in this parish."

The Association met in February 1885 and voted in favour of a compromise although it went well beyond the Rector's original cautious Lenten suggestion. It proposed that Sunday evenings in general should be free to all parishioners though the less well-attended Matins should continue with rented seats as before; no more seats should be rented out in the future; and all seat holders who were in principle supportive of free seats should give up their claim. To appease his opponents the Rector suggested that parishioners would probably sit Sunday after Sunday very much in the same part of the church "and no right-minded person will knowingly put any impediment in the way of their doing so", perhaps a hint that the lower orders may not be too pushy.

The *Essex Herald* on Tuesday, March 24th printed the Rector's Sunday sermon on the extremely pertinent text: "For even Christ pleased not Himself." [25] Frank Johnson told his congregation that he could, if necessary, give names of some of the poorer people "who had been moved from seat to seat until they had left the church in despair." A letter to the editor in the same edition explained that the problem had been exacerbated by the removal of the galleries. The choir used to occupy the west gallery and school children the north and south galleries which left space for the poor downstairs. When the galleries were removed the choir was relocated to the chancel and the school children and organ to the main body of the church, ousting the poor. However the writer noted:

"The only time there appeared to be crowding is on Sunday evenings when one of the curates, who is a popular preacher, draws contingents from the surrounding villages."

The gifted preacher in question was almost certainly Harry Darwin Burton: in 1892 he would be appointed Diocesan Missioner in the brick-fields near St. Albans where his rousing sermons, honed in Chelmsford, were to pack his iron mission church with working men.[26]

In the midst of this war of words Thomas Gepp, the Rector's Warden, died. At the Rector's suggestion it was agreed that the new appointee should serve only three years.[27] Frank Johnson immediately invited Frederic Chancellor to fill the position, ostensibly a strange choice. Perhaps the Rector wished to precipitate a parish warden election which might return a free-seater while leaving himself with the option of reining in Chancellor or sacking him if he did not moderate his stance.

But hopes on the electoral front seemed to have backfired when Thomas Gepp's son, Walter, won the Chelmsford vote leaving Frederick Veley, representing Moulsham, as the Rector's only ally. However, once Walter Gepp and Frederic Chancellor came under resumed fire from the free-seaters, Gepp changed his view. He had witnessed the groundswell of opposition at the Free Church Association meeting and came out in support of the Sunday evening compromise. He was accused by traditionalists of treachery but vigorously defended himself: it was his duty as an elected representative to take note of popular feeling. Perhaps he had also been in thrall to his late father and could now take his own line.

Frederic Chancellor showed no deference to his Rector and for two years continued to oppose reform. The annual Vestry Meeting in 1885 was a very tetchy affair. The *Essex County Chronicle* of April 10th gave a blow by blow account of the acrimonious public spat between Rector and Rector's Warden. Chancellor alleged the Rector had told him to quit as warden even though he still had one year left of his allocated three; Frank Johnson disagreed, asserting that there had been an "understanding." Chancellor retorted that the "Rector may have put a different construction upon what I may have said to that which I intended"; the offended Rector demanded an explanation as "it is reflecting on my honour." Chancellor quoted the Rector as saying: "I wish I could persuade you to fall in with the arrangement: if we cannot come to an arrangement I shall have to find another churchwarden"; the Rector confirmed it but insisted that Chancellor had agreed.

Chancellor abandoned this unproductive line of one man's word against another and fell back on his interpretation of the law, quoting an 1800 Act of Parliament which said that seats should be "appropriated to those who had the best claim and right": no churchwarden, Chancellor proclaimed, could ignore the law. However, a letter in the *Essex Weekly News* of April 10th pointed out that the 1800 Act had been superseded by a legal judgement in 1825 and a report of a House of Lords Committee in 1858 both stating that pews were a common right of all. Meanwhile another correspondent to the *Essex County Chronicle* pointed out the blindingly obvious:

> "The chief speakers seemed only to be concerned about their legal rights and privileges . . . There is nothing in the Bible or Book of Common Prayer that will justify the setting apart of seats."

Frank Johnson had the bit between his teeth: he gave Chancellor the push as Rector's Warden and appointed William Dennis, a man who favoured compromise. In the annual election of 1885 Frederick Veley stood again as parish warden for Moulsham while Frederic Chancellor, undeterred by his sacking, took on the turncoat Walter Gepp for the Chelmsford warden's position. Although Veley was elected unopposed at the Vestry Meeting all eyes were on the contest for Chelmsford in which a show of hands gave Gepp only a narrow victory over Chancellor by 35 votes to 34. Not within living memory had an election at the Vestry Meeting failed to go through on the nod. Chancellor's supporters asserted their legal rights and demanded an official poll of all ratepayers in which each voter had from one to six votes to cast depending on the value of his property. In an open vote surely Chancellor would overhaul Gepp using this weighted method of voting? The gloves were off. The disconcerted William Duffield, who had lived in Chelmsford for 40 years, claimed he "had never known anything which had caused such strong feeling."

The polling station was opened at the Charity School in Church Street, on the northern edge of the churchyard, on Friday April 10th from 10.00 a.m. to 5.00 p.m. and on Saturday April 11th from midday to 8.00 p.m.. On the Friday evening when the poll closed for the day Chancellor was in the lead with 276 votes followed by Gepp on 228 with Veley on 217. Chancellor appeared to be in pole position to be elected as parish warden for Chelmsford; Veley, as the sole candidate for Moulsham, was a shoo-in. But if the multiple votes were taken out of the equation Gepp had 193 people voting for him, Chancellor only 155 and Veley, a matter of academic interest only, 151.

The poor who had been earning their pittance at work on Friday would come into their own on Saturday; some of them earned a bit extra by carrying sandwich boards round the streets or handing out election literature. According to the *Essex Herald* of April 13th:

> "Cabs, buses and wagonettes were liberally embellished with placards . . . Church Street was crowded with noisy partisans who shouted vociferously for their respective candidates."

There were other crowds outside the newspaper's High Street offices where running totals of votes cast for each candidate were posted. The landlords of the Lion and Lamb Hotel and the Railway Tavern favoured the common man and loaned their vehicles to Gepp and Veley. Many saw this as an opportunity for a bit of fun on a sunny day whether or not they had a vote. The paper observed:

> "The people were not at all averse to coming for a ride on such a fine afternoon. Many who appeared at the table were disqualified, either through having had parish relief or from an insufficient residence . . . The halt, the maimed and the blind were all represented."

At the final count Gepp had 838 votes, Veley 756 and Chancellor 699. It was the highest poll ever taken in a parish election: over two-thirds of potential votes were cast. It was a veritable trouncing for Chancellor who had been outmanoeuvred by the Rector. The *Essex Herald* reckoned that the majority for Gepp over Chancellor, 139 using the multiple vote system, was 268 if each voter were taken at equal value with just one vote to his name.

Chancellor's humiliation might have been even worse had there not been tactical voting by Non-Conformists who turned out in large numbers to support him under the mischievous slogan, "Chancellor and Disestablishment." They hoped his victory would drive away the poor to their chapels and foment such a public uproar that the cause of Anglican disestablishment would prosper. The Rector was alert to the danger and in May 1885 wrote:

"It is for the welfare of the Church in future . . . that the vast masses to whom the franchise is to be extended should see that the Church cares for them . . . and that they should be so welcomed into her bosom that they will defend her against the attacks of unbelievers."

It was a shrewd point. Many male agricultural labourers had received the parliamentary vote in 1884 as their industrial brothers had done in 1867. Two-thirds of men now had the vote. The Rector wanted their voice to be heard in Church as well. If Chelmsford's obdurate pew-renters continued to snub them they might join the disestablishment camp of "unbelievers."

In May 1885 a judge in York found that churchwardens could not sue a pew holder for arrears in rent as the charge was illegal.[28] In the same year the Convocation of Canterbury voted for free seats in town churches where potential congregations were greater in number than seats available and there was a growing band of professional and business men who were prepared to pay for a well-placed pew. Country churches usually had a smaller number of key families who could have their pick of the best seats and still leave plenty of room for servants and labourers.[29]

A year later resentment continued to simmer in Chelmsford. The *Essex County Chronicle* of April 30th 1886 again printed an account of the annual Vestry Meeting. The Rector was still beating his head against a wall:

"Some of the leading parishioners are as strongly as ever opposed to the change. It is scarcely fair to say (as some say) that they are turned out of their church in the evening, because they are asked to take their chance of a particular seat once in the day with 1,000 other parishioners, many of whom have no appropriated seat at all."

William Dennis complained of deliberate sabotage by the sidesmen who had refused to assist the churchwardens by labelling seats that were free. But there was one slight improvement for non-fee payers: they were no longer kept outside until five minutes after the service started but admitted when the bell ceased tolling just prior to the service. Even so Frederic Chancellor claimed that not a single poor Chelmsford person had entered St. Mary's as a result of the changes: instead they had been flocking in from the neighbouring villages of Writtle and Great Baddow to hear Harry Burton's lively Evensong sermons. Chancellor petulantly asked:

"Was it intended that the people of Chelmsford should be turned out of their seats and that 'foreigners' should take their place?"

Frank Johnson would not let him get away with that:

"It had been their lot to be driven to the outside fringe of the Church and it was not likely that after years of this they would come back again at once."

Chancellor was not used to being crossed but had met his match.

The fruits of Frank Johnson's hard won triumph were revealed in the number of Easter communicants which soared from 428 in 1883 to 830 in 1888.[30] But it is unlikely that many of the new worshippers were from amongst the poorest classes. Sartorial elegance at church was the expected norm. Working women might cover their dowdiness with a shawl but labouring men had no such convenient camouflage. Both knew they would not fit in and preferred not to expose themselves to social disapproval.[31] In 1886 the Men's Guild, recognising that the congregation appeared "stiff rather than sympathetic and congenial", invited the lower classes to a meeting to give their views and identify their needs; not surprisingly very few attended.[32]

Rector Frank Johnson:
Chelmsford Cathedral Knightbridge Library

However, some services were arranged to allow for the duties of live-in domestic staff. In April 1883 the *Parish Magazine* reported:

> "It has been ascertained on enquiry that an occasional celebration of Holy Communion at 7.00 a.m. at the last Sunday of the month during summer would suit the convenience of those in service who cannot well be spared at a later hour."

Taking advantage of the long hours of summer sunlight those below stairs would therefore be able to take Communion early and avoid the awful sin of delaying their employers' breakfast. On Ascension Day an even earlier service was held at 5.00 a.m. for those who had to go early to work: 45 took advantage.

While the pew rent row raged Frederic Chancellor, in 1882, personally paid for the restoration of the south porch and the chamber above it; access to the latter would now be via a hidden staircase off the porch near the south door leading up to an internal upper doorway housed in a delicate gallery; the unsightly external brick stairs and door were demolished. The chamber served as a document store and had long been a home for the library bequeathed in 1677 by John Knightbridge, a native of Chelmsford and Vicar of Spofforth in Yorkshire. It had previously functioned as a military harness and gunpowder store[33] and had also served since 1660 as a registry for the Archdeacon of Essex.[34] Chancellor might have financed the restoration regardless of the circumstances but it earned him an illuminated memorial from 696 grateful parishioners[35] and, he may possibly have hoped, votes in the pew rent controversy.

There were other alterations. The two treble bells loaned to the new daughter chapel at St. John the Evangelist, Moulsham in 1837 were taken back when the tower of the new Church of St. John the Evangelist was built in 1883, making the St. Mary's peal of ten once more complete.[36] With extra space provided by the north aisle extension the marble pulpit was moved in 1884 out of the chancel to the nave arch on the north side making more room for new oak choir stalls and further enhancing the congregation's eastward view of the chancel which was paved and enclosed with screens of hammered iron-work.[37]

Outside, the churchyard had been closed to burials since 1857 with the last interment that of Mary Reynolds aged 95. New cemeteries had been consecrated on the fringe of the town at Rectory Lane in 1856 and Writtle Road in 1886.[38] In 1881 many of the slab gravestones were flattened, the churchyard planted with trees, shrubs and flowers, and the pathways edged with iron railings. In the following year, the New Street wall was lowered to give the public a better view from the east.[39]

Churchyard after the 1881 improvements:
Chelmsford Cathedral Knightbridge Library

There would be no more monuments although in 1909 special permission was given for a memorial cross to be erected to Frank Johnson and his wife, Emily, who had died within a month of each other in 1908.[40]

The 1880s had been a stormy decade. But if Frank Johnson had not freed up his church St. Mary's would have encountered difficulties 20 years later when cathedral status beckoned.

CHAPTER 3

The Charitable Church

While some of the congregation were uneasy about worshipping with the poor they were nonetheless charitably dutiful towards them. Charity could be the difference between life and death in an era when there was no welfare state and the workhouse was a dumping ground not a solution for poverty. Mary Reynolds' longevity had been exceptional: the average age of burials recorded in the first three decades of St. Mary's *Parish Magazine* was a meagre 42 with 28% being children under 10. The well-organised system of District Visitors would have ensured that the church kept in touch with its poorest parishioners and, even given the predisposition of some of them to lecture the poor on their way of life from a lofty moral platform, there would have been other kindly Christian souls who brought genuine compassion and practical help.

A prolonged agricultural depression hit England from 1870 when cheap North American grain began to flood world markets and forced down farm land values and agricultural wages. Many farm labourers deserted the country for the towns: the 1901 census revealed that 201 Essex parishes had smaller populations than in 1851.[1] Chelmsford was therefore in the midst of a sea of rural poverty. Harvest Festivals had real meaning as the gifts of produce were recycled to the poor. In 1879 the *Parish Magazine* noted that the bad harvest would necessitate "a muted Festival in a purely agricultural county like ours."[2] In 1894 the Bishop of St Albans urged the observance of the three Sundays of Rogation to bless the crops.[3] This was not just symbolic: divine benevolence was crucial. In September 1912 the triumphal processional harvest hymns were dropped after torrential rains destroyed the crops.[4]

The Coal Club enabled poor parishioners to pay a monthly subscription and receive back coal in the winter that had been purchased at cheaper summer prices: this would help agricultural workers on short time in the winter months though, the worse the conditions, the more likely claimants were to outnumber the resources available. The Chelmsford Blanketing and Clothes Club operated on a similar principle[5] and wealthy benefactors could make additional gifts to either club. Some church services were dedicated to raising money for tickets for the Chelmsford Infirmary to be given to the poor who needed treatment they could not otherwise afford.

Severe winters tested all these charities beyond their limits. The January 1891 *Parish Magazine* reflected:

> "Christmas of 1890 will long be memorable for its severe cold and deep snow. On Christmas Day 1890 . . . at 8.00 a.m. the thermometer stood at four degrees [Fahrenheit] below zero—36 degrees of frost."

It did not relent. The April 1891 *Parish Magazine* noted:

> "Seldom has there been such a protracted period of severe weather as in December and January last, causing a great deal of want and suffering among those who were thrown out of work."

The detrimental effects of alcoholic intemperance on the domestic budgets of the poor, the stability of family life and the incidence of crime, were persistent themes countrywide in sermons and pamphlet literature. Charity money would be given to the "respectable" poor defined at best by church or chapel attendance or at least by sending the children to Sunday School, demonstrating an absence of drunkenness and showing appropriate gratitude. The first meeting of the parish's Church of England Temperance Society had taken place in 1881, though there had been a town Temperance Society since 1838. The aim of the Church's organisation was temperance rather than absolute abstinence which was reflected in its three sections of members: total abstainers; partial abstainers bound by certain defined restrictions; and a section for those anxious to further the cause but who felt they personally did not require definite rules.[6]

In November 1892 the Rector brought his congregation's attention to the Church of England Waifs and Strays Society urging support to enable these children to be reared as Anglicans. There was also a Girls' Friendly Society to

befriend young working girls of respectable character whether they worked at
home, in service or in shops and factories: its aim was to stop young women
falling into prostitution especially rural girls leaving home at 14 to take up
urban employment. In 1894 they had a new meeting room over Mr Dace's
shop in New London Road. At the same time a Church Institute for young
men was opened: it had one room for lads and another for those at work
with its implicit temperance agenda of keeping them out of the pubs.[7] One
month later a Reading Room for factory girls was opened.[8]

It was as important to ensure that children were taught Christianity as
it was to keep their parents away from the demon drink. There had been
a Church of England National School in Chelmsford since 1812.[9] It was
relocated in 1841 from its previous site at the back of the churchyard in
some old wine vaults to a new site donated by Lady Jane Mildmay and
with a new name, the Victoria Boys' and Girls' National Schools.[10] They
were fee-paying and quite separate from the nearby Charity School which
had been set up in 1713 to give a much more rudimentary free education
and clothing to 80 pauper children and was funded by wealthy benefactors
and the proceeds from collections at St. Mary's annual Charity School
sermons.[11] When state elementary education became compulsory in 1876
the need for the Charity School diminished: in 1884 half its assets were
handed over to build a new boys' National School and the other half used
as an endowment to fund pupils' access to secondary education.[12] In 1883
the dual purpose St. Peter's infant school and mission church was dedicated
at Rainsford End, in the newly expanding suburb to the west of the town,
where St. Mary's redundant terracotta font, recently replaced by a marble
one, was installed: a more substantial iron church was built on land at the
back of the school in 1892.[13]

Sunday School was an important provision in the days before
state-provided education took over responsibility from church and chapel.
However its standards in teaching basic literacy were patchy and, inevitably,
attendance slipped when the 1902 Education Act expanded state elementary
and secondary education under county and county borough supervision.[14]
Financial rewards were offered for good attendance and the summer Sunday
School outing to the seaside could also be an inducement to stay on: in
1914 625 children and parents from St. Mary's and St. John the Evangelist,
Moulsham went to Clacton on a special excursion train.[15] From 1901 a
Church Lads brigade for older boys offered greater attractions with its
drills and uniforms that may have made its compulsory bible class more
bearable.[16]

In 1895 Frank Johnson was elevated to the suffragan Bishopric of Colchester and was replaced by Henry Ashton Lake. He was a graduate of Corpus Christi College, Cambridge who trained at Gloucester Theological College and came to Chelmsford from an incumbency at Castle Hedingham after curacies in Staines and Cuddesdon. For some years Frank Johnson had contributed financially towards the payment of St. Mary's three assistant clergy. He said that he did not want to shirk his responsibility but urged the parish to share in the financial burden otherwise it would be impossible for the rector to be anyone else than a man of independent means.[17] Henry Lake tried to follow his example and personally guaranteed to pay for one curate for five years.[18] Yet, ironically, the congregation continued to raise money for clergy in foreign missions, missions to seamen down in Essex's dockland and the Additional Curates Society to staff the poorer urban churches. Henry Lake was also to discover that the rector, by virtue of having traditionally received tithe rents, was responsible for the repair of the chancel roof, the parish being restricted to responsibility for the nave: in 1905 he could pay for repairs only through fund-raising activities.[19]

The old Craig and Hancock 1772 hand-pumped church organ became one of Rector Lake's first concerns: it had possibly not taken kindly to its earlier removal from the west gallery, first to the south-west corner and then to the north east corner of the church. Frederick Frye, organist since 1876, had complained to the churchwardens that many of the small pipes were blocked by dust, others were out of tune, some notes of the lower octave were "decrepit and speechless"[20] and several collapsing pipes had to be supported by cord or wire. The pedal organ had one stop only, a powerful double-diapason: "as this stop forms the bass of the softest accompaniment, as well as the loudest, the result is often extremely distressful." Eventually, in 1900 a Norman and Beard hydraulic organ was installed. Hydraulic power had the advantage of being silent and cheap. The quantity of water used was not great: 660 gallons were consumed at the three services on a Sunday.[21]

Sir Frederick Bridge, Organist at Westminster Abbey, gave an inaugural recital on the new organ at its Dedication Service when gratitude might also have been expressed to the Rural Dean, Canon H.E. Hulton of Great Waltham,[22] who had given £1,000 (over £84,000 in today's money) to restore the roofs of the north and south aisles. Unfortunately, a subsequent recital on May 2nd 1900 by Walter Alcock, Organist of Holy Trinity, Sloane Square and Assistant Organist at Westminster Abbey, had to be cancelled as an incident at the water works had deprived the town of one third of its water supply and the hydraulic organ pumps of their pressure. In the late summer of 1902 seven Sunday evensongs were also deprived of the organ due to lack of water pressure. This was dry eastern England and low summer rainfall exposed the weakness of a hydraulic system. In November 1910 a new electric organ-blowing apparatus was installed which reduced running costs by one-third and guaranteed continuity of service; the whole church was lit by electricity from 1911.[23] Walter Alcock returned for a more successful recital in December that year.[24]

On January 1st 1898 Frederick Stannard died: he had been parish clerk for 40 years under four incumbents. The February *Parish Magazine* observed that he had "witnessed the change from the black gown to the surplice in the pulpit, from a mixed choir in the west gallery to a surplice choir in the chancel, from a monthly to a weekly and even more frequent celebration of the Holy Communion."

In fact he had seen a minor revolution in Anglican worship. The Church of England had moved away from long sermons with the principal emphasis on moral teaching, salvation by good works and only rare Holy Communions at the major festivals, all underpinned by a horror of any practice that smacked of Rome, to embrace a more catholic style of worship centred on prayer and the sacraments, albeit not without scandalised protest from the evangelical wing. Although it had not always been a comfortable transition, the influence of the Oxford Movement of John Henry Newman, Edward Pusey and John Keble in the middle of the 19th century and the ensuing struggles over what were deemed to be appropriate rituals that were consonant with the Book of Common Prayer, had a lasting effect. By the third quarter of the 19th century many churches, including St. Mary's, had moved to weekly Holy Communion with robed priests and choirs, a congregation facing eastwards to the altar rather than to a pulpit on the north wall and a growing acceptance that religious art and candles enhanced the sense of spiritual wonder and piety. Nonetheless congregational susceptibilities needed to be watched: when St. Mary's had moved to a robed choir Archdeacon Mildmay had left the decision to the churchwardens' approval.[25] In that instance they did not exercise a veto, although, as we have seen, they tried to reassert their power during the pew rents' controversy.

Henry Lake represented that more Anglo-Catholic or High Church strain. The redecoration of the church in 1904[26] introduced, on the north side of the clerestory, angels bearing musical instruments with murals of the Nativity, the Magi and the Presentation in the Temple. At the east end, round the window behind the altar, were the nine instruments of the Passion; the scourge and reed, lantern, seamless robe, spear and sponge, cross, nails, hammer and pincers, ladder and Judas' bag of silver. On the north side of the chancel were the Choirs of Angels and the four Archangels and on the south side were paintings of the Flight into Egypt, the Return from Egypt, the Finding in the Temple and Christ Subject to his Parents. The design on the east side of the chancel arch represented the Adoration of the Lamb in the Blessed Sacrament which would catch communicants' gaze as they returned to their pews from the altar rail. All were accompanied by appropriate scriptural texts. With other biblical scenes and flowery tendrils already adorning the side chapel walls, the patronal festival on the Feast of the Blessed Virgin Mary, which Henry Lake had inaugurated in July 1896,[27] and the regular Eucharist would now be celebrated in a more sacramental ambience.

As the paint dried the Bishop of St. Albans decided that Essex needed its own diocese and cathedral.

Canon Lake's decorated chancel looking west; Chelmsford Cathedral
Knightbridge Library

CHAPTER 4

The Poor Relation

The industrial revolution changed the face of England. Population centres shifted away from the old medieval woollen areas of the southern chalk downs, East Anglia and the south west, to the new urban industrial heartlands of Lancashire, West Yorkshire, the north-east and the midlands. There was a parallel population explosion: the headcount virtually tripled between 1751 and 1851. The great rural 15th century parish churches, many built from medieval wool fortunes, therefore bore witness to a former economic age, most of them in areas that were now of static or declining population. Owen Chadwick, the great church historian, observed:

> "About the beginning of Queen Victoria's reign or a few years before, it was discovered with surprise that England, if a Christian country, contained multitudes of citizens who were not Christian. It dawned upon the public that England was no longer a country of villages and godly poor."[1]

Only London's relative position remained unchanged. It was still the capital and the financial and commercial hub of a growing Empire but was expanding rapidly. Huge new docks would soon be springing up along the Thames on the Essex shore, its casual workers packed into cheap and insanitary tenements.

The new industrial towns were a largely unknown and frightening prospect for predominantly middle-class church-goers. William Blake caught the mood; his "dark satanic mills" conjured up the enslavement of vast numbers in ignorance, squalor and moral degradation without the traditionally binding social influence of church and squire in tight-knit village communities. For several decades after the defeat of Napoleon the political and ecclesiastical establishment feared that these industrial centres would be infected by the contagion of atheistic republicanism spreading from a revolution-prone Europe. Indeed, with Europe peppered by revolutions in 1830-1 and England suffering economic depression and rioting, the majority of bishops in the House of Lords opposed even a very modest extension of the vote in the Reform Act of 1832[2] which nudged the electorate up to a mere 625,000 male property owners. They feared that any extension of political liberty could degenerate into anarchy, as it had done in France in 1789. Rather, their imperative was to build churches in the industrial jungles in order to inculcate moral teaching and respect for authority. Political repression and Christian exhortation went hand in hand.

It took more than half a century for England's leaders to take a more proactive stance. Fear of revolution had subsided. In 1867 a second Reform Act redistributed parliamentary seats to enfranchise male householders in the new industrial towns. Politicians seeking power would now have to respond to their needs. The shortage of schools in the new urban areas, with which even the Anglican and Non-Conformist churches, despite their best voluntary efforts, could not keep pace was not addressed until 1870 when rate-levying School Boards were created in areas where no elementary church schools already existed. Social reforms in housing and public health also gathered pace in the 1870s.

It should therefore be no surprise that the Church of England was also late to respond. The pattern of dioceses in England and Wales still reflected the rural economy of medieval and Tudor England. The 17 Old Foundation cathedrals* hallowed by the Normans were supplemented in 1541-2 by Henry VIII's six New Foundation cathedrals: Westminster (but only briefly as Queen Mary gave it back to the Benedictines in 1550 before Elizabeth I reclaimed it in 1579 as a Royal Peculiar), Chester, Peterborough, Gloucester, Bristol and Oxford. Their great abbey churches were salvaged from the carnage of monastic dissolution but were the only addition to the ancient pattern of English dioceses.

---

* The Old Foundation cathedrals comprised Canterbury, London, Rochester, York, Winchester, Lichfield, Hereford, Worcester, Durham, Exeter, Lincoln, Chichester, Norwich, Ely, Carlisle, Salisbury and Wells.

Although the Church of England did not start major restructuring until the 1870s the unwieldiness of the 4,100 square miles and two million people of the Diocese of Chester did require some early attention. The new dioceses of Ripon and Manchester were carved out of it in 1836 and 1847 respectively. Both had old collegiate churches blessed with ancient constitutions of dean and chapter and venerable cathedral-like buildings so outward adaptation was straightforward. The representation of bishops in the House of Lords was stabilised by amalgamating the dioceses of St. Asaph and Bangor and also those of Bristol and Gloucester. The act of parliament creating the Diocese of Manchester anticipated further new creations and set a ceiling of 26 bishops in the House of Lords with guaranteed places for the two archbishops and the bishops of London, Durham and Winchester; other bishops would take their place in order of accrued years of service as diocesans.

By the 1840s no one doubted that the inflated Diocese of London, which included Essex, had grown too large for Bishop Charles James Blomfield to handle. But the subsequent makeshift solutions were messy and created as many problems as were solved. Essex was used as an expendable pawn in a larger ecclesiastical game of chess and was twice sacrificed to the needs of other dioceses.

Essex was vast with slow internal transport networks. In the coastal salt marshes vicars often left ill-paid curates in charge rather than expose themselves to ague, a form of malarial fever. Bishop Blomfield gently remonstrated:

> "There are two well-known preservatives against ague: the one is a good deal of care and a little port wine: the other, a little care and a good deal of port wine. I prefer the former, but if any of the clergy prefer the latter, it is at all events a remedy which incumbents can afford better than curates."[3]

If vicars were thin on the coastal ground, bishops were almost invisible. As Chadwick says:

> "Parts of distant Essex . . . can hardly have seen their bishop for decades, perhaps not for centuries, perhaps never. Bishops used to confirm children only in the largest centres, sometimes a thousand or more children at a time, by raising their hands in the pulpit over the heads of the entire assembly. Now bishops

went into little country churches and prayed over the head of each individual."[4]

That change in episcopal style was due in no small measure to Samuel Wilberforce, Bishop of Winchester (1869-74), who left his palace in horse and trap and on the new-fangled railways to get out and about in his diocese.[5] Today he is remembered more as Bishop of Oxford (1845-69), when he opposed Charles Darwin's theory of evolution, than for his later pioneering work in the parishes but he had heralded a new era of pastoral rather than princely bishops for whom accessibility to their scattered flocks would matter.

In the same vein Bishop Blomfield felt it would make sense to create a coherent and accessible metropolitan Diocese of London by absorbing the urbanised parishes south of the Thames that were the responsibility of the Canterbury, Winchester and Rochester dioceses and jettisoning Essex which had been in the Diocese of London since Saxon times. Canterbury and Winchester could absorb the losses comfortably but only the Rochester Deanery would remain in the Diocese of Rochester. In 1846, therefore, Essex (temporarily minus the nine parishes of the Barking Deanery which followed in 1867) and Hertfordshire, which had been divided between the dioceses of Lincoln and London since Norman times, were transferred to Rochester as makeweights. This geographical nonsense was pointed out, in gentlemanly fashion one assumes, when 440 Essex and Hertfordshire clergy wrote to Bishop Blomfield regretting the change.[6] As a discrete diocese for Essex eventually hove into view 60 years later, that criticism was reinforced:

"The vicissitudes of Essex, that diocesan Cinderella, now the poor relation of the family of London, now of Rochester, must have meant much spiritual starvation."[7]

One could make an argument that the Diocese of Rochester was superfluous to need but it was a venerable ancient, the second oldest diocese in England, founded in 604, the same year as the Diocese of London and only seven years after St. Augustine founded Canterbury. The acquisition of Essex and Hertfordshire would revive Rochester given that its abolition was inconceivable not least amongst proud Kentish men living under their 99th bishop and eager to make a century or more. So the change went ahead. Danbury Palace, just four miles east of Chelmsford, became the Bishop of Rochester's residence as he could not continue to live in Kent and be accessible to the majority of his flock north of the river. His former residence, Bromley Palace, was sold to a local businessman.

Bishops George Murray and Joseph Cotton Wigram accepted this strange arrangement but not so Thomas Legh Claughton who was consecrated as Bishop of Rochester in 1867. He acknowledged that he was principally bishop of Essex and Hertfordshire. To reach his cathedral in its isolated Kentish enclave he either had a very long dog-leg rail and road journey from Essex through London or had to take the Tilbury to Gravesend ferry, an impossible trip in stormy weather. Rochester Cathedral would rarely, if ever, have been visited by those who lived north of the Thames. He strongly advocated that Essex and Hertfordshire should have their own diocese.

The new Diocese of St. Albans, therefore, was created in 1877, one of six new dioceses to emerge in the period 1876-88. In the south west it was at last acknowledged that the Bishop of Exeter could not exercise meaningful pastoral care over such an immense area as Devon and Cornwall and so Cornwall got its own Diocese of Truro in 1876. Four dioceses emerged in the industrial heartlands: Liverpool, carved out of the Diocese of Chester in 1880, Newcastle out of Durham in 1882, Southwell, covering Nottinghamshire and Derbyshire, out of Lincoln in 1884 and Wakefield, a further sub-division of Ripon, in 1888.

The see town for the Diocese of St. Albans would inevitably be situated in Hertfordshire: that was where the money was. For the last 20 years a group of Hertfordshire businessmen had been agitating for St. Albans Abbey to be converted to a cathedral and had offered to put up the cash based on estimates drawn up by George Gilbert Scott who was trying to effect repairs to the dilapidated and structurally unsound abbey church. When that cash ran out the irascible architect Edmund Beckett poured £30,000 of his own money into the project (£2.3 million in today's money) on the condition he could do what he willed. Demonstrating himself to be "a man of arrogance and bile",[8] he subsequently wrote a record number of rude letters to *The Times* deriding critics of his architectural decisions. His victims included Rector Mildmay's successor as Archdeacon of Essex, Alfred Blomfield (son of Charles James Blomfield), who had rashly raised an eyebrow at what happened to the west window.

Bishop's Stortford (what more appropriate name for a bishop's seat?) on the border of Essex and Hertfordshire, with its excellent railway connections was the only, though not really competitive, alternative. St. Albans, named after the first British Christian martyr, prevailed. The Diocese of Rochester would receive some Surrey parishes in south-west London from the Diocese of Winchester by way of compensation. Winchester House in fashionable St. James' Square was redundant now that the diocese had lost its London parishes and would be sold to provide an endowment for the new St. Albans see: the Bishop of Winchester would still have Farnham Castle and would not be homeless. Bishop Claughton, Rochester's 101st bishop, was translated to become the first Bishop of St. Albans. He had already served the people of Essex and Hertfordshire for 10 years and would do so for 13 more.

Communications between Essex and Hertfordshire would pose a constant problem. Danbury Palace was not near a railway station and, in any case, railway lines (and most main roads) ran on a north-south axis to and from London, not laterally. Bishop Claughton therefore conducted interviews, institutions and examinations in London which was equally accessible to the whole diocese.[9]

There was a need to establish an equitable relationship between the two counties. Chadwick puts it succinctly: "Essex had the population, the acres, the Bishop's Palace. Hertfordshire had the money, the cathedral and the name."[10] The Diocesan Conference was held in each county alternately. The suffragan bishopric created in 1882 was awarded to Essex and attached to Colchester, one of the historic towns listed in an act of Henry VIII defining the places that might have suffragans. Alfred Blomfield was consecrated in this role. Now the northern half of the county could get to know him. The southern half already knew him well as Archdeacon of Essex.

By 1888 Bishop Claughton was totally blind and had been in ill-health for some years. Decision-making passed more and more to Frank Johnson, the Bishop of Colchester. Bishop Claughton resigned at the age of 81 in 1890 and lived on in Danbury Palace until his death in 1892 when the Palace was sold to raise money for a residence for the Bishop of Rochester. That meant that the Bishop of Rochester would now have a home but the Bishop of St. Albans would not. John Wogan Festing, the second Bishop of St.Albans, compromised by living in Endsleigh Street in Euston with easy access to the London rail termini that could catapult him quickly into the main centres of his Diocese. He was inevitably criticised for this and compromised in 1896 by renting St. Albans Rectory for the summer months. He probably accepted the criticism without demur: "he was so silent by nature that often, at a diocesan gathering, he had not a word to say and would do nothing but sit and smile and stroke his face."[11]

This taciturn bishop was faced by the huge challenge of ministering to the spiritual needs of London-over-the-Border, a phrase in common usage in the 1890s, first coined by Charles Dickens over 30 years before[12] to describe the new industrial areas of Thames-side Essex which each year sucked in thousands of impoverished workers. The Victoria and Royal Albert docks had placed Essex at the heart of imperial trade; there was a huge new railway works at Stratford; East Ham and West Ham were centres of the chemical industry; and the Beckton gas works in the isolated Essex marshes began to serve London's needs, the largest works of its type in the world. The associated poor quality housing for all these developments brought a huge influx of potentially Christian souls.

Bishop Festing's priorities were new parishes for London-over-the-Border each with its church, parsonage, school and clergy and, as was the case for all bishops, supporting poor rural clergy whose incomes from tithe and glebe had been savaged by the agricultural depression that had hit England from the 1870s. Beautification of St. Albans Cathedral, the appointment of a salaried dean and chapter to emulate the ancient cathedrals and a new residence for the Bishop would all have to wait. The Bishop of St. Albans Fund raised £190,000 in 15 years (over £16 million in today's money).[13] Except for setting aside some cash to buy a piece of land for a future bishop's house (though with no idea when it would be built) all the money was spent on London-over-the-Border.

St Cedd's original Cathedral of St. Peter-on-the-Wall on the isolated Essex coast: photo by Tony Tuckwell

As the 19th century drew to a close it was clear that the fusion of Essex and Hertfordshire could not last. The population of the Diocese of St. Albans, three-quarters of them in Essex, was greater than those of Ely and Norwich dioceses combined: it was literally a killing job for a diligent pastoral bishop. Many of Essex's poor industrial workers had scant knowledge of the Christian gospel of salvation and no church in their midst. St. Cedd, the first Bishop of the East Saxons, had undertaken the initial conversion of the people of Essex in the 7th century, incorporating his modest cathedral in the wall of an old Roman fort: it would need a reconstituted bishopric and cathedral in the 20th to evangelise the new territories of unbelief.

CHAPTER 5

The East Anglian Plan

In 1903 Edgar Jacob, the Bishop of Newcastle, became the third Bishop of St. Albans. Unlike Bishop Festing, who had died in office at the end of 1902, he was a great talker and communicator.[1] He had first-hand experience of ministering to the urban poor and would empathise with the needs of London-over-the-Border. He had cut his teeth in a curacy amongst the slums of dockland Bermondsey and after a spell in India had served for 18 years in the Hampshire naval dockland parish of Portsea where the population doubled during his tenure of office; he started with one curate and a dilapidated church and ended with 18 curates and the new church of St. Mary's designed by Sir Arthur Blomfield (another son of the former Bishop of London, Charles James Blomfield) with half the money donated by W.H. Smith, the great bookseller and future cabinet minister. During seven years in Newcastle Bishop Jacob was equally successful in persuading leaders of commerce and industry to invest in diocesan projects.[1] He, therefore, not only had the common touch but was also able to appeal to the Christian conscience of the wealthy. He was an inspiring visionary with an ideal background for tackling the problems faced by his new diocese.

He quickly saw that, with Essex's Thames-side population expanding relentlessly, the county needed its own diocese. According to Ernest Gray, the M.P. for West Ham North:

> "The two once tiny villages of West Ham and East Ham had become within the last 30 years densely-populated areas . . . and . . . had grown in that time from 30,000 to nearly 300,000 . . . on . . . land which 30 years ago was a marsh."[2]

In concert with the bishops of Ely and Norwich, Edgar Jacob presented a scheme to the Convocation of Canterbury in 1905 for an overall reorganisation and refunding of their dioceses. Redistribution of endowments, principally from Ely, underpinned the scheme. The timing was determined by the retirement in 1905 of its octogenarian bishop, Lord Alwyne Compton. He supported the scheme but a younger bishop would be better placed to handle the transition and future planning.

The 1901 census figures (see Table 1) told the story of the population explosion in London-over-the-Border.

Table 1: dioceses in 1901[3]

Diocese	Counties	Population 1901	Benefices	Population per benefice	Clergy
Ely	Cambridgeshire Huntingdonshire Bedfordshire West Suffolk	531,152	567	937	763
Norwich	Norfolk East Suffolk	731,075	890	821	1,006
St Albans	Hertfordshire Essex	1,336,267	630	2,121	1,015

Table 2: proposed dioceses in 1907

Diocese	Counties	Population 1901	Benefices	Population per benefice	Clergy
Ely	Cambridgeshire Huntingdonshire	222,103	252	881	325
Norwich	Norfolk	458,596	598	767	686
St. Albans	Hertfordshire Bedfordshire	424,064	303	1,400	451
Suffolk	Suffolk	407,123	473	861	537
Essex	Essex	1,088,857	461	2,362	735

The Diocese of St. Albans averaged 2,121 residents to each benefice compared to just 821 in Norwich and 937 in Ely. In the proposed new scheme finalised in 1907 (see Table 2) Norwich and Ely would reduce even further to 767 and 881 respectively; a new diocese in Suffolk would fit neatly into this pattern of small village and market town livings at 861; but St. Albans would still average 1,400 and Essex 2,362. Both Essex and Hertfordshire were experiencing the growth of commuter settlements and Essex would be solely responsible for London-over-the-Border.

Both the existing and proposed structures masked the true size of London-over-the-Border's population and the extent of its clerical shortage as census enumerators almost certainly did not make contact with all the shifting dockland population. Moreover, if one were to separate the rural and small town parishes of Essex, about 80% of the county's total, whose average populations per living would have been comparable to Ely, Suffolk and Norwich, the number of residents per living in London-over-the-Border would have been up to 20,000 and would be destined to remain high while church building constantly played catch up.

Ely's wealth was the key to the plan. Proceeds from the sale of Ely House, the bishop's town house in Mayfair, and cuts in current episcopal stipends would help finance the two new county dioceses proposed for Essex and Suffolk. The Bishop of Ely would reduce his princely stipend from £5,500 per year (£461,000 in today's money) to £4,000 (£335,000); the bishops of St. Albans and Norwich, starting from a lower but still comfortable level, would lose £500 each (£48,000). Ely might have sacrificed even more financially but it would still embrace the University of Cambridge, the training ground historically for many Anglican clergy and an internationally-renowned centre for Protestant theological studies which, it was argued, would demand a great deal of a bishop's time. The new Bishop of Ely, Frederic Henry Chase, came from the post of President of the Queens' College, Cambridge and the Norris Professorship of Divinity, as though to underline the point.

Ely's financial sacrifice would be matched by a 60% reduction in its territorial extent. Its diocese would now be confined to Cambridgeshire and tiny Huntingdonshire. It had experienced major communications problems with its parishes in Bedfordshire and West Suffolk, similar to those between Essex and Hertfordshire. So Bedfordshire would replace Essex in the Diocese of St. Albans, a more logical link, as Bedfordshire and Hertfordshire were well connected by north-south rail communications with St. Albans 37 minutes from Bedford by the Midland Railway and Luton just 15 minutes away. West Suffolk would be combined with East Suffolk, taken from the Diocese of Norwich, to form a new Suffolk diocese. Given that the Church of England was an established church with many county links, not least associations with the military colours of shire regiments, it was logical to make diocesan and shire boundaries coterminous; the territorial link might make people more aware of and loyal to their cathedral.

Norfolk was the fourth largest county in England. The city of Norwich, which had grown rich on wool, was for centuries one of the largest in pre-industrial England and contained more medieval churches than any other city north of the Alps. The Diocese's rural population was scattered in a historically large number of benefices which, had they been evenly spread, would have been sufficient for one every three square miles.[3] They made very heavy travelling demands on their diocesans which would be only marginally eased by the amputation of East Suffolk.

Meanwhile, the population in Essex and Hertfordshire increased by a further 37% between the censuses of 1891 and 1901; in London-over-the-Border the figure was an enormous 62%; by contrast the increase for England and Wales was only 8.2%. So Essex's need for its own diocese was becoming desperate though it would still have over twice the population of its neighbouring rural dioceses, an imbalance that was likely to worsen as London's population spilled inexorably eastwards. In simple mathematical terms there would be an argument for a further subdivision in the near future with one diocese for rural Essex and another for its metropolitan area. On the other hand financial necessity might require continued association of impoverished East London with the relatively wealthier shire areas of Essex.

The emergence of new bishoprics in the 1870s had forced serious thought on the issue of how much income was needed for a new diocese to be viable. The Bishoprics Act of 1878 recommended an assured minimum annual income of £3,000 (£227,000 in today's money)—in effect a £100,000 endowment (over £7.5 million) invested at 3%—rising to £3,500 (£264,900) within five years with an additional £500 per annum (£37,900) if no bishop's house was available. It was hoped by those supporting the East Anglian reorganisation that £2,500 (£189,000) for the diocese and £300 (£22,700) for the house might be acceptable; the vital need for restructuring meant there would probably be some flexibility. St. Albans already had the land on which to build a bishop's house but Essex and Suffolk would start from scratch.

On May 14th 1906 the first of a series of Essex fund-raising meetings was held at the Shire Hall in Chelmsford; the Lord Lieutenant, Bishop of St. Albans, High Sheriff, Mayor of Chelmsford and Bishop of Colchester were present. Led by Mr Charles E. Ridley and other gentlemen of the district

£20,000 (£1.68 million in today's money) was raised. Essex and Suffolk now proposed to unite forces to complete their funds.[4]

While the money came in the location of the cathedrals had to be decided. In Suffolk the town of Bury St. Edmunds with the ancient abbey church of St. Edmundsbury would provide a simple solution: it was less straightforward in Essex.

CHAPTER 6

Is Braintree the Hub of the Universe?

In 1906 Bishop Edgar Jacob invited those churches that aspired to become Essex's cathedral to submit applications. He kept his own views to himself at this stage not wanting to influence the Essex parishes whose vote he would seek on the relative merits of the candidates.

He specified the information he wanted so that it could be tabulated in neutral style for the parochial electorate. Was the church big enough? Candidates must state their church seating capacity and whether there was scope for extensions. Could the congregation generate sufficient income to support the style of worship expected of a cathedral? Annual income from church collections must be declared excluding Easter Sunday, which was usually the congregation's offering to the incumbent, and special services. Were there any restrictions on attendance at services? Candidates must reveal whether any pews were still reserved for families who paid rents. Would the Bishop be able to appoint the Dean? Candidates must confirm whether there was a lay patron who owned the advowson which in many cases had passed to purchasers of monastic property at the Reformation. Were there suitable meeting places for diocesan conferences? Candidates must identify local public buildings that would fit the purpose. Finally, would the cathedral be accessible on a return day trip? Hence the almost obsessive interest in rail communications in which the Bishop himself was well versed: he had travelled widely in Essex and understood how long it took to reach the rural west, the south east round Tilbury and Southend and the north-eastern Tendring peninsula round Clacton. He wryly described Essex's problems in a House of Lords debate:

"If anybody is acquainted with the means of locomotion . . . he will know perfectly well that they are based on the principle that every sane man desires to go to London in the morning and return in the afternoon and to go nowhere else."[1]

For the aspiring applicants success would bring considerable prestige to what it was assumed, incorrectly, would immediately become Essex's first city. As mayors envisaged their elevation to a lord mayoralty and local businessmen scented a commercial opportunity not a little civic pride and prejudice emerged in the ensuing campaign.

Seven towns entered their churches in the race. Three were in London-over-the-Border: the old abbey church of St. Margaret's in Barking; the Borough of West Ham with the parish churches of either All Saints' in West Ham or St. John the Evangelist in Stratford; and St. Mary's in Woodford. Four were from the more rural part of the county: St. Mary's in Chelmsford; St. James' or "another church" in Colchester; St. John the Baptist, Our Lady and St. Laurence in Thaxted; and yet another old abbatial foundation, Holy Cross in Waltham Abbey.

By mid-November the seven had submitted their applications and on the 26th of that month the Executive Committee of the Essex and Hertfordshire Bishopric Fund met to read them. The printed summary eventually provided to the parishes by Bishop Edgar Jacob in early January 1908 was based largely on this information.[2] The Executive Committee would meet in February to consider parish responses and make its recommendation for formal acceptance by the full General Committee in March.

Not divulged to the parishes, however, were the private discussions between the Executive Committee and the three man deputations from each of the competing towns who were invited in alphabetical order to Church House in Westminster on December 18th 1907. The Bishop wanted to seek clarification on information they had already provided and to give them the chance to make any other comments they felt were relevant. The discussions were recorded verbatim[3] and added a fascinating, if not always flattering, gloss.

Barking

Barking described itself as a still growing town of 31,000. The church could seat 1,000 all free and the site of the old abbey to the south could be purchased to extend the building. The Bishop of St. Albans owned the advowson but the annual church collection of £250 (£20,600 in today's money) was modest. Nor were there any local hotels or suitable conference venues though there was a large site set aside for a future Town Hall; while awaiting its completion East Ham Town Hall, just four minutes by train from the church, could be used, or, if one wished to remain in the parish, the public swimming bath could be floored over in winter and 1,000 seats installed though the Vicar of Barking admitted that it would not make "an elegant hall." However, Barking had distinct transport advantages: it was quickly accessible to the south-eastern corner of the county on the London, Tilbury and Southend line and it was linked directly by rail with the great mass of population in West Ham and via a connection with the Great Eastern Railway (G.E.R.) at Ilford to Chelmsford and Colchester. It also had history on its side: Barking Abbey had been very powerful in Saxon and medieval times and a suffragan bishopric of Barking had been created by Bishop Edgar Jacob in 1901.

In interview the Vicar made a compelling point that "it would be a magnificent thing for the Church to place this cathedral in the midst of the poor." When asked by the Bishop whether there was "sufficient public spirit and church feeling among the inhabitants of Barking to rise to the responsibilities of a cathedral"—in other words were their pockets deep enough—the Vicar got precious close to reminding his diocesan of the parable of the widow's mite:

> "Of course, they are poor people but they are absolutely indefatigable at giving and a large number of poor and small offerings might accomplish it, if I may say it with all due respect, according to their means, far in excess of the upper classes . . . We have no wealthy population in the district, My Lord . . . You see the Beckton Gas Works are our richest people and you know what companies have to be."

He did: the shareholders' dividend would come first. But on purely Christian arguments the Vicar would seem to have been ahead on points.

Could all the people of Essex reach Barking with ease? The Vicar was reassuring:

> "In a few weeks time we shall be on the District Railway, the electric system . . . They have built an enormous railway station recently. It was just opened on Sunday."

The Vicar was optimistic about prospects for church extensions. The adjacent old abbey site was owned by Sir Edward Hulse who had already donated part of the land for an infant school and the Dowager Lady Hulse had recently given £20 (£1,650 in today's money) for the Renovation Fund, a taste of possible future largesse. The Vicar reckoned that financial security might be further enhanced by ongoing annual population increases of about 1,500 brought about by the continued expansion of the new coke, gas, rubber and chemical industries, although it is doubtful whether their working class labourers would have been avid churchgoers.

It had been a good pitch and the Vicar, as the main spokesman of his three man deputation, refrained from commenting critically on other rival bids. But he could sense that they were not in the running so he played the long game. He acknowledged the strength of Chelmsford's case and saw Barking as the answer for metropolitan Essex when the continued population explosion required a further sub-division:

> "The feeling in the neighbourhood is that the ideal is to have your cathedral in the middle of the county . . . The probability is that in the course of a very few years it will be absolutely necessary to subdivide again . . . In that case we think Barking the ideal . . . It would catch all the Tilbury line, all that part of the county on the river, which no other place would."

Chelmsford

The high-powered Chelmsford deputation took the floor: Canon Henry Lake, Rector of St. Mary's; Frederic Chancellor, in his seventh term of office as Mayor of Chelmsford; and Sir A.B. Pennefather, Chairman of the Diocese of St. Albans Finance Committee and soon to have the same responsibility in the Diocese of Chelmsford. They were probably unaware of Barking's endorsement.

They described Chelmsford as a small market town of 18,000 but with a population of 105,000 within a 12 mile radius. St. Mary's took a handsome £600 annually in church collections (£49,500 in today's money) and, no thanks to Chancellor, boasted 1,000 free seats. The church could be extended eastwards into the churchyard. The Bishop of St. Albans owned the advowson. Moreover, Chelmsford was the county town and the geographical and communications centre of Essex with ample meeting places: the Shire Hall Ball Room would hold 500, its Picture Room and the Grand Jury

Room 200 each, the Corn Exchange 1,000, the Drill Hall 1,200 and the Mechanics' Institute 250. There was plentiful accommodation at the three principal hotels—the Saracen's Head, the White Hart and the Bull—plus the smaller Lion and Lamb. Chelmsford had been accustomed until recently to lodging people for the Assizes. Chancellor explained:

> "It has been dropped in the last few years but formerly it was a common thing for almost every shop-keeper down the High Street to put up a barrister or somebody, a witness or whatever."

Frederic Chancellor was the giant in this game: apart from his political clout he had a large architectural practice in London and Chelmsford and was one of the most significant laymen in the Diocese having been Honorary Architect to the Diocese of Rochester in 1859 and from 1871 to 1877 and to the Diocese of St. Albans from 1877 to 1902. During his career he restored over 90 churches and nearly 80 parsonages in Essex alone. He was used to getting his way:

> "An autocrat and a person who was not easily approached; inevitably clothed in a frock coat, top hat and red carnation, he was a stickler for etiquette."[4]

Those characteristics had been forcibly displayed during his opposition to free seats 25 years earlier, one of the rare occasions he did not get his way. As a consummate politician he now portrayed open access as a virtue and prepared an exceptionally detailed case which promoted Chelmsford's undoubted strengths while at the same time occasionally massaging the facts and undermining the cause of those he had identified as his principal opponents.

At interview Chancellor came straight to the point presenting a list of selected cathedrals and their floor areas based on choir, nave and aisles but excluding transepts, concentrating his attention on the central areas that would be used for public occasions. On this basis Chelmsford's church had a floor area of 9,418 square feet which, at a cost of £5,600 (£462,000 in today's money), could be enlarged to 12,216, not far short of Rochester's 12,600, well in excess of Chester's 10,875 and just ahead of Carlisle's 11,988. He reckoned it would be well over twice the area of Oxford or the would-be cathedral at Waltham Abbey though it would not reach the grand proportions of Gloucester or Lichfield. To support his case he had already drawn up a costed plan for additional vestries, a Chapter House and a 50 feet extension of the chancel. This was all smoke and mirrors: taking into account total floor space, Chelmsford, if chosen, even with extensions, would still be England's smallest cathedral.

Transport was Chancellor's trump card. Chelmsford was connected directly by rail to nearly every point in the county, bar the west, with direct trains to Stratford, Colchester and Tendring and, with one change at Shenfield, to Southend; all travellers to St. Mary's were within a five minutes' walk of the railway station. On the other hand he noted that "in the present day the railway does not seem to be of such importance . . . as the motor car" and calculated that the 105,000 people who lived within 12 miles of Chelmsford might travel easily by road for the day to diocesan festivals. He was slightly ahead of things in 1907 when the car was still the rich man's toy but would soon be proved right: 200,000 registered motor cars in England and Wales in 1914, when the Diocese of Chelmsford was formed, turned into well over one million by 1930.[5] Indeed, the whole county was within 25 miles of Chelmsford except for the Tendring area in the far north-east for whom a cathedral at Colchester would be the ideal solution.

He anticipated the problem of north-west Essex's isolation, having trialled a rail journey to Ashdon near Saffron Walden:

> "I went from Chelmsford to Marks Tey and along the Sudbury line to Bartlow. I think it took about two hours . . . I had a trap to meet me . . . to go to Ashdon which is about one and a half miles from Bartlow station."

As for west Essex he was confident that very soon:

> " . . . the Ongar line will be carried to Chelmsford. Some time ago a deputation from the corporation of Chelmsford . . . urged [upon the G.E.R. directors] the necessity . . . of continuing that line to Chelmsford."

But when Canon Henry Lake took the floor the wind seemed to go out of Chelmsford's sails. His references to the poor areas of East London were uniformly pessimistic: "London-over-the-Border is the great bane of the Diocese" was his uninspiring opening. Bishop Edgar Jacob, who had triumphed over such adversity in Portsea and Newcastle, must have winced: it was the great mission of the Diocese and the very reason for its creation. Henry Lake then proceeded to highlight divisions in West Ham's ranks, perhaps under instructions from Chancellor to home in on a rival's weaknesses: "what has struck me . . . is that London-over-the-Border themselves are not united as to whether the cathedral should be there." In what other way could West Ham's case be scuppered? With a nudge and a wink he seized upon the new metropolitan Diocese of Southwark, created in 1905:

> "It so happens that I said to a friend of mine, whom probably you all know—who has certainly worked for 40 years in Southwark and is one of the canons of the Cathedral—'London-over-the-Border is our great burden. What is your experience?' He said . . . 'First everybody in London in our part looks to St. Paul's Cathedral, especially the people who work in London; secondly, if you ask me what is our influence on the actual place of Southwark I am afraid it is nil; and thirdly . . . money . . . is a perfect burden and the reason is that the country parts of the Diocese feel they have no cathedral.'"

Canon Lake concluded disingenuously: "I did not want the Committee to feel we were trying to press Chelmsford; we wanted them to take as broad a view as possible for the good of the whole Diocese." One very much doubts that that was the impression received.

Canon Henry Ashton Lake:
Chelmsford Cathedral Knightbridge Library

Henry Lake was uncomfortable and at one stage, the report says, petered out inarticulately. As a gentlemanly cleric unused to politicking he was out of his depth. Certainly the Bishop might have hoped for greater enthusiasm for Christ's mission to the poor from the man who had been an honorary canon of St. Albans Cathedral since 1904 and would eventually become Sub-Dean in the new cathedral.

Colchester

The good people of Colchester had been the most God-fearing in the country as measured by the 1851 religious census when 89% of them attended Sunday services, just under half of them Anglicans,[6] but their cathedral deputation did not seem aware of this happy statistic.

They were a much bigger town than their arch rivals, Chelmsford, with 45,000 inhabitants and another 104,000 Essex people within a 12 mile radius. There were an additional 3,000 men based at the Colchester military garrison and the deputation advised that new lunatic asylums would swell the population further "but that is not a thing to boast about." St. James', where the Bishop of St. Albans owned the advowson or, rather indecisively, "another church", were proposed as the cathedral. The deputation was vague on seating accommodation: they claimed St. James' could seat 800, all free, but when the figures were queried they seemed unsure as they were reliant on the Rector's calculations and he was not there. However, there was room for enlargement and local Liberal M.P., Weetman Pearson, the tycoon owner of the Pearson oil and construction conglomerate, had promised £1,000 (£82,500 in modern values) towards the costs: alternatively there was a site nearby which could be used for a newly built cathedral. Maybe the mysterious other church would swing it for Colchester? The Bishop required them to reveal their hand. It was all very anti-climactic. St. Mary-at-the-Walls was the card up the sleeve but it provided only 500 to 600 seats and could not even match St. James' meagre annual collections of £125 (£10,300). However, public assembly rooms and accommodation were Colchester's strength, even better than Chelmsford's: the new Town Hall seated 800, the Corn Exchange 1,500, a Drill Hall 1,000, a new Co-operative Hall 900-1,000 and the Masonic Hall 300. Mass catering was on hand: the Cups Hotel could feed 200, the Red Lion 400, the George Hotel 200 and a temperance hotel 200.

Colchester's historic claim was strong: it was the first Roman town in Britain and for a short while the Roman capital. Even more to the point

Henry VIII had nominated the town as one of an exclusive group of 26 that could be represented by a suffragan bishop if required. Two had been appointed by the Bishop of London in Tudor times (1536-41 and 1592-1608) but the title then went into abeyance until the Bishop of St. Albans revived it in 1882.

The Colchester deputation was immediately on the defensive on the issue of transport. While it would be a good centre for Tendring in north east Essex and easily accessible by rail from Chelmsford, its main G.E.R station was well-removed from the town centre even though it had recently been linked by a tram service. The far-flung people of Southend were totally opposed to Colchester but the deputation countered with the information that a bill had recently been passed in Parliament to facilitate direct communication from Colchester to Southend through Maldon or possibly via Mersea Island: this was their equivalent of Chancellor's Ongar line to Chelmsford, one of the many golden hopes of new rail and bus lines that successive deputations were to dangle before the Bishop. Access from west Essex posed an even greater problem: the deputation had manfully worked out a series of cross-country rail routes—via Halstead or Saffron Walden on the Colne Valley Railway to meet up with the main London to Colchester line at Marks Tey; via Cambridge; or via Witham and Bishop's Stortford—but the panel concluded that these very long cross-country routes of two hours with few trains in a day would make return day trips problematic: it might be just as well for the people of west Essex to go into London on the Cambridge line and then out again on the G.E.R. line through mid Essex.

Crucially the vast mass of the population in London-over-the-Border would be 60 miles away. The deputation asserted that the Bishop did not need to live in Colchester: "Essex is really an ellipse with two foci, one in Colchester, the other at Stratford." They instanced Suffolk where the cathedral was proposed at Bury St. Edmunds but the Bishop would reside in Ipswich. But those two towns were separated by only 27 miles. In any case, it was not a question of how Essex people could get to the Bishop—as their Father in God he would go to them—but how they would get to their cathedral.

When asked if there were any other matters they wished to raise the deputation urged that the Church of England should grab the Colchester name for the new diocese before the Catholics did so: they were restructuring their huge Archdiocese of Westminster and, like their Anglican rivals, seeking to make a separate diocese in Essex.

"We regard with some apprehension the great progress that the Roman Catholic church are making in our district . . . If the Church does not take the opportunity of making Colchester the great centre of a cathedral, the Roman Catholics probably will, inasmuch as they, perhaps more so than the Protestants, have a very great love for the old associations . . . and for what may be termed the continuity of Christian life and policy . . . They have purchased very large properties in Colchester lately . . . There is a very large teaching staff of the Sisters of Mercy . . . and they have established very large girls' schools . . . and a good many are brought over from France to be educated there. And then at Clacton they are making enormous progress and in every part of our district they are purchasing property regardless of expense and evidently on a very strong propaganda."

The old Puritan parliamentary stronghold that had attacked local royalist Catholic gentry in the Civil War was still paranoid: the Catholics must be kept at bay. This was an extraordinary diversion which really bore no relevance to the issues and elicited no questions. In any case the Catholics chose Brentwood.

Thaxted

Thaxted had the weakest case on paper. Barely more than a village, its population had declined by over a third—to 1,659 in 1901 from 2,556 back in 1851[7]—as impoverished agricultural labourers drifted to the towns. The Parish Church was its crowning glory, perhaps the finest church in the county architecturally and with a seating capacity estimated at 2,500, all free: it would not need any structural alteration. Thaxted was at pains to point out that it would cost £200,000 (£16.5 million in today's money) to build a similar-sized cathedral elsewhere though such grandiose plans were not on the Bishop's agenda. A site was also on offer for a bishop's house. On the down side Daisy, Lady Warwick, owned the advowson and wanted to hang onto it; church collections totalled only £40 annually (£3,300); there were just two hotels and negligible public meeting space with the school seating just 300 and the Guildhall 50; and the nearest railway station was five and a half miles away at Elsenham.

The Thaxted deputation had an unenviable task. So they started with their obvious strength, the magnificence of the church and tried to make a virtue out of its isolation—"there is a certain charm in peace and quietness . . . an atmosphere that is particularly suitable to spiritual life and affairs"—not unlike Holy Island with which they made a comparison. They too suggested that the Bishop could live down south in mission territory but that would not make the cathedral any more accessible.

They were in huge difficulty on rail and bus transport. G.E.R. promised to build a short branch line connecting with the main Cambridge line at Elsenham: the line did, in fact, open in 1913[8] but connected Thaxted only with the thinly populated western part of the county. In the meantime the deputation was confined to exploring bus routes:

> "We propose that there should be a motor service from Braintree through Bardfield, through Thaxted and then on to Saffron Walden . . . I am told by a business man there is very little doubt that it would be a commercial success."

The Bishop's panel turned to the very large population 40 miles away in Southend. The deputation suggested that they would come up by train to Braintree 14 miles away and then on to Thaxted by a 40 minutes bus journey or they could go in to London and come up by the Cambridge line to Saffron Walden eight miles away and another bus, but the panel doubted that the people of Southend would be able to come and go in a day. Similarly, when asked about Harwich and Clacton in the north-east of the county, the deputation suggested that they too would go by train to Braintree and then on by bus to Thaxted.

The Bishop summed up: "I suppose the great difficulty about Thaxted is its accessibility?" "Not with these new systems, my Lord" came the logic-defying response. The Bishop's patience seemed at an end. Envisaging most of Essex descending on the nearest bus link at Braintree, he retorted with resigned irony: "you speak as if Braintree was the hub of the universe." It would be a long day and they were only just over half way through. Perhaps this was the last session before lunch.

It did not get any better. One of the panel asked about the choir, probably already knowing the answer. The Vicar admitted it was "very bad but we have an exceedingly good organ" but then had second thoughts: "I hope that is not going to be put down as 'very bad' because I should not like my choir to see that. I should rather say my choir is quite as good as that in any other country place." The arrival of Gustav Holst, who was to make Thaxted musically renowned, was still ten years off. For the time being the

Vicar reassured the panel that the patron of the living had choral music at heart: "Lady Warwick, as patron of the living and owner of a great deal of property all round, begged me to say how she would give her interest and influence strongly on this." But when asked whether she would allow the Bishop to appoint his Dean, the Vicar had to be honest: "I do not know that she would surrender the patronage." As a former mistress of Edward VII, when he was Prince of Wales, and soon, in 1911, to use their billets doux in an attempt to blackmail George V, she would not have been a safe or suitable pair of hands.

Waltham Abbey

Waltham Abbey was a small town of 6,000. Holy Cross Parish Church could seat only 600-800, all free. The principal employer was the huge Royal Gunpowder Mills. With the government owning much of the land there were few substantial private landowners to support the church. The end of the Boer War in 1902 had diminished demand for gunpowder and many of the population moved elsewhere for work: church collections had therefore declined from their former £300 per year (£24,800 in today's money) to £250 (£20,600). The town would also struggle to accommodate diocesan meetings: the Town Hall could seat 600, a private hall 300 and an old chapel 150 and there were only two hotels.

Getting to Waltham Abbey would be a challenge as the town lay on the south-west fringe of the county. Its railway station was one mile from the church at Waltham Cross in Hertfordshire on the line from London to Hertford which ran on the Hertfordshire side of the River Lea and would be of marginal use to an Essex diocese. A new tube line to connect directly with Stratford (and thereby overland to mid and north-east Essex) had been proposed but in the meantime the bulk of the Essex population would have to come into London and out again on the Lea Valley line to Waltham Cross. But the Abbey could boast the tomb of King Harold: no other rival could match that!

The Waltham Abbey deputation played with a straight bat. Ely, Peterborough, Norwich and St. Albans cathedrals were magnificent Norman structures so "it would be maintaining the dignity of East Anglia if a cathedral is to be added which would in like manner belong to the Norman period." They pointed out that the Abbey had been considered by Henry VIII as one of his New Foundation cathedrals in the 1540s.

The Bishop commented that seating capacity was small for a cathedral. The choir and transepts had been destroyed at the time of the Reformation, leaving just the old nave but, taking the modern Lady Chapel into account, the deputation said they could seat 1,000. However, the Lady Chapel could be reached only from an outside door and was on a raised level. The private owner of the 16 acres of the old monastery would be prepared to sell land at a modest price so that extensions could take place for a new chancel and transept. Asked whether this would be very expensive, given the need to blend with the age and magnificence of the Norman building, the deputation was hopeful of local support: recently they had raised £2,500 for a tower (£206,000 in today's money) to which the War Office had made a large contribution.

The advowson, in the hands of a five-man trust, also presented problems. Two of them were in the three man deputation, but they said they could not speak for the willingness of the other three to surrender patronage to the Bishop who inevitably observed: "that is one of the difficulties of the situation."

West Ham

With its population of 309,000 the Borough of West Ham represented the heartland of London-over-the-Border and Chelmsford's chief rival. It had nominated two churches as potential cathedrals: St John the Evangelist, the parish church of Stratford, where the Bishop of St. Albans owned the advowson, and All Saints', the parish church of West Ham itself, where the Vicar was patron but had promised a transfer to the Bishop. St. John the Evangelist had 1,000 seats of which 70 were rented out; All Saints' had 1,050, 450 of them rented. Both churches could be enlarged and both took a substantial £450 annually in collections (£37,100 in today's money). There were three hotels and for meetings Stratford Town Hall could seat 1,000, the Council Room 250, the Education Office 150 and the Technical Institute 800. Stratford was very accessible by rail: Plaistow underground station was within the Borough; there was an overland line from Southend with its station seven minutes by tram from the Town Hall; and Stratford Central Station on the main G.E.R. line through the heart of Essex was just five minutes' walk from St. John the Evangelist Church and 15 minutes from All Saints'. Indeed, the West Ham deputation was keen to point out that Essex County Council sometimes preferred the convenience of Liverpool Street station's Great Eastern Hotel over Chelmsford for its meetings. G.E.R also allowed through expresses to stop at Stratford on special occasions.

Unfortunately, in interview the Mayor of West Ham started in a state of bumbling disorganisation. He had tried randomly to sound out the Borough's clergy: a meeting of the Barking Deanery included clergy who were principally not from West Ham and, in any case, took place prematurely before Barking had put forward its candidature; a meeting in Ilford also contained non-Hammers and the cathedral issue had not been advertised as an agenda item so many who would have liked to express a view were absent; and there had been a "sort of Church Council meeting" in Upton Park. For what it was worth the majority of the few who voted at these meetings supported Chelmsford.

The Mayor then fell victim to hyperbole, claiming that Stratford Broadway could be reached by tram by one million Essex people in half an hour. A panellist corrected him: London-over-the-Border's population was only 800,000; the Mayor replied that growth was so rapid that it was difficult to be exact; the Bishop eventually settled on 750,000. The Mayor escaped to firmer ground by promising free or reduced cost use of the Town Hall and the Education Office committee room.

All Saints' was the longest church in Essex and rough plans had been prepared by George Gilbert Scott for further enlargement but Bishop Edgar Jacob commented:

> "I do not think myself it would be wise with the enormous needs of
> the living people to spend . . . very large sums on the architecture
> of the cathedral."

Although collections were substantial the Bishop still sought reassurance that the people of West Ham would be able to finance a cathedral and its special services. The Mayor conceded that most of the moneyed class lived miles out at Forest Gate with only a few close to hand.

The Bishop then asked for comment on "a sort of idea in the county, that if the cathedral is put at West Ham, the county of Essex is out of it altogether", noting that it would be "purely and totally a town affair." By way of comparison he repeated Canon Lake's concern that the Diocese of Southwark was struggling, a somewhat hasty judgement as it had been up and running for only two years. Nonetheless the Bishop queried whether country parishes would give much financial support to a cathedral if it seemed to focus too much on London. The Mayor, who had lived in Southwark for nine years earlier in his career, acknowledged that Southwark Cathedral was taking time to establish its identity: some Southwark junior clergy preferred visiting St. Paul's just across the Thames for spiritual sustenance and the cathedral was less central to local life than would have been the case had it been at Woolwich or Camberwell. Even so he had no doubt that the impact of Southwark Cathedral on the life of the district would grow. It had been helped by the generosity of the Bishop of Worcester, Charles Gore, who had given large sums out of his private fortune—he was the brother of the Earl of Arran—so that the cathedral "was a very elaborate building with elaborate musical services." As for the new Essex diocese, the Mayor doubted whether the unbeneficed clergy in the mission chapels, where churches had not yet been built, could afford trips to a cathedral outside London-over-the-Border: for many years these iron mission huts would continue to serve the spiritual needs of West Ham as its population increased each year by about 18,000, equivalent to the total population of Chelmsford.

Canon Richard Pelly, Vicar of All Saints', spoke movingly of the Church's mission:

> "We have been considering the cathedral from the point of view of the clergy and those who can go about the country in motor cars, but I do want the committee very earnestly to consider the great number of poor people . . . We do want the church to be the church of the poor as well as for others . . . That is the whole beginning, the middle and the end of our claim for West Ham."

But, he confessed, they still had pew rents: it was because of West Ham's poverty and they guaranteed a minimum income. Bishop Edgar Jacob was adamant: "they are illegal, totally illegal in a parish church." Canon Pelly asked the Bishop to order their abolition as he had tried it unsuccessfully with leading members of his congregation. The Bishop, who harboured an as yet unexpressed preference for West Ham, was disappointed: "well, I swept them all off at Portsea as being illegal." In the end it was the incumbent's willpower that mattered. Frank Johnson, the Bishop of Colchester, who was sitting alongside his diocesan, would have empathised: he bore the scars of that experience from his time at Chelmsford in the 1880s.

Woodford

The wealthy parish of Woodford on the edge of Epping Forest claimed 15,000 souls and rising. London merchants and bankers lived here in luxury residences, 200 of them within one mile of St. Mary's Parish Church. In its time Woodford had provided three Lord Mayors of London.[9] The advowson was in the hands of Lady Henry Somerset who owned large estates in Herefordshire and Surrey and was renowned for her work for the British Women's Temperance Association. The church seated 900 and could be enlarged: £3,000 (£248,000 in today's money) had been guaranteed by the congregation for this purpose. Collections realised a substantial £500 annually (£41,300) and additional income was generated by renting out all the pews. The church already put on a daily choral evensong. There were three hotels but public meeting space was negligible: the Memorial Hall and a gymnasium could seat just 400 each. There was a choice of two houses for a bishop's residence: either the Rectory or one offered by local magistrate, Mr J.R. Roberts. There were good rail links with West Ham, a direct line to Ongar and a loop line via Chigwell to Ilford to connect with the G.E.R. main line to the rest of Essex but the church was half an hour's drive away from the nearest London, Tilbury and Southend station.

The plutocratic residents of Woodford were well-insulated from the criminal haunts of London but, with pharasaic casuistry, paraded London's criminality as the very reason for placing the cathedral in their midst:

> "Over half the fines and the fees at Petty Sessions come from Becontree and London-over-the-Border . . . it would show that we wanted a cathedral . . . more than those righteous parishes in the rest of the county who do not produce so much crime."

Following that perverse logic surely West Ham should prevail? But, they argued, a cathedral in West Ham would be overshadowed by the docks and the huge Town Hall whereas in Woodford it would be "the essence of the thing."

As for accommodation, one deputy offered:

> "I cannot suppose that any of your clergy, my Lord, would stop at licensed houses and if they do not we have got the finest temperance hotel. It is within pistol shot of that house where you are now living."

That was true even if the means of measurement were somewhat chilling. The Bishop came clean. To ensure easy access to London-over-the-Border he had, in truth, lived in Woodford since 1904 and Chigwell prior to that. Indeed, his knowledge of the local tram and rail network was impressive:

> "You could drive to either Walthamstow or Leytonstone and get on the Tilbury Line down to Southend and you could drive to Tottenham or Ponder's End in half an hour or less and get on that [Lea Valley] line . . . The tram from Woodford High Road takes you right to Stratford Broadway and also down the Ilford Road right to Clapton. You could also get to Loughton via Whipp's Cross."

All this hit a sore spot with Frank Johnson, the Bishop of Colchester: he would have preferred that the Bishop had lived at Liverpool Street's Great Eastern Hotel. The Woodford deputation had stirred up a small hornet's nest: whether it did their case any good is doubtful.

Back on the main agenda, offers of hospitality were profuse. The rich house owners close to the church "would be only too proud and well able and delighted to entertain any guest who may be quartered on them." As for a bishop's residence, "we have this handsome offer of Mr Roberts to give a choice of two good houses." They calculated what this offer in kind would save the Diocese:

> "It has been talked about that a sum of £300 p.a. [£24,800 in today's money] would enable the Bishop to live where he liked to for which you would need capital of £10,000 so we are virtually offering £10,000 [£825,000]."

Moreover, the congregation were very keen to subscribe to anything they were asked to support such as the curates' stipends which they financed out of offertories and voluntary subscriptions. And Lady Somerset, with condescending generosity, was prepared to offer the advowson to the Bishop provided the cathedral was in Woodford.

But what about the pew rents? The Bishop took a softer line than with West Ham. He jested familiarly: "I believe those wonderful parliamentary pews [private pews granted for life] are done away with?" However, the churchwardens still continued a private business in fixed term renting accumulating £350 a year (£28,900 in today's money): non-subscribers sat in the galleries unless they were guests of a renting family. The Bishop reasserted that pew rents were not legal though without the fervour that he had employed with the West Ham deputation. These were his seriously rich neighbours. They were not likely to be leading contenders for the cathedral prize and, come what may, their continuing financial support would be important for the new diocese.

Bishop Edgar Jacob summed up: "you consider that Woodford being a little outside . . . has considerable advantages over the very thick of London-over-the-Border?" The Rector replied:

> "Yes, my Lord and we consider ourselves that it is much better for people coming to diocesan meetings . . . especially the poorer people who come out a little from that densely populated part to a place which is brighter and better for their bodies as well as their souls."

It had been an arduous day. The Reverend John Ellerton had ended his life 15 years earlier as Vicar of the Essex parish of White Roding: the first line of his famous hymn, *The day thou gavest Lord is ended*, might have echoed in prayerful gratitude in the current Bishop of St. Albans' mind that night.

CHAPTER 7

A Mess of Chelmsford Pottage

June 30th 1907 had been set aside as the day when Essex parishes would bring the question of the cathedral before their congregations.[1] Intercessions were offered during the previous week. From July the race would be officially on.

At a public meeting in Chelmsford on October 9th, in the Ball Room of the Shire Hall, Frederic Chancellor presented his *Memorial of the Mayor, Aldermen and Burgesses of the Inhabitants of Chelmsford setting forth the reasons why Chelmsford claims the honour of being chosen as the cathedral site for the new Diocese of Chelmsford*. It included the basic facts that the Bishop was later to incorporate on his electoral broadsheet. But it also reminded people of the county town's other attributes: the Shire Hall had been the centre for county business for 600 years; the town hosted the Lord Lieutenant's public county meetings, the Assizes and County Council and County Education Committee meetings; it was the headquarters of Essex Police; the business of the two archdeaconries of Essex and Colchester had always been transacted in Chelmsford; and ordinations had been frequently held in St. Mary's when Danbury Palace had been the Bishop of Rochester's residence. Within a 25 miles radius there were 454 churches: no other competitor could reach half that figure.

Chancellor had also been doing his own selective polling. A circular letter had been sent to incumbents, churchwardens, justices of the peace and other "gentlemen": 651 were in favour of Chelmsford, 48 for Colchester and 31 split between the rest. This was a scam as the majority approached came from Chelmsford and its hinterland. It was a politician's tactic: ignore your opponents and identify your own vote.

Similar biases appeared elsewhere: everyone was for his own town and wanted to do down his rivals. At the Colchester public meeting no one had a good word for Chelmsford. The insult was reciprocated by Chelmsford. The editor of the Chelmsford based *Essex County Chronicle*, Thomas Thompson, a keen supporter of Chancellor and official seconder of the *Memorial*, wrote condescendingly:

> "We have nothing to say against Colchester but some of the claims advanced in favour of that place have been quite quixotic . . . There are two or three very graceful edifices in Colchester but they are mere cockleshells compared with St. Mary's at Chelmsford."

The St. Mary's *Parish Magazine* for October 1907 took a more detached view:

> "The Mayor has already received numerous promises of support. In the meantime it should be the prayer of all that God will so guide the minds of those who have to settle the question that their decision may be what is really best for the work of the *whole* Diocese."

However, as we have seen, its author, Canon Lake had been privately pre-empting God by urging that West Ham would not be the solution.

A General Committee was set up by Frederic Chancellor to support Chelmsford's case.[2] It was not meant to be an executive body—that would be a smaller inner group—but it would be socially powerful. Its promoters undoubtedly hoped that the cachet attached to membership would make it more attractive to be seen to be a member than not. Wykeham Chancellor, Frederic's son, acted as secretary; he sent invitations to join the Committee and approached others for money to help defray administrative costs.[3]

Despite the huge support that Frederic Chancellor secured for his *Memorial* from his hand-picked gentlemen contacts, not all replies to Wykeham Chancellor's invitations were as cordial. Refusals covered a variety of reasons: no longer resident in Essex; too busy; not well-informed about the issues; preferred another town's candidature; wished to keep an open mind; too ill, old or deaf; or were Non-Conformist.

Some were more pointed. The Vicar of Gestingthorpe up on the Suffolk border wrote:

"Thank you for your open letter re Chelmsford as the cathedral city which with the pamphlet from Colchester have gone into the waste paper basket as I think the Bishop is far better able to judge which will be the most convenient centre than I am."

A curate at Castle Hedingham could not care less: he had received notice to quit from the Vicar and was off to Halifax. The Vicar of Saffron Walden on the county's north-west Cambridgeshire frontier was indifferent: "I beg to decline . . . because Chelmsford is nearly as inaccessible as St. Albans." A reply from Writtle Wick near Chelmsford started: "As I have quite enough to attend to and really don't much care whether Chelmsford becomes the cathedral city or not . . ." and continued in the same sardonic vein. A resident of Broomfield, just to the north of Chelmsford, was unimpressed: "Chelmsford is about as wild cat a scheme as Colchester." A cynical correspondent from Walmer in Kent added:

"All the championing for the honour of being the cathedral city is merely a longing on the part of those in office for higher positions . . . I fancy I see the flutter of excitement when the 'Dear Dean' of the ladies of 'The Close' begins to live in the hopes of those who are sighing for halcyon days."

Tribune, a London newspaper, in its edition of October 21st 1907, had little time for Chelmsford:

"From a geographical sense [Chelmsford] is the centre of the county but . . . during the last 40 years not one new parish has been instituted in Chelmsford whilst on the other hand in London-over-the-Border 40 new parishes have been installed."

Charles Banham, Honorary Secretary of the Colchester Cathedral Site Committee, objected in the next edition to this assumption of a two horse race:

"Your account in Monday's *Tribune* omits all mention of Colchester. Colchester is by far the largest town in extra-metropolitan Essex . . . From its position of ready access, its great historical associations, its numerous available churches and its modern importance as the metropolis of the greater part of Essex, Colchester is indubitably the most sensible site for the new cathedral."

In the national press the *Morning Post*, on December 18th 1907, supported West Ham:

"To place the new cathedral in any distant part would be to give it to the comparatively few, whilst by far the larger majority would never see it or feel its daily influence. It is the thousands of the toiling, industrial and working classes who are most in need of spiritual help."

The *Church Times*, on December 20th 1907, confined itself to a simple statement of facts about the seven contestants but quoted Chelmsford's population as only 13,000 which sparked a response from the vigilant Frederic Chancellor on January 3rd 1908, correcting the figure to 17,000: he had forgotten that he had formally declared 18,000 to the Bishop. To the Mayor of West Ham such puny numbers were laughable: in the *Church Times* of January 10th he put the shire small fry in their place:

"The population of West Ham is more than one quarter of the county . . . If they were to add together the cathedral towns of Winchester, Salisbury, Wells, Truro, Ely, Peterborough, Durham, Chester, Rochester, Canterbury, Bangor and Llandaff they would have a town the size of West Ham . . . In population and rateable value West Ham is now the seventh town in England."

The Stratford Express reported on West Ham's public meeting on January 22nd 1908. Bishop Edgar Jacob had by now let slip his view that the inexorable eastward advance of London would require a further subdivision of the Essex diocese in the not too distant future. West Ham, it seemed, would have its cathedral one way or another but they would prefer it now. Their supporters quoted the Bishop's own book, *The Divine Society*: "it is a real misfortune that so few of our cathedrals are to be found in great towns." Canon Pelly countered the whispers that urban dioceses could not support a cathedral's finances: only 20 years ago Newcastle had been preferred over Hexham yet Newcastle was viable. Southwark too denied the rumour and its bishop supported West Ham's case. Another clergyman reasserted the Church's true mission:

"He had been told that West Ham was poor and was everything that a cathedral diocese should not be . . . What was the Church working for? To preach the gospel to the poor."

Not surprisingly West Ham's public meeting endorsed its own candidature without dissent. However, the numbers attending were very small in proportion to its population. The Church may be working for the poor but the poor mostly did not attend churches or public meetings.

By mid-February it was all over. The *Daily Mail* on February 11th 1908 reported that the Executive Committee of the Essex and Hertfordshire Bishopric Fund had received the views of the parishes and unanimously recommended Chelmsford to the Bishop's General Committee which would meet on March 5th to rubber stamp the decision. When they did the bells of St. Mary's were rung in celebration.

Of the 461 parishes, 388 sent in returns, only five of them declining to state a preference. Chelmsford was placed first in 191 parishes, Colchester in 101, West Ham in 63, Woodford in 13, Barking in 8, Waltham Abbey in 6 and Thaxted, having voted for itself, managed 1:[4] the second and third place preferences were not needed.

Recriminations soon began. The *South Essex Mail* on February 14th was ruefully ironic:

"We understand that the clergy and laity of the villages would prefer the venerable old town . . . Chelmsford is dignified, if such a word may be applied, and aristocratic: it has a beautiful parish church, a fine market and considerable commerce. In and around the town many well-known families reside . . . Dr Jacob will no doubt be thankful to go to Chelmsford just because of its old world air and its peaceful surroundings. But our surprise . . . is that the Church herself has missed a glorious opportunity of identifying itself with the workers, the toilers, the poor of Essex . . . Can the new Essex diocese 'feed the multitude' of Essex men and women . . . as well at Chelmsford as at West Ham? . . . She cannot and we deeply regret her want of judgement and her neglect of a golden occasion."

The *Stratford Express* the following day did not mince words: it loathed the decision and was scornful of the clergy:

"If it had been left to the people . . . there cannot be the slightest doubt that West Ham would have got an overwhelming majority . . . Small semi-private meetings have been held at which only a dozen people have been present and, influenced by the clergy, they have passed resolutions in favour of Chelmsford . . . In one case the vicar of a church quite close to West Ham refused to accept the decision of a meeting of parishioners because he did not consider the meeting representative . . . In some cases the clergy have . . . refused to allow petitions in favour of West Ham inside their churches. A few . . . have even refused to call a meeting. Certain it is that the population majority said to favour Chelmsford does not exist except on paper . . . The Church . . . has sold her birthright for a mess of Chelmsford pottage."

The paper also sensed that money had triumphed over mission:

"The fact that the county families of Essex have subscribed the larger part of the money should not count in settling the question where the cathedral is to be . . . The clergy are alone to blame for the decision to make a small country town of 15,000 in the wilds of Essex the cathedral city and to leave 800,000 people of London-over-the Border without the aid and inspiration of which the cathedral, we are told, was to be the unfailing source."

To make his point the editor, careless of Frederic Chancellor's feelings, had even shrunk Chelmsford's population.

The Bishop asked his returning officer, Canon Kenneth Gibbs of Aldenham Vicarage, Watford, for a detailed analysis of the poll.[5] The Canon's comments show that the process did indeed lack clarity. The Bishop had given the parishes useful summaries of the candidates' applications; he had helpfully suggested that they decide on London-over-the-Border or the country and then choose the prime candidate in the sector for which they had opted; he had also invited second and third choices which might help if it were a close run thing; but he had not said who should vote, leading to an inconsistent variety of practice.

One case supported the *Stratford Express'* suspicions. In St. Edmund's, Forest Gate the vote was decided by the Vicar and churchwardens with Chelmsford first and West Ham second but the Vicar wrote to Canon Gibbs to say that a meeting of the congregation would by a considerable majority have reversed the order. However, there were other instances of parishes which rode roughshod over their incumbent: in one Leytonstone and two Wanstead parishes clergy who would have put Chelmsford first were ignored by their churchwardens and congregations who plumped for West Ham. It happened in the country areas too: at All Saints', Stanway the vote went for Colchester which was just three miles away, even though the incumbent preferred Chelmsford; at St. Paul's, Clacton on the north-east coast the vote went for Colchester despite the incumbent preferring West Ham; at Stebbing, in north Essex, the congregation voted for Chelmsford, overriding the incumbent who preferred West Ham and the curate who spoke up for Thaxted. Contrary to the *Stratford Express'* view the people seemed to triumph over the clergy reasonably frequently.

Sometimes Canon Gibbs had to interpret the vote. The Shalford return recorded both churchwardens voting for Chelmsford and the Vicar for West Ham: Canon Gibbs went with the majority so the Vicar lost. In other small country parishes that sent multiple returns representing different pressure groups he returned the ballot papers asking for just one response.

Others were confused by the Bishop's statement that there would soon be another subdivision of the Diocese. St. Michael's, Walthamstow voted for Chelmsford first but added a note that if it were definite that the new Diocese were soon to be split then they would have chosen Colchester leaving West Ham to pick up its cathedral seat later; the Vicar added that several other parishes agreed. On the other hand, out in the country, Great Dunmow had voted for West Ham because, when the next division occurred, they knew they would get their country cathedral. Many parishes made the point that as Bishop Edgar Jacob lived in London (and it was assumed he would continue to do so as the new Bishop of Chelmsford) the cathedral must be in the country.

The parishes of Chingford, Greensted Green and South Weald in the south-west of the county and Farnham in the north-west near Bishop's Stortford, refused to vote and demanded that the question be settled by the Bishop: other parishes made the same remark and voted under protest. In Braintree the Vicar wanted to boycott the vote but was overridden by his churchwardens who made the return.

In the Stour Valley parishes on the Suffolk border there were strong feelings for Colchester. Dedham said Colchester "would represent the *County* feelings and tradition which London-over-the Border could not be said to do"; Belchamp St. Paul voted for Colchester and urged that north Essex should prevail because those living further south in the county had, for a thousand years, been living nearer their cathedral whether in London, Rochester or St. Albans. Further south, in the Colne Valley, St. Andrew's, Halstead took a more detached view: it voted for Colchester because of the expected further subdivision of Essex but noted that Chelmsford would be the best choice if this did not happen. Ideally these parishes and many others would have liked to record two votes, the first for a unitary diocese, the second, anticipating a further subdivision, voting for two cathedrals, one for the country and the other for the metropolitan area. Canon Gibbs wrote to the Bishop:

> "Doubtless many vote for Chelmsford who would agree that Colchester would be best for north Essex and the result is that one feels that the *mere* votes leave one uncertain as to the opinion of the people who give them."

The dread of any bishop must be the voice of a predecessor or, barring that, his son: P.L. Claughton, the Vicar of Halton near Witham and son of the first Bishop of St. Albans, was strongly for Thaxted because the "population and convenience of Thaxted ought not to be considered but the Honour and Glory of God." Canon Gibbs informed Bishop Edgar Jacob that the son "is quite sure that his father, the late Bishop, would have voted with him."

It was a skewed voting system. Canon Gibbs expressed his reservation to the Bishop: "I daresay that West Ham by itself has as large a population as a hundred of these little country parishes." That was true but in population terms Chelmsford was still well ahead: the 191 parishes voting for it represented 428,375 people (according to the 1901 census) compared to West Ham's 63 parishes with a population of 321,677. On that score Colchester could have no argument: the 101 parishes supporting its case were mostly tiny rural communities in the north of the county representing a population of only 120,567.

So, that was that. Chelmsford had been declared the winner. In the *Essex County Chronicle* of April 3rd the Bishop admitted that he would have voted for West Ham and would live there "as an Essex Bishop must live near London, nearer than Chelmsford, if he is to administer a diocese without unnecessary fatigue."

All that remained was for Bishop Edgar Jacob to be enthroned as the first Bishop of Chelmsford. But it would take another six years for parliament to pass the relevant legislation: he would then be too ill for the challenge.

CHAPTER 8

A Parliamentary Marathon

The Church of England's original structures and Prayer Book were defined in statute law and could only be changed by statute thereby placing the Church at the mercy of governments and how much parliamentary time they were prepared to spare. As the new century got under way it was in very short supply. With most men having the vote responsive governments now devoted a great deal of time to educational, social, employment and public health legislation and were also distracted by the immensely divisive issue of Home Rule for Ireland that had seen Irish members of parliament filibustering to hamper government activity and give publicity to their cause.

An Enabling Act to give the Church of England the right to regulate its own internal administrative structure without queuing for parliamentary time would resolve the problem but that would not come until 1919. It was certainly needed: between 1880 and 1913, 183 out of 217 Church of England parliamentary bills were dropped because of lack of time; three-quarters of them were never even discussed.[1] It was a matter of indifference rather than hostility. As one church historian put it:

> "The less ecclesiastically interested or party-minded or theologically informed the average M.P. was, the less likely he would be to see the point in change of any sort. Let the Church exist, so long as it does not cause trouble."[2]

Life became even more complicated after the Liberal landslide victory at the 1906 General Election when a more specifically anti-Church feeling surfaced. The Liberals' strength lay in industrial England where more people

81

attended Non-Conformist chapels than Anglican churches and in Wales where worshippers were overwhelmingly chapel. The Liberal leadership could not ignore these religious realities especially where they affected educational policy.

In both England and Wales Non-Conformists were disgruntled with the Conservatives' 1902 Education Act which made the county and county borough councils, created in 1888, responsible for school provision thus abolishing the ad hoc school boards set up in 1870 to raise money for schools where church schools did not exist. The Act also brought within the councils' scope all voluntary schools, the vast majority of them Church of England, but as a compromise they were permitted to retain their distinctive religious instruction lessons with an opt-out conscience clause for parents who objected. In many rural areas in England and throughout Wales the Church of England voluntary school was often the only one providing elementary education and Non-Conformists took umbrage at subsidising Anglican doctrine through taxation. In 1906, therefore, the Liberals sought to reverse the arrangement by enforcing non-denominational religious education lessons with an opt-out for parents who wanted specific doctrinal teaching by their own clergy for which a room would be provided on the school premises. Many of the bishops were vocal in their opposition and instrumental in whipping up public demonstrations.

St. Mary's *Parish Magazine* in March 1906 quoted Bishop Edgar Jacob's reaction to the Education Bill:

> "The rights of the state do not include . . . the right to trample on the religious convictions of those who have steadily maintained that definite religious belief is at the root of character and have made great sacrifices to be able so to teach."

The Archbishop of Canterbury, Randall Davidson, was reported in the May 1906 magazine:

> "The only shred of former rights preserved is that on two days in the week teachers other than those belonging to the school may give denominational teaching at the cost of those to whom the buildings belong."

Thomas Stevens, the first suffragan Bishop of Barking, protested in *The Times* of April 13th:

"Never has the authority of Parliament been asserted as brutally as in this bill for riding roughshod over our sacred trusts . . . These trusts are trusts for God, not for man . . . I cannot rob God, nor will I."

A mass meeting was held at Chelmsford's Corn Exchange on May 21st with up to 1,000 present and another followed on October 27th. Such nationwide public demonstrations were used by the hereditary Conservative peers to justify their demolition of the bill in defiance of the democratically elected House of Commons, a fate they dealt out to a wide range of Liberal bills over the next three years. Most of the bishops, by their stance, were seen as Tory henchmen.

In this fervid atmosphere parliamentary enthusiasm for a Bishoprics Bill to give life to the new dioceses of Chelmsford and St. Edmundsbury was unlikely. The bill was introduced in the House of Lords on March 3rd 1909. If the Lords approved, which inevitably they would, it would lie on the table of both Houses of Parliament for 30 days and, if not objected to, would be carried into immediate effect by an Order in Council. If objections were raised time had to be found for a debate in the House of Commons which gave the opportunity for what Bishop Edgar Jacob termed "malcontents" to lay ambushes and talk out the bill.

Circumstances were on the side of the obstructionists. An immense constitutional crisis erupted in April 1909 that lasted two years and prevented much cherished government legislation seeing the light of day, let alone the small issue of east of England bishoprics. It started when Chancellor of the Exchequer, David Lloyd George, presented a budget designed to raise taxes on the rich to pay for naval expansion and the new old age pensions. The House of Lords rejected it. Their defiance of the constitutional convention that the Commons alone decided taxation precipitated an election in January 1910 which produced a virtual dead heat between the two major parties, leaving the Liberal government dependent on 82 Irish and 40 Labour members of parliament. The Lords caved in on the budget but a further constitutional impasse arose when George V, rather than appoint a legion of Liberal peers to ensure the passing of legislation which would reduce the power of the House of Lords, asked the government to seek a further electoral mandate on this issue. If they won, the Conservatives in the Lords might concede. A second election in December 1910 produced an almost identical outcome but still with a large anti-Conservative majority. Sure enough sufficient Conservatives in the Lords backed down allowing the 1911 Parliament

Act to pass by 131-114 votes, the majority including 13 bishops but two bishops voted against and 11 abstained or were conveniently absent.[3] The Conservatives thereby protected their in-built majority but with diminished powers. The Act replaced the Lords' veto with a two year delaying power though this could still be used to destructive effect in the last two years of a parliament. The Conservative die-hards who had remained adamant in their opposition featured members of the Cecil family, leading Anglican laymen who were at the same time promoting the abortive Bishoprics Bill: politics and religion had become counter-productively intermingled.

The Parliament Act left the way open for Church disestablishment in Wales including the diversion of its £270,000 endowments (£20.8 million in today's money) to secular use. Inevitably another confrontation with the government loomed led energetically by the Archbishop of Canterbury. Only three bishops held back from the fray; one of them, Charles Gore, by this time Bishop of Oxford, commented dryly that only in Welsh lunatic asylums was there in effect still an established church such was the desertion of the Anglican Church by the sane Welsh. To the neutral the case seemed open and shut: Anglicanism was an English import foisted on Wales; Welsh bishops had, for the last 150 years, been Englishmen; often the parson and the schoolteacher were the only Anglicans resident in a Welsh parish.

The bishops organised a national campaign to raise public awareness. This was the thin end of the wedge: Irish disestablishment in 1871, Wales now, next England. The Dean of St. Asaph spoke at the Shire Hall in Chelmsford on November 14th 1913. On June 30th 1914 simultaneous evening services in St. Mary's, Chelmsford, Holy Trinity, Springfield and St. John the Evangelist, Moulsham were followed by a procession to Bell Meadow in the centre of town to rousing cornet-accompanied hymns including *The Church's one foundation*, *Onward Christian soldiers* and *O God, our help in ages past*. The resulting assembly of 4,000 people passed a Resolution of Solemn Protest as their part of a national demonstration.

It was all to no avail except to make many Liberal members of parliament even more disenchanted with the Church of England and its business. A Welsh Disestablishment Bill was introduced in 1912 and passed by the House of Commons. The Lords rejected it but it would automatically become law in 1914, although the onset of war delayed its implementation until 1920.

Although the Parliament Act seemed to have resolved the immediate constitutional deadlock a series of unprecedented crises between 1911 and 1913 continued to push non-essential issues to the parliamentary sidelines. On the international scene the provocative antics of Kaiser Wilhelm II in

Morocco, German naval expansion and the descent of the Balkans into open war dominated debate and, as tensions heightened, required an Official Secrets Act to combat espionage and legislation to control aircraft over U.K. territory. At home two years of the worst strikes in Britain's history involving miners, seamen, railwaymen, dockers and firemen brought the troops out on the streets; the Home Rule Bill for Ireland led to the formation of the Ulster Volunteers and a threat of civil war with Conservative leaders and some army officers backing the Ulstermen; some suffragettes turned to violent activity and hunger strikes in pursuit of votes for women; and scandal erupted when government ministers used inside information to buy shares in an American subsidiary of Marconi just before the parent company was awarded a lucrative government contract. And then there were other crucial Liberal reforms still awaiting parliamentary time, with many Conservatives, bruised by their recent constitutional defeats, in retaliatory mood: national insurance to provide the working man with medical and unemployment benefits was vigorously opposed by Conservatives as an unwarranted interference with the free market and a sop to the emerging Labour party; attempts to improve working conditions in shops and mines offended the largely Conservative owners who would have to pay something towards the costs; and introducing the payment of members of parliament so that the House of Commons would no longer be the preserve of those with independent means seemed to those on the right to be yet another nail in their political coffin. In this context the fact that the Bishop of St. Albans was ill and overworked would not have been a matter of concern for many members of parliament.

In 1913 the Church rethought its strategy, combining the Sheffield Bishopric Bill, which had also fallen foul of the budget crisis in 1909, with the reorganisation of East Anglia's bishoprics: one bill would stand more chance than two. In the meantime the Diocese of St. Albans was becoming ever more unwieldy: the 1911 census revealed that Essex's population had increased by a further 30% since 1901, compared to 11% across the whole country. Assuming non-metropolitan Essex roughly matched the average national increase then London-over-the-Border's population had rocketed ahead at a rate approaching 60%.

On August 11th Bishop Edgar Jacob set off on holiday, resigned to further delays,[4] but within three days it was all over. Prime Minister Asquith insisted on a "truce of God". He would give government time to the Bishoprics Bill and employ parliamentary sleight of hand to get it through provided both sides restrained their extremists and allowed each others' bills to pass into law. On the one side a group of Non-Conformists and some Liverpool Evangelical Anglicans, who disliked the way bishops had allowed the advance of ritualism in Anglican services, had been harassing Church Bills and using parliamentary procedure to talk them out of time: on the other flank zealous Anglicans had been ambushing Non-Conformist Chapel Bills. Behind the scenes Lord Hugh Cecil consulted the parliamentary leader of the Non-Conformists, Liberal M.P. Charles Allen, to try to quieten things down.[5]

Previous Bishopric Bills had been started in the House of Lords; this one was launched in the House of Commons. Out of the blue the bill to give life to the bishoprics of Chelmsford, St. Edmundsbury and Sheffield passed through its Commons second reading on August 12th. Asquith made no prior announcement of the reading, catching its opponents off guard. Government business managers struck again organising a third reading of the bill in the early hours of the morning of August 13th when even fewer members of parliament were present. Both readings were starred by government whips so that 64 ministers turned up to vote and outnumbered the zealots. The Prime Minister was sharp with those politicians who wanted to continue the fight: the bill raised no question of religious principle; it was an internal administrative measure for which all the money had been found privately; and it was only fair to let it go through in return for the 15 Nonconformist bills that were in the pipeline. It passed its third reading and was sent to the Lords where it went rapidly through all its stages on August 14th.

It had been a marathon race decided by a sprint in the last hundred yards or as Bishop Edgar Jacob preferred:

> "The story of the passage of this Act through the House of
> Commons may seem like a story of bargains between parties and of
> human infirmities and efforts and surprises, but no Christian man
> can doubt that there has been an unseen Pilot of the ship."[6]

In his September diocesan letter the Bishop made it clear that, although in 1906 he had declared himself ready to take on the burden of the new Essex Diocese, his weakened heart was now not up to it:

> "Two years ago, after the severest pressure of my life, my health
> broke down and I was obliged to spend the winter on the Nile . . .
> but I shall be 69 in November next and my doctors are agreed

that I must not attempt to organise Essex as the first Bishop of Chelmsford. That must be left to a younger man."

There merely remained the completion of financial and administrative formalities. The Bishoprics Act of 1878 sought an assured annual income for a new diocese of £3,000 (£227,000 in modern values), rising to £3,500 (£264,900) within five years, plus an additional income of £500 (£37,900) if there were no bishop's house. By 1913, as had been hoped, the bar was set lower at not less than £2,000 (£153,000). However, the Essex and Hertfordshire Bishopric Fund had collected enough to establish an endowment that would realise £3,100 annually (£238,000) and would encompass the stipends of the suffragan bishops, leaving some over to kick-start the funding of another diocese should there be a further subdivision.[7]

The question of the bishop's house had also been resolved. It proved to be a disappointment for West Ham as Chelmsford would now get both bishop's house and cathedral. In 1909 the Essex and Hertfordshire Bishopric Committee had purchased Guy Harlings on the other side of New Street to the east of St. Mary's from the executors of Frank Johnson: he had bought it in 1895 when he became Bishop of Colchester.[8] It was assumed that this expansive site would accommodate both the new bishop and the rector, the former in an 18 roomed house yet to be built with a "motor shed" attached and the latter in Guy Harlings itself with a small stable for his horse and trap.[9] Come 1914, however, the first bishop would chose the cheaper option of living in Redgates (renamed Bishopscourt), a large house close to All Saints' Church, Springfield, just a mile north of St. Mary's,[10] leaving Rector Henry Lake on his own in Guy Harlings. The Ecclesiastical Commissioners approved the financial arrangements on December 18th and the Order in Council constituting the Diocese of Chelmsford was signed on January 14th 1914. A second Order in Council formalising the boundaries of the dioceses of Essex and Suffolk was signed on March 7th.

On January 27th 1914 John Watts-Ditchfield, the Vicar of St. James-the-Less in Bethnal Green, received a letter from Prime Minister Henry Asquith inviting him to become Chelmsford's first bishop despite the rumour in the *Manchester Guardian* three days earlier that the Archbishop of Brisbane was to be appointed.

In 1897, when John Watts-Ditchfield had been installed in impoverished Bethnal Green, the *Holloway and Hornsey Press* had written:

"The world in these days is apt to sneer when a clergyman accepts a 'call' . . . but where a man accepts a 'call' which involves the amount of uphill work which the Rev. J.E. Watts-Ditchfield is having to face at St. James', Bethnal Green even the bitterest sceptic and the most confirmed sneerer must admit the sincerity of the man."[11]

Similar sentiments might have applied to the challenge of his bishopric. He had done heroic work in his slum parish where most of the men, if employed at all, were casual labourers in the docks on a small or irregular wage and the women worked in sweated industries. He targeted the men believing that if he could win them over their families would follow. His success was such that his book, *Fishers of Men,* published in 1899, ran to three editions. He and his wife, Jane, were extraordinarily diligent home visitors: she helped with the housework and children if the men were out while he sought out the men in the pubs. Accompanied by a brass band, his visits excited huge interest. He preached on street corners amongst the barrow-boys and held summer open air services in Victoria Park, the East End's equivalent of Hyde Park. In 1903 the *Daily News* religious census revealed that 1,699 people attended St. James-the-Less, more than double the number of any other Anglican church in the Borough.[12]

His industrial exhibitions to highlight the abuses of sweated labour and high rents caught the attention of the *Daily Graphic* on May 9th 1904:

"The Vicar of St. James-the-Less has organised in . . . the heart of Bethnal Green, an exhibition . . . the inspection of which arouses mingled feelings of painful surprise and unexpected pleasure . . . Surprise and pleasure because it shows specimens of as fine marquetry and other furniture, silk-weaving and other industries, as can be seen anywhere: pain because . . . the making . . . has been carried out by poor people for a remuneration which is a scandal to humanity."

He was an inveterate raiser of funds from wealthy philanthropists to finance church restoration, a parish hall, sporting facilities in the derelict churchyard, a medical mission, a temperance billiards club and a settlement for ordinands as a base for mission work in the East End. His people loved and respected him: a meagre 26 Easter communicants in 1897 had grown to 915 by 1914 and the Sunday Schools had an average attendance of 2,000 with 150 teachers.

He had an international reputation too. He received an invitation from the Church of England Men's Society to visit Australia in 1912. Again he preached his doctrine of men first as the basis for true family faith. The Western Australian *Daily News* of April 27th wrote:

> "The Rev J.E. Watts-Ditchfield shoulders a Sheffield-steel blazing weapon in the shape of a warm and convincing personality . . . There is a twinkle in his eye that tells of the utmost good humour . . . He is a man's man. Superficially he gives the impression of one who is not merely inured to the world but lives in it through sheer joy of association."

The Sydney *Daily Telegraph* on June 22nd wrote:

> "He is a man who would never waste breath or bandy words about how a thing should be done. He just does it . . . It takes a diamond to cut a diamond. It takes a man to catch a man."

In August he transferred to New Zealand, preached in Honolulu on the way to Canada and in a succession of towns as he travelled across the continent from Vancouver to New York. He arrived home in November 1913 having travelled 35,000 miles and addressed 470 meetings. The expanses of Essex would be modest by comparison.

He was on the evangelical wing which was not well-represented on the bishops' bench. The *Church Times* of February 6th 1914 commented:

> "He is regarded as a leader by the younger clergy of that school which latterly has shown signs of impatience with the rigid traditions and dry Protestantism of the older men . . . Those who know him best decline to believe that as a diocesan bishop he will fail to perceive that there are equally loyal churchmen in the ranks of those with whose principles of churchmanship he is not in full sympathy."

He did indeed perceive them but there would be some bumpy moments en route.

He was consecrated as a bishop on February 24th. His first engagements were at St. Nicholas', Colchester on March 8th and at All Saints', West Ham on March 15th, diplomatically giving pride of place to the two major towns that had lost out in the race for the bishop's seat. In the absence of the Archbishop of Canterbury he was enthroned in Chelmsford Cathedral on April 23rd by William Walsh, Bishop of Dover. Fears of militant suffragette activity, even the burning down of the Cathedral,[13] came to nothing though *Votes for Women* literature was being sold in the street,[14] an activity which some regarded as indecorous. The Bishop detached himself from the procession after the service to address the crowds from The Gun outside the Shire Hall, thus setting a precedent for his successors:[15]

> "I can assure you, as far as I can, that I shall simply live and die for the good of this county of Essex."

In his diary he wrote:

> "So ends a week never to be forgotten. Farewell to Bethnal Green. Welcome to Chelmsford. I held one curacy, one vicariate and I shall probably live and die at Chelmsford. Lord, make me faithful."

CHAPTER 9

Town or City

Much to the chagrin of the locals Chelmsford's new cathedral did not bring city status in its wake. The widespread assumption that the two were inextricably linked seemed to be backed by historic precedent. The Normans had moved a number of cathedrals from small Saxon towns to places of much greater significance and when Henry VIII created his six New Foundation cathedrals they were all in places adjudged to be cities or, as in the case of Westminster, a settlement to which he immediately granted city status. Consequently the great 17th and 18th century lawyers, Edward Coke and William Blackstone, upheld that a city was defined by "ancient prescriptive receipt" because of its centuries old possession of the royal gifts of an incorporated charter as a borough and a diocesan bishop's seat. The new industrial centres could aspire to the former by taking advantage of the 1835 Municipal Corporations Act to secure borough status complete with their own elected councillors, aldermen and mayor. They could display their economic eminence by erecting great Victorian town halls that still dominate the centres of so many of the great conurbations. But God prevailed over mammon. City status, an ecclesiastical rather than a secular gift, remained out of reach.

However, when new cathedrals began to emerge it was discovered that cathedral and city status were not legally identical twins. There were two distinct processes as was demonstrated when the Diocese of Manchester was created in 1847. While Parliament created the diocese, a separate petition for city status to be granted by Letters Patent[1] had to be made to the monarch via the Home Office. Manchester did not get round to this until 1852. Ripon, which had inaccurately been calling itself a city since 1836, eventually decided to regularise its position too and formally received city status in 1865. So, for a few years Ripon and Manchester were the first cathedral seats not to be cities, a temporary procedural hiccup that was soon rectified.

St. Albans, with a population of only 8,298, became the first interesting test case. Though smaller places such as Wells, Ely and Lichfield were cities they were regarded as quaint medieval anomalies. An internal civil service memorandum was scornful of St. Albans' pretensions:

> "I don't see why, because they have a bishop, they should be made
> a city, when it is only a fourth or fifth rate market town in point
> of population."[2]

But Home Office ministers ignored the advice and stuck with tradition: St. Albans was enshrined as a city in 1877 as was Truro, another small town. For the moment the linkage of city status to a cathedral seat had been maintained but government circles began to question whether by default the Anglican Church alone should continue to define this privilege.

The first break with tradition came in 1878. It was announced that there would be four new bishoprics, in Liverpool, Newcastle, Southwell and Wakefield. Liverpool and Newcastle proved straightforward as they were great regional centres and amongst the largest towns in England for whom city status would be a commensurate ecclesiastical and civic honour. But it was the choice of Southwell that broke the link.[3] Nottingham would have been the better choice in population terms for this new Nottinghamshire/Derbyshire diocese but ancient rivalry meant that Derbyshire churchmen refused to bend the knee. The Church compromised and chose Southwell with its glorious Norman Minster and negligible population of 2,897. It was not even an incorporated borough and therefore was not eligible to apply for city status. So, in 1884, it became the first English Anglican cathedral not to adorn a city.

Wakefield's case also raised some eyebrows. Leeds, with its population of over 175,000, was furious that it had not been chosen for the cathedral seat. Wakefield, with only 31,000, was the recipient and applied for city status. The Home Office decided to follow precedent and made the grant. After all, it could not recognise St. Albans and Truro and ignore Wakefield which was larger than the two of them combined. But this would be the last time a borough would be promoted to city status merely because it had a cathedral.[4] Leeds had to lick its wounds until 1999 when the Church woke up to the fact that it was indeed populous and renamed the Diocese of Ripon as the Diocese of Ripon and Leeds though the latter still had no cathedral.

In Ireland and Scotland there was no established church so city status would be a purely secular award: Belfast received Letters Patent in 1888 to join Dublin, the seat of British government in Ireland and long regarded as a city, and Londonderry which had been granted a city charter by James I; Dundee in 1889 joined Glasgow, Edinburgh and Aberdeen which were considered cities by ancient usage. In England and Wales the change from sacred to secular criteria was signalled when Birmingham was granted city status in 1889. Other industrial centres of the north and midlands soon followed: Sheffield and Leeds in 1893 and Bradford, Nottingham and Hull in 1897. Birmingham, Sheffield and Bradford would, in the new century, also become cathedral seats but the others remained unashamedly secular. Leicester tried for city status but failed as its population of 123,000 was relatively small by comparison. West Ham had a greater population than Leeds, Bradford and Nottingham but the Home Office decided that the London metropolitan area should be limited to its two historic cities of London and Westminster. On that same basis Southwark was denied city status in 1905 thus becoming the first cathedral town to fail in its application for city status.

In 1907 the Home Office imposed a minimum population qualification of 300,000 for aspiring cities. Cardiff, Wales' largest town with about 180,000 people, just squeezed in before the new qualification became operative, greatly helped by the support of Edward VII who had been Prince of Wales for sixty years. That royal favour could now be a deciding factor was demonstrated immediately after the war when George V successfully bestowed his favour on Leicester after a royal visit. In the 1920s he did the same for the naval bases of Plymouth and Portsmouth even though they did not reach the newly lowered population qualification of 250,000: the affection of the monarch, who was a former naval officer, sufficed. George VI did the same in 1937 for the 50,000 inhabitants of Lancaster to celebrate his accession as their Duke thereby creating a huge exception to the population rule.

The fate of Southwell and Southwark and the population criterion applied to secular city awards had clearly not filtered through to Chelmsford in 1914. The town clerk was even surprised to find that he had to obtain Letters Patent by petition to the Crown: his first letter was sent to the Patent Office but, having nothing to do with inventions, was forwarded to the Home Office. They replied authoritatively:

"The creation of the Bishopric of Chelmsford does not give the borough any claim to the title of city and . . . the Secretary of State cannot hold out any hopes that he will be able to recommend compliance with the prayer of the Petition."

Bury St. Edmunds also applied. A Home Office memorandum of March 16th 1914 summed it all up:

"For a long while the Home Office acted on the principle that any town which became the seat of a new bishopric was entitled to an application to be made a city. This rule was broken through in the case of Southwark when the title was specifically refused . . . It is perfectly clear that no encouragement should be given to the idea that the possession of a new bishopric in itself gives a town any claim to be granted the title of city and that minor towns like Bury St. Edmunds (16,785), Chelmsford (18,008) and even Ipswich (73,932)—which is sure to apply if the authorities know that Bury St. Edmunds has applied—should certainly not be made cities." [5]

Even the newly published *Chelmsford Diocesan Chronicle* in February 1915 could not find anything notable to say about its new cathedral:

"The Cathedral of St. Mary . . . unlike the vast majority of English cathedrals is absolutely unconnected with any of the great events which go to the making of history, nor is it associated with the names of any man or woman of conspicuous importance in the annals of the English race. Its walls neither contain the shrine of any saint, nor do they guard the remains of any prelate, statesman or warrior of renown. Even the questionable distinction of having stabled Cromwell's horses is not one that Chelmsford's church can boast, nor does it contain a single battered image to testify that it was an object of special concern to the commissioners of Edward VI. It has, in fact, lived a tranquil, unobtrusive life . . . in perfect keeping with the quiet, agricultural neighbourhood in which it stands . . . No mention of its church is made in the Domesday Survey."

If the Diocese could not get excited why should the Home Office bother?

It would take another 98 years and the opportunity presented by Elizabeth II's Diamond Jubilee before Chelmsford could call itself a cathedral city.

CHAPTER 10

Willingly to War

The enthusiastic crowds who greeted the enthronement of 52-year-old John Watts-Ditchfield as Bishop of Chelmsford on April 23rd 1914 reappeared on August 4th to cheer Britain's declaration of war on Germany. But for the new Diocese of Chelmsford the financial drain of war was to have a severe impact on its capacity to build new churches in London-over-the-Border and made any lingering prospects of major cathedral enlargement a pipe-dream. St. Mary's was therefore confined to the few minor improvements that it had been able to make as a pro-cathedral in those euphoric months between the passing of the Bishoprics Act and the formal creation of the Diocese. Nor were the fates benevolent. A major gas explosion in 1911 ripped up pews and a section of stone floor when a workman unwisely sought the source of a gas leak with a lighted taper;[1] precious cash had to be diverted to reparation rather than embellishment.

Chelmsford's new cathedral would remain a parish church in appearance but that did not preclude trying to greet its first bishop in style at his enthronement. However, the bells had not rung since Whitsun Day, May 26th 1912. The unsteady internal oak frame of the bell tower needed to be rebuilt in steel. The opportunity was taken to recast all the bells and add two more to match the 12 bell peals of St. Mary's, Saffron Walden and Holy Cross, Waltham Abbey; it would not do to be third best in the Diocese. A four day fete was held in the Corn Exchange in April 1913 to raise funds. The new treble and tenor bells were private gifts, the latter from the Essex Bellringers. The weight of the 12 bell peal would be nearly seven tons compared with just over four for the old 10 bells. A new floor was installed in the tower to deaden the sound inside the church. In the bell chamber itself special louvres reduced noise in the streets below, carrying the sound further over the town. At the same time the clock installed in 1893, replacing its 1768 predecessor, was thoroughly overhauled and a large part of its cast iron works renewed in steel. It now needed winding twice a week instead of daily. Chimes and heavier hammers for striking were added.[2] The bells and clock were dedicated by Edgar Jacob, Bishop of St. Albans, on September 27th 1913. The church was filled with over 1,300 people, one fifth of them from the Essex Association of Bellringers. Organist Frederick Frye composed a special hymn, *Lifted safe within the steeple*, for probably its only rendition. The bells rang for seven hours until 10.00 p.m. which would have tested the new noise abatement systems and possibly the patience of local residents. In the following week 800 curious people climbed the tower to see the cause of all the excitement. A new St. Mary's Guild of Bellringers was formed and rang the Bishop of Chelmsford in seven months later at his enthronement. From the old oak bell frame were carved a Prie Dieu for use by the clergy and the arms of the Bishop of Chelmsford which were to be affixed to his chair.[3]

Opening Day of the four day fete, April 19th 1913:
Chelmsford Cathedral Knightbridge Library

To house the honorary canons the North Chapel or Mildmay Chapel was converted into a Canons' Chapel. A pair of oak doors was inserted in the side oak screen to give access to the sanctuary and a new iron grille screened the chapel from the church on the western side. The seats for the archdeacons were placed in the south side of the sanctuary in the sedilia or inset stone niches.

The Service of Installation for 13 canons took place on June 12th 1914.[4] The five Essex clergy who had been honorary canons in the Diocese of St. Albans, one of whom was Henry Lake, were automatically included in this number which would eventually reach 24 when, it was assumed, they would constitute themselves as a Chapter governing the life of the Cathedral under a Dean. Until then, by default, the Bishop himself fulfilled the role of Dean. The full Chapter would take some time to emerge. During the Diocese's first year the founding act of parliament limited the Bishop to appointing no more than eight honorary canons, men who had given long and honoured service to the Essex part of the Diocese of St. Albans. In addition established cathedrals normally had at least four diocesan-financed permanent residentiary canons who performed specific roles, for example as Precentor. Chelmsford Cathedral's Precentor from its inception was an honorary canon, John Barrow. He was financed by the Parish without any additional stipend from the Diocese until 1917 when £225 was granted (£9,830 in today's money) but without residentiary canon status. £50 (£2,190) was also given to the churchwardens for additional expenses incurred in carrying out diocesan duties.[5]

The Bishop's new Pastoral Staff was an early casualty of the war. The commission had been given to Bertram Reynolds who had designed the Primatial Cross for the Archbishop of York[6] and was to be presented by the Church of England Men's Society at Easter 1915. It was to have been made in Belgium but all contacts were severed after German occupation. At one stage there was a rumour that the Germans had even commandeered the cross for the value of the metal.[7] The work was transferred to English silversmiths who struggled to obtain the raw materials[8] but the Staff eventually arrived for Holy Week 1916.

Local pride in Essex's new diocese was quickly eclipsed by the unfolding horror of war. The men, whom John Watts-Ditchfield had always made his priority to secure for Christ, were now more likely to be found on the Western Front than in their local pubs. Squaring the pressures of patriotism with the teaching of the Sermon on the Mount proved a complex challenge. A number of enthusiastic clergy saw this as a holy war and used their pulpits to urge their men to go and fight, a responsibility which they, exempt from military service, did not have to share. They made many of their fellow clergy wince with discomfort and created a chasm between themselves and their parishioners. Indeed, one historian is firmly of the view that the war deepened the alienation of the majority of the English male population from the life and practice of the churches in general.[9]

The Cathedral took a humble and prayerful approach to the outbreak of war and foresaw its vast implications. The *Parish Magazine* in September 1914 reflected:

> "The British Empire at War! . . . It seems hard to realise that we have taken up arms to defend justice and righteousness . . . The war . . . will surpass all previous wars in the gigantic size of its operations. The sight of whole divisions of our Territorial Forces passing through the streets and remaining billeted on the inhabitants, the commandeering of horses and vehicles from every source . . . are among the incidents that we can never efface from the memory."

On August 5th there was a quiet Service of Intercession that peace might soon be restored. On August 8th the colours of the Essex Regiment (Territorial) were laid solemnly upon the altar followed by an evening outdoor service at The Gun in front of the Shire Hall when members of almost all the religious bodies in the town took part. It was poignant that this weapon, captured from the Russians during the Crimean War, should be the focus of public sentiment at the start of another conflict. On August 9th, the first Sunday of the war, a muted evensong was said until the Third Collect with organ music only beyond that point. Each Wednesday was marked as a day of supplication with a special service at night. In accordance with the Archbishop of Canterbury's request August 21st was a National Day of Prayer. The names of parishioners' friends and relatives on active service were regularly posted in the porch and prayers offered for them individually. Their names and regiments were also read out before the Intercessions at daily Evensong and the bi-weekly midday service: Monday, Essex (Fortress) Royal Engineers; Tuesday, Army Service Corps; Wednesday at noon 5th Essex A Company and at 5.30 B Company; Thursday, Essex Yeomanry and Officers; Friday, at noon the Royal Navy and at 5.30 non-commissioned officers and private soldiers serving in all other regiments; Saturday, those who had fallen. The Tenor Bell was rung as a Peace Bell each weekday from August 31st for a short time after midday. On September 22nd an organ recital took place in aid of the Belgian Refugees Fund but the Church of England Temperance Society Annual Meeting on October 20th suffered reduced attendance as many members had troops in their houses and could not get away. A military hero of a former era, Field Marshal Earl Roberts of Kandahar and Pretoria, died and the Cathedral was placed at the military's disposal for a memorial service at the same time on November 19th as his funeral at St. Paul's Cathedral.[10]

The first Diocesan Conference on October 27th lasted only one day and was transferred to Chelmsford from Southend where all public buildings had been commandeered by the military, a slight damper for John Watts-Ditchfield's first such occasion. The Bishop testified to the exemplary conduct of the soldiers, urging that in towns and villages where they may be camping or billeted, provision be made not only for amusement but for quiet writing and reading and that the clergy be on the alert to provide such services as may be desirable. He appealed for money to provide 50,000 Prayer and Hymn Books for the troops and for the use of motor cars on Sunday in the neighbourhood of Chelmsford to enable chaplains to get out to the camps to take services. The suffragan Bishop of Barking informed the Diocese that the Government had agreed to waive the 10 shillings stamp fee on a marriage licence in the case of soldiers below commissioned rank who wished to be married at short notice before being sent abroad provided that the diocesan registrars reduce their fees to 10 shillings too: he advised that they should.[11]

By 1915 the invasion of neutral Belgium and alleged war atrocities had greatly united Christian opinion in Britain.[12] The horrors of trench warfare had yet to make themselves fully felt. But, despite the prevailing enthusiasm, the Archbishop of Canterbury in 1915 refused a government request for the clergy to appeal from the pulpit for recruits for Kitchener's Army[13] and defended clergy non-combative status: involvement in fighting would be incompatible with ordination vows and the spiritual leadership of the clergy would be vital for the right conduct of the war and a true peace.[14] This was reiterated by John Watts-Ditchfield in a letter to *The Times* on February 23rd with the additional pragmatic argument that "even in peace the number of clergy where they are most wanted is clearly inadequate." But the clergy in general were drawn from the same schools and social circles as the political and military leaders and many of them disobeyed the Archbishop, using their pulpits to urge the men to fight: public opinion was hard to resist, some lay patrons would have wished it and many clergy had sons who were in uniform. As a result the clergy were increasingly seen as leading cosily from behind. Aware of this, the Church volunteered from 1915 not to accept any men for ordination who were of military service age. As the Vicar of Harwich put it:

"It was a cheap form of religion which consisted in possessing a set of doctrines which enabled one to escape from one of the disagreeable duties of life."[15]

The Rector of Navestock agreed:

"It is difficult to exhort laymen to a form of national service from whose risks and dangers you are free yourself. It is difficult to ignore the spiritual influence which Roman Priests and Presbyterian Ministers have gained by sharing the chances of the field." [16]

He matched words with actions and joined the Volunteer Reserve Force. Though there were many brave Anglican chaplains, Captain Guy Chapman despaired of the Anglican Church as an institution:

"The Church of Rome sent a man into action mentally and spiritually cleaned. The Church of England could only offer you a cigarette. The Church of Rome, experienced in propaganda, sent its priests into the line. The Church of England forbade theirs forward of Brigade Headquarters, though many, realising the fatal blunder of such an order, came just the same."[17]

The blood-chilling jingoism of Arthur Winnington-Ingram, Bishop of London, was uncomfortable for many Christians and untypical of the episcopacy. In 1915 he urged on British men:

"Band together in a great crusade—we cannot deny it—to kill Germans. To kill them, not for the sake of killing but to save the world; to kill the good as well as the bad; to kill the young men as well as the old; to kill those who have shown kindness to our wounded as well as those who crucified the Canadian sergeant, who superintended the Armenian massacres, who sank _The Lusitania_ ; and to kill them lest the civilisation of the world should be killed."[18]

The redoubtable Dean Inge of St. Paul's Cathedral protested:

"The mental processes of the Bishop are, for a man in his position, of almost childlike simplicity."[19]

By contrast Chelmsford's John Watts-Ditchfield took a more thoughtful Christian stance:

> "The lessons of the Sermon on the Mount must be forced home with a new power illustrated as they will be by the horrors of the War."[20]

The Bishop of Colchester, Robert Whitcombe, also took a reasoned line while not doubting the need for retaliation against unprovoked attack:

> "While Christ was against personal vengeance for selfish ends . . . his command does not involve turning the babies' and the widows' left cheek to be smitten by a ruthless foe. On the contrary, Christianity justifies coercion against cruel barbarity."[21]

He also had some practical thoughts for the clergy:

> "Leave the favoured few and look after the many. Services must be decreased rather than increased, that clergy may have more time going about doing good. The services must be simple and congregational, such as those outside, driven in by the stress and storm without, can understand."[22]

The Bishop of Barking, Thomas Stevens, wrote feelingly:

> "The countryside seamed with trenches: the cathedral city [sic] transformed into a garrison town; holiday resorts, like Southend, with its huge hotel, turned into a vast military hospital and at intervals visited by hostile aircraft; churches darkened by order and evening service suspended till this has been done."[23]

The harder patriotic line was more likely to surface amongst the parish clergy: the Cathedral's own Canon Lake edged towards it, warning of "slackers and shirkers . . . We all know them."[24] But he was not as forthright as Canon David Ingles of Witham who represented the white feather brigade:

> "I shall forever be ashamed of my parish if she does not send out all her young men and those of the proper age to fight. I want

to see all the single men from 19-35 years clean out of Witham Parish . . . I believe this war is a visitation sent from God."[25]

His son, Major Alexander Ingles, was killed in action nine days after his father's call to arms.[26]

In July 1915 the *Essex County Chronicle* started to print full casualty lists of Essex men on the first Friday of each month: on July 19th there were 1,200.[27] The Cathedral's own Roll of Honour representing those of the parish on active service reached 1,000.[28] By late 1916 shopkeepers were unable to obtain enough mourning materials to meet demand.

What was to be done about the needs of London-over-the-Border in such straitened times? In 1915 the Diocese observed:

> "It is now more than 47 years since the London-over-the-Border Fund was removed from the Diocese of London [to the Diocese of St. Albans]. At that time the population was about 97,000 contained in 23 ecclesiastical parishes . . . The population is now estimated at 920,000 in 68 ecclesiastical parishes."[29]

But Essex's Londoners were disadvantaged compared to their fellow workers who still found themselves in the Diocese of London:

> "Our neighbours in East London have the wealth of London at their back. We have no fairy godmother of that sort."[30]

The Diocese pleaded for money for London-over-the-Border so that the bereaved families of servicemen had a church to receive them and did not have to "sit in darkness."[31] But resources were diminishing:

> "Several of our largest and most loyal supporters have been compelled to reduce their contribution owing to the war and its heavy claims."[32]

The war eventually became horribly enervating in its effect. Numbers attending services in the Cathedral reduced during Lent 1915 owing to illness in the parish, billeting in almost every house and torrential rain in January and February.[33] But the frustrated Bishop found these excuses unacceptable:

"I really wonder whether we have grasped even a faint idea of what thousands of our lads are passing through at the front. If we did should we find the Services of Intercession so sparsely attended even by Christian people? . . . Cannot Christian men give a lead? . . . If they are not abstainers can they not become so for the period of the war?"[34]

Divisions caused by continuing ritualist issues plainly annoyed the Bishop, not just because he was an evangelical but also because they showed Anglican disunity at a time of national crisis: "what would the man in the street think of any unseemly wrangle on ritual questions during the war?" He had in mind the Consistory Court case brought by the parishioners of St. James', Colchester, a recent aspirant to cathedral status, against their rector, Charles Naters (formerly a curate at St. Mary's, Chelmsford 1889-93), unhappy at the Anglo-Catholic practices he had introduced. In 1916 William Padbury introduced incense at Cressing, conducted the first sung mass in the church, put candlesticks on the altar and, some said, instructed pupils at the church school to cross themselves. George Gresley, Vicar of Shenfield, provoked one churchwarden to resign because he introduced Anglo-Catholic practices: the vicar himself was forced to resign in 1917 because of his unpopularity. At least in Thaxted, another of the cathedral aspirants, Conrad Noel, Vicar since 1910, with his unusual combination of Anglo-Catholicism and Communism, left his advocacy of ritualist practices and the hanging of the Red Flag until the war was over.[35]

As the stalemate on the Western Front continued Bishop John Watts-Ditchfield held a united act of intercession at The Gun in front of the Shire Hall in Chelmsford on July 17th 1915 with the band of the 2nd/7th Warwick Regiment in attendance. On August 4th 1915, the first anniversary of the outbreak of war, the Cathedral held a memorial service for those who had fallen to match the one in St. Paul's attended by King George V and Queen Mary; such annual commemorations would continue until 1918. In August 1915 the *Parish Magazine* backed the thrifty message of the Parliamentary War Savings Committee to eat less meat, be careful with bread, waste no food, economise on imports such as tobacco, petrol and rubber, think before spending anything and, if possible, grow one's own vegetables: in his New Year message Canon Lake added the caveat that economies should not include "work for God and His Church."[36] Rather more proactively, in 1916, the Sunday School children agreed, or had been persuaded, to give the cash cost of their prizes to war funds.[37] The Cathedral also sought to revive the Church Lads' Brigade, formed in 1901 to promote "reverence, discipline and self-respect and all that tends to Christian manliness."[38] It had been subsumed with other cadet organisations in 1914 for war training: a successful appeal was made at the beginning of 1915 for £30 (£2,250 in today's money) to get the Brigade re-started. After one year it had 70 members but experienced a rapid turnover as lads left for the army or munitions work and struggled for leaders as officers were quickly called up for active service. Even so by the end of 1915 they had a pretty full programme: Sunday Bible Class; Monday social club; Tuesday band practice; Thursday ambulance section; Friday company drill and signalling; Saturday football.[39] In October 1916 all public buildings were commandeered for war use but the Brigade was rescued by Thomas Hay, Headmaster of Chelmsford's Grammar School, who allowed weekly drill in the school's gymnasium.[40]

Many activities were cancelled: cathedral choir and Sunday School outings; the Church Congress at Southend as coastal Essex was too exposed to attack; and the Bishop's Primary Visitation for 1916. Unlit streets reduced attendance at the Temperance Society and Church of England Men's Society evening meetings[41] and the latter were eventually to find themselves bereft of members after military call up and the demands of war work had taken their toll. The Christmas Social Tea and yuletide tree were cancelled and a much contracted *Parish Magazine* was published on cheaper paper. Instead of seasonal celebrations National Days of Supplication were held over the New Year weekend.

During 1915 there had been a national restriction on the frequency of church bell ringing to avoid disturbing the daytime sleep of the munitions workers on the Saturday night shift;[42] practice nights experienced similar restrictions. The Guild of Bell-ringers maintained their dexterity by meeting together to ring hand bells.[43] However, on Sunday, January 1st 1916 a full muffled peal at the end of the service was permitted in memory of the fallen; there was another half-muffled peal on June 13th when the Cathedral was placed at the disposal of the army for a memorial service for Secretary of State for War, Lord Kitchener of Khartoum, who had drowned on the torpedoed *H.M.S. Hampshire*. It would be another two years before the initial Allied breakthrough in early 1918 on the Western Front gave cause for unrestrained bell-ringing but even then the Bishop sensitively demurred:

> "Even while the bells were ringing a merry peal, telegram messages were being received in hundreds of homes. Far better wait until Peace is declared and the Angel of Death has completed his toll."[44]

It was a wise as well as a humane decision: the German counter-offensive that followed in the spring of 1918 nearly snatched victory for them from the jaws of defeat.

With an average of nearly 3,000 British men dying daily during the five months of the Battle of the Somme, July to November 1916, the Bishop needed to make some decisions on war memorials in the Diocese's churches. The Convocations of Canterbury and York had recommended that dioceses should set up advisory committees including in their ranks those with some artistic knowledge whose advice could be sought: 16 were quickly established though they did not include Chelmsford.[45] Even so the Bishop was clear that he wanted proportion and artistic merit:

> "The largest monuments in Westminster Abbey are frequently to the memory of men whose deeds were the smallest and who were the soonest to be forgotten . . . We must therefore consider carefully what impression the memorial will make on the worshippers in 2000 A.D."

He was against memorial tablets to one man though this would be waived for an individual who had greatly distinguished himself in the field of battle or who had held a prominent place in the Church. The strongest reason in his mind was their manifest unfairness:

> "One striking feature of the war is the union between 'duke's son and cook's son'. They fight together and they die together. Are they to be separated in the parish church? . . . There should be preparations made for the erection in each parish church *at the end of the war and not before*, of one Roll of Honour . . . Such a course is more in accord with the spirit of the Church, which should know no class distinctions. This, however, will not exclude the pious offerings of windows, choir stalls, prayer desks etc. as commemorative gifts for the adornment of the House of God."[46]

So far the Church as an institution had been reacting to the war. It now moved to a proactive phase but with mixed results.

CHAPTER 11

The National Mission

In the autumn of 1916 the archbishops, Randall Davidson of Canterbury and Cosmo Lang of York, launched the National Mission of Repentance and Hope in an attempt to spur the Christian conscience of the nation in response to those, like Horatio Bottomley, editor of the ultra-patriotic *John Bull* magazine, who argued that the Church of England was not rising to the needs of the hour. Although Bottomley was a crook, jailed after the war for embezzling the funds of small investors in his Victory Bond Club, at the time his jingoism had considerable resonance. The National Mission was a remarkably ambitious project given the internal rivalries of churchmanship and the degree of clerical, parochial and diocesan isolation in the days before telephones and electronic media made centralisation so much easier.

Archbishop Lang explained the rationale but his choice of words was unfortunate:

> "We have called a National Mission of Repentance and Hope;
> Repentance because we are called to bid men and women
> everywhere to repent of their sins which have stained our
> civilisation and brought upon it the manifest judgement of God;
> and Hope . . . because when the old order will have gone and
> the duty will be laid upon the nation of seeking a new order in a
> new world, we must present before the minds of the nation the
> one hope, Christ, His Mind, His Spirit, for the rebuilding of a
> new world."[1]

Hope was fine but the idea that the sins of the slaughtered dead on the Western Front, on the beaches at Gallipoli or at the bottom of the Atlantic were the victims of God's judgement was too much to take. The Archbishop came across as an Old Testament prophet, crankily insensitive to many of his listeners.

Bishop John Watts-Ditchfield took a similar line at St. Paul's Cathedral. The Allies could not ignore their own faults: Russian pogroms against the Jews, Belgian brutal exploitation of the African population in the Congo, British opium wars in China, and the French separation of church and state which he interpreted as the overthrow of God and religion. And on the home front he expected people to look to their own sins:

> "Neglect of Sunday, the prevalence of intemperance and impurity, the hasting to be rich, the division among the classes and the masses: the Church had lost her proper hold on the nation. After 16 centuries of possession, she had only five per cent of her men as communicants."[2]

The non-churchgoing population was scarcely likely to be attracted inside to receive such a damning indictment.

As most of the men were inevitably elsewhere on war service female missionaries would be trained to target women who did not attend church. John Watts-Ditchfield was chairman of the national committee that had oversight of women's work. In tune with the times the archbishops' call was phrased in military terms:

> "We are raw recruits like the men who came in their millions to serve their King and Country . . . The Church, like the Army, has its rules, its discipline, its common life . . . And there is no age limit in the Christian Army . . . The King of England has shown his interest in all the men who are serving in his army but he cannot know them all individually . . . But our King in Heaven knows all his soldiers . . . The Christian Army has its Roll of Honour, its 'noble army of martyrs' . . . A soldier who deserts his post is shot, because one desertion may endanger the whole line. Our Commander does not shoot his soldiers. He forgives them but his cause is endangered wherever they fail."[3]

Not all churchmen were persuaded. Hensley Henson, Canon of Westminster Abbey and, from 1917, Bishop of Hereford, who had been as influential a parish priest in Barking between 1888 and 1895 as John Watts-Ditchfield had in Bethnal Green,[4] commented:

> "If religious revival is to take place, I suspect that it will come from outside the Church and not from inside . . . Those who are running about the country exhorting little companies of puzzled women have no vision of any larger teaching than that which has passed their lips for years and is now admittedly powerless. A dervish-like fervour cannot be maintained and is not really illuminating or morally helpful."[5]

In the Diocese of Chelmsford Bishop John Watts-Ditchfield gave the National Mission his full attention. As an evangelical it was his natural territory, with drink and gambling as his prime targets:

> "No nation can be regarded as Christian with a drink bill of 160 million and . . . with a turnover of some 50 millions in the bookmakers' hands."[6]

He listed the other evils to be overcome: venereal disease, cruelty to children, the appalling conditions in city slums and the prevailing spirit of materialism. In the March 1916 *Diocesan Chronicle* he excused himself from all weekday parochial engagements for the rest of the year to concentrate on the National Mission.

But the idea that women should bear the brunt of spreading the word riled those on the Anglo-Catholic wing who included Andrew Clark, Vicar of Great Leighs, a few miles north of Chelmsford. He protested that the bishops had "lost any sense of manly or true feeling" and were "enslaved to the whine and insincerity of cant":

> "The old women of the episcopal bench are devising old-womanish National Missions and relays of women preachers, but will not move a finger to lighten the Church service of dreary incrustations of a bygone age . . . or allow . . . reasonable alternatives for intolerably long and weary psalms and lessons for the day."[7]

That the Church was mired in the Prayer Book of 1662 was, for him, the reason why people did not come to church.[8] His reaction was mild in comparison with other Anglo-Catholics who envisaged women priests in the offing. The Bishop of London, super-patriot Arthur Winnington-Ingram, this time writing in a more reasoned vein in the *Manchester Guardian* of August 17th 1916, expressed incredulity:

> "With hundreds of women taking classes for girls and children and even boys in churches every Sunday it was not a great concession to allow them during the few weeks of the mission to enlarge their classes for women and girls."

But the Anglo-Catholic outcry forced the Bishop of Chelmsford to redefine his position. He did so nationally in *The Times* on August 22nd. He had wanted women to speak in church, where a spirit of reverence could be engendered, rather than in noisy and inadequate public buildings. But he knew he had to compromise if he were to save the Mission:

> "The natural man would say, 'Resist the unfair agitation, largely begotten of ignorance and prejudice'. But such a spirit would surely wreck the mission for no blessing could rest upon it conducted on such lines."

He therefore conceded that women would be licensed to speak only to audiences of women and girls with no stray males allowed in; they would not have the same faculty to preach as that given to male lay readers; and they would be denied access to the pulpit, lectern or chancel steps, traditional rostra from which men expounded the Gospel. However, the Bishop had been angered by the Anglo-Catholic response:

> "Surely this is the work of the Devil . . . What is lamentable is the keenness and zest with which we seem to have fastened upon a point which could be made contentious. It is only too characteristic of one of the least attractive features of our Anglican Church life."[9]

Nonetheless, he had been taking a hard line against ritualist issues in the Diocese and was now experiencing a counter-attack: the strength of the opposition stunned him. When the storm broke he was on holiday in

Teignmouth. The *Essex County Chronicle* contacted him to apprise him of the "unseemly discussions" taking place in Essex which were threatening the Mission.[10]

Although the Mission was scheduled for a national launch in October an early start was made in London-over-the-Border to take advantage of the weather. On September 13th and 14th Luke Paget, Bishop of Stepney, was invited to address missioners earmarked for West Ham. Each mission consisted of groups of three women:

> ". . . from comfortable homes, many not strong and some no
> longer in their first youth . . . who . . . gave up ten days of their
> time to walk in the chilly damp lanes and stand about at cottage
> doors for hours, happy to suffer the tiredness."[11]

They would go only where the incumbent invited them. Despite the Anglo-Catholic backlash demand exceeded supply. On September 18th, in a special Evensong in Bishopscourt Chapel, the Bishop gave a farewell address to a batch of missioners destined for the East End and administered Holy Communion to them the following morning at the Cathedral. The Diocese's early start was prescient: the official launch service in the Cathedral on October 2nd was hit by heavy rain so that the outdoor procession had to be abandoned. Five other diocesan centres followed with their own formal launches: West Ham on October 3rd, Saffron Walden October 4th, Leyton October 6th, Colchester October 11th and Southend October 12th.

The precise timing of the mission in each parish would be decided by the incumbent. The parishes in Chelmsford invited their missioners to visit from December 7th to 12th, raising public awareness with a procession on December 2nd. The Cathedral's robed choir took a circular tour through Springfield, Great Baddow and Moulsham, picking up their parish contingents and that of Widford as they went, culminating in a mass procession up Moulsham Street and High Street with the Bishop leading the way accompanied by the Mayor, Town Clerk and Mace Bearer representing the Borough. Processional psalms were sung and ten cantors chanted the solemn Litany as the procession made its way to the final assembly point at The Gun for the Apostles' Creed, a few words from the Bishop and the blessing and National Anthem. It was said that onlookers "received the witness with the greatest reverence and the soldiers stood to attention." According to the *Parish Magazine* there were good congregations throughout the six-day Mission and a daily children's service was attended by 400-500.[12]

The evaluation of the National Mission by the Diocese was less rosy. In the January 1917 *Diocesan Chronicle*, one writer claimed:

> "It has undoubtedly succeeded as far as the small minority of churchgoers are concerned. To them it has been an inspiration . . . Indifference, not antagonism, is still the state of the large majority."

A second writer criticised the timing: religious fervour and cold weather were incompatible bedfellows and tub-thumping missions had had their day:

> "This is a large country parish . . . The Mission was held in the second week of December . . . It requires a good deal of resolution to forsake the fireside to attend a meeting which may be a mile or a mile and a half away . . . My impression is that many people associated it in their minds with the perfervid exhortations, crude and exaggerated utterances and strong emotional appeals of evangelical missions of a former day which the spread of education has made irrational and suspect . . . Few, if any, attended the services and meetings of the Mission who were not church people."

A third correspondent felt that men who had experienced battle would be more credible missioners:

> "Talking in the ordinary way is no use. A band of mission friars, after the war, gathered from ones who have seen service, might do a great work in the highways and hedges."

And this was echoed by a fourth correspondent who feared the Church lived in its own cocoon:

> "What weakens the power of the Church is the apathy of the dislocated units out of touch with the whole body, the self-contained parson's freehold and its autocracy, very often a long way from human sentiments and ideals."

A fifth writer observed:

> "Our parishes are desperately full of neutrals. They never attend church but they are not opposed to the Church. They simply leave it alone . . . Often they are good fellows enough, living respectable lives and outside religion the parson is often on good and even friendly terms with them. They may respect his office but they ignore his ministry. They like their children to be taught the Bible and to attend the Sunday School because they rightly think that religion is the best guide to a good and upright life. But ask them to come to church and they evade the question or put you off with a vague promise which they have no intention of keeping."

Writing much later in the October 1918 *Diocesan Chronicle* the Rural Dean of St. Osyth reflected:

> "This time of trial and loss has . . . not brought any great accession of numbers to the Church . . . and only on rare instances is it felt that the National Mission has been productive . . . There is no evidence that Intercession Services are greatly frequented nor that the Church in this locality is able to exercise her prophetic office in any arresting manner . . . Sometimes one meets with alienation from all religion on the ground that, if God really ruled, the war would not have occurred at all. There is little antagonism to the Church but much indifference."

At the 1918 Diocesan Conference one layman took a more pragmatic view of the qualities required of rural clergy:

> "What is the good of a philosopher in a village rectory? You wanted a man who could build a stack and enjoy a rat hunt."[13]

The issue of the role of women in the Church did not end with the last rites of the National Mission. The war work of women in jobs previously regarded as a male monopoly had done as much as all the pre-war agitation of the Suffragettes to persuade politicians that at least some of them deserved the vote. At the Diocesan Conference in 1917 the Bishop said that women had performed heroically in the last three years:

"Resource, restraint and endurance had marked their actions and the traditional view of women's place in the life of the Church was gone forever. The State was about to recognise women's part though tentatively."

He said that they must be allowed more parochial responsibility but theology and governance were different matters:

"Many . . . lacked equipment for dealing with wider questions . . . In many parishes the girls and women would be, for some years to come, least equipped for governing powers."[14]

The motion was eventually carried that women should be allowed to attend diocesan and deanery conferences. Arguments raged on both sides. Guy Rogers, Vicar of West Ham, who had been awarded the Military Cross for his bravery as an army chaplain on the Western Front, asserted:

"The Church must not lag behind civil and secular progress . . . It was common justice . . . The Church accepted women's money . . . No taxation without representation was a time-honoured principle. Were women fit to be patrons of livings and yet not fit for diocesan conferences?"

Sir A.B. Pennefather of Chelmsford said that the Church Missionary Society had hotly opposed women's entry into their organisation but they now had 24 seats; they did not drive men away and spoke purposefully. Another speaker asked:

"As a Church . . . we had blindly opposed Wesley and blindly opposed science; were we to treat the women's movement in the same way?"

But others saw an increase in women's role as "uncatholic" and the first step towards women priests, quoting the scriptures and the ancient church fathers to support their case: the arguments of the modern era had an early dress rehearsal in 1916-17.

Canon Lake was a tolerant man of the Anglo-Catholic wing and responsible for orderly services in the Cathedral. Although he had let slip a comment that the Bishop was making October 1916 a very busy month what with the Mission, ordinations and other special services, he loyally kept his counsel on wider issues and confined himself to hopes for victory in the war:[15]

> "We had hoped that by the end of 1916 we might have welcomed some of our brave lads back at the end of the war. Such was not the case. This disappointment must not in any way weaken our determination to go through with the war at any cost until the brutal savagery of German militarism has been decisively overcome. As one of our lads wrote to me from the trenches—'everybody out here is longing for peace but all know that it would be wicked to those who have made the supreme sacrifice if we were to patch up an unsatisfactory peace'."[16]

As submarine warfare and the stalemate on the Western Front worsened the Bishop's attitude towards the country's enemies seemed to be hardening. In January 1917 he wrote:

> "Peace can never come until punishment has been meted out to those who have filled the world with horror and stained the earth with blood. There must be no premature peace, leaving our children to fight again a battle which their fathers shirked. It must be a war for the end of war and the Prussian spirit must be forever crushed."[17]

A few months later he returned to the theme:

> "'Germany spoke with contempt of our army and she in her turn is finding that on land we are her most terrible foe . . . The Lord who slew the Assyrian foe is still on the Throne."[18]

At the same time he deplored the contradictions of government policy:

> "They ask us to close down our services on Sunday in order that people may work seven days a week and then keep the public houses open on Sunday that men may drink."

But with food shortages and the need to sustain levels of energy he was sympathetic to those who could not fast in Lent as they had done in former years.[19]

With military conscription being introduced in 1916 the exemption of the clergy came under close scrutiny but John Watts-Ditchfield was adamant:

> "The clergy . . . are rendering the nation the greatest of all services
> by helping to build up its moral and spiritual strength."

He suggested that rural clergy were sustaining the war effort by encouraging parishioners to grow vegetables[20] although this modest achievement was unlikely to convince the critics. The issue would not go away. Many clergy were becoming restless in their desire to become engaged in war work of some sort. The dreadful explosion at the Silvertown Munitions Factory in West Ham in January 1917 that killed 73 and injured over 400 only pointed up the contrast. In February 1917 the Bishop wrote:

> "I must ask the clergy *not* to enter upon any outside work . . . without
> consulting me *before* they make any definite arrangements."[21]

A crisis point was reached in April 1918. The U.S.A. had entered the war a year earlier but took a year to train up an army and equip it. The Germans therefore threw all their reserves into a massive offensive to win the war before fresh American troops descended on Europe in insuperable numbers. The Allies barely saved Paris. In desperation the Government introduced a Manpower Bill to extend conscription to new categories of men up to the age of 51, including clergy. Public disgruntlement that it had taken so long led John Watts-Ditchfield to write to *The Times* on April 15th pointing out that nearly 4,000 clergy nationally had so far forsaken their exemption to serve as forces' chaplains or in other supportive roles through the Church Army or the Y.M.C.A. so that "no one who knows their readiness to serve can rightly accuse the clergy at home of cowardice or shirking danger." He pointed out that successive prime ministers and the late Lord Kitchener had urged that clergy should stay at home to minister to their parishes. Now they could be called up but would not be asked to fight. However, he urged caution about their recruitment. The absence of fathers on active service left a moral vacuum that the Church Lads' Brigade and the Scouts were partly filling but it also needed the secure backstop of the local parson. He quoted a serviceman: "we are all thankful that the wife and kids will have the padre at home if we don't come back."

But in May 1918 the Bishop responded to the pressure from the clergy themselves, writing to about 250 Essex clergymen under 51 years of age asking them to volunteer for some form of non-combatant service even if not called up. He even went so far as to say that although he could not call upon them in view of their ordination vow to join the actual fighting line, he would not debar it. However, all offers of service had to be filtered through him as he had to look after the needs of the Church, especially in the undermanned parishes of London-over-the-Border. He noted that already nearly 100 diocesan clergy had gone to the Front, over 70 of them forces' chaplains. He recognised that "the honour of those under 51 remaining needs to be protected" and sought to dispel rumours about his own chaplain who had, on three occasions, offered himself for military service but had been rejected on medical grounds.[22]

The Church was on the defensive. It sought to rebalance perceptions. It had its own heroes. The July 1918 *Diocesan Chronicle* reported that two clergy had been killed on successive days: George Bishop, Curate of St. Mary's, Plaistow 1913-14, Chaplain attached to the Northumberland Fusiliers, died on May 27th 1918 aged 34; the following day 31-year-old Richard Colborne, Curate of St. Edward's, Romford 1913-15, who had been gassed and his sight affected earlier in the war, lost his life. In May 1919 the *Diocesan Chronicle* commemorated chaplains Edward Robson, drowned on *H.M.S. Aboukir* in the North Sea in October 1914 and Vincent Bonnington who died in 1917, both Essex clergy, and cited 41 clergy sons who had been killed. In a much later obituary it was noted that Canon Arthur Sacré, Vicar of All Saints', East Hanningfield 1892-1917, had acted as a Territorial Chaplain, served at Gallipoli though well over 50 years old and had been invalided home.[23] In the September 1918 *Diocesan Chronicle* the Archdeacon of Colchester again defended the clergy; he had 232 of them in the north of the county, only 63 under 51 of whom 17 were medically unfit, 24 had already been engaged in war work and several more were preparing to serve.

Aware of the public perception of a privileged clergy, the Bishop also arranged that clergy glebe land, a plot of land attached to a living which the incumbent could farm or more likely rent out, was sold by auction, thus removing another perceived social barrier:

"'It is probably better that the parish priest should not be a landlord. Double relationships are generally well avoided and the 'squarson' really belongs to an older order."[24]

On November 11th 1918, after over four years of fighting, with more than 700,000 British Empire soldiers dead and 1,663,000 wounded, the war ended. The Bishop detected an irony:

"'In his German home the composer of the hymn *Now Thank We All Our God* little realised how hundreds of thousands of English people would join in singing with full hearts on such an occasion as last week."

There was hope. People flocked to church at the Armistice.

"Never have our churches been more crowded . . . Force can defeat a nation in arms but it can never really conquer the world. Only Christ can be the world conqueror . . . but . . . it is sad to report that scarcely any of the party leaders are Churchmen . . . Churchmen have not taken and are not taking the lead in the political, social and industrial reconstruction of England."[25]

The development of the function and buildings of the new Cathedral had been put on hold. Its routine of services had held up but its parish organisations and activities had been greatly hampered by the absence of the men. The cathedral tower, one of the air-raid look-out points for bombing raids by Zeppelins and Gothas to which Essex had been particularly vulnerable, had happily emerged unscathed.[26] The Coal Club had found great difficulty in getting supplies[27] though the Cathedral had done its bit where it could, collecting fruit and hundreds of eggs for local hospitals.[28]

During the war Canon Lake had tried to encourage his readers with the words of the psalmist:

"We went through fire and water and Thou broughtest us into a wealthy place."[29]

They had truly come through fire and water but the country was well nigh bankrupt.

CHAPTER 12

The Crusading Bishop

On Armistice Day, November 11th 1918, a special service was held in the Cathedral; every seat was taken and there were 300 standing. The Bishop had his own views on the cause of victory:

> "It was said that England's wars were won on the playing fields of Eton. I doubt it. I would rather say they were won in the English Sunday Schools and Bible Classes, where boys and girls learned the great lessons of sacrifice and unselfishness."[1]

He was a man of straightforward faith who believed that modern German theological scholarship, which was turning parts of the testaments from miraculous story into mythical allegory, had reaped its own awful reward:

> "Germany has been made what she is by a watered down faith which is really no faith at all. The preaching of a non-miraculous Christianity cannot produce any lasting good. The so-called *New Theology* does not save souls . . . The revivalists in the history of the church have been old-fashioned in their faith."[2]

He was one of them.

The impact of war continued. Medals for good attendance at Sunday School were awarded to only half of those eligible due to the scarcity of metals.[3] However, the singing of the National Anthem at the end of Sunday services was ended;[4] it was becoming a formality and now that the war was over the change would not appear unpatriotic.

Bishop John Watts-Ditchfield;
Chelmsford Cathedral Knightbridge Library

With the end of the war the Enabling Act in 1919 ensured that the delays that befell the Bishoprics Bill between 1909 and 1913 would not be repeated. The Church would now have its own decision-making pyramid with the elected Church Assembly at the apex, in which members of the laity were represented for the first time with, below them, democratically chosen diocesan and ruridecanal conference delegates and parochial church councils. The Church Assembly, with its three houses of bishops, clergy and laity, would deal with all matters bar theology and doctrine which remained the preserve of the clergy in the Convocations of Canterbury and York. All proposed legislation would be referred to the Ecclesiastical Committee at Westminster, comprising 15 members from each house of parliament, which retained the right of veto.

Given that some women had received the parliamentary vote in 1918 and could be elected to the Church Assembly, John Watts-Ditchfield did not want the issue of women's ministry in the Church to lag behind:

> "'We have admitted laymen to speak in our churches with certain restrictions and are we to deny godly women a similar privilege?'"[5]

In March 1919 a Diocesan Women's Council was formed. On April 16th 1920 St. Mary's, wearing its parish church hat, elected eight men to the Chelmsford Ruridecanal Conference and ten men and four women to the new Parochial Church Council.[6]

The Bishop had also been heartened by the way the war had bridged some denominational differences. He had started life as a Methodist and yearned for greater unity:

> "I am most hopeful respecting organic union . . . I pray that the bigots and narrow partisans on both sides may not again frustrate the will of the Church's Lord . . . I am not here advocating the 'interchange of pulpits' . . . I do not think it is allowable as our constitution now stands . . . at the regular and ordered services as found in the Prayer Book . . . but at other services. It seems out of keeping with the spirit of love . . . that there should be no united gatherings for thanksgiving unless they are held in a theatre or cinema or hall."[7]

Within the Diocese he identified three immediate priorities for the Church in peacetime Essex. The first two, the needs of London-over-the-Border and the development of the Cathedral, were not contentious; the third, his dismay at the country's addiction to pleasure after the horrors of war, received a more mixed reception.

The needs of London-over-the-Border still remained acute. The Bishop had his shopping list. More cash was needed to raise clergy stipends in general to a proper level, most particularly in the London area whose ill-paid clergy, he claimed, were exploited:

> "It is mere hypocrisy if the Church is to protest against sweating if she herself allows her own agents to be paid as they are."

34 new permanent churches were needed and 13 were still half-built, each new one requiring an accompanying parsonage and parish hall. Southend had also grown rapidly. To fill the gaps he wanted a less socially exclusive ministry:

> "The ministry of the poor . . . opened to the poor . . . No man called by God must find the door to the ministry barred from lack of means."[8]

121

The Bishop also bewailed the limitations of the Cathedral:

> "Nothing has been done to make the Cathedral suitable for its
> new position in the Diocese. Its canons sit in a little chamber
> behind the organ. At an ordination, wet or fine, candidates must
> robe some distance from the Cathedral and walk in their robes
> through the street as there is no vestry accommodation. There is
> no Chapter House and no room for diocesan purposes. Canon
> Lake has done all he could to further the work, but the east end
> must be extended and a Chapter House erected."[9]

His point was amply proven in May 1923 when the first Diocesan Clergy
Synod was held in Chelmsford. Local hospitality was not in doubt as offers
of accommodation well exceeded demand. However, clergy had to make do
with the nearby Corn Exchange as a waiting and reading room, the Shire
Hall as a robing room and toilet facilities were scattered along the quarter
mile route from the railway station.[10]

Above all John Watts-Ditchfield was alarmed at the way the nation was
relaxing into recreation and pleasure after the strains of the war:

> "I am no kill-joy . . . It may be that the Puritans went to an extreme
> that cannot be defended . . . But when I find the *most* conspicuous
> notices on church boards and in porches relate to whist drives and
> dances I am tempted to ask 'Is this of Christ?' . . . Dancing and
> whist drives may or may not be beneficial . . . but I have never
> known a soul converted through either."

St. Mary's congregation, with its tradition of social occasions, may have
been a little disconcerted. Then the Bishop laid into smoking:

> "During the war I realised what it meant to our lads in their
> weary hours of waiting and suspense but . . . the cigarette is seen
> everywhere . . . No respect is paid to the feelings of non-smokers.
> The labels in the carriages on railways are persistently ignored and
> aged and invalid people are forced into carriages filled with foul
> smoke left there by English gentlemen . . . Youths are rarely seen
> without a cigarette between their lips and their growth physically
> and mentally is impeded, as every medical man would testify . . .

Frankly I deplore the spread of cigarette smoking among young girls . . . It may be that the time has come for clergy and those who work among lads, to eschew the cigarette habit altogether and keep to the pipe."[11]

He returned to the theme a few years later:

"Pleasure is rampant. It has invaded the Church . . . The cigarette is lighted immediately before and after the most solemn services. It is easy to deride the Puritans but the Puritans were men of grit."[12]

For the Diocese there was now the serious question about the function of the Cathedral. While every cathedral contained its bishop's seat and conducted special diocesan and civic services, the wider purpose of a cathedral in relation to its diocese and locality was uncertain. A new diocese could start from scratch without carrying quantities of historical baggage. On April 23rd 1919 a paper on the *Cathedral of the 20th Century* was read to the Cathedral Chapter by Canon F.W. Galfin.[13] Some thoughts were practical such as quarterly Chapter meetings rather than one ineffective annual gathering. Ideas for the areas of responsibility for the residentiary canons bore some resemblance to what actually emerged many decades down the line at Chelmsford. On a more revolutionary plane he advocated the abolition of deans "who though they are often very good men are quite useless officials." He also regretted the supermarket affect of cathedrals: they had the best preachers and music and tended to empty local churches of their congregations. It was all interesting stuff but as Chelmsford did not yet have a dean, full complement of residentiary canons or a choir of any great reputation, it was pretty unthreatening.

In May 1919 the *Diocesan Chronicle* reported that the Bishop had appointed a Cathedral Extension Committee, though the evangelical in him was never at ease with the idea of ornate churches:

"God will not judge our churches by the beauty of their decorations or services but by the miracles of grace performed in the name of Christ. At the end of the year it may well be in our stocktaking to put down how many infidels and drunkards have been converted within the last twelve months."[14]

The continuing needs of London-over-the-Border led John Watts-Ditchfield to launch his Bishop's Crusade to raise £400,000 in four years (£14.3 million in today's money), adapted in 1920 to £500,000 over 10 years (£15.7 million).[15] He committed himself fully to the Crusade leaving parochial matters to his suffragans. But he was concerned about the motivation of donors. Back in 1913, in a lecture to University of Cambridge undergraduates, he had condemned some philanthropy as hypocritical:

> "Some, while living the life of modern Sodom, will pose as philanthropists and their gifts will swell the exchequer of the hospital or even of the university."[16]

He wanted givers to be pure in heart without a whist drive or a dance in sight:

> "Both may be perfectly legitimate forms of recreation but . . . I have never heard of either being opened by a prayer . . . I want offerings as a result of *self-denial* and not because of a night of amusement."[17]

He urged the rich to make bequests in their wills:

> "During the year hundreds of wills of Essex people have been proved and not half a dozen have contained any bequest to that Church of which the testators were members."[18]

And he reminded the working class to "remember your sixpence."

The cathedral congregation supported the Crusade but did not regard the Bishop's restrictive covenant as applicable to other more local financial needs. Thus the Parochial Fund benefited from the New Year Social Tea, inaugurated in 1888 to raise money for the Victoria Schools and reinstituted at the Corn Exchange in 1920 after a five year war gap, with 650 present: another 400 attended a whist drive the next day.[19] A tea of similar dimensions was held at Easter and a summer fete during Patronal Festival weekend in early July where every variety of entertainment was provided. Nonetheless, the congregation did respond to the Bishop's specific Self-Denial Weeks in October 1920 and 1921.

Many of the Bishop's Essex flock did not agree that fun and fund-raising were incompatible but he was unrelenting:

> "I have received so many letters in respect of my observations on the raising of money for church purposes by means of whist drives etc . . . The sum of £10 or £20 is raised [£313 or £626 in today's money] and everyone is full of congratulations. Is the spiritual life any higher? Contrast this with a week of special prayer and self-denial . . . Bazaars and sales of work are on a different footing . . . but . . . I never sanctioned anything like a raffle . . . sweepstake or any other form of gambling."[20]

While arguments raged about the morality of various forms of fund-raising Canon Lake continued to pay £180 annually out of his own pocket (£5,640 in today's money) towards the £450 (£14,100) for St. Mary's two curates. The St. Mary's Finance Committee protested that this burden was unfair and should be shared by the congregation especially as they benefited without cost from the services of the Precentor whose annual stipend was paid by the Diocese:

> "Times have changed: it is no longer for the few to give much as for the many to give more. It is done in other places. It is time Chelmsford got over its spoiling."[21]

But what was to be done about the Cathedral? Charles Nicholson, resident of Southend, was appointed to produce plans for a new building. He was one of three brothers who contributed significantly to the beauty of Anglican churches and their services: Archibald was a stained glass artist and Sydney, organist at Westminster Abbey, would found the Royal School of Church Music in 1927.

Charles Nicholson's plan soon emerged. He would retain the current building and construct an extension to the north that would fill most of the churchyard on that side to produce a magnificent structure, doubled in size, with two towers at the west end. The half that comprised the old church (including one of the towers) would continue its parish function and could, if required, act as an overflow for major diocesan events and services.

Exterior of Charles Nicholson's planned new Cathedral: original in Chelmsford Cathedral Knightbridge Library: photograph by Mervyn Marshall/David Lloyd

Interior of Charles Nicholson's planned new Cathedral: original in Chelmsford Cathedral Knightbridge Library: photograph by Mervyn Marshall/David Lloyd

The existing organ would be re-sited in a loft between the cathedral quire and the old church's chancel so that it could serve both and a new large organ would be built at the west end of the cathedral nave. The ground floor of the new West Tower or Canons' Tower would act as a Chapter House until a new one was built elsewhere. The extended Cathedral would seat 2,000 people and would be comparable with Manchester, Llandaff, Wakefield and Newcastle. It would take seven or eight years to complete the minimal amount of building to make it functional at a cost of about £120,000 (£3.75 million in modern values) but that would still leave the west porch, the new Canons' Tower and permanent vestries to be added subsequently at an unspecified cost. It could be decades before the whole project would be completed.[22]

There were warnings that "other needs might have a prior claim"[23] such as the Church Central Fund established in 1919, for which the Diocese of Chelmsford had to raise £8,500 (£305,000 in modern values) and had so far sent only £927 (£33,200); the Bishop's Crusade Fund; and the longstanding London-over-the-Border Churches Fund. The Cathedral Extension Committee was understandably enthusiastic for a new building: "cannot Chelmsford emulate Truro's yet bolder achievement?"[24] Over a 30 year period Truro had built the first new English Anglican cathedral since the Middle Ages but such a luxury could never be seriously considered by Chelmsford. Schemes of northward extension that Nicholson also proposed for Sheffield, Bradford and Portsmouth cathedrals fared no better, though Sheffield did eventually accept a modified plan in 1931 to adapt the existing parish church and swivel it from an east-west to a north-south axis with the east and west ends of the old church providing the cathedral transepts, a project that took 35 years to complete.[25]

In the meantime piecemeal improvements were made. Frederic Chancellor had died in 1918 at the age of 92 and in September 1920 a memorial screen was dedicated to his memory "adding just that majesty and dignity that the south aisle seemed to require."[26] The Church Council decided that the Cathedral's War Memorial would take the form of a three-light window designed by Charles Nicholson in which the patron saints of the Royal Navy, Army and Royal Air Force would be represented plus the badges underneath of the Essex Regiment and the Royal Air Force; a tablet in Portland Stone would record the names of the fallen.[27] The middle light of each of the eight south clerestory windows would receive a representation of either a singing or a censing angel and the lights on either side representations from The Song of the Three Children. Two of these windows were given by Canon Lake and his sister, Mary, as a thank offering for their 25 years' service; another was in memory of William Dennis, former churchwarden, who had navigated the church through its pew rent controversy.[28]

A new wooden bishop's chair, with its ornate back soaring towards the ceiling, and a memorial to the chaplains and sons of clergy who fell in the First World War were dedicated by the Archbishop of Canterbury, Randall Davidson, in 1922, the first visit to Chelmsford of the Primate of All England. The bishop's cathedra was a memorial to the former Rector and Bishop of Colchester, Frank Johnson and his wife.[29] Critics detected a contradiction. John Watts-Ditchfield responded:

> "It has been challenged in some papers as being contrary to an address I delivered in which I strongly deprecated at the present time any expenditure on the ornamentation of churches or on organs or in fact on anything we could do without."

But, he explained, the sum of £500 (£37,400 in modern values) had been raised prior to 1914 as a memorial to Frank Johnson and it was only that money with interest that was being spent.[30]

As things returned to some form of normality after the war, the absence of men from church continued to be noticeable. A Church of England Men's Society discussion—"Why men don't come to church"—was only moderately attended, thereby begging its own question.[31] There were 821 names on the electoral roll in 1921 but only 281 were men;[32] they had been scattered to the winds by the war and had not returned to worship. Chelmsford Cathedral was not treading in the footsteps of its Bishop who was soon to become national chairman of the Society.

Music must have played its expected part in cathedral worship but it receives few mentions in the *Parish Magazine* or the *Diocesan Chronicle*. On December 31st 1922 the choir of 16 men and 16 boys gave a beautiful rendering of carols after Evensong.[33] The tradition of a Christmas Eve Festival of Lessons and Carols had not yet arrived: it had started at Truro in 1880, was first held at King's College, Cambridge in 1918 and its first broadcast would be in 1928. But on Sunday November 11th 1923 the choir sang at the unveiling of the town's war memorial in Duke Street by Admiral Sir Roger Keyes of Zeebrugge.[34] Indeed, the choir's annual outing to the seaside seems to have received more coverage in the *Parish Magazine* than its singing. The Cathedral was as yet only the former Parish Church with a different name; the clergy and choir had a new status but not necessarily a new mind-set.

For the congregation an honour had been bestowed but plenty of evidence would accrue over the years to show that they found the concept of sharing with the Diocese a difficult one to handle.

At a national and diocesan level the new political structure of the Church gave an opportunity for its different wings to voice their views. Some felt it would exacerbate splits by giving floor space to the fractious. At the Diocesan Clergy Synod the Bishop seemed to recognise this reality. He wrote:

> "Some of the speakers left me with the impression that in certain quarters after the manner of the Bourbons 'we have learned nothing and forgotten nothing' in spite of all the changes that have occurred in the world in the last hundred years."

However, he acknowledged that it was:

> " . . . an excellent piece of discipline for us clergy to have to listen in silence to the expression of opinions with which we entirely disagree. This surely ought to help us realise what the layman in the pew has to suffer when we ourselves are in the pulpit."[35]

But at the Synod the Bishop was clearly not well: no sooner was it concluded than he had to enter hospital for surgery from which he never recovered. While on his sick bed he sent a note of greeting and fellowship to an Anglo-Catholic Congress meeting, an appropriate last official action by a man who had striven to build bridges even though his outspokenness sometimes offended. He died on July 14th 1923. Canon Lake was summoned home from a holiday in Switzerland. The Archbishop of Canterbury, Randall Davidson, conducted the funeral service at the Cathedral on Thursday, July 19th followed that evening by a memorial service. Authority had been given for the Bishop's burial in the churchyard and for his wife to follow him when her time came.

The funeral procession started from Bishopscourt in Springfield, where the Bishop's body had lain, led by the police and followed by the cross bearer, all the town clergy and churchwardens. The pall bearers were specially chosen and included the first priest and last deacon whom he had ordained and his old curates from his Bethnal Green days. The funeral service, which the Bishop had himself arranged, was delayed by an hour until 2.15 because of trouble on the railway line. Nonetheless at 1.40 the official processions began with the Chelmsford Corporation and past and present mayors of

Chelmsford; the mayors, or their deputies, of Colchester, Maldon, Saffron Walden, Southend, Harwich, East Ham, West Ham and Bethnal Green; representative Non-Conformist ministers; diocesan clergy; rural deans; the cathedral choir and clergy; the honorary canons; the bishops of London, St. Albans, St. Edmundsbury and Ipswich, Bangor, Barking, Colchester and Nassau; the Archdeacon of Southend; and finally the Archbishop of Canterbury and family mourners. After the service the public were able to file past the open grave.[36]

John Watts-Ditchfield had not been an identikit bishop. The son of a Lancashire shoemaker and Wesleyan minister on the Wigan Circuit, he was not confirmed as an Anglican until he was 27 and was ordained at St. Paul's Cathedral two years later. With this background and no university education he could not have been more different from his episcopal colleagues. At the time of his death half the bishops were connected with the peerage or the landed gentry by birth or marriage; almost all had been privately educated, nearly half of them at ten of the leading public schools; and with very few exceptions they had all graduated from Oxford or Cambridge universities. As one historian noted, while not living in their own bishops' palaces, staying at Lambeth Palace while attending an episcopal meeting or dropping in at the House of Lords, they might well be at one or another of the great aristocratic homes across the country.[37]

John Watts-Ditchfield was probably less well-versed in diplomacy than some of his peers. The August 1923 *Diocesan Chronicle* wrote:

> "He was so obviously genuine and sincere. If he said it he meant it. He was quick to express himself and, perhaps, like St. Paul, not always equally ready to listen. At his enthronement he pronounced 'Essex for Christ'. Others would not have used the phrase. They would have felt it too bold, too impossible. With him it was just characteristic . . . He retained so much of apostolic faith in the power of the Gospel of Christ to win the world."

Another obituary writer in the *Diocesan Chronicle* revealed the suspicion with which his emergence had been greeted:

> "The appointment had come as a surprise and many in Essex were slow to see the wisdom of it . . . Certain early utterances were severely criticised and called forth vigorous protests . . . It was only by degrees that our Bishop won his way."

In other words he trod on some toes: perhaps some of them had needed a good stamp. But the essence of the man triumphed:

> "It was the atmosphere of prayer and intercession in which he lived, it was the affectionate nature of the man, forgiveness of heart, which did much to break down any opposition or disloyalty."[38]

The Times of July 16th called him:

> "An unconventional prelate . . . He had won the respect of the huge artisan population in the Diocese . . . But he secured no strong financial support. No doubt the war was largely responsible for this."

The *Daily Telegraph* gave qualified praise:

> "There have been many bishops in recent years more learned, even more statesmanlike . . . but . . . none possessed of a greater love of souls."

The local papers were less lofty. The *East Anglia Daily Times* observed:

> "His preaching was characterised by the fervour of the old Wesleyan Methodist type."

The *Essex Weekly News* remarked on his industry and accessibility:

> "He preferred to do work himself which might have been delegated . . . He was probably the most unconventional prelate who ever sat on the episcopal bench. He never believed, as some have done, that the dignity of a bishop must be hedged round by a barrier of aloofness."

There is no doubt that he overestimated the degree of conformity he could expect from his clergy of varied churchmanship backed by their freehold security of tenure and, in some cases, support of lay patrons. Some certainly felt that his moral and doctrinal pronouncements were somewhat menacing and rigid in tone: in bald print they do come across in that way.

After all the formal obituaries had been published, a heartfelt letter from "A Grateful Father" appeared in *The Times* on July 20th. One son had been killed on active service and buried in Belgium in 1914, the other wounded at Passchendaele in 1917, hospitalised for two years and then ordained deacon and priest in 1923 by John Watts-Ditchfield:

> "For nearly two years this large-hearted Bishop's care and interest
> in this soldier clergyman was beyond all praise. Nothing was a
> trouble to the Bishop . . . A real 'Father in God' interest was shown
> in my wounded son."

The pastoral dedication of clergy is by its very nature confidential: such documentation is rarely found.

The Bishop's father's favourite maxim was "better to wear out than to rust out."[39] In both senses of the phrase his son had followed this precept religiously.

CHAPTER 13

Exhaustion, Extension and Excursions

The September 1923 *Parish Magazine* announced that 52-year-old Guy Warman, Bishop of Truro, had been appointed as the second Bishop of Chelmsford; he was enthroned on October 11th. He had been a great friend of John Watts-Ditchfield, especially within the Group Brotherhood, of which Warman was a co-founder in 1905, which tried to develop a less fundamentalist evangelical response to the challenges from science, philosophy and literary criticism of the Bible.[1] However, both men asserted their evangelical credentials by declining to wear mitre or cope, though Guy Warman eventually conceded to a cope for ordinations. Canon Lake, as a High Churchman, trod warily and, to avoid invidious comparison, rarely wore his full vestments.[2]

The rural Diocese of Truro may have seemed far removed from the challenges of the Diocese of Chelmsford. However, Guy Warman had the right grounding. A north Londoner by birth he had graduated from Pembroke College, Oxford, been ordained in St. Mary's, Chelmsford in 1895 by the Bishop of St. Albans followed by his first curacy at Leyton and then two northern incumbencies in Birkenhead and Bradford in between which he served as Principal of St. Aidan's Theological College in Birkenhead.

The *Parish Magazine* was optimistic:

> "He is a comparatively young man and therefore likely to possess the necessary strength for such a work as our difficult diocese presents. His previous experience . . . has fitted him for dealing with very large populations."

Bishop Guy Warman at The Gun after his enthronement,
October 11th 1923: *Daily Sketch*, October 12th 1923

He described the task he was taking on:

> "There are a million people in London-over-the-Border, rural
> Essex with as large a population as Cornwall, the ever-growing
> seaside resort of Southend and the largest housing scheme in the
> country, that of the London County Council at Becontree."[3]

Following in the footsteps of John Watts-Ditchfield he called for
"aggressive evangelicalism" and warned of a "recrudescence of paganism"
through immersion in pleasure and materialism as people sought diversion
from the memories of war:

> "The great mass of the people of this land have either considered
> or found no use for religion or have accepted at the hand of others
> the notion that it is useless."[4]

It was not an auspicious time for the St. Mary's congregation. The
struggling Church of England Men's Society had been disbanded nine days
before Guy Warman's enthronement, "though it is to be regretted", wrote

Canon Lake, "because other parishes look to the Cathedral to give them a lead."[5] All was not well with the choir either. Although the adult singers had purchased their own new choir desks and a benefactor and former choristers had clubbed together to do the same for the choirboys,[6] sporadic attendance and variable quality were affecting performance. The *Parish Magazine* was constrained to comment:

> "An honourable position carries with it honourable responsibilities and we would like to see all members of the choir who can manage it coming regularly and punctually to choir practices . . . It is not merely a matter of knowing the music, but of learning to adapt oneself to other people's limitations."[7]

The congregation was urged to underpin descant singing:

> "We have tried it lately with some of the better-known hymns in the Cathedral . . . but the congregation must do its part which is singing the melody lustily and with a good will and then the effect should be one full of inspiration."[8]

Perhaps the choir needed new leadership and singers. In 1926 Frederick Frye would celebrate his 76th birthday and 50th year as organist and choirmaster; he would continue in the post for a further 16 years. In the same year Mr Catt, secretary to the choir since 1886, would mark his golden jubilee as a choir member.[9] For the last 40 years his Choir Minute Book had concentrated almost solely on the annual outing and choir dinner and music was never mentioned.[10] They were not the only old retainers. The Verger, James Oswick, would die in harness at the age of 75, having held office for 27 years: the *Parish Magazine* described him as "brusque, downright and genuine to the core",[11] in other words, a somewhat prickly character who did not mince words.

It was common for clergy to serve until they dropped as it was not until 1949 that a Church Dignitaries Retirement Measure enabled some form of retirement with pension. Frederick Frye's organist's position, with its £100 annual salary (worth £4,450 in today's money), was, like clergy posts, also held in freehold for life.[12] Octogenarian bishops were not uncommon. Christian charity made it difficult to suggest that people who had passed their peak should hand over the reins especially where the loss of remuneration may cause genuine hardship. Moreover, voluntary unsalaried office holders often relished their status; demotion would entail loss of face and social standing.

Although there seemed to be a lack of energy in the congregation, it was essential from a diocesan viewpoint that the Cathedral began to function as the mother church. In 1924 Canon Lake was made Sub-Dean so that he at last had a formal role in the Cathedral while still retaining his parish title of Rector.[13] A year later the *Diocesan Chronicle* talked up the Cathedral's efforts:

> "During the last few weeks the Cathedral Church has been in special ways fulfilling its function as the mother church of the Diocese . . . an ordination, a great territorial service, the jubilee service of the Girls' Friendly Society, the annual festival of the Church of England Men's Society, the annual gathering of the diocesan bell-ringers and a great service for the Mothers' Union . . . It is good to know that the parishes of the Diocese are to be remembered in prayer day by day in the Cathedral and that plans are being made whereby the Cathedral shall be similarly remembered in the churches of the Diocese."[14]

That practice had been in operation since the summer of 1924; two parishes were remembered at the altar each day so that all 476 would be covered in a year.[15]

Chelmsford was also living up to its hospitable claims made when the cathedral town contest took place. In 1925 the Diocesan Conference was held in the town for the second successive year: "Chelmsford's hospitality never fails . . . There is a growing feeling that . . . Chelmsford is the right place for the annual meeting."[16] But the Diocese was not keeping pace with other dioceses' electoral roll registrations: only one in 14 of its communicants were registered compared to one in 12 nationally[17] which cost the Diocese three seats in the Church Assembly House of Laity.[18]

The first critical analysis of the Cathedral's role came in June 1926. The Church Assembly set up a commission of enquiry into the property and revenues of the Church; a sub-committee came to Chelmsford led by Ernest Pearce, Bishop of Worcester.

It reported that Chelmsford still had no legally constituted Chapter though it did have 24 honorary canons.* By implication, therefore, the Bishop must be Dean because Canon Lake had been made Sub-Dean, but no formal declaration of the Bishop's position had been made nor any definition of the responsibilities that each role entailed; legally this left the Bishop with no more jurisdiction in the Cathedral than in any other parish church. The sub-committee observed that there was happily no friction "but the situation should be made secure from the hazard of less cordial relations." There was also confusion over Canon Lake's two titles of Sub-Dean and Rector. How did the one fit with the other? Could a future Sub-Dean be appointed who was not Rector or vice-versa? Again, legal positions needed to be clarified.

The sub-committee also noted that "so far nothing has been done to provide for the appointment of preachers on a cathedral basis" and that

---

* Honorary canons' stalls were named after St. Cedd; Sigeberht, King of the East Saxons; the Venerable Bede; St. Aidan, first Bishop of Lindisfarne; St. Augustine, first Archbishop of Canterbury; Samuel Harsnett, Vicar of Chigwell, Rector of Shenfield and Archbishop of York; St. Benedict; John Beche, Benedictine Abbot of Colchester who was hung for resisting the dissolution of the monasteries; John Leche, Vicar of Saffron Walden and founder of its Grammar School; Edward the Confessor, builder of Westminster Abbey which formerly owned the manor of Moulsham; St. Edmund, King of East Anglia, martyred by the Danes; St. Botolph, a seventh century monk after whom St. Botolph's Church in Colchester is named; Theodore, Archbishop of Canterbury who did much to unite the Roman and Celtic churches; Justus, first Bishop of Rochester; Mellitus, first Bishop of London and first missionary to the East Saxons; St. Alban, first British martyr; St. George, whose saint's day marked the enthronement of the first Bishop of Chelmsford and the annual Chapter meeting; St. Erkenwald, founder of Barking Abbey; St. Thomas of Canterbury; Maud, Queen of Henry I who financed the bridging of the River Lea at Stratford; King Harold, buried at Waltham Abbey; St. Osyth, martyred by the Danes; St. Helen, mother of Constantine the Great, alleged discoverer of the True Cross; St. Ethelburga, sister of Erkenwald and first Abbess of Barking.

The Rector's Stall was dedicated to St. Peter-ad-Murum; the Precentor's was named Restitutus, reputedly an early bishop in the Christianised Roman Empire who attended the Council of Nicaea in 325; and the two Archdeacons stalls were named after Aubrey de Vere and Henry Bourchier, [19] the first earls of Oxford and Essex respectively.

there was no role for the honorary canons. It suggested a rota which would give the Bishop and Rector their fair proportion of services but also offer an opportunity for the canons to preach once in every two or three years.

The Sub-Dean's stipend caused concern. Canon Lake did not have an official residence but paid rent out of his own stipend for the use of Guy Harlings as a rectory; he also subsidised the curates which left him with net pay of about £250 a year (£11,100 in today's money) which the commission described as "ridiculous." He should, they said, receive £500 (£22,200) as Sub-Dean from the Church's central funds or the "Bishop will be shut up in his choice of Rector to men with considerable private means", precisely the point that Frank Johnson had made 30 years before.

Then there was the question of the parish's needs which the sub-committee calculated as a rector and two curates. There were in fact three clergy named as curates but one was the Precentor (a cathedral, not a parish, role) who was paid £250 annually by the Diocese, one was employed full-time at St. Peter's Mission Church in west Chelmsford, leaving just one full-time curate for St. Mary's, though the Precentor clearly also chipped in with some parish activities.

Finally the sub-committee delved into the murky shadows where parish and diocesan financial responsibilities interfaced. £3,000 (£133,000 in today's money) had been set aside for distinctly diocesan services and events in the Cathedral but this excluded the cost of incidental printing, cleaning, lighting and heating which continued to fall on the parish. Furthermore, although the capital cost of planned extensions to the Cathedral would be borne by the Diocese, the cost of additional insurance would fall on the parish. The parish was getting a raw deal.

Bishop Pearce's report concluded:

> "This hardly-pressed Diocese is wise to move slowly in the development of its Cathedral and, because of the problems with which London-over-the-Border is faced, the Cathedral deserves the practical and intelligent sympathy of the Church at large."[20]

This somewhat vacuous statement was making virtue out of an inevitable necessity: it was not wisdom that had dictated slow development but the impoverishment of a devastating war and its effects on a county not renowned in better times for its riches.

Reference had been made to extensions on which work started in the summer of 1926 as a memorial to John Watts-Ditchfield. The chancel was to be extended eastwards by 17 feet, only one-third of the distance proposed by Frederic Chancellor in Chelmsford's cathedral bid. This would provide two additional bays to give more room for the choir and enable the honorary canons' stalls to be moved out of their hidey-hole in the Mildmay Chapel. But some of the congregation did not welcome these developments:

> "Many of the older members of the congregation may not be very eager for this new move. They love the Cathedral as it is and as they have known it for many years."

To sugar the pill Canon Lake explained that the money required had been raised from the whole Diocese "and is, in fact, a gift to the parish" while he also dangled before his resentful critics the prospect of another project, the building of proper vestries, although the money for that embellishment had yet to be raised:

> "It must have been felt by all that our vestry accommodation—where the vestries are simply a portion cut off from the church by the organ so that the organ protrudes into the church and reduces space and dignity there and in which no sound can be made [in the vestry] without its being heard by the congregation—is most unsatisfactory."[21]

Canon Lake's attempt to pour oil on troubled congregational waters would perpetuate confusion. The new extension was not, as he claimed, a gift to the parish, even though the congregation would get free use of its benefits week by week, but an investment by the Diocese in its mother church. And the unsatisfactory state of the pokey vestry, a longstanding problem which the parish had not been able to rectify, was again to be resolved by diocesan money. Congregational enjoyment of the glamour of cathedral status needed to be accompanied by an acceptance that the Diocese would expect a return for its investment.

The town was very interested in the new building development: it would mean work for local businesses. But Sir Charles Nicholson chose a firm from Stamford which caused some disgruntlement. History was repeating itself as John Johnson had been equally unpopular in 1800 for going far afield. The old foundations at the east end were in an unsatisfactory state and needed strutting and shoring up for which Nicholson may have felt local firms lacked sufficient experience.[22]

The work was finished by the end of 1927. Congregational gifts added further lustre: Dr Theodore Waller, the late churchwarden, was commemorated by his family in the painted glass of a clerestory window[23] and to enhance the high altar, an anonymous donor gave new altar rails which were beautiful specimens of 17th century carving.[24]

On April 24th 1928, almost to the day of the anniversary of his enthronement, a life-size statue of John Watts-Ditchfield was unveiled by his widow in the extended chancel and the diocesan and suffragan bishops and the honorary canons took their places in their new stalls for the dedication of the extension. In his address Bishop Guy Warman affirmed:

> "The Cathedral is the mother church of the Diocese. It should be
> the centre of our diocesan life. It should offer homely welcome . . .
> The facilities of modern transport are fast making it what it would
> desire to be."

He also wanted the Cathedral to be a symbol of unity in a divided church:

> "The creation of the Church Assembly and of the Parochial
> Church Council has given . . . larger scope for and greater publicity
> to our differences . . . This Cathedral, now enlarged, must become
> the prayer centre of a praying Diocese."[25]

In a more light-hearted vein at the Diocesan Conference the Bishop jested:

> "He was reminded of a lady who had indulged in the extravagance
> of a new hat. She immediately discovered there were many
> other new things she needed. He had a similar feeling about the
> Cathedral." [26]

The Bishop recognised the desperate needs of London-over-the-Border but, even so, accepted that the Cathedral's new vestry could not wait. This, it was suggested, should be in a two-storey building. Its southern wall would commence 12 feet from the Cathedral's north wall and would connect with the Cathedral by a passageway so that minimum adaptation would be required should Nicholson's grand plan for doubling the size of the Cathedral eventually be given life. The vestry project and the cleaning and removal of the organ, would cost £5,500[27] (£245,000 in today's money).

The town also lent a hand. The Cathedral was a diocesan responsibility but its tower clock was of public value. Its condition was dangerous. An appeal from the *Essex Weekly News* and the *Essex County Chronicle* raised 20% of the cost of restoration.[28]

While these grand events were unfolding around them life for the youth of St. Mary's Parish seemed to be on the up. The Young People's League was started in 1925 by the curate, Hamish Gray, for those over 14 who had just left school for work.[29] Its birth was made possible by the opening of the new Cathedral Hall in November 1924 at the west end of the churchyard, all the money contributed by parishioners. Hitherto parish organisations had to use the Victoria Schools and they had restricted availability. The Hall proved a welcome money-spinner with 191 lettings between October 1925 and March 1926. In particular, the ever-popular New Year Socials could be held there rather than in the expensive and freezing Corn Exchange.[30]

60 young people immediately joined the Y.P.L., as it became known.[31] In July they made an excursion eastwards to Beeleigh, near Maldon; some went by bus, others cycled with the warning that the road from Danbury to Maldon was "the worst in England."[32] In the evenings the girls engaged in raffia work, dancing and studied literature and singing; the boys indulged in bell-ringing, ju-jitsu and boxing; and there were joint plays, dances and debates.[33] The separate boys' and girls' sections soon merged and one old member remembered that it was like a matrimonial bureau.[34]

The Sunday School too was seeing happier days. The July 1924 Sunday School outing went to Felixstowe:

> "280 children made the trip from the parish . . . accompanied by 33 teachers and 48 parents. About 80% of the children from the Cathedral went on the outing. Many of them bathed, more of them paddled, all of them ate and drank unceasingly, just a few of them were lost and only two of them (of whom no report has yet reached the writer!) left behind."[35]

The following year discipline in the Sunday School had improved to such an extent that "the teachers were anxious to undertake the entire control of the children in church." Their new-found courage would "relieve Mr Alexander of what has been a very thankless task, heroically and indefatigably carried out for many years."[36] This reluctant martinet, churchwarden Charles Alexander, could now relax during the service without requiring eyes in the back of his head.

"Suffer little children to come unto me" may have been an inspiration for Sunday School teachers but for many children the attraction of Felixstowe or other coastal resorts was the real inducement. Children with 75% attendance were eligible to join the summer outing for just one shilling (5p: £2.22 in today's money); the less dedicated would have to pay one shilling and sixpence (7½p: £3.33). Public collections helped subsidise the trip so that mothers with three top attending children could accompany them free; mothers with two children paid two shillings (10p: £4.44); and with one child three shillings and sixpence (17½p: £7.77).[37] A train full of St. Mary's children and parents plus those from the mission church of St. Peter's, St. John the Evangelist, Moulsham and London Road Congregationalist Church, unloaded 1,000 customers at Clacton in July 1925.

In August a more sedate group of 50 members of the Rector's Bible Class went to Clacton:

> "There was a break at Colchester, the reason given being the charabanc. Others however seemed to need refreshing besides the vehicle . . . After being photographed, the party dispersed. What each did is not recorded. This was perhaps the best course to take."

The Guides had their sixth annual camp at Steeple Stone, out in the remote Dengie Peninsula, wedged between the Blackwater and Crouch estuaries and the North Sea, with a Church Parade at St. Lawrence. The Scouts and Cubs camped at Little Easton Park near Great Dunmow at the invitation of Daisy, Countess of Warwick.[38]

Word may have got round that the Clacton trip had been something special as the number of Sunday School classes increased from 12 to 19: there were, strangely, more boys than girls which reaffirms the suspicion that inspiration was more earthly than spiritual. Clearly the boys found it was going to be a long wait till they reaped their summer seaside reward: indiscipline returned and Charles Alexander must have wondered whether he would be recalled to front-line duty:

> "On Sunday mornings pushed away in a corner out of sight of their Superintendent where they can see nothing of what is going on, a good deal of the service is lost to them and they are apt to be fidgety and difficult to control . . . The girls have shown a

decided improvement—but we are sorry to say this does not yet apply to the boys."[39]

The fun and games were threatened by the ten day General Strike in May 1926 which caused huge national divisions. However the parish's main concern was not the grinding poverty of the miners (they got short shrift) but the possible impact on the Sunday School treat. The strike may have caused the diocesan Clergy Synod to be postponed from June to September but children were tougher nuts to crack: "may we never have another one!" the *Parish Magazine* exclaimed, referring to the strike, not the treat. The Rector craved a return to normality:

"The country as a whole behaved splendidly and here in Chelmsford the order observed was admirable. Any amount of our people enrolled as 'Specials' . . . We shall all pray that the nation may emerge from the conflict stronger and more united than ever before to face the perplexing problems of the 20th century . . . Provided this interminable and wasteful coal strike is well over, we [the Sunday School] hope to go to Dovercourt by train on July 21st."

They did and St. Mary's yet again made its annual contribution to the economy of Essex's seaside towns. And to make sure that those children who were lucky enough to have holidays away from Chelmsford kept the faith and accumulated credit for the following year's trip, they would be awarded attendance marks if they could bring a paper, signed by a responsible person, to say that they had attended a church or Sunday School elsewhere. As for the other youth organisations, the Cubs camped at Walton-on-the-Naze and the Guides at Heybridge while the Cathedral Scouts went by ferry to the Belgian battlefields though "many of the boys decided they would have preferred to have travelled by airship, as they would not have been ill for quite so long."[40]

Then, suddenly, in September 1928 Guy Warman left the Diocese to become Bishop of Manchester in the midst of the Prayer Book crisis, in which a divided Church of England had marooned itself. The country also suffered fierce class divisions exacerbated by the General Strike. Bishop Warman connected the two and was horrified that a disputatious Church was not setting a good example:

"Certain newspapers . . . pamphlets and . . . speeches foretell a period of strife, of disruption, even of catastrophe for the old Church of the land . . . Will those who love such honoured words as Anglo-Catholic, Evangelical and Liberal be able to live together? . . . We want to be in a position to tell more and more miners and mine owners alike that they are members of the family of God and that there is a Christian solution of their family problem. We cannot expect to be in that position if we find ourselves unable to handle our own family matters in the same family spirit."[41]

The Bishop had played a leading role in the work on the Revised Prayer Book. The 80-year-old Archbishop Davidson had delegated much of the administrative work to him so he had borne the full brunt of internecine strife as Evangelicals and Anglo-Catholics went for each others' throats. Maybe he found committee work more congenial. He was naturally of a somewhat private and retiring disposition and some clergy, it was said, found it difficult to get beyond his shyness.[42] Posterity has fared no better: he had no time for biographies of bishops and left no diary and very few private papers.[43]

The Anglo-Catholics had made considerable inroads on the ritual and style of church worship over recent decades. The First World War had played its part. Prayers for the dead were welcomed by a grieving public who had no time for evangelical claims that they smacked of chantry superstition. Dying Anglican soldiers in the trenches had lacked the benefit of a reserved sacrament, unlike their Catholic colleagues. The Revised Prayer Book, which emerged after an extraordinary 21 years of protracted discussion, would permit continuous reservation of the communion bread and wine in circumstances approved by the local bishop. Pleased Anglo-Catholics were predictably opposed on religious principle by fervent evangelicals and, more cautiously, by folk who just liked the Book of Common Prayer as a beautiful text that they had always known.[44] By offering the revision as a substitute rather than an alternative for the Book of Common Prayer the reformers left the way open for anti-Rome hysteria to be whipped up.

The 1919 Enabling Act was designed to allow internal administrative and organisational changes to be made without full parliamentary debate but any change to the Book of Common Prayer, introduced in 1549 and redefined in 1662 by statute, would still require parliamentary approval. A parliamentary ambush, all very reminiscent of the Bishoprics Bill 20 years before, was led by two evangelical hawks, the Home Secretary, William Joynson-Hicks and the Solicitor-General, Thomas Inskip. They were both members of the Church Assembly where they had resoundingly lost the debate but launched a second attack in the House of Commons. They were backed by assorted parliamentary Protestant malcontents, especially evangelicals from Wales and Presbyterians from Scotland and Ulster, plus, by way of variety, one Communist Parsee. This motley coalition defeated the Prayer Book proposals twice in 1927 and 1928 even though the Prayer Book would apply only to England. But their fear of the Vatican and its authoritarian ways was so ingrained that they believed they were protecting British political liberties. Outside Parliament the dissidents had been led by 80-year-old Edmund Knox, former Bishop of Manchester, who came out of retirement to address meetings in the Albert Hall and elsewhere and to organise a protest memorial signed by 300,000 communicants, an act which Hensley Henson, Bishop of Hereford and a liberal reformer, derided as "an army of illiterates generalled by octogenarians."[45] Those millions who were indifferent to the Church would have breathed a sigh of relief that they were not involved in such pin-headed theological arguments.

The Church proposed a compromise which may have proved illegal had it been challenged: a bishop could approve the use of the Revised Prayer Book in his diocese but must also leave the old Book of Common Prayer intact for those who wanted to continue with its usage. Over a few years, by stealth, the Revised Prayer Book gradually came into use. Canon Lake wrote in December 1928, for the January 1929 *Parish Magazine*, that the proposed new Prayer Book would probably become a permanent standard of worship "meeting some of the needs which a Prayer Book of nearly 300 years old cannot possibly meet." Some new services were already in use:

> "In our Cathedral services some of the 'permissions' . . . have already been adopted e.g. the new lectionary, the special intercessions etc. There may be others which, with the goodwill of the congregation, may be helpful. They will not be introduced without explanation."

By the time most people had read those words Canon Lake was gone, dying suddenly at the age of 81 on January 7th 1929. The *Parish Magazine* in February said:

"He had won the affection and esteem of all classes in the community . . . Tolerant and fair to men of all parties, Canon Lake was a definite High Churchman whose own personal life centred round the daily celebrations and the daily offices. His Wednesday evening intercessions, his two Sunday Bible Classes, his monthly Communicants' Class for men, were all features of his activity that he was loath to hand over to another and he kept in active harness almost to the end."

He remained essentially the parish priest, comfortable with the sacraments but ill-at-ease with his cathedral role which had never, in fact, been clearly defined. As a High Churchman he was unfailingly loyal to his two evangelical bishops though he found their Crusades not entirely to his nature. In August 1925 he had written in the *Parish Magazine* that the Bishop's Crusade in October was going to clash with the annual Society for the Propagation of the Gospel meeting and sermon; he commented that these must not suffer but added, almost ruefully, that "still, the call for the Bishop's Crusade each year seems more pressing." Ironically 1929 was to be the last year of the Crusade.

It was a month for final farewells as the *Parish Magazine* also recorded the death of Sir John Caesar Hawkins who had been Rector from 1878 to 1880.

The Cathedral and its Diocese would now be in new hands.

CHAPTER 14

Rector to Provost

Henry Wilson, graduate of Corpus Christi College, Cambridge, Rector of St. Mary's Church, Cheltenham (and prior to that curate in Hampstead and vicar in Kingston-on-Thames), reacted with mock modesty to his invitation to become the third Bishop of Chelmsford:

> "It is a curious fact that I did not know the post was vacant and so slightly was I versed in lofty matters that I tossed the unstamped envelope aside with a mild malediction, thinking that it contained a bill."[1]

Conscience pricked him: he opened the envelope, acquitted himself of the sin of debt and on St. Paul's Day, January 25th 1929, was consecrated as a bishop at Westminster Abbey. With remarkable consistency he, like his two predecessors, was 52 years old when elevated to the Essex see. He was enthroned in Chelmsford Cathedral by Cosmo Lang, Archbishop of Canterbury, on February 12th. James Inskip, the Bishop of Barking, whose half-brother, Thomas, had sabotaged the Revised Prayer Book in the House of Commons two years earlier, stood in for the late Canon Lake. Working at a distance from his bishop's base in Walthamstow was difficult: administrative hiccups and a biting cold wind on the day itself left 100 seats empty.[2]

Henry Wilson's frank inaugural address showed a willingness not to mince words that would characterise his episcopacy. In the wake of the rows over the Revised Prayer Book he remarked:

"The clergy were, not without cause, popularly regarded as defenders of a theological system rather than as examples of Christian living . . . Men and women today knew a Christian when they saw him . . . It seemed sometimes that the things to which we devoted our greatest zeal were those on which we were divided among ourselves; and the outside world looked on with contempt."[3]

The new bishop was from the Liberal Evangelical wing of the church. He did not have much time for the Broad Churchmen, by this time called Modernists, who, as experts in textual and historical criticism, were increasingly wedded to a non-miraculous version of the Bible: in his later autobiography he described them as "agnostics clinging to the hem of Christianity."[4] But nor had he allied himself with those more extreme Evangelicals who had opposed the Revised Prayer Book. Anglo-Catholics he credited with having brought dignity and piety to church services but regarded them as mainly a clerical movement whose few outstanding parish clergy, such as Robert Dolling in Portsmouth or Arthur Stanton in Holborn, made an impact because of their "magnetic force and manifest saintliness"[5] not their theology and would, in his view, have had a following whatever they had taught. He wondered whether:

". . . in these days when pastoral work is hard, uphill, disappointing and often depressing, some of the [Anglo-Catholic] clergy have not found what psychologists call a 'defence mechanism' or 'compensation' with an emphasis on the sacerdotal character of their ministry."[6]

He asserted that the "kind of service presented in the best ordered Evangelical Churches is the one most congenial to the English people" and was dismissive of the growing school of thought that wanted to substitute sung Eucharist for Matins. But he acknowledged that Evangelicals were now rather cowed and "under the weather."[7]

On February 21st, a few days after the bishop's enthronement, *The Times* announced that William Morrow, Vicar of All Saints', Wandsworth would be the new Rector of St. Mary's and Sub-Dean of the Cathedral. He had been a curate for 10 years in West Ham and then spent 15 years in two incumbencies at North Woolwich and Forest Gate; with a quarter of a century's experience in London-over-the-Border he certainly knew the Diocese's mission territory well. In 1919 he became Vicar of Clifton in Bristol where his wife, Lucy, died very suddenly, precipitating his move in 1925 to Wandsworth. He was installed in Chelmsford on May 7th 1929 and would be supported by his sister, Frances, just as Canon Lake had been by his. He had formally resigned as an honorary canon when he left the Diocese in 1919[8] but was immediately reinstated to an honorary canon's stall on his return.

Bishop Henry Wilson in sporting vein:
Chelmsford Cathedral Knightbridge Library

William Morrow, like his diocesan, was also firmly on the evangelical wing.[9] He never lit candles on the high altar and immediately requested permission not to wear a cope. That was no problem for Henry Wilson who had once declared: "you would never get me to wear one of those things." As a bishop, he wore a black chimere over his rochet rather than a showy red one.[10]

The Bishop was outraged that the Rector was still expected to pay for his curates:

> "It is *scandalous* that the Rector should pay . . . curates. This is a relic of the bad old days . . . A little application of up-to-date methods will put this right."[11]

He was as good as his word and the Rector was at last relieved of this financial burden.

The new Rector's personality was more colourful than his vestments. A Dubliner with a sparkling wit, he had been a keen rugby player and Alpine mountaineer. His bishop declared that he had "never met anyone who had found it possible to fall out with him."[12] One member of the congregation remembered him well:

> ". . . a jovial Irishman with a beautiful singing voice: he could call on a fund of splendid Irish jokes . . . living in Guy Harlings with his sister, Miss Morrow, a lady who thought her brother's sermons gave 'a very excellent discourse.'"[13]

The Church Council decided initially that the new vestry block, broom cupboards and all, should be dedicated to the memory of Canon Lake though in the end it was considered more fitting that just the Chapter House should be the late Sub-Dean's memorial.[14] The Cathedral Extension and Lake Memorial Fund prospectus tried to whip up the enthusiasm of potential donors, observing that other parish church cathedrals, notably Leicester, were adapting and adorning their buildings leaving Chelmsford in their wake.[15] The Bishop dedicated the extension on November 18th 1929. Only half the money had been collected so, pending further contributions, the outstanding amount was financed by an interest free loan from the Diocesan Church Building Committee.[16] Designed by Sir Charles Nicholson and supervised by Wykeham Chancellor, who had taken over his father's architectural mantle, the new rather four-square building was made of stone and flint to fit in with the rest of the Cathedral; block floors were laid with bagac hard wood from the Philippine Islands; doors and fittings were made of oak. The spacious choir vestry was accessible from the main body of the Cathedral and via an external door to the churchyard; internal stairs led to an upper Chapter House; the ground floor also contained a bishop's room and offices and a small Muniment Room where it was hoped a diocesan archive would be developed.[17]

The next project was the refurbishment of the North Chapel, known familiarly by most as the Mildmay Chapel or since 1914 the Canons' Chapel. The honorary canons no longer needed it so it would be dedicated to private meditation and prayer; to that end the high altar was transferred to the chapel and was replaced by a new high altar and rails in memory of Arthur Duffield, which was donated by his family with altar linen worked by their friends.[18] It was based on a 15th century perpendicular design by Wykeham Chancellor[19] whom William Morrow infuriated by refusing to allow its candles to be lit.[20] The 17th century high altar rails, presented to the Cathedral seven years before, were adapted to stand in the Lady Chapel or South Chapel.

The Vestry Extension: photo by Tony Tuckwell

No sooner had these projects been completed than an unexpected windfall from the will of John Keene, former chairman of Pearl Assurance who died in 1932, opened up new possibilities for the town and Cathedral. John Keene's widow, Lavinia, provided £25,000 (£1.38 million in today's money) for building new almshouses, opened on October 11th 1933 in Broomfield Road to the north of the town. Another generous gift of £20,000 (£1.11 million) was made to the Cathedral:[21] £6,000 (£332,000) was earmarked to be invested in perpetuity for a series of lectures on social and economic questions and matters of practical religion to be delivered twice a year in the Cathedral, though they would not get going until 1954; choral scholarships to King Edward VI Grammar School were endowed but these ceased when fee-paying ended in maintained secondary schools in 1946; and the large uncommitted balance enabled Canon Morrow to renovate the organ which had been coated in thick dust and mortar during the recent vestry extension work. It would also be shifted just a few feet further north out of the aisle into the transept where the cramped vestry had formerly stood, thereby providing an uninterrupted view down the north aisle to the re-ordered Mildmay Chapel and the splendid 16th century Thomas Mildmay Memorial which had been hidden behind the organ since 1900. The organ specification was sorted out by Walter Alcock who had moved on from Westminster Abbey to Salisbury Cathedral since his last involvement when the hydraulic system dried up: during the organ's installation services would be accompanied on a grand piano.[22] Whilst his brother was working on the building extensions and the organ was out of commission, Sydney Nicholson's Festival of Music, held at the Cathedral in October 1932, necessarily concentrated on unaccompanied singing.[23] Continuing construction work on vestries and chapels ensured that for the best part of four years, until April 1933, the Cathedral was closed except for services.[24]

The old organ was used for the last time on September 4th 1932 and the reconstructed one, built by Hill, Norman and Beard, was used for the first time on Good Friday, April 14th 1933. It had four manuals rather than three, 51 stops instead of 37 and a greater body of tone and variety of colour, including clarion and flute. The keyboards had a 61 and the pedals a 30 note range, enriched by the addition of three stops, including a sub-bass of 32 feet tone. A new carved organ case was designed by Wykeham Chancellor. The whole thing cost £3,250 (£180,000 in today's money).[25]

On Easter Monday five days vacuum cleaning of the Cathedral started to get rid of the dust that had accumulated after four years of building work. There was a last minute hitch when part of the ceiling collapsed but not, thankfully, during a service.[26] Wykeham Chancellor took immediate charge of the renovation: it cost nearly £300 (£16,600 in today's money) but he could persuade the Diocesan Board of Finance to contribute only £50 (£2,770).

The organ in its new position from 1933:
Chelmsford Cathedral Knightbridge Library

The Dedication Service for the new organ was held on April 29th, with the Bishop of Manchester, Guy Warman, returning to his former mother church as the preacher and the newly knighted Sir Walter Alcock on the organ. The following week organ recitals were given by some of the foremost English organists—Reginald Goss Custard of Alexandra Palace and St. Michael's, Chester Square; Ernest Bullock of Westminster Abbey; George Thalben Ball, of Temple Church; and Ernie Cook of Southwark Cathedral—and lunchtime organ recitals were started on Fridays, the busy market day in Chelmsford. [27]

The Keene bequest also financed the restoration of the 1749 spire. The lead had perished exposing to the weather the eight oak posts, especially on the south and west faces, which carried the superstructure for at least half their length. It could no longer safely support the remaining three and a half tons of lead covering and, indeed, was visibly leaning when viewed from the west.[28] Wykeham Chancellor proposed replacing the lead with lighter and tougher copper that would catch the sun's rays and turn an attractive shade of green. At the same time the weather-vane would be repaired and gilded. The *Parish Magazine* described its delights which were not easily observable from ground level:

> "It may not be generally known that the weather-vane is copper and represents a flying dragon with open mouth and protruding tongue and is a fine example of 18th century workmanship. It is entirely hand wrought and the detail is exceptionally good—its total length is 6'6" while the ball immediately beneath is 1'10" in diameter."[29]

This was not the first time the spire had caused concern. Frederic Chancellor had declared it to be unsafe back in 1874 when the *Chelmsford Chronicle* had advocated its removal: the resale value of the lead would have more than covered its demolition cost.[30] But, although many people found it amusing—it was locally known as "the candle extinguisher"[31]—any suggestion that it be removed was resisted: they liked its familiarity, wisely so as even the critical eye of that architectural guru, Pevsner, calls it "charming."[32]

In 1930 St. Mary's Parish shrank in size when the new District of the Church of the Ascension,[33] centred on St. Peter's mission church, was carved out of it. Situated in Primrose Hill at the west end of town, the mission church, which had replaced a makeshift room originally acquired in Compasses Terrace in 1879, was licensed in 1883 and rebuilt in iron in 1892. As the town was also expanding northwards, another iron mission church, All Saints', was built in 1905 on the corner of Broomfield Road and Stanhope Terrace and in 1929 a mission hall was erected in King's Road to the west of All Saints' to serve the new Boarded Barns Estate.** The District of the Ascension had a population of 7,000 in 1930 and an electoral roll of 288 with the usual imbalance of 97 men and 191 women.[34] With St. Mary's newly truncated parish limits Canon Morrow reinstituted the old custom of Beating the Bounds, though for symbolic reasons not, as in days of yore, to ensure that people knew who would be liable for church rates and in which churchyard they could expect to be buried.[35]

** In 1962 the new Church of the Ascension was built, with its vicarage in Maltese Road and St Peter's was closed. At the same time All Saints' became its own parish, absorbing the developing Woodhall Estate and part of Writtle.

In 1929 the parish was hit by a series of tragic drownings. 16-year-old Leonard Harvey lost his life in the River Chelmer. Three other members of the cathedral congregation drowned in the act of saving others: George Dawson, also 16, in Belgium while saving a fellow cathedral scout in recognition of which his parents were awarded a gift from the Carnegie Fund and a brass tablet in the Cathedral was dedicated to his memory;[36] 23-year-old Winifred Lacey in Jersey while going to the aid of a friend in difficulties; and 27-year-old Reginald Joyce in the River Can while rescuing a small boy.[37] On a less sombre note 14-year-old Bob Clark had saved two small children who fell into deep water at Baddow Meads for which he was later awarded a silver watch from the Carnegie Fund. But whose hero was he? There was some ill-will when the scouts claimed him as theirs and organised the presentation: the family had requested that it be made at the Cathedral as he had not joined the scouts until after the rescue.[38] In 1930 another scout, 13-year-old Geoffrey Bateman, was killed by a bus and, with rare grace, his parents exonerated the driver: the Rector wrote: "we know they are right but such magnanimity on the part of those who suffer . . . deserves to be placed on record."[39]

As Rector, Canon Morrow spoke his mind more directly than Canon Lake. He pursued the issue of parishioners making their wills:

> "Have we made our will? If not, are we aware that it is the duty of the clergy to urge us to do so? The service for the Visitation of the Sick is quite explicit about it. 'If the sick person has not before disposed of his goods, let him be admonished to make his will'. What trouble is caused by this selfishness (for no other word is strong enough) which omits to perform this duty until it is too late. Relatives and dependents, of course, have first claim, but the needs of our Parish Church or the extra-parochial needs of the Church at large should not be lost sight of where sufficient surplus funds are awaiting disposal."[40]

For evangelical Christians the British Empire, considered by many to be at its height in the 1930s, was still the vehicle to civilise the world. Canon Morrow wrote in the October 1931 *Parish Magazine*:

> "The spirit of patriotism . . . seems to be a decaying principle in so many lives today . . . It is not from any spirit of jingoism that I say this. It is because we believe that England has a destiny to

fulfil among the nations that I am a true patriot. Let us strive in our own lives to be citizens of the Kingdom of Christ and then we are certain to be Christian patriots."

In May 1932 he continued on the same theme:

"There is not a place where our traders have invaded that has not been 'occupied' by the Messenger of the Lord of Hosts. If it had not been for Christian missions, Uganda and Kenya would never have been ours today . . . The missionary has paved the way in all directions for the man of commerce. I do most earnestly ask our businessmen to weigh the matter of their responsibility . . . and become more and more keen on this great part of the Church's work."

Whatever the material benefits of Empire to the mother country the world was soon engulfed in the Great Depression of the 1930s. Bishop Henry Wilson felt it had been aggravated by:

". . . waste and over-indulgence in pleasure on the part of those whose lives are never menaced by the grim prospect of poverty and anxiety for the future . . . Frugal living, harder work, less pleasure-seeking would do us all good and the money this saved would have a steadying influence on the industries of our land."[41]

His economics were not very sound: the moneyed classes' spending provided employment for the less well off.

The Bishop also shared Canon Morrow's belief that the Empire was a means to universal Christian salvation:

"It is designed in God's purpose to be an instrument for the betterment and uplift of the world . . . He gave it to us because in his wisdom He believed that we would use the trust aright and in entire obedience to His will."[42]

When the Nazis bludgeoned their way to power in Germany and the Japanese imposed savage military control over Chinese Manchuria he contrasted their brutality with the relative benevolence of the British Empire:

"Our Empire is a trust from God and as such it is our duty to endeavour to discharge the trust aright. It is the fashion in certain quarters today to heap scorn upon this kind of sentiment . . . It is a very simple thing to point out that the acquisition of a great deal of the British Empire is distinguished by actions which are not always capable of defence, but the fact remains that the influence of the British Empire upon the nations under its control has not only been just but also uplifting."[43]

But in these increasingly troubled times he took a step back from the happy-go-lucky patriotism that had engulfed the nation back in 1914:

"Many people feel that the world is trembling on the brink of another disaster like that of 1914 . . . War is a sin . . . I do not think this necessarily means a definitely pacifist attitude or a disparagement of the military calling . . . Our sailors and soldiers are our national police whose duty it is to defend us against individuals who 'run amok'. The most peaceful people I know are sailors and soldiers and the most war-like during the war were the fire-eaters who stayed at home and arranged precisely how all the enemy nations should be dealt with, from the seclusion of their armchairs."[44]

Economic difficulties hit the mission in London-over-the-Border which remained understaffed. The 1931 census showed that Essex's population had risen a further 19.4% over the previous decade, predominantly in the metropolitan south of the county; James Inskip, the Bishop of Barking, referred to "the multitudes who pour into Essex as sheep without a shepherd."[45] The Diocese's Church of England Men's Society responded by raising money towards the building of a new church, St. George's, Barkingside; the Mothers' Union did the same for St. Elizabeth's, Becontree.

Clergy recruitment still posed a challenge. Merging rural parishes and redeploying some of their clergy to the urban areas, a Church Assembly suggestion, was not necessarily the answer: most country priests were elderly "who if they were dislodged from their benefices would be unable easily to accommodate themselves to crowded working-class parishes."[46] A report commissioned by the Church Assembly showed that out of the five largest dioceses two had more clergy than Chelmsford though Manchester, with twice the Diocese of Chelmsford's population, had fewer.[47] Not surprisingly young married clergy were reluctant to take their wives and children to the polluted atmosphere of industrial towns. But Bishop Wilson also had his own views on priorities for young clergy: a new ordinand should learn his job before getting married:

> "Young officers in the army and navy are not supposed to marry until they are 30 . . . I shall not accept for ordination any young man who will not promise to refrain from matrimony without my special consent until he has served three years."[48]

Could the Diocese raise more money for clergy stipends? A report from the Additional Curates Society showed that the Diocese of Chelmsford in 1930 received £3 from this central fund for every £1 it generated itself.[49] But raising extra cash locally was easier said than done in such harsh economic times. Canon Morrow wrote:

> "It is sad to hear that in our own town there are nearly 2,000 out of work . . . I am hoping to do more in the coming winter for the unemployed. I shall be glad to hear of concert parties or friends who might get up a concert in the Cathedral Hall. I am afraid the distress will be very acute, especially if the winter should be a hard one. Anyone that can help with money, clothes or boots etc. or getting up concerts will be most welcome to our ranks."[50]

Three concerts and a sale of work in aid of the Mayor's Unemployed Fund were held that autumn in the Cathedral. Perhaps there was a need for more doughty characters like Mrs Dennis, the 83-year-old widow of the late churchwarden. She had raised over £3,000 [51] (£148,000 in today's money) for clergy stipends in the poorer parts of the Diocese and was a fierce product of the High Victorian era. When she died in 1930 Canon Morrow wrote:

> "Mrs Dennis was what might be called 'an acquired taste' but beneath a rather rugged exterior there lay a heart of gold . . . She gave herself wholeheartedly to . . . increase the support given by the parish to the Assistant Clergy Fund. The younger generation,

she always felt, was not pulling its weight as the older had done; and if her method of approach was not always the happiest, her keenness and enthusiasm were never in doubt."[52]

And what about mission work within established parishes such as Chelmsford? A diocesan report on evangelism said that parochial missions lasting ten days were indispensable but were hampered by clergy shortages. It was impractical to invite experienced missioners if it meant leaving their own parishes short-handed. But the report also echoed the criticisms of the 1916 National Mission:

> "The kind of religious emotionalism which once appealed to very uneducated people, when religious enthusiasm was a novelty, now no longer appeals and in many cases repels."[53]

Other problems were identified: the lack of long-term preparation; confusion of purpose as to whether the mission's keynote was evangelistic, devotional or educational; and the tendency of people to shy away from churches whereas they might be attracted to meetings in cinemas or the open air.

The clergy were badly affected by stipend reduction as the agricultural depression hit tithe income to the Church. This ancient land tax was a vexed political question. The Tithe Acts of 1918 and 1925 had done something to reduce the burden, saving tithe payers £14 million (£623 million in modern values) by stabilising the charge but at the cost of a 10% reduction in clergy pay. However, plummeting agricultural income in the 1930s still left farmers exposed. At a meeting of tithe-payers in Chelmsford's Shire Hall one speaker protested: "no Church could thrive on an injustice: it did not matter to what denomination a farmer belonged, he had to pay for the benefit of the Church of England".[54] The local press reported harrowing cases of distraining orders placed on farmers who had no money to pay the tithe. A sympathetic Bishop Wilson was saddened that the Church was seen by some as "Shylocks who were determined to have the full pound of flesh" and referred to a manifesto in a recent by-election which stated that "England is the only country in Europe where the Church still saps the blood of the farmer."[55] He knew his rural clergy unfairly bore the brunt of criticism for a situation they had not created, calling them "the salt of the earth . . . quietly doing their duty, generally wretchedly underpaid, often misrepresented."[56]

The Tithe Act of 1936 eventually enabled the tithe to be commuted to an annual capital charge attached to the land to be paid in annuities over 60 years. This would end tithes in the long run but the Diocese calculated that it would immediately reduce clergy incomes by yet another 10% because of the level at which the capital charge had been set.[57] As a result the Bishop had to offer a country parish to eight or ten clergy before someone accepted as a rural stipend was usually in the region of only £350 a year (£18,500 in today's values) and there was generally a very large and old vicarage to maintain:

> "Nowadays people have lost their money and . . . do not belong to the 'moneyed' class . . . Particularly in Essex the anti-tithe agitation has added enormously to the difficulty . . . A clergyman . . . will almost inevitably find himself entangled in a very delicate situation with some of his leading parishioners." [58]

The Bishop could already foresee the need to group five or six parishes under one minister.

Amidst the dust of building projects, the terrible economic conditions of the Great Depression, the lack of money for London-over-the-Border and the difficulties of recruiting clergy, the Church was about to regularise the governance of the new parish church cathedrals, especially those like Chelmsford that had not inherited ancient collegiate structures of dean and chapter. Seven more new dioceses and parish church cathedrals had joined the ranks since the intake of 1914: Coventry in 1918, Bradford in 1919, Blackburn in 1926 and Portsmouth, Guildford, Leicester and Derby in 1927, making 20 new parish church cathedrals since the first modern creation of Ripon in 1836. Derby now became the smallest English cathedral, displacing Chelmsford from that envied position.

In 1931 the Church Assembly passed the Cathedrals Measure which stipulated that the incumbent in a parish church cathedral should be called the Provost and that a Cathedral Council should be set up which would be distinct from the Parochial Church Council; the two councils would co-exist, each catering for this novel arrangement whereby parish church cathedrals had to look in two directions simultaneously. Canon Morrow explained that the main change for the Parochial Church Council would be the loss of most of its financial control but reassured his congregation that, by way of compensation, it would have good representation on the Cathedral Council.[59] In his New Year's Letter for 1932 he wrote:

"It is no light matter to be at the head, not only of a parish church, but of a cathedral. There is so much to be thought out and arranged . . . There are two factors which are uppermost in my mind. The first is that I shall do all in my power to preserve the rights of the parishioners and the dignity of the Parochial Church Council. The second is the confidence which I have in the congregations to do their part to make our dear old Cathedral a centre for the whole Diocese and to support the work of the Parish and Diocese with that unity of spirit and liberality in service that they have done in the past . . . It has been a real joy to me to see the large congregations, not only on Sundays, but upon other occasions when the diocesan side of affairs was more emphasised than the parochial."[60]

The consultative process took a while. In the June 1934 *Parish Magazine* Canon Morrow advised:

"The next great occasion will be the sealing of the statutes of the Cathedral when they have obtained the Royal Assent: at that stage the Rector will be installed as Provost."

In October 1934 he reported that the Cathedral Chapter and the Parochial Church Council were going through the final draft of their constitutions which were to be presented to the next meeting of the Church Assembly and, assuming their acceptance, to lie on the table of the House of Commons for a month: this time they would not be ambushed by political malcontents. The request that the three churchwardens and seven elected members of the Parochial Church Council should also be members of the Cathedral Council had been accepted by the Cathedral Commissioners which would give the parish almost equal representation.

Provost? Dean? There was confusion in the minds of the congregation. The Rector explained that the designation of Provost, rather than Dean, was because the position was in the gift of the Bishop not the Crown,[61] though that only half solved the problem of nomenclature as he still retained the titles of Rector and Canon. Meanwhile, the Rector-cum-Canon-cum-Provost observed, "there remains the great work to be done of synthesising the parochial and the cathedral ideals until they emerge into a real union"[62] and hoped that "it may now only be a matter of time when it will be the City of Chelmsford."[63]

On July 2nd 1935 everything except city status came to fruition. The honorary canons met William Morrow at the west door and presented him with a copy of the four Gospels and of the Cathedral Statutes; he was then presented to the Lord-Lieutenant and the Mayor, representing the county and town. On taking the oath he knelt before the Bishop who read the commission appointing him Provost. Then the Mandate of Instruction was handed to the Archdeacon of Southend who placed the Provost in his stall of St. Peter ad Murum. The statutes were clear that the Rector of St. Mary's would always be Provost of the Cathedral. Provost Morrow explained it all in the August 1935 *Parish Magazine* including the etymology, "provost" deriving from a word which means "placed over." But he regretted that his cathedral responsibilities would divert him from home visiting.

Provost William Morrow:
Chelmsford Cathedral Knightbridge Library

On October 31st Royal Assent to the Statutes was granted just before the historic service to commemorate the 21st birthday of the Diocese which the Marconi wireless factory, just down the road from the Cathedral in New Street, relayed to the Cathedral Hall for those parishioners who did not have seats. The procession of about 500 clergy led by Cosmo Lang, the Archbishop of Canterbury, "created a great impression in the town." Ever aware of symbolism the first meeting of the Cathedral Council in the Chapter House was held on April 23rd 1936 on the 22nd anniversary of the enthronement of the first bishop.

CHAPTER 15

The Bolshie Bishop

In the February 1935 *Parish Magazine* Provost Morrow bewailed the large numbers who supported St. Mary's social events but not the Cathedral's services or other voluntary work. The following month he noted that, of the 30,000 people in the town, hardly 5,000 attended a place of worship on Sundays and that many of the 1,100 names on St. Mary's electoral roll were only "paper members." It was, as Bishop Wilson wryly observed, the church of the majority, "the church which most people stay away from."[1] But when functioning as a cathedral for major national commemorative events, such as the Silver Jubilee service for King George V and Queen Mary on May 6th or for the Armistice Day two minutes' silence, the place was packed. The Provost knew that for many the Anglican Church was still identified with their sense of nationalism:

> "I think that deep down in the hearts of the English nation there is the belief in the necessity of emphasising the solidarity of our nation. By this means our colonies are assured that we stand shoulder to shoulder in defence of order, freedom and righteousness."[2]

The routine Sunday by Sunday religious apathy of Chelmsford's population was not untypical. Of the inter-war period one church historian wrote:

> "The principal intellectual . . . orthodoxy of England . . . was a confident agnosticism . . . It starts with an emphatic presupposition

164

of disbelief, from which—if you were reasonably intelligent—only the clergy, Roman Catholics and a few eccentric neo-medievalists were expected to be exempt."[3]

The combined effects of Darwin's evolutionary discoveries, textual and historical analyses that cast doubt on the literal truth and authorship of parts of the Bible, the new insights into psychology and the carnage of the First World War had all dented belief; motorised transport was also opening up weekend alternatives to church-going. Meanwhile the two wings of the Church, seemingly oblivious to the general decline, continued to snipe at each other over issues of ritual.

There were attempts in Chelmsford to recapture lost ground. On July 21st 1935 a Church Army mission preached en route to Southend from Salisbury. The Provost wrote enthusiastically about their charismatic leader:

> "Few could fail to be touched by the splendid testimony of Captain Renes who 25 years ago was bantam champion boxer and who had won hundreds of cups and belts in America and elsewhere . . . I at once recalled our Bishop's words when he said that the Church must be more aggressive . . ."[4]

. . . by which, almost certainly, he did not mean fists first.

To try to win over the minds of the men the Provost held a monthly men's service. On December 1st 1935 the Church of England Men's Society organised a service with lessons read by the two directors of the Hoffman's ball-bearings factory, music from its band's instrumental soloists and the bells rung by its men.[5] On February 2nd 1936 there was a service for the male employees of the Crompton Parkinson electrical engineering company's "Arc Works",[6] and on April 5th one for the Marconi Wireless and Telegraph Company.[7] Later that year the Council of Meat Traders joined in the monthly men's service to give thanks to the Church for its successful lobbying against the opening of meat retailers' businesses on Sundays.[8] And in the same spirit of evangelism the first of a series of open air services was held at the Recreation Ground on June 16th [9] and another at The Gun in front of Shire Hall on July 21st.[10]

To capture the young there was a concerted effort in 1936 to open an Anglican secondary school in the centre of the town to which the Church's junior schools could send their children. This once again raised the spectre of Non-Conformists paying rates to subsidise grants to Anglican schools though it was the required capital cost of £36,000 (£1.91 million in today's money) that scuppered the scheme.[11] More successfully, plans were drawn up to merge the Victoria, Widford and St. John's church junior schools into one mixed school. "We shall have to raise at least £12,000", (£636,000) the *Parish Magazine* warned in June 1938. Mrs Lavinia Keene gave £5,000 (£265,000) and another £4,000 (£212,000) was raised from the sale of the Victoria Road site (the parishes of Widford and St. John's Moulsham would retain their own capital gains). A grant from the National Society and the Diocesan Committee for Religious Education left the parish needing to raise just under £3,000 (£159,000); it did. The foundation stone was laid on September 19th 1938: the new merged institution was called The Cathedral School.[12]

For many in England the bishops seemed out of touch. Episcopal attitudes were still predominantly Victorian in outlook and manner. Most bishops saw their dioceses as their own fiefdom: in the words of one bishop; "there are forty-three diocesan bishops, forty-three oracles, each from his own Delphi."[13] At the very top the Archbishop of Canterbury, Cosmo Lang, was an aloof High Churchman whose "patrician style made him seem remote and snobbish to ordinary people."[14] His close relationship with the aristocratic Cecil family and their relatives, who seemed to chair every important Church committee, ensured that the Church was run on high Tory lines and was more sympathetic to Anglo-Catholic views.[15]

Bishop Henry Wilson fitted into the autocratic, though not the aristocratic, mould. He was fiercely independent and passionate about his beliefs. He did not suffer fools gladly, for him a fairly broad stream of humanity, and was sometimes caustically cynical, a trait he acknowledged in his later years. He recounted how he was visited by the former Archbishop of Canterbury, Randall Davidson, after his appointment to Chelmsford had been announced. Davidson advised:

"Remember that you have been chosen a bishop because you represent a certain point of view. It has all too often happened that new bishops disappoint us by losing their characteristic and distinctive quality. Never be afraid to stand alone and say what you think."

Henry Wilson reflected:

"I valued those words greatly, although in some ways they were unnecessary, for by temperament I am not inclined to take opinions from others and I always feel uneasy when I find myself agreeing with the majority."

He regarded *vox populi* as "usually the safe road . . . crowded with dull, unimaginative, unadventurous people who plod along in monotonous security." He disparaged those who looked before they leapt: "'jump and you'll get there' appeals more to me."[16]

Those of "frothy religious sentiment" who dwelt on the fringes of the Church were to be challenged not wooed. He parodied their lukewarm beliefs in such a way that they probably felt more comfortable staying where they were:

"'I believe in God the Father because I believe there must be a God of some kind; a sort of eternal good nature and easy-going tolerance. I believe that Jesus Christ lived a holy life which I ought to admire and I believe that I ought to obey the teaching of the Sermon on the Mount. I am not quite clear what it contains, but I imagine no one can really be expected to live up to it. I have great reverence for the Cross but I do not pretend to understand what it means. I am not quite sure whether I believe in life everlasting, but if there is such a thing I believe that somehow or other everything will turn out all right for everybody in the long run: at any rate, I hope so. Amen . . . This religion which means that in practice we shall all 'muddle through into heaven' and that we must all subscribe to the local hospital to cover a multitude of sins, is certainly not Christianity. I have heard it described as 'the religion of the hot-water bottle'."[17]

Nor were those within the Church exempt from his critical eye: "it is the absence of enthusiasm in that circle of real adherents that is so distressing."[18] It is no wonder that his monthly letter in the *Diocesan Chronicle* was eagerly awaited by the press for whom it often provided good copy, not just in the nationals but also in the regional press as far away as Hull and Nottingham.

He was an inveterate correspondent to *The Times* where he banged the drum for his £150,000 appeal (£7.4 million in today's money) for the needs of London-over-the-Border. On March 1ˢᵗ 1930 he had described south Essex:

> " . . . rapidly becoming one unbroken city stretching from London to Southend . . . In Dagenham and Becontree . . . there are nearly 100,000 people . . . A large proportion of these people are unemployed and most are poor . . . I am issuing an appeal . . . to build new churches . . . to keep the people of England and particularly their children, in touch with the old Church of the land."

Through *The Times* he was clearly aiming to tap into the wealth of the establishment and London corporations but was also successful in securing the regular patronage of the Royal Family though names and amounts were not revealed.[19] He renewed his appeal to the nation's conscience on February 20ᵗʰ 1931:

> "The newcomers are Londoners and for them we must provide nine permanent churches, an average of 14,000 people to each church . . . The times are bad, but the policy of drift in this matter will make the times worse, for an irreligious democracy is the greatest danger which faces our country today."

On April 10ᵗʰ 1933 he wrote to say that the Diocese was still short of its target:

> "Most people are finding it very hard to pay their way but thoughtful people are becoming even more convinced that the healing of our troubles lies much more in the spiritual than in the economic. In a word we are not balancing our spiritual budget."

In another letter to *The Times* of January 14ᵗʰ 1936, in response to the objections of London's conservationists to the demolition of All Hallows, Lombard Street, he calculated that the proceeds from the sale of land could finance over 20 churches in London-over-the-Border and cheekily pleaded that "the mother Diocese of London might remember the needs of her poorest and youngest daughter." No such luck: the church was demolished in 1937 and the cash diverted to London's own church-building programme.

Ten years on, on April 10th 1947, he responded to a comment from the Diocese of Southwark, which claimed that Metropolitan London had two dioceses, with a reminder that, in fact, it had three:

> "For the Diocese of Chelmsford (which incidentally has always claimed and with the best reason, the title of 'Cinderella'), has a population of about 1,500,000 East Londoners . . . which has been tipped into Essex."

He was always ready to remind London that it could offload its population but not its moral and spiritual responsibilities.

In truth, he probably enjoyed going into print with the well-turned phrase. He was a naturally gifted writer with a very good grasp of history. His first-class brain, an eye for detecting others' fallacies and a combative temperament meant that those who did not construct a careful argument were likely to be dismantled incisively in a manner that Dean Swift would have relished. One can see why his obituary claimed that "when he was ordained the world lost a first-class journalist."[20] Provost Morrow captured him well:

> "It was always a cheering experience to see him jauntily walking up the High Street, his hat cocked at that particular angle which so exactly typifies his joyous and triumphant outlook on life."[21]

Amongst his victims were those who sought to torpedo the bishops' collective attempts to admit Non-Conformists to Holy Communion services. They received a powerful historical put-down as Bishop Wilson produced copious precedent to show how Dissenters in times past frequently attended Anglican communion to escape civil penalties for non-conformity. He poured cold water on the "fantastic manipulations" of those who opposed "the charitable proposals of the bishops."[22]

The summer of 1936 saw him at his most richly idiosyncratic. The nation was treated to his views in *The Times* on the "trick-riding" of cyclists, one with a six foot ladder across his shoulders and a pail in his hand, another with a baby's cradle strapped to the rear mudguard and a third, a fellow clergyman with a pile of books under his arm: he called for some "exemplary prosecutions" of cycling offenders.[23] Ten days later he wrote suggesting that nine well-worn hymns be eliminated from the repertoire for the next twelve months:

"Why, for instance, should such a hymn as *O God our help in ages past* be worked to death? . . . Whenever there is a service of national or civic importance, when the mayor comes to church and we want to be a little religious but not too much so, this hymn seems to be regarded as quite essential."

He also had it in for *Praise my soul the King of Heaven* and *Now thank we all our God* which "I have even once sung three times on the same day": such was the lot of the peripatetic bishop. Others on the execution list were *All people that on earth do dwell, We love the place O God, City of God, Ye watchers and ye holy ones, The Church's one foundation* and *Lead us Heavenly Father*.[24] The idea lingered on. In 1948 he added *Thy hand, O God, has guided* which he feared he would soon be singing in his sleep.[25]

But he may have gone too far when he suggested that the persecution endured by Christians under the yoke of European totalitarianism, if applied in England, would act as a stimulus to religion. One appalled correspondent suggested that he might be prime candidate for the firing squad himself while others had a broader list of offending clerics whom they felt would not be missed.[26]

As is not uncommon today, a bishop's pronouncement on political, social and economic issues will raise the hackles of those who feel that he is stepping outside his proper territory, even though there are very good New Testament precedents. Bishop Wilson declared himself against party political intervention but claimed:

"The line between moral and political questions is now almost inextinguishable . . . Quite certainly the old taunt against the bishops that they are experts in tight-rope walking is no longer true. The old countryman's advice to the young cleric would appear to be quite out of date—'And never to speak right out and thou't be a bishop yet.'"[27]

He was particularly outspoken against Fascism and Nazism at a time when appeasement was government policy. The Spanish Civil War polarised international opinion as Hitler and Mussolini intervened to back General Franco's military uprising in July 1936 against the left-wing Republican government which was backed by the Soviet Union. In the Anglican hierarchy only Cyril Garbett, Bishop of Winchester, and Henry Wilson, who described his politics as a "very pale blue",[28] took a strong line. Archbishop of Canterbury, Cosmo Lang, a personal friend of Neville Chamberlain, who became Prime Minister in 1937, supported the government line of inaction. In 1937 in the House of Lords Bishop Garbett denounced the Luftwaffe's bombing of Guernica but in 1938 Bishop Wilson went much further: he uncompromisingly supported the Spanish Republic at a rally in London and excoriated the Vatican for its collusion with Franco and the accommodations it had reached in Italy and Germany with the Fascist and Nazi dictatorships. Those on the political right dubbed him the "Red Rev" and the "Bolshie Bishop"[29] because he took them to task for claiming that the Republicans were slaughtering Catholic priests. He argued that the Spanish Republic had permitted religious freedom from its inception in 1931 and that atrocities started only after civil war had broken out in 1936 and the rule of law disintegrated: "a revolution, like a boiling pot, throws up scum." [30] His facts were wrong: the murder of clergy and the burning of churches had started in 1934 before Franco's military coup. The Bishop found himself in conflict with the redoubtable William Inge, former Dean of St. Paul's and pungent columnist for the *Evening Standard* who, however, was equally naive in accepting at face value Franco's propaganda and, like Pope Pius XI, ignored the murder by Franco's troops of pro-Basque clergy in northern Spain.[31] Inge woundingly labelled those who had killed nuns as the Bishop's protégés:

"It is really rather horrible to find a bishop championing men who, acting on instructions from Moscow to exterminate the middle class, have slaughtered, at a low estimate, 200,000 helpless and harmless people."[32]

The Bishop fought back:

"Dr Inge thinks it 'horrible' for an Anglican bishop to plead for fair play for an unpopular and despised minority. I hope nevertheless that I shall have the courage to remain a 'horrible' person to the end of my days whatever that cost may be and I can assure him that the cost is pretty heavy."[33]

A year later he again took the British Government to task for observing strict neutrality in Spain:

"If we accept . . . that it is better to allow violence to triumph than to take risks to restrain it, we are committed to a principle of submission to any and every demand of the dictators."[34]

Churchill in his political wilderness could not have put it more eloquently. Two pro-Fascist organisations, the United Christian Front, sinister advocates of the Nazi myth of a Jewish-Communist international conspiracy, and the Friends of Catholic Spain kept up their bombardment in the letters columns: the apparently friendless bishop fell silent. His colleagues had warned him that he might ruin himself professionally by his lone stand but he stood firm:

"It was a disagreeable affair though some satisfaction was derived from the fact that most of the people attacking me were the type whose praise I should not have received without misgiving. A little later I had further compensation when the gentleman who had been attacking me was incarcerated for subversive behaviour in 1940."[35]

That "gentleman" was Archibald Ramsay, a Conservative M.P and founder of the despicable United Christian Front. The day after war broke out Ramsay issued his scurrilous anti-semitic parody *Land of dope and Jewry*: When a Nazi spy, uncovered in the American Embassy, proved to be a personal friend Ramsay was locked up for four years as a security risk.

The Bishop received further snubs when he became President of the Council of Anglo-Soviet Unity in 1941 after the German invasion of the Soviet Union. He retaliated:

"Even the mildest exhibition of friendship towards the Soviets is always regarded as profoundly suspicious. It was also noticeable that many of the people who were shocked at the 'godlessness' of Russia were not conspicuous themselves for their 'godliness'."[36]

However, later in the war he fell for Soviet propaganda, swallowing wholesale Stalin's assertions: that his victims in the infamous show trials were Nazi spies;[37] that the Soviet Union would respect the independence of the countries it so-say liberated in 1944-5;[38] that it would allow religious freedoms;[39] and that a no-nonsense Soviet occupation of Germany would be beneficial for its inhabitants.[40] His isolation did not bother him: coming from an Episcopalian family in Presbyterian Scotland he reckoned he was used to being in a minority.[41]

Back in the Cathedral Provost Morrow in his role as Rector was struggling to balance the parish's books. He described the economic problems of 1935 which are strikingly familiar 75 years later at the time of writing:

> "The economic position . . . is still difficult . . . The reduction
> in the rate of interest has fallen most heavily on the thousands of
> people whose incomes are 'fixed'. On the other hand the banks
> are 'chock full' of money, only waiting to spend when times are
> more settled. For the first time, as far as I can see at present, we
> are threatened with failure to balance our budget."

He suggested that hundreds in the congregation could give a penny or two more (about 25p or 50p in today's money) to cover the £1,510 deficit (£83,600). A leaflet dated December 1934 from the Provost and the churchwardens said:

> "There is an idea in the minds of some people that, owing to
> the munificent gift of Mrs Keene, the parish does not need
> any help. Such is not the fact. That large sum WAS NOT
> GIVEN FOR PAROCHIAL PURPOSES AND IS NOT,
> NOR WILL BE, ADMINISTERED BY THE CHURCH
> COUNCIL."[42]

It was in 1935 that Chelmsford Cathedral music began to emerge out of its parish shell. In March the Bishop appointed as Director of Diocesan Music that champion of English music, Martin Shaw, formerly master of music at St. Martin-in-the-Fields, who had worked with Ralph Vaughan Williams in editing *Songs of Praise* and *The Oxford Book of Carols*. The appointment was for two years on an experimental basis but in fact lasted ten. Frederick Frye had by this time been 59 years in office as organist and the parish and diocesan roles needed separating pending the time when he would be replaced by an energetic younger man with suitable cathedral experience who could combine both. But it was Russian music that first took centre stage: on April 29th a Russian Orthodox Church Choir of seven men, members of the Orthodox Theological Academy in Paris, whose patron was Archbishop Cosmo Lang, sang in Chelmsford Cathedral. They bore testament to the horrors of totalitarianism: "one did not know where his father was and another believed a sister and her husband were prisoners in the mines."[43]

On May 24th, Empire Sunday, came the first radio broadcast from the Cathedral, seven years after the first B.B.C. broadcast of a religious service and 15 years after the very first public broadcast when Dame Nellie Melba's voice emanated over the airwaves from the radio masts of the Marconi factory in New Street. The Provost wrote:

> "Those who were in the immediate zone of Chelmsford heard the first part indistinctly but then a 'click' came into their receivers and the Bishop's address was wonderfully clear and distinct. But those who heard from a distance heard the whole service from beginning to end beautifully. I have heard from Bishop Auckland, Dublin, Chesterfield and other places all expressing the pleasure the broadcast gave them . . . I am very much hoping to hear in a month from the Reverend Donald and Mrs Marsh who are living among the Eskimos at Eskimo Point about two degrees from the Arctic Circle. It is one of their great joys—the only white people for miles around—to hear the strokes of Big Ben! I am sure they will be thrilled at hearing voices from so near home."[44]

Economically it was not a propitious time for any further enhancements of the Cathedral. There was some tinkering at the edges: in 1935 Adolphus Maskell, a churchwarden since 1891, presented a canopied and carved Provost's stall designed by Wykeham Chancellor as a memorial to his wife;[45] Charles Ridley, a former Deputy Lieutenant, High Sheriff, chairman of the Essex Hunt Club and fund raiser for Chelmsford's hospital, left a legacy of framed portraits of Frank Johnson, Bishop of Colchester, and bishops Claughton and Jacob of St. Albans;[46] in 1938 the Chapter Seal arrived and was deposited for safety in Barclays Bank;[47] in 1939 Mrs Keene paid for microphones in the Cathedral and the Friends of the Cathedral was formed, at a minimum subscription of one shilling (5p: £2.42 in today's money), to raise money to beautify the cathedral.[48]

National and international crises piled thick and fast on top of each other. The joy at George V's Silver Jubilee in 1935 turned to sorrow at his death in January 1936 and then various degrees of disappointment and desolation as Edward VIII's abdication hit the headlines. In the January 1937 *Parish Magazine* the Provost's New Year letter, in epiphanal vein, referred to the contemporary incidence of three kings in one year though nowhere in it could he bring himself to mention Edward's actual name nor the act of abdication:

> "The second [king] passes out, alas, not in the sleep of death, but in the silence of oblivion, which shrouds him in the cloak of a nation's dismay, disappointment and benumbing amazement at his failure . . . I would, however, close this letter by commenting on the amazing way in which the whole nation and Empire bore itself in the face of an unique crisis. With marvellous self-restraint and calm patience it awaited events and accepted the inevitable with a magnificent solidarity . . . Oh that this national expression of deep purity of character may demonstrate itself still further in the New Year. May it bring a revival of personal religion in every home."

Unconfined joy returned with the coronation of George VI and Queen Elizabeth. In his parish letter of May 20th 1937 William Morrow described:

> ". . . the millions assembled along the route . . . to testify their loyalty to their newly-crowned King-Emperor . . . It is quite manifest that the religious nature of the ceremony had impressed itself upon all . . . It may or may not be reserved for King George VI to bring back again in its entirety the old theocratic ideal which Israel . . . lost when they asked for a king, but we shall pray . . . that the reign . . . may succeed in bringing all his subjects to the crowning of that 'other King—one Jesus'."[49]

However, that very Empire that the Provost extolled was under a darkening cloud as the dictators expanded their ambitions in Europe. They could be countered by Christian dedication at home:

> "One could write a long letter on world affairs and social problems, but these seem to be so very fully dealt with in magazines and the press generally that the space here provided can be best used by dealing with parochial matters. 'Get the parishes right and the country will be right' is a timely, if optimistic, slogan . . . The number of communicants on Christmas Day was a record for this parish . . . but when we compare those large congregations

with our weekly numbers and especially the daily celebrations, the result is not so cheering. We average 100 on Sundays and 25 on weekdays . . . I want to speak to the men of the parish. We have a 'live' branch of the Church of England Men's Society . . . Our numbers are at present 40 but, alas, several are paper members."[50]

The Munich crisis in September 1938 brought a temporary surge in attendance at services[51] but a year later, on August 15th 1939, William Morrow's monthly letter criticised the B.B.C.'s decision to broadcast John Buchan's *The Thirty-Nine Steps* at Evensong time: "I fear they have yielded to the clamour of those who never darken the door of a church except for a wedding, a baptism or a funeral."[52]

The peace that Prime Minister Neville Chamberlain had bought at Munich in September 1938 through the sacrifice to Hitler of Czechoslovakia's fortified frontier German districts was greeted joyously, though it was more the relief of postponement than escape. Bishop Wilson was received in silence when he pointed out to a League of Nations meeting in Colchester the moral bankruptcy of constant concessions to dictators that only whet their appetites for more.[53] Memories of the last war were still vivid and the Luftwaffe bombing of the Basque town of Guernica in 1937 had demonstrated the vulnerability of civilian populations to air power. Britain's hair's breadth escape in the Battle of Britain in 1940 owed much to the two years' breathing space that the Munich settlement gave to allow an accelerated build up of armaments and air defences.

It was during this armed peace that Chelmsford was due to celebrate its Silver Jubilee as a Diocese. Anniversary services were held in the Cathedral on April 23rd 1939 when war seemed inescapable: within the previous month Hitler had contravened the Munich agreement by invading the remainder of Czechoslovakia, Britain had given a formal military guarantee to Poland and Mussolini's Italy had invaded Albania.

A great pageant had been planned, *Judgement at Chelmsford*, words written by Charles Williams and music composed by Martin Shaw, illustrating the story of Christianity in Essex. It was due to be performed at the Scala Theatre in London from September 25th to October 7th with three Saturday matinees and 13 evening performances. Special trains would be laid on from Chelmsford, return fare 2s 1d (11p: £5.04 in today's money), on September 23rd and October 4th. Theatre seats would cost five shillings

(25p: £12.10), two shillings and sixpence (12½p: £6.05) and one shilling (5p: £2.42).[54]

But on Friday September 1st Germany invaded Poland. 80 double-decker buses arrived at Chelmsford bus station with 4,000 London evacuees, 2,543 of them destined for Chelmsford and the rest for other Essex towns.[55] On Sunday September 3rd Britain's ultimatum to Germany expired without response and Neville Chamberlain announced that Britain was at war with Germany.

The great pageant was cancelled.[56]

CHAPTER 16

Wearily to War

On September 20th 1939 William Morrow wrote to his parishioners:

> "I know that regarding this terrible war we as a nation have entered
> it with clean hands . . . We know who is the aggressor . . . We
> do not need any excuse or apology when we say we are fighting
> for the freedom and righteousness of the world which alone can
> bring peace. We pray that Hitler and all his accomplices will be
> brought before the Bar of the Nations and reap the due reward
> for all their tyrannical injustices and hideous cruelties."[1]

A month later in his letter of October 21st the enormity of Nazi evil
had begun to register:

> "Our nation has been deceived by perfidy and intrigue, simply
> because our leaders could not descend to those sordid depths of
> the Hitler crowd, who are apparently incapable of understanding
> those codes of honour, truth, fair dealing and justice which alone
> can interpret a nation's true position and ideals."[2]

He quoted from the Bishop's letter in the October *Diocesan Chronicle:*

> "The outbreak of the last war was signalled by an angry belligerent
> spirit . . . Instead of the songs of defiance of 1914 we are chanting
> the *De Profundis* . . . We must pray for victory before we pray for

peace. Victory means the victory of righteousness . . . 'Hitlerism must be destroyed' must be the slogan of this war."

Air-raids were expected and feared. The Cathedral Hall was commandeered as a hospital to deal with the injured. The parochial Coal and Blanketing Clubs were wound up as the state took over responsibility for social welfare and it became impossible to buy up summer coal. However, District Visitors still visited their allotted streets, "ministering to those whose loved ones are serving their country and bearing those gifts of sympathy and tact that are so comforting in these days of anxiety."[3]

The 15th century cathedral windows had not been designed with blackout in mind, so Evensong was immediately brought forward to 4.00 p.m.,[4] and then 3.00 p.m. in November as the nights drew in,[5] until March 10th 1940 when there was enough daylight for normal times to be resumed; the following October, the Cathedral reverted to the winter pattern of earlier evening services and later morning Holy Communion services.[6] The factory and men's services, which had normally been held on Sunday afternoons, were cancelled during the winter months and confirmation classes moved from Wednesday evening to Sunday afternoon.[7] Tragic circumstances led to the resumption of a Hoffman's service as a one-off event when, on December 19th 1944, the factory received a direct hit from a V2 rocket: four days later a memorial service for the 30 victims was held in the Cathedral.[8]

As in the First World War, cathedral activities were disrupted or curtailed. Military service depleted the number of Sunday School teachers so that classes were suspended until December 1939 by which time revised arrangements had been made. The traditional New Year social teas were abandoned. The Young People's League had to relocate from the Cathedral Hall to the Cathedral School, but on Saturday afternoons only.[9] However the Ministry of Food then took over the building so that pupils and teachers moved back into the old Victoria National School buildings and would stay there until April 1947.[10] The Young People's League moved temporarily to the Girls' Friendly Society rooms in Legg Street[11], just to the north of the churchyard, before finally settling in the premises of the local Toc H organisation;[12] however, their activities dwindled as most of the young men were involved in military or civilian war service, not least on the cathedral roof as fire watchers.[13] For the same reason the Church of England Men's Society meetings were suspended and the Patronal Fete in July was cancelled. The Pan Anglican Lambeth Conference was postponed and with it the overseas bishops' visit to the Cathedral. Wykeham Chancellor's building repairs remained unfinished because of difficulty in securing materials.[14] However, the Cathedral Scouts tried to be positive, taking on the collection of waste paper and cardboard (but not, they were advised, carbon paper and grease proof paper) in response to the Government's appeal to reduce shortages.[15] These same shortages caused the *Parish Magazine* from July 1940 to cut its size from twelve to four pages and, to maximise the flow of information, its print diminished to a minute font size; from September 1940 the Rector's letter was restored to normal font "to help our readers" who, however, would still have to squint at the rest.

In September 1940 War Minister, Anthony Eden, instigated the Local Defence Volunteers and the Bishop, who had suggested the idea of a "town guard" as early as June 1939, led by example: he was one of the first in Chelmsford to join what would become the Home Guard.[16] Mrs Dorothy Wilson was also busy supporting the war effort, undertaking to raise £350 (£14,900 in today's money) for a second mobile canteen for use amongst the troops in Essex to match the one bought by Mrs Keene.[17]

In the daughter Parish of the Ascension in west Chelmsford the war interrupted plans to build a new church in Maltese Road next to the vicarage: the land had been purchased[18] but no further progress could be made. However, Ashley Turner, the Anglo-Catholic Vicar, raised the need for reservation of the sacrament, an issue that had caused great division in the Church, evangelicals considering that it smacked of transubstantiation and Romish veneration of the Real Presence. However there remained the practical issue of how clergy could administer Holy Communion to those dying of injuries sustained in air raids. The Bishop, who had already expressed the view that the "faithful parish priest moving among his people while an air raid is taking place" would be in the front line,[19] wisely gave the Church of the Ascension permission for continuous reservation during the period of the war. Ashley Turner sought to reassure readers of the *Parish Magazine* which continued to serve both parishes of St. Mary's and the Ascension; he wanted to be able to give Communion to the sick and wounded at the shortest possible notice and had no other ulterior motive:

> "It seemed to me that the uncertainties of the future in relation
> to air raids made it desirable that the Blessed Sacrament should
> be easily and quickly available . . . There will always be those
> who see in a development like this 'the thin end of the wedge'. I
> have assured the Bishop that my request to him is entirely bona
> fide."[20]

The Provost's end-of-year commentary on the war bore its own doleful testimony, deepened by the death of his helpmeet and sister, Frances, in November 1939:

> "The war has developed almost into a world war. The centre of gravity is being shifted one fears to the Near East . . . Things look at present far from promising . . . Germany . . . has resorted to the most diabolical methods by which she ruthlessly destroys all shipping she can and cares not whether they are neutral or otherwise."[21]

For the army this was still the Phoney War with, as yet, no direct engagement of British and German troops but those with a memory of the First World War feared the worst. In February 1940 the Provost wrote:

> "Millions of soldiers are facing each other at close range . . . It is no spirit of cowardice that I say when the clash does come the death toll will be enormous . . . We have gone to war in the assurance that there never was a time in our history when the conscience of the nation was clearer . . . We are verily Crusaders in the highest sense of the word. The old Crusaders had but one object: to win an empty sepulchre out of the hands of the infidel. We are imbued with a more serious motive. It is nothing less than our determination to redeem humanity from the rule of tyrants and an infidel more cruel and heartless than the Saracen."

The Cathedral's Easter 1940 intercessions were for victory, the wounded and the relatives of the fallen, the protection of the United Kingdom from bombardment by air, the Finns (invaded by the Soviet Union in November 1939) and saving other smaller nations from merciless aggression, in the hope that the message of Easter would guide and influence the world towards the paths of peace.

In the meantime, while those paths seemed unattainable, the Church of the Ascension, in the June 1940 *Parish Magazine*, advised on procedures should an air raid warning sound during a service:

> "A short pause will be made to allow any who have duties to perform and who wish to do so to leave the church; the service of Holy Communion will . . . be continued after the pause;

181

members of the congregation are strongly urged to decide now what they would do if a warning is given while they are in church; remember that, should such a situation arise, we can help others by our calmness; remember that we have a special responsibility as Christians to show our faith in God by steadfastness and unselfishness in times of danger."

In October the Vicar added a further refinement:

"When a siren prevents the start of a service the clergy will be in church ready to start 15 minutes after the all clear if this does not make the service more than one hour late."

Clearly the Vicar was referring to the Archbishop of Canterbury's general advice for churches which was published in the *Essex Chronicle* on August 30th 1940 and which the Cathedral too would have followed. That advice also recommended that clergy should stay in the church during an air raid ready to resume the service after the All Clear and that the congregation should be dissuaded from leaving when an air raid warning sounded if firing could already be heard.

Provost Morrow certainly reinforced government messages which some locals seem to have ignored:

"'Stay put' is the command we have all been asked to obey in case of air raids. It was very thoughtless of hundreds to leave their homes and walk about the roads. They were in danger themselves and were a source of danger to others. The Fire Services and Ambulance Services would have been seriously hampered in doing their duty were the people to have been hurt. It is therefore selfish of any people to leave their homes . . . until the 'All Clear' signal is given."[22]

And what about the children during night-time air raids? Margaret Turner, wife of the Vicar of the Ascension, had sound advice for the parents of the two parishes:

"I would like to suggest that you keep near your shelter . . . either an old mattress or a couple of blankets and pillows. At the very beginning of the sounding of the siren (if not as a routine job before going to bed) put these down. Then make your children lie down on this improvised bed with as little delay as possible and firmly tell them to go to sleep. Small children who do not wake at the sound of the siren or are only partially roused should be carried. It is essential that all this is done quickly and calmly, as the children will settle to sleep much more readily if they are not thoroughly awakened by excitement and delay. If necessary give them a drink and a biscuit. Then put a shield round the light and refuse to talk to them. The children will soon get used to this procedure and will sleep through any but the worst air raids . . . The lifelong damage to nerves which the unsettlement (and the noise) of air raids may do to children can certainly be lessened if those who have the care of children keep themselves calm and do all that they can to ensure them undisturbed sleep."[23]

In the summer of 1940 France had fallen. The evacuation at Dunkirk had provided some uplift of spirits, but Britain was alone. In the August 1940 *Parish Magazine*, Provost Morrow wrote:

"*Punch* last week had an amusing commentary upon our 'Isolation'. The picture describes the coast of England and two soldiers on watch. One says to the other, 'So our poor old Empire is alone in the world.' The other rejoins, 'Aye, we are, the whole 500 million of us'."

Like many he was inspired by Churchill's oratory:

"Mr Winston Churchill said in his broadcast on July 14th: 'Now it has come to us to stand alone in the breach and face the worst that the tyrant's might and enmity can do. Bearing ourselves humbly before God, but conscious that we serve an unfolding purpose, we are ready to defend our native land against the invasion by which it is threatened. We are fighting by ourselves alone. But we are not fighting for ourselves alone. Here in this strong city of refuge which enshrines the title deeds of human progress and is of deep consequence to Christian civilisation; here girt about by the seas and oceans where the Navy reigns; shielded from above by the prowess and devotion of our airmen, we await undismayed the impending assault'."

The Provost then quoted another broadcast of imperial defiance by Professor Vincent Harlow of the Ministry of Information on July 15th:

"There are over 500 million people who have not bowed the knee to the modern Baal whose shrine is at Berchtesgaden! Nor will they: they will stand together until they have swept this pestilence from the earth. Hitherto Hitler has swept from victory to victory because he has been able to fire his obedient people with a dynamic spirit—a will to conquer. He will not be finally overcome until that dynamic force is matched by one greater than his own. We and our partners overseas have it within us—the flaming spirit of a crusade—a crusade inspired by the individual spirit of man in free and equal association marching to destroy the mass hypnotism of a tyrant which kills the soul."

The Provost commented:

"These two quotations have in them the assurance of victory, final and complete. They both rely on God and 'if God be for us, who can be against us?' . . . These anxious days call with insistent voice the whole nation to definite prayer and consecration. It is to me astonishing to find the hundreds of young people in our town, apparently totally indifferent to the claims of God upon their whole life. They evidently do not realise that it is **for them** that we are fighting."

In Chelmsford Bishop Henry Wilson's reputation as a scourge of Nazism and Fascism went before him. On June 19th 1940 a German Heinkel 111 bomber crashed in flames in the grounds of Bishopscourt in Springfield: local rumour had it that the Bishop had brought it down with his shotgun. Fittingly he officiated at the joint funerals of the three Luftwaffe airmen who were killed in the crash and buried in the Borough Cemetery.[24] But other bombers got through. On October 17th 1940 the Cathedral was filled to overflowing for the funerals of the Mayor of Chelmsford, John Ockleford Thompson, his wife Emma, their son Lieutenant-Colonel Thomas Cloverley Thompson and their grandchildren, eight-year-old Audrey and one-year-old Deana, who were all killed by a direct hit on their New London Road home when a lone Luftwaffe raider jettisoned two bombs over the town; a servant, Alice Emery, also died.[25] Bishop Henry Wilson and Provost William Morrow officiated at the Thompson family funeral. "Tragedy follows tragedy in this insane war", wrote Provost Morrow, "three generations wiped out by one fell stroke."[26] News of other losses drifted in: 33-year-old Lance Corporal Dick Gilbert, formerly a choirboy and Young People's League member, died of wounds in the Middle East in November 1941;[27] with hindsight we now know that 25-year-old Lance-Sergeant Charles Chancellor, Wykeham's son, had been killed in Greece in April 1941[28] even though, as late as September 1942, the *Parish Magazine* was still reporting him as missing, presumed dead.

It is the nature of wars to kill young men while older men are able to live out their full lifespan. In February 1942 the *Parish Magazine* announced that Frederick Frye, organist and choirmaster for the last 66 years, was seriously ill with bronchitis and that he would retire on June 30th. An appeal was made for £500 for nursing fees (£18,200 in today's money) but he died in September, aged 91. With the balance left over from the appeal a simple memorial was erected on the north wall near the organ door through which he used to enter the Cathedral.

Frederick Frye: Chelmsford Cathedral Knightbridge Library

Everyone was expected to contribute to the war effort. 2,000 feet of iron railings in the Cathedral churchyard were removed for scrap in 1942.[29] The Cathedral itself was only a quarter of a mile from the Marconi wireless factory site and half a mile from Hoffman's ball-bearings factory, both enemy targets. In June 1941 the *Parish Magazine* reported that the Government had undertaken to give free cover against war damage for the fabric of churches and a special insurance at 30 shillings (£1.50: £72.50 in today's money) per £100 (£4,840) for furniture and effects up to a value of £10,000 (£386,000). At this point 130 churches in Essex had already been damaged or destroyed so the Diocese strongly advised taking out the insurance: the more churches that took part the lower the premiums would be. The Cathedral complied and spent £134 (£5,180) on fire equipment such as ladders, buckets and appliances. In July 1941 the Provost appealed to the parishioners for £234 (£9,000) towards the high insurance costs and hoped that non-churchmen, for whom their Cathedral was an important symbol, would also contribute: "many have said, 'I hope the Jerrys won't get that.'"

Provost Morrow was also appealing for fire-watchers. In April 1941 he asked:

> "Who will volunteer to protect the church of your ancestors in response to our Lord's question, 'Could ye not watch with Me one brief hour?'"

In July 1941 he wrote that there was only a little band of 12.

> "I happened to be in a cathedral city a few days ago and found that they have 92 constantly watching! I hope I shall not have to appeal again for the protection of the chief place of antiquity in our town."

The Young People's League provided the recruits: three of them became local heroes. On April 15th 1943 incendiaries were dropped in the New Street area close to the Marconi factory and one landed on the Cathedral roof: 18-year-old Dennis Hance, 17-year-old John Copsey and 15-year-old Albert Pearce were on fire watch. Dennis recalled:

> "The fire watch used to be on the roof of the Cathedral vestry which was within 200 yards of County Hall, on top of which was the air raid siren. Being so close you were able to sleep [at the Cathedral in a storeroom] as the siren would wake you up and, if need be, you could then go onto the Cathedral roof to

fire watch . . . On the night of 14th to 15th April . . . we watched
a small incendiary come down on the roof . . . It had ignited on
impact with the north aisle roof . . . John . . . got hold of the
stirrup pump nozzle. I was the charlie in the middle operating
the pump and poor old little Albert was running up and down
the ladder with buckets of water. Despite spraying water . . . for
about five minutes it was still burning . . . but John eventually
went over to it, kicked it and it went out . . . The Government
felt there was a need to give the Fire Guard some publicity and a
boost . . . The three of us lads on duty were invited to Cannon's
Restaurant in Duke Street where we met a scriptwriter from the
B.B.C . . . She duly wrote a script which exaggerated the incident.
A few weeks later the story was broadcast . . . The story was in
the local papers and also got through to the German press and
the *Illustrated London News* . . . The Cathedral Chapter felt they'd
better do something about it too, so they gave us £15 each, which
was a lot of money in those days [£526 in today's money] . . . I
used it to buy three architectural books and the Provost . . . wrote
a thank you message."[30]

The Provost's attempt to tell his parishioners about these heroics was
censored until the June *Parish Magazine* although a scorched pew in the
north aisle and charred repairs in the roof acted as silent witnesses.[31]

As the fortunes of war began to turn in 1943 the Bishop was in
pugnacious form. In the January *Diocesan Chronicle* he poured scorn on
the Italians whom he likened to condemned murderers:

"The wretched Italians will get just as much out of their
'cooperation' with Germany as does the criminal when the bolt
is pulled!"

Vichy France's Admiral Darlan decided to cooperate with the Allies
after Montgomery's inspired victory at El Alamein and was derisively cast
aside:

"Darlan is about as straight as a corkscrew . . . He has seen the
red light and he wants to be on the winning side."

He reserved his most biting punning sarcasm for Pope Pius XII:

"The European fence is decorated with many figures, both pious and non-pious, who have loudly declared their neutrality—until they are quite sure which side is going to win!"

In May, as the Allies swept across North Africa towards Spain General Franco began to make less hostile sounds. After his bruising encounter with Franco supporters in 1938 the Bishop relished his revenge:

"The fall of Tunis and Bizerta was signalled by a speech from General Franco in which he appeals for peace in unison with the voice of the Pope. Franco, when democratic government was being garrotted in Spain . . . told the world that we had lost the war and had better capitulate. Now he (and presumably the Pope) appeals to the 'conscience of the nations' . . . Historians will have an interesting task in unravelling the very tangled web of Vatican politics: its friendship with Japan and its association with the . . . marionettes of the Axis powers: and there is little doubt that General Franco has been living up to the congratulatory benediction sent him by the Pope when he suppressed *(for the time being)* the Spanish Democratic Government."

In September he rejoiced at the fall of Mussolini and seems to have well-nigh endorsed assassination:

"The fall of Mussolini is a proof of the inevitability of democracy . . . Had the assassin who chipped Mussolini's nose* with a bullet . . . been more efficient, it is probable there would have been no European War."

He would not let the Vatican off the hook. In November he reminded his readers that:

---

* Violet Gibson, an Irishwoman, fired three shots at Mussolini in April 1926, but, from virtually point blank range, she only grazed his nose. Having moved from Ulster Protestantism through Christian Scientology and Theosophy to Catholicism, she claimed she was acting on God's orders. She was pardoned by Mussolini and sent back to England to be interred in a lunatic asylum.[32]

"It is wise to remember that there is a Japanese Ambassador at the Papal Court and perhaps the Pope, who has promised to address himself to the 'warring nations' will for once say something which is not a platitude to Ken Harada [Japanese Ambassador] . . . The Japanese certainly need a little mild admonition."

His concern that the governments of Catholic countries were invariably anti-democratic was reiterated in 1944:

"The religious forces in the Latin nations of Europe are all reactionary in their outlook and their progressive elements are largely non-religious. Have England and America sufficient Christian force to meet the need? If not, the peace will fail again."[33]

He took issue with the Government's edict that church bells should be silenced and used only as an invasion warning:

"I always regarded it as an emergency measure of rather doubtful value. It is not everyone who can ring a bell. The whole process of discovering the approach of the invading force, wakening the custodian of the church, opening the church building and ringing the bells, would appear to be so complicated that when at last the ringer approached the church he would probably be greeted by a contingent of the enemy who would naturally make straight for the church since that was known to be the place from which the warning would be given . . . I have always felt that the firing of a rocket would be a much more effective warning. However that may be, it is most desirable that the authorities should . . . restore a traditional feature of our national life which has definitely contributed to the decay of church-going."[34]

Politicians were berated for opening theatres on Sundays:

"Any intelligent observer could see that it was inevitable and it is indeed a safe prophecy that it will not be long before a demand for horse-racing on Sunday will be voiced . . . As a nation we owe far more than we ever realise to the strict religious traditions which held the field unchallenged in the past . . . I am convinced that the Puritan contribution is responsible for the iron in our blood and our backbone of steel."[35]

He returned to the theme a few months later, blaming the fall of France and the collaboration of the Vichy Government on the decay of national religion. He demolished a correspondent in the *Daily Telegraph* who had erroneously identified the Immaculate Conception as one of the miraculous Anglican beliefs that people rejected: the Bishop was at pains to point out that it was a "Roman dogma" and not to be confused with the Virgin Birth, a fine distinction that would have been lost on the majority of his readers. That very likelihood led him to deplore "the . . . ignorance of people generally as to what the Christian Church *does* teach": by "Christian" he meant "Anglican" as, for Henry Wilson, Catholicism was beyond categorisation. In despair he declared "emphatically and with good reason, that many of our people (and communicants too!) could not pass an elementary test on this subject."[36]

But the Church's task of ministering to the people, difficult enough in peace-time, was now hindered by a dire shortage of clergy: one tenth of the Diocese's clergy had enlisted as forces' chaplains at a time when ordinations had petered out to almost nothing.[37] One of them, George Parry who parachuted into Normandy on June 6th 1944, was killed when the Germans re-took the dressing station where he was ministering to the wounded. The Bishop honoured him: "George died in the likeness of his Master for the men he loved and served." His parents, who lived in Leytonstone, had now lost two sons in the war.[38]

However, he felt the Government was definitely on the right lines with its Education White Paper which would eventually give birth to the 1944 Butler Education Act. The Bishop shunned the Protestant sectarian past: "schools should not be proselytising centres where little Non-Conformists are converted into little Anglicans."[39] But he welcomed the proposal that half the cost of reconditioning church schools should be borne by the state.

January 17th 1944 was Provost Morrow's Golden Jubilee as an ordained minister. It must have been a relief to him as well as the families of his parish to be able to write on January 21st:

> "I rejoice with all those who have had letters from their loved ones. Although still prisoners of war, that gnawing feeling of uncertainty and anxiety has given way to thankfulness that their loved ones are alive."[40]

The Cathedral again came close to disaster on June 18th 1944 when a V1 rocket motor suddenly cut out overhead. Fire watcher Dennis Hance was with one of the Cathedral's clergy, William Mitchell:

> "We stood there looking at each other for about 10 seconds before there was an almighty crump as it came down and exploded. The doodlebug landed by the open air baths only a few hundred yards short of and in line with, the Cathedral."[41]

The Provost's attempts to describe what had happened were again subject to censorship and did not appear in the *Parish Magazine* until July 1945:

> "Well do I remember this date in June last year! At 6 a.m. on a beautiful Sunday morning I was rudely awakened by a terrific roar and, looking up towards the windows [of the Rectory], found them smashed to bits and even the shutters shared the same fate. At first I did not know what precisely had happened. It suggested to my dazed brain that the whole house might be coming down. But gradually I heard shouts saying that all was well."

The Bishop referred to the indiscriminateness of these flying bombs in the August 1944 *Diocesan Chronicle*: "another Nazi blunder . . . that will inevitably further embitter the attitude of the Allied nations." A few months later, on December 7th, he and his wife had a narrow escape when a V1 exploded near Bishopscourt, blowing in the windows as he was pulling down the blackout; he suffered 16 cuts to his face from glass fragments but his eyes were unaffected.[42]

And amidst all this chaos, after a two year delay, a new Cathedral Organist and Choirmaster was appointed. On August 21st 1944 the Provost announced that, as from November 1944, James Roland Middleton, Sub-Organist of Chester Cathedral, Organist and Choirmaster of Mold Parish Church and a music master at Chester City High School and Alan County School, Mold, would lead the Cathedral's music; he had a doctorate in music from Durham University and was an F.R.C.O.[43]

In 1944 the Allies continued their advance from their D-Day bridgeheads and overran German air and missile bases in northern France while the Eighth Army pushed northward through Italy. The Ministry of Food found that it no longer required the Cathedral Hall but the Cathedral School building would remain out of action until 1947. The blackout could also be modified and restricted street lighting was permitted in Chelmsford, so cathedral services could revert to their normal times. The Bishop wrote:

> "The lifting of the blackout has not only been a great blessing but is symbolic of the lightening of the darkness which has bathed the world in gloom for the past six years . . . I mean six, for the miserable year which preceded the war when everyone who could see further than the end of his nose knew that war was coming, was nearly as bad as the five years of war. To see the inevitable approaching is sometimes worse than the realisation."[44]

As the defeat of Nazism loomed men still died. On January 6th 1945, the memorial service for Chelmsford's M.P., Colonel Jack Macnamara, who had been killed in action in Italy,[45] took place in the Cathedral.

The Pope's call for Christian charity by the victors incensed Bishop Wilson. It was not so much the message but the messenger that annoyed him:

> "It was not in the best taste to exhort Londoners to display 'the Christian sentiments of charity, forgiveness and mercy' at this time of day, for, apart from the fact that generosity of spirit is a notable characteristic of our people, it is difficult to remember one single word from the Pope in condemnation of the Nazis when they swept London with destruction. He is to be congratulated that his frequent appeals that Rome might be saved met with a response, but those appeals were not forthcoming when other cities were in danger or if, as we are told by some, pious regrets were expressed, they were uttered *pianissimo* . . . One of the painful features of the war has been the pitiful failure of the Vatican to give any spiritual direction to the nations whose religion, if they have any at all, is derived from Rome. Apart from vague and equivocal platitudes the Popes during the war have had nothing to say . . . The abominable ferocity . . . in Abyssinia was unrebuked and General Franco and his fellows were addressed by the Pope of that time as 'dearest sons of Catholic Spain' . . . Nor have the 'dearest sons of Catholic Spain' even yet been exhorted to release the hundreds of their fellow countrymen who are still languishing in prison because their political opinions do not coincide with

those of the Spanish dictator . . . The plain fact is that Vatican politics are anti-democratic."

And in the same article he was clear that retribution should be visited on the enemy's leaders:

"It would be wrong for me to seek revenge on someone who has injured me and particularly so if I intend to exact the penalty by my own hand. But it is right for me as a Christian citizen to require that society shall punish a criminal who has injured someone else . . . for vindictiveness does not enter into the case at all . . . In the New Testament the idea that forgiveness means escape from the consequences of wrongdoing does not appear at all . . . The converted drunkard or roué is forgiven but he frequently dies of cirrhosis of the liver or venereal disease. That appears to be God's way of dealing with us . . . It is clear that no one is capable of receiving forgiveness unless he is forgivable . . . unless he is penitent . . . The widespread idea that God is an easy-going and eternal good nature who lets everybody off and is never severe on anyone has not one jot of support in Scripture."[46]

He was spoiling for a fight with the Church's critics. One of them, Viscount Hinchingbrooke, Conservative M.P. for South Dorset, heir to the Marquisate of Salisbury and member of those influential Anglicans, the ubiquitous Cecil family, urged that the church should win back worshippers by showing religious films and playing gramophone recordings of top orchestras to augment "music from a timeless harmonium or wheezy organ." For good measure he also castigated the Church's leaders of the last half century as "incompetent men who will not fight for their faith or their ideals."[47] Bishop Wilson, who certainly did not fit that description and was not in thrall to the aristocracy, brushed the viscount aside as a lightweight exponent of gimmickry:

"He had recently delivered his soul regarding the futility of the clergy in a harangue which did more credit to his courage than his intelligence . . . This sort of attack might do a great deal of good, only we must have much more of it and more ably delivered. Nothing would be more bracing than a real organised attack on the Church. We are living too soft and taking things too much for granted . . . But it would have to be real persecution and not twaddle about turning Church services into cinema shows and concerts or popularising worship with the aid of stunt-workers and sensationalism in the pulpit."[48]

For the last six years London's sheer survival had been the aim. Now evangelical work in London-over-the-Border could start afresh but steps would have to be retraced as 321 churches, 176 parsonages, 83 halls, 62 schools and 23 other buildings had been damaged. Of these, 14 churches, 10 parsonages, 12 halls and five schools needed complete reconstruction.[49] There would be a large financial shortfall as government grants would not suffice to cover all war damage; church schools required improvements and extensions to meet the standards demanded by the 1944 Education Act; and money was also needed to fill the woefully depleted ranks of the clergy and pay them a reasonable stipend. In November 1944 the Bishop had hazarded £150,000 as the target (£5.15 million in modern values): "equal to the amount which would be needed to keep the European War going for about 40 minutes!" In March 1945 it was set at £400,000 (£13.5 million).

As victory in Europe approached William Morrow wrote to his parishioners:

> "There is a feeling of bathos in anything I may write. At the same
> time it is only right that it should be chronicled as a great event
> in the history of our nation and, therefore, of our parish . . . We
> are, we devoutly hope, freed from an intolerable doom. Had
> Hitler won we would have suffered even more than the worst
> concentration camps. Hitler hated us because he envied us . . .
> On Sunday June 10th I intend to pay a tribute to our Cathedral
> watchers. Then on the morning of June 17th we shall remember
> the Royal Air Force . . . I then hope to do honour to the other
> branches of the Forces."[50]

Victory came sooner than he had anticipated. On V.E. Day, May 8th, hourly services of thanksgiving were held which filled the Cathedral all day: "it was a wonderful gathering but", the Provost wrote, "how to turn that volume of thanks into dedication and service for God is the problem."[51] For one of the Cathedral firewatchers, John Copsey, who had subsequently joined the army, it was a huge problem. He wrote that the war had affected servicemen's outlook. They did not discuss religion. About two-thirds of them had lost touch with their home church and the old pew-rent mind-set still lingered:

> "I have heard several young men say they have lost their faith in God since joining the army. They have seldom been in a church since joining up . . . The Church has either made no attempt or only a feeble attempt to keep in touch with them . . . I have been told of cases where soldiers have entered a church for the first time and have later been asked to leave the seat in which they are sitting because it is the particular seat in which some lady or gentleman has sat for many years . . . I very much regret to say that I have seen it happen in my own church. Incidents like these have been the cause of many soldiers not attending church."[52]

Another young man, Roy Poole of the Royal Air Force, wrote to the *Parish Magazine*:

> "Most of the men think that the main things are prayers, good thoughts and good deeds and that the Church is not a great necessity to Christian life. The great companionship and friendship of the R.A.F. today is the result of the keeping of the commandment 'Love they neighbour as thyself' . . . One point which troubles many of them are the references in the Bible to fighting and killing and some of them have lost their faith since joining up because they say they cannot fight a war and keep those Commandments as well."[53]

The Provost might well wonder how thanksgiving could be transformed into service to God.

CHAPTER 17

Dirt, Damage and Departures

The Cathedral, like many public buildings, was in a sorry state by the end of the war: lack of money and materials had enforced neglect. Wykeham Chancellor, the Cathedral's Honorary Architect, was no longer available to advise as he had died, aged 80, towards the end of 1945. In 1939 he had intended to give the money for a new west door; in 1950 his widow, Mabel, fulfilled this wish as a memorial to their son, Charles, who had been killed in 1941. The Diocese collected money for an interior western vestibule as their memorial to Wykeham; at the same time the de Vere star and boar and the Bourchier reef knot on the west front were painted in colour.[1]

Many windows had been damaged by bomb blast. Most of the new glass would have to be clear as stained glass was too expensive. Restoration would take much time and money. One small cosmetic improvement was made when three pews were removed at the front of the nave to give more space for those officiating at large services.[2]

There was considerable repair work to do on the Cathedral Hall after the Ministry of Food's wartime occupation. Ironically when all dilapidations had been completed it could not be used as there was no heat:[3] the severe winter snows and cold of 1946-47 blocked transport networks and froze stockpiles of coal at the pitheads, so many power stations were forced to close down. The March 1947 *Parish Magazine* could not be published as the printers suffered similar problems. Petrol had been rationed since September 1939: acute shortages in 1947 saw the Bishop's allowance reduced to 600 miles a month, only one-third of the distance he normally travelled.[4]

Choral vestments were shabby. New choir surplices and choirboy ruffs appeared on Easter Day 1946 but the cassocks continued to be threadbare and "holy". To re-equip the full choir would be complex as clothes had been rationed since 1941 when each person had been limited to 66 coupons per year, cut to 48 in 1942, 36 in 1943 and a threadbare 24 in 1945: a boy's cassock would consume seven coupons and a man's eight:

> "These can only come from the congregation and we might consider if a levy of one coupon per member or even one per family will not soon bring in all that will be required."[5]

By October sufficient had been collected for 12 boys' and 18 men's cassocks but the singers still had to wait for materials to become available. They would also need a good instrument to accompany them: the cleaning and restoration of the organ, on which no significant work had been done since its installation in 1933, was completed in the summer of 1947 and George Thalben Ball returned for another celebratory recital on October 30th.[6]

The men's purple cassocks were inaugurated on Quinquagesima Sunday, March 2nd 1947, when the Royal School of Church Music chose to visit the Cathedral to report on the newly accoutred choir's standards. The choir was rated as A (good) or B (moderate) in all aspects of its performance; the humiliation of a C (poor) was comfortably avoided. Four As were given: for blend, clearness of said words, interpretation ("musicianly without being fussy") and demeanour ("from the moment the choir appears one is aware of a subtle change in the church"); nine B+s: for boys' tone, men's tone ("at times it is a little laboured"), balance ("a little more weight in the alto line would be an advantage"), attack and unanimity ("not quite so good at mp and p"), clearness of sung words ("you must watch your vowels: keep them pure and keep them open on long notes"), emphasis ("don't be afraid of this business of emphasis in singing: we all use it freely and effectively in conversation!"), and chanting and phrasing ("a little more consistency needed"); and two Bs: for intonation ("boys tended to sing a shade flat at times") and breath control ("one or two boys show their breathing too much.") The boys, unlike the men, did not have their new cassocks until later in the year so perhaps they were less inspired. Roland Middleton was doing his best to educate the congregation with a series of informative articles in the *Parish Magazine* on hymns, canticles, psalms, anthems, responses, carols and the organ; he had also instituted a full Choral Evensong on Saturdays.[7]

The great Silver Jubilee pageant, *Judgement at Chelmsford*, postponed in the autumn of 1939 when war broke out, was revived. On May 31st 1946

The Times carried an article appealing for amateur dramatic talent, both on and back stage, with auditions that summer. From June 14th - 28th 1947 there were 16 performances at the Scala Theatre in London. *The Times* reviewer, who by happy chance was also the librettist, explained that Chelmsford was personified as a 25-year-old girl "come to take her place among the great sees" and was required to show with what energy she had followed God in her present and past life:

> "The pageant makes admirable stage pictures of Chelmsford at the various crises of its spiritual life . . . achieving in the final scene of atonement a massive and impressive assemblage of colour and sound."[8]

The choir was trained by Roland Middleton; the actors were largely from Barking, Romford, Wanstead, West Ham and Southend as they had easier access to London for rehearsals. Princess Alice attended on June 27th. Another royal acknowledgement followed on September 28th when Princess Mary, the Princess Royal, sister of George VI, came to the Cathedral for the dedication of the Red Cross Banner.[9]

It took much longer for the Cathedral's glass to be sorted out. In February 1949 the *Parish Magazine* reported:

> "The modern glass has been a welcome improvement and was similar to that used in St. Paul's and St. Martin-in-the-Fields, admitting a maximum of light. The east window and Hanbury memorial windows will now be restored and this will involve the use of plain glass for about six months while the restoration is in progress. It is hoped to mend all the broken windows in the clerestory, to make the former Gepp window like those on the north side and place in the tower window a completely new design in stained glass. These renovations are not expected to be completed for 15 months."

In December 1949 there was a progress report:

> "The designs for the stained glass windows to be placed in the west window (under the tower) and the two side chapels . . . have been approved by the Cathedral Council. The west window will depict the Nativity and the figures chosen for the east windows are St.

Cedd and St. Alban in the North Chapel and St. Osyth and St. Ethelburga in the South Chapel. The work will be undertaken by the A.K. Nicholson Studios."

There was a disagreement with the Gepp family. All the money received from the War Damages Commission had been used on the west window: the Gepps protested that their window should have been insured separately.[10] It therefore took longer to repair than had been anticipated and was not dedicated until 1971, at the last Assize Service before the judicial reforms that gave Chelmsford its own Crown Court and ended the 800-year-old office of Sheriff: Thomas Gepp, the window's dedicatee, had been Under Sheriff.[11]

Parish life revived slowly. The Church of England Men's Society was re-started in 1946. The Provost wrote:

"This is the most important of the societies in the Church. Man is the breadwinner. His influence in the home counts for everything."[12]

There were 350 communicants on Easter Sunday 1946 but numbers did not hold up, much to the disappointment of the Provost:

"I was, ever since the victory, much depressed and amazed at the sparse attendance of most of the congregation at Holy Communion. From the splendid numbers on Easter Day they have dwindled to a miserable number . . . It is constantly my aim not to **drive** my friends to come to the Holy Eucharist, but to show them rather what they are missing when they do not come."[13]

Such adult matters would not have bothered the children as their Sunday School outing was soon back in operation in the summer of 1946.[14] But as late as April 1949 the *Parish Magazine* was appealing for bell ringers to supplement the handful of regulars, tempting volunteers with the added attraction of a 13th bell, to give a "flat sixth", donated in 1947 by Frederick J. French as a memorial to his father.[15]

St. Mary's was still barely recognisable as a cathedral. The development of the building had been very limited, there were as yet no residentiary canons to match those of the ancient sees and the choir had only just begun to blossom. The financial problems of blitzed London-over-the-Border made any immediate resolution of these issues unlikely. That a parish, not a cathedral, magazine, was issued monthly confirmed that St. Mary's roots were still local rather than diocesan. But, to be fair, the exact purpose of a cathedral in England still remained somewhat vague. In May 1949 the *Parish Magazine* published an article by the Provost of Derby describing his vision. It was printed without comment which presumably meant that there was some degree of acceptance by Provost Morrow.

The Provost of Derby acknowledged that for a cathedral "most of its worshippers live in and are members of some other parish" but he did not question whether robbing Peter to pay Paul was desirable. As beacons of excellence and high culture visitors from parish churches in the far-flung corners of a diocese should not expect to find in a cathedral what they already have in their own church:

> "So cathedral services should be models and ideals of worship, an inspiration to all who visit it . . . Its organist and choir should endeavour to give examples of the best church music of all ages and types . . . irrespective of whether the congregation can understand it or not. It is highly desirable that we should all from time to time have the opportunity of this kind of education."

He paid close attention to the performance and presentation of services: "the ceremonies too, even the manner of walking, standing and sitting of the ministers and singers, should be most carefully performed." He wanted to see a variety of clergy preaching: "in a mother church, a large number of representative clergy should have invitations to preach", but he did not see it as a two-way process with cathedral clergy going out into the parishes. He then answered a frequently asked question:

> "Why are cathedral congregations not much larger? The answer is two-fold: first, because the number of people capable of appreciating cathedral worship is limited; secondly because the cathedral is not a rival to the parish churches."

The first answer was patronising and reflective of class and educational divisions of the time and the second was contradicted by his admission that cathedrals attracted their congregations from other parishes. Overall he painted an elitist and self-regarding picture which assumed that deferential parishes would continue to pay their quotas and, rather like provincials visiting the Royal Shakespeare Company, be dazzled by the quality of the performance even if they did not completely understand it. In the mid 19th century Prebendary Perry of Lincoln had described a cathedral as "an extraneous ornament or decorative addition to the diocesan edifice":[16] the Provost of Derby had not advanced very far from that position.

Bishop Wilson, now in his 70s, was still in combative epistolary form. His monthly letters in the *Diocesan Chronicle* encompassed moral outrage about the evils of the atomic bomb and, as ever, feelings of high dudgeon provoked by what he saw as the inadequacies of politicians, clergy, congregations, methods of evangelism, church governance and, no surprise, the Vatican. His own undiminished sense of being right seemed to be even more emphatic, with a continuing sardonic edge. When commenting on the retirement or elevation of colleagues, he wrote: "I am not given to praising people (perhaps I do too little of that!)"[17]

On the dropping of atomic bombs on Hiroshima and Nagasaki he was crystal clear in his condemnation:

> "It is quite impossible . . . to defend this kind of warfare. When the flying bombs and rockets were falling upon us we charged the Germans with the indiscriminate slaughter of non-combatants . . . It seems that human progress today is rather like that of the Gadarene swine . . . progressing pretty rapidly . . . to an abyss!"

He responded to his critics the following month by quoting a letter he had received from a British serviceman:

> "For the last 3½ years I have fought in Burma and I have seen many horrible things. The brutal savagery which characterised the war in Burma was a man to man affair. The best man in a hand to hand struggle always won . . . The 14th Army fought the Japanese and beat them and they had a respect for the tenacious bravery of the beaten foe—something many people will never understand . . . My Lord, we share your deep disgust . . . Where will the world look to find humanity when England is part and parcel to such a monstrous breach of all that is right, humane and decent?"[18]

On a less idealistic level were the Bishop's negative observations on the political process as the country prepared, in the summer of 1945, for its first general election in 10 years:

"I have only once attended a political meeting and that was 39 years ago. A more futile business I never witnessed. About 90% of the audience were of the same political hue as the candidate . . . and if he had told them that the moon was made of green cheese they would have shouted agreement . . . I left wondering how any sensible person could think it profitable to attend such a silly business."[19]

His remarks inevitably created a stir. The *Manchester Guardian* leader on May 22nd 1945 reminded him that the 1906 electoral process that he derided had produced a Liberal government that had introduced old age pensions and national insurance. They warned him that "holding aloof from the British way of deciding issues . . . is showing little citizenship and less courage." Predictably the bishop scorned the "twitter" in the press:

"Among others the *Manchester Guardian* honoured me with a leader and the *Sunday Dispatch* contained an article by Dr C.E.M. Joad, both of which were unfavourable to my point of view. I am afraid I remain impenitent."[20]

Joad felt the Church should have supported the Labour Party because of the Atlantic Charter which became the founding document of the United Nations and the Beveridge Report which advocated universal social welfare from "the cradle to the grave": the Bishop retorted that the Atlantic Charter was compiled by Winston Churchill, a Conservative, and President Franklin Roosevelt and the Beveridge Report by a Liberal which would, according to Joad's logic, require a vote against Labour. It was very clever to score points off Joad, one of the celebrated Brains Trust panel on B.B.C. radio, but it was possibly not the best use of a bishop's time. He returned to his jaundiced view of democracy for the 1950 general election:

"Both parties would no doubt confidently assert that the angels are on their side, but I incline to the view that the angels would be no more than interested spectators, perhaps not very interested! . . . Bloggs must assure his following in the most definite terms not only that he is altogether right, but that Scroggs is absolutely wrong and probably a fool and a knave also; and so the inevitably unedifying contest must go on and on."

"I have written rather cynically", he admitted. His final rider—"we can thankfully claim that in no country in the world is government so clean and honest as in our land"[21]—seemed a pale afterthought.

He was at his most constructive, though not necessarily effective, as a driving force on the Archbishops' Commission on Evangelism, chaired by Christopher Chavasse, Bishop of Rochester, whose report, *Towards the Conversion of England*, emerged in 1945. Its most striking proposal was for a massive advertising campaign of evangelism to cost £1 million over five years (£33.7 million in today's money), a rather naive belief by the commissioners in the modern miracles of marketing given their deploring of other modern influences, namely humanism, secular education and science and technology. One historian considered that the Commission "appeared to have little sense of the Church being prepared to 'listen to the world' and to appreciate the world's own particular insights."[22] The Church Assembly declined to set up the recommended permanent Council on Evangelism and was supported by Archbishop Geoffrey Fisher's damning words:

> "Everyone seemed to distrust schemes or organisations for the promotion of evangelism—and I share that distrust."[23]

Bishop Wilson, in his own Diocese, was adamant that evangelism must be based firstly on a rekindling of the devotion of those within the Church whose grasp of religious teaching, he still felt, was tenuous:

> "If we have only a small fraction of the people professing the Christian religion, let us see at least that they know what their religion teaches."

He was uncomplimentary about the clergy:

> "Generally speaking preaching is of a poor quality . . . If our preachers were better more would come to listen."

He accepted that the public mood might be unreceptive to missions:

> "An evangelist 30 or 40 years ago could speak about sin, penitence, judgement, personal responsibility to God and the after-life, with the assurance that his hearers accepted these things as truth."

Bishop Henry Wilson spreading the Word at Clacton-on-Sea:
Chelmsford Cathedral Knightbridge Library

But his sense of history was deserting him: that had not been the experience of the 1916 National Mission. The religious press then had a go at the Commission's report, commenting that bishops were too remote to support their clergy in evangelism. In March 1946 Bishop Wilson wrote:

> "Now, to be frank . . . I doubt that the parish clergy really want the Bishop 'popping in' to see them at all kinds of unexpected times . . . Nor do I find any great eagerness on the part of the clergy to attend meetings at the summons of the Bishop."

If he intended to criticise them face-to-face as he did in print that was not surprising:

> "The best of them feel that they do not want to be taken from their work and the less good find excuses for absence. Yet we are told they are all clamouring to attend synods and conventions!"

Clearly some critics had been harking back to a golden age of bishops in yesteryear. That approach inevitably got short shrift:

> "The bishops' . . . predecessors are enhaloed with that dubious glory which often is generously given to the past, but I doubt very much if these almost saintly figures and monumental scholars of 50 and a 100 years ago would be equal to the task which their inconspicuous successors have to face. I met one of these great men in the early days of my ministry. He never even shook hands with me, for it was his practice to take no notice of curates!"[24]

Modern methods of church government did not impress him. Of the Diocesan Synod in 1947 the Bishop said:

> "If talking could save Church, State and the clergy we should all be quite secure! But laying aside all cynicism . . ."[25]

Of the Church Assembly's discussion of establishment in 1949 he wrote:

> "The debate struck me as poor and unreal and distinguished by arguments largely based on imaginary grievances."

He saw establishment as:

> ". . . a precarious survival from an age long since dead . . . We should use the time left to us to build up in every parish a clergy sustentation fund."[26]

He rejected the criticism that discussing disestablishment and disendowment would hasten the day. He was uncompromising on the need for every parish to build up a clergy sustenance fund from quarterly, half-yearly or annual collections, as happened everywhere in the Anglican Communion bar England. Central Church funds had been diminished by the effects of the 1936 Tithe Act and the loss of share dividends following the post-war nationalisation of railways, coal, electricity and gas. He reassured readers that "'none of the money will go 'out of the parish': the bugbear of many good people."[27] By the end of the year parishes were protesting that they could not meet the needs of the diocesan quota as well as the sustenance fund.[28] This left the Diocese of Chelmsford as the largest English consumer of the resources of the Additional Curates' Society funds, many congregations labouring under the misapprehension that the Society would provide for all needs.[29]

Behind his hypercritical exterior the Bishop's personal sense of Christian passion and justice remained as strong as ever. He commented on the rumour that the two starving orphans to whom he and his wife had offered hospitality at Bishopscourt were German, pointing out that they were, in fact, French:

> "The positive fury with which we were attacked was extraordinary! . . . I wonder would God really be very angry with people who fed starving German children? . . . It is a curious psychological fact that the most furious and belligerent people are civilians."[30]

When, a year later, he suggested that people send part of their extra Christmas rations to starving people in Germany, he received an abusive response.[31] Yet within a year the Soviet Union had blockaded West Berlin and an air lift of food and other essential supplies became its very lifeline.

His barbed response to the Roman Catholic Church's ban on mixed marriages and the perceived elevation of papal authority above that of the scriptures, remained as evangelically firm as ever. His criticisms were undoubtedly sharpened by his awareness of the considerable Irish influx into the industrial complexes of the East End and as seasonal agricultural workers on Essex farms;[32] they would all look for leadership to the Roman Catholic Diocese of Brentwood, created in 1917, which also claimed spiritual authority over the people of Essex.

Papal teaching declared mixed marriages to be "degrading the holy character of matrimony, involving as it did a communion in sacred things with those outside the fold."[33] Bishop Wilson called this an advanced form of papal aggression:

> "There is an old saying that when the Roman Church is in a minority she is a lamb; when in equality she is a fox; when in a majority she is a tigress. We are in the second stage thanks largely to the steady annual recruitment the Roman Church receives from Ireland."[34]

The Bishop may have written in harsh terms but it was in the context of a longstanding climate of cold war between the two churches which was as mutually paranoid as its secular equivalent between communism and capitalism. Catholics were not usually allowed to join non-Catholic clubs.[35] Father Donald Colger, speaking of his appointment as a Catholic curate in Chelmsford in 1936 recollected:

> "It was considered daring (and not desirable) to be on speaking terms . . . The dear old Church of England was considered a fair target of sardonic remarks and even beastly ones . . . Non-Conformists were, of course, even outside this."[36]

In the war of trading insults they had come up against a heavyweight in Bishop Wilson. When Monsignor Ronald Knox's translation of the New Testament appeared, approved by "all the Archbishops and Bishops in England and Wales" (meaning the Roman Catholic hierarchy), Bishop Wilson was incensed at their assumption that they were the only legitimate priesthood in England:

> "We touch a level of insolence and bad taste which is symptomatic of the confident aggression which distinguishes the Roman Church in England today."[37]

His response was probably exacerbated by the fact that the Monsignor, son of the evangelical Edmund Knox, former Bishop of Manchester, had betrayed his roots by converting to Catholicism in 1919.

For a while the shared war-time experience of family members killed and injured or rendered homeless by bombing had united people of different denominations. Theological posturing at the top gradually began to lose touch with the grassroots. While the Pope prevaricated, Cardinal Arthur Hinsley, the Roman Catholic Archbishop of Westminster, showed that Catholic leaders could also be patriots: he took a strong stand against the dictators, forming the Sword of the Spirit in 1940 to unite Christians internationally for justice in peace and war and, as an avuncular patriotic Yorkshireman, he struck a chord across the country. But he was openly reprimanded by the Pope for joining in public with George Bell, the Bishop of Chichester, to say the Lord's Prayer. When the question of joint prayer was raised again George Beck, the Bishop of Brentwood, wrote to *The Times*:

"The Catholic saying 'Thy Kingdom come' would be praying for the conversion of all men to Catholicism: the non-Catholic evidently would not subscribe to this petition."[38]

He reminded Mervyn Haigh, Bishop of Winchester, who had resurrected the issue, that Catholics regarded him as a layman; ditto the Bishop of Chelmsford. Bishop Wilson retorted with icy clarity. He said the Roman Catholic Church was:

"... based upon a conception of God as an ecclesiastical potentate, very exacting about rules and regulations, who deals with the souls of men almost always, if not entirely, through an institution. According to the most extreme (and perhaps most logical) form of this theory, for all practical purposes God is thought of as almost in retirement and all the business is conducted by the institution and its officers, God Himself being surrounded by a zareba of ecclesiastical ceremonial and preciseness which can be penetrated only by officials and officers specially and exclusively appointed."[39]

The Bishop's disillusion with Catholicism did not spread to great men in other faiths. Mahatma Gandhi's assassination in 1948 elicited a rare encomium:

"Future generations will describe him as one of the three or four greatest men who have ever lived. He was not called by the name of Christian but in fact no one on earth so fully lived according to the teaching of our Lord as did he . . . I regret that the Church missed the chance of expressing its grief at the loss of this holy man."[40]

He was firm in his views that revision of the Prayer Book had gone far enough. As congregations declined there was a move to make services more relevant and appealing on the assumption that presentation was the problem. Bishop Wilson described the Prayer Book as:

"... the best sample of Christian public worship in the vernacular which has ever been achieved . . . In fact it is unusual for our people to hear this service in its entirety with its perfect balance and dignified language. Revisers of the Prayer Book abound. Inspired by such laudable motives as 'shortening the service', making it 'more up-to-date' and more appropriate to 'modern needs', they introduce unctuous emphasis on words and phrases, cut down and introduce and as a result destroy the dignity, melody and balance of a perfect structure. Lessons are chosen to suit the incumbent. Psalms are shortened . . . It is now become a widespread habit to indulge after the Third Collect in a freedom from all adherence to the Prayer Book and to make use of a wide variety of modern prayers, the subjects of which are often petty and the language sentimental and unworthy."[41]

He referred to:

". . . 'critics' and 'candid friends' who cloak themselves under the ample folds of the garment called 'putting our house in order' . . . But I am positive that the right procedure is first of all to recover our own unity and loyalty for the Church and needful reformation can then be more easily and effectively carried out."[42]

On the world stage anxiety about the length of a sermon appeared somewhat irrelevant. In 1948 the Soviet attempt to starve the French, American and British sectors of Berlin into submission, frustrated by a superbly organised round-the-clock Anglo-American airlift, brought Bishop Wilson face-to-face with the realities of Soviet rule compared to the more rose-tinted view he had formerly held. With the Soviet army maintaining an iron grip on East Europe and communism on the verge of triumph in China, he now feared that half-hearted Anglicanism was no match for the dedication of the revolutionary left:

"The criticism so often levelled at us is that we Christians are no different from and no better than others and this criticism is fortified by the absence of discipline in our habits, the casual and irregular way in which we discharge our religious duties and the slight sacrifice (if indeed any sacrifice) we are prepared to make for our faith . . . I was frequently told . . . by chaplains in the services that while means of conveyance were provided for Roman Catholics who wished to go to Mass on Sundays, no such facilities were offered to our men . . . The common assumption was that 'C. of E.' was rather a slack body whose adherents were rarely in earnest . . . This is typical of a widespread opinion . . . Flabby Christianity is no cure for anything and confronted by red-hot Marxianism [sic]—and all Marxianists are red-hot—it will be driven from the field at once."[43]

The war had been an exhausting experience for those who lived through it. On September 21st 1948 Provost Morrow wrote to his parishioners: "I have been told by my doctors that I must surrender my charge which I have loved for 19 years."[44] A month later, on October 21st, he advised: "my doctor had to speak in somewhat stern language." He reflected nostalgically on the pre-war factory services for the workers of Marconi's, Hoffman's, and Crompton Parkinson's:

> "It was a great encouragement to me to speak time after time to a Cathedral filled with employees . . . I was on the point of resuming them when a crisis came and my 'last bolt was shot!"[45]

For some time his letters to his parishioners had exuded an air of almost desperate sadness. He was dismayed by the industrial unrest after the war protesting that "some system which savours of anarchy"[46] had been substituted for law and justice: "our nation is losing its character for patriotism . . . pure selfishness dominates in all classes."[47] As Parliament debated the divorce laws, on which the Church opposed any relaxation, he expressed the view that "a wave of infidelity is sweeping over the country . . . Free love is openly advocated."[48] The solution lay in "the Heathen . . . 'drinking in' the message of Jesus and his love", but he felt himself stymied by "the apathy of our congregation towards the command of our Blessed Lord when he said 'Go ye into all the world and make disciples of every creature'."[49]

He spoke the same evangelical message as the Bishop who wrote affectionately: "he is one of my oldest friends . . . he is wise not to strain his health by another winter in office."[50] William Morrow moved to Sutton Valence in Kent whence he wrote immediately to his former congregation:

> "I am here in this **small** house and **large** garden! I cannot change the descriptions but am trying my best to redeem the garden from a waste to a pleasant prospect . . . I miss dear old Chelmsford. I hear no noise of the factory workers passing . . . I see very few

'prams' here . . . Perhaps when one gets used to the conditions we shall be glad to listen to the bleating of sheep and the lowing of the oxen."[51]

He died in 1950.

In February 1949 it was also announced that Roland Middleton would be moving back to Chester Cathedral as Organist and Master of the Music, a post he would hold until 1964. The *Parish Magazine* sang his praises. He had completely transformed the music of the Cathedral:

> "Owing to many different circumstances the music had fallen to a very low level when, in November 1944, Dr Middleton took up his work. It is fair to say that he started completely afresh and had to build up a choir from very small beginnings."

Illness and promotion had taken away the Provost and the Master of the Music; on March 4th 1949 the Cathedral's Consulting Architect, Sir Charles Nicholson, died; in 1950, the Precentor, William Dawe, moved on to take up his own parish.

That just left Bishop Henry Wilson; in the July 1950 *Diocesan Chronicle*, he announced his retirement at the age of 73. It was not his health, he insisted, just that "you can't teach an old dog new tricks", a truth which had been apparent for some time. As one observer said, "he retained a boyish delight in puncturing popular pretensions":[52] at times he did it amusingly, at others he often came across as self-righteously insensitive, delighting in his own cleverness. Few bishops would wish to match his rich range of dismissive adjectives. He was even condescending about his successor, Falkner Allison, who had been his junior at Dean Close School in Cheltenham:

> "If some angel visitant had whispered in my ear, 'This boy will some day succeed you in a certain bishopric to which in a few years you will be called', I should have regarded it as a fantastic dream. Indeed, when I was confidentially told of his appointment, it was a complete surprise to me: for I had the impression that the responsible people were looking elsewhere."[53]

The second oldest bishop seemed bemused at being succeeded by the youngest. As was his wont, his first thoughts revealed the inner man, even if he did go on to praise his successor's scholarship which could be matched by "few of the present bishops", thus irritating at least 13 of them who had been Oxbridge dons.[54]

The Bishop of Colchester, Frederick Narborough, referred to his diocesan's "complete freedom from pomposity and spontaneous outspokenness."[55] Those whose pungent commentary scourges the mighty are often viewed affectionately by more humble onlookers who admire their hero's audacity and eloquence. Thus it was for Henry Wilson whose verbal missiles aimed at wielders of power were counterbalanced by "his kindness and interest in the affairs of ordinary people"[56] and the championing of his see town: he was therefore made a Freeman of Chelmsford on October 30th, accepting the honour with a tribute to his parish clergy whom, it has to be said, he had not always described in such glowing terms:

> "I receive the honours, I receive the dignities, I have enjoyed the hospitality of the distinguished and the eminent. But they [the clergy] are the people that do the work . . . I know the uphill character of their tasks. For the most part their names will never be known."[57]

But he still had time for one more attack on progress:

> "The exchange of 'the British Empire' to 'the Commonwealth of Nations' has always struck me as mealy-mouthed and rather smug, for I believe our Empire has been the greatest civilising influence apart from the Christian faith, in human history."[58]

Nor did he pull any punches in his final letter to the Diocese. Of the Christian faith he said:

> "'I always believed it to be a revelation given by God . . . but a visitor from another world would rarely realise this if he frequented religious assemblies or read the reported utterances of eminent clergy or ministers."

He ended with a confident assertion of his faith:

> "I believe that truth is invincible and error certain to die, though it may live long."[59]

CHAPTER 18

All Change

On January 22nd 1949 Canon Charles Kempson Waller was installed as Provost of the Cathedral and inducted as Rector of St. Mary's Parish. He had been educated in the county, at Felsted School, graduated from St. John's College, Oxford and trained at Wells Theological College. This was a homecoming. His father had been churchwarden at St. Mary's and was commemorated in a window. As a young man, Charles had been greatly influenced in his high churchmanship by Canon Lake whose cope he wore for the first time on Ascension Day,[1] a break from the self-denial of his evangelical predecessors. All but six years of his ministry had been spent in the Diocese, in Barking, Dagenham, Hornchurch and Wanstead. He had even married into the Diocese, to Marion, grand-daughter of Thomas Stevens, the first Bishop of Barking. Not since 1895 had Chelmsford known a Rector's wife. The proliferation of possible titles continued to confuse:

> "Shall we learn **not** to call him 'Canon' but either 'Rector' or 'Provost'? Well we must try . . . Provost Morrow was known affectionately as 'Canon', a title which, he said, he had given up in 1935."[2]

While he never neglected the parish, the renaming of the *Parish Magazine* as the *Cathedral Review* in 1949 was symbolic of an eye on the wider horizon.

Like his predecessor the Provost wanted commitment. He warned against "Religious Individualists" who took no part in the worship or activities of the Church or only that part that suited their personal convenience and taste; "Religious Organisationists" who gave themselves to an organisation they liked and any services dedicated to it but not general worship; and "Religious Parochialists" with no vision of Christian life outside their parish in the Diocese or the mission field.[3] One hopes that, after reading this, there were some left who still felt themselves to be within the fold. He sought his congregation's support for the special appeal for the Mission to Seamen whose Institute at Tilbury had been bombed and was sinking into the marshland and encouraged them to read the S.P.C.K. book *Why Trouble the Heathen?* as those of other or no faiths were still aggressively known.[4]

Provost Charles Waller: Chelmsford Cathedral Knightbridge Library

In 1949, as one of his first acts, Provost Waller appointed the well-qualified 39-year-old Stanley Vann, B.Mus., F.R.C.O., A.R.C.M. as Cathedral Organist and Choirmaster, to follow Roland Middleton. It was a popular choice: "those most discerning little people, the choristers, decided after an acquaintanceship of only 20 minutes that Mr Vann is their man!"[5] He had been Assistant Organist at Leicester Cathedral and Chorus Master of the Leicester Philharmonic Society under their illustrious conductors, Sir Henry Wood and Sir Malcolm Sargent. He then moved on to All Saints', Gainsborough and Holy Trinity, Leamington Spa, the latter interrupted by war service in the Royal Artillery. He was a very good organist but had earned his reputation as a superb choir trainer, especially in psalm singing. Choir discipline was strict and, for the boys, started the moment they set foot in the Cathedral.[6] He supplemented his income from his Cathedral post with the Professorship of Harmony and Counterpoint at Trinity College, London.

Music was in very good hands but the building was still in a mess which it was hoped would be rectified when Stephen Dykes-Bower, who lived in the Diocese, at Quendon near Saffron Walden, was appointed as the Cathedral's Consultant Architect in 1950. His parallel appointment in 1951 as Surveyor of the Fabric at Westminster Abbey, with the most significant collection of monumental sculpture in Britain to care for, must have provided an interesting contrast to Chelmsford.

In June 1950 Dykes-Bower produced a detailed report on Chelmsford's needs:[7]

> "Of all the parish churches which have, with the creation of new
> sees, been raised to cathedral rank, none presents greater problems
> of adaptation . . . It is still not large enough to accommodate great
> diocesan gatherings; it remains in form and aspect, a typical parish
> church; and internally its arrangement precludes the distinctive
> ethos of cathedral worship."

He knew that an enlargement could not be afforded though he regretted that Nicholson's eastward extension of the sanctuary had not gone at least one bay further:

> "For better or worse the common conception of a cathedral is
> that of a building of great size and splendour—the pride of the
> county, to which a visit is a privilege for many people, particularly
> in the villages, eagerly looked forward to and long remembered
> afterwards . . . A cathedral certainly should not evoke expressions
> of universal disappointment."

The cumbersome Victorian pews were a major obstacle. The Incorporated Church Building Society laid down six feet as the minimum width desirable for the nave gangway: Chelmsford's was barely four and a half feet and the aisle gangways were even less:

"Along such narrow paths no procession can move with dignity. And it is largely on this account that a first view of the interior . . . is so unimpressive: the general appearance would not flatter a parish church, still less does it suggest a cathedral."

An Easter time view of the cluttered interior:
Chelmsford Cathedral Knightbridge Library

He recommended an immediate removal of those flanking aisle pews that were even further advanced than the front row of pews in the nave and sinking the heating pipes below a new stone floor designed to match the walls; in the long-term the pews should be scrapped in favour of chairs to make the Cathedral seem lighter and larger.

The Cathedral lacked usable side-chapels. He thought it needed a Lady Chapel comparable to those in the older cathedrals but neither the Chapel of the Holy Ghost (South Chapel) nor the Mildmay Chapel (North Chapel) were large enough. He therefore recommended a new Lady Chapel in the outer north aisle. In the Chapel of the Holy Ghost the east window was not central in the east wall: the seating should therefore be centred on the window and a stone floor should be laid to replace the mixed tile and wood flooring.

In the chancel the choir sat as a parish church choir, with the Provost and Precentor opposite each other, like vicar and curate, leaving the honorary canons penned in a block of stalls east of the altar rails. In the sanctuary the suffragan bishops and the Archdeacon of Southend occupied seats set into the thickness of the wall and knelt at projecting faldstools "which would disgrace a mission church"; opposite them the large gothic bishop's throne, with chairs on either side, meant that "there is very little effective sanctuary left and the whole aspect of the chancel is one of muddle and confusion." He recommended setting the altar rails a bay further east to enlarge the choir proper so that it could accommodate clergy and choir in new stalls; the sanctuary would be shorter but, containing only the high altar and bishop's throne, would appear larger.

Sanctuary with the heavy choir stalls, statue of Bishop John Watts-Ditchfield (back right) and the towering Gothic bishop's throne (back left): Chelmsford Cathedral Knightbridge Library

The chancel furniture needed a complete overhaul. The honorary canons' stalls, designed by Sir Charles Nicholson, and the Provost's stall, designed by Wykeham Chancellor, were impracticable and should be transferred from the cathedral to the Chapter House: older cathedrals had canons' stalls in both, one for services, the other for chapter meetings. The "cumbrous" choir stalls were declared "unworthy of a cathedral": the choir should have new three-tiered oak stalls and pews with the back row on either side set within the thickness of the arches, to seat a choir of up to 26 boys and 22 men. A seating plan for the honorary canons, suffragan bishops, the Archdeacon of

Southend, any visiting emeritus canon, the Provost and Precentor, cathedral chaplains, visiting preachers and the Chancellor and Registrar, would accommodate up to 90 people; it would suffice for all civic and diocesan occasions and, should an afternoon daily Choral Evensong develop in the future, seat both choir and congregation. A new chancel floor should match Nicholson's floor in the sanctuary.

Dykes-Bower liked the east window and the easternmost window in the south aisle, all by Clayton and Bell: they "deserve to be and will in time be recognised at their true worth." The east windows of both chapels and the west window of the nave, damaged in the war, were in the process of receiving new stained glass. But he confirmed that clear glass elsewhere would lighten the interior.

He detested the internal paintwork:

> "The stonework throughout is dirty and discoloured; the plaster is a sickly cream in the nave and a nondescript grey in the aisles; the walls of the chancel and the Chapel of the Holy Ghost are decorated with nineteenth century wall paintings. The absence of any one unifying colour contributes perhaps more than any other single factor to the disappointing appearance of the interior . . . Nor would any person of normal taste tolerate in his private house plastered walls so unsightly as those of this Cathedral."

The densely decorated Chapel of the Holy Ghost:
Chelmsford Cathedral Knightbridge Library

He advocated white lime-washing which would "be a transformation, making the building seem larger, brighter and twice as restful . . . and the change would induce a sense, not of coldness, but of radiance." The ribs of John Johnson's nave ceiling—an example of early nineteenth century fan-vaulting—should be painted in gold and red and blue, with white infilling and the cherubs and other clerestory ornaments picked out in gold.

As for the other furnishings, a new font raised on just one step should be set centrally on the line of the axis through the side tower arches, to replace the multi-stepped one at the west end of the south aisle which impeded processions. Extraneous cupboards should be cleared. A new lectern was desirable. "In both the Chapel of the Holy Ghost and the Mildmay Chapel, the altar furnishings could scarcely be worse." Regimental colours, hung in the north aisle, were of varied decorative merit and needed some thought, though he had no proposals at this stage.

The organ's position in the north east corner was problematic:

> "Though it sounds overwhelming to the player at the console,
> it does not speak effectively into the body of the Cathedral . . .
> When the organ is next due for rebuilding, it might be desirable
> to design the instrument in two portions—the softer departments
> of pedal, choir, swell, solo and a divided great accompaniment
> section remaining, as now, against the north wall and the heavier
> section of the great and pedal, with the solo reeds, transferred to
> a loft placed across the blank bay at the west end of the nave in
> front of the tower arch. A well-designed organ-case here could be a
> fine feature of the Cathedral. The whole organ would be playable
> from one console in approximately its existing position."

The virtue of the Dykes-Bower report was that it could be tackled in self-contained sections which would not prevent the rest of the Cathedral being used. However, the largest task, the re-arrangement of the choir, would be quite costly and did not occur until the great re-ordering of 1983, though not in the form he suggested. Nor did the new Lady Chapel take off as an idea. Not surprisingly the cheaper and more easily achieved improvements came first.

Dykes-Bower urged Chelmsford on:

> "Blackburn is completing a big scheme of structural enlargement.
> Portsmouth and Sheffield have already proceeded some way with

even more ambitious plans. Guildford is building a completely new cathedral. Bury St. Edmunds has restored and re-decorated its nave and has plans for erecting a new choir and ancillary buildings. Derby has carried out much sumptuous internal beautification. Newcastle and Wakefield, which were earlier in the field and quick to make themselves true cathedrals, are continuing with further good work."

He concluded that "by comparison with what other parish church cathedrals are doing, the scheme is modest." That was true, but if the Diocese had not had to respond to the migration of hundreds of thousands of Londoners into Essex, it too might have indulged in architectural dreams.

In the meantime Provost Waller began to take the Cathedral gently in a High Church direction. He introduced the Sacrament of Penance in 1949 for those who wished to use it:[8] private confession was clearly provided for in the Book of Common Prayer but, as a so-called Roman practice, had not traditionally been used although it became much more normal in the 20th century as High Church practices spread. He introduced a Christmas Eve Midnight Communion in 1950 and experimented with Parish Communion on the first Sunday of the month starting from January 7th 1951,[9] held early and followed by a breakfast provided at a cheap cost. This was a nod in the direction of the Parish and People movement: since its inception in 1949 its leaders had argued that the Eucharist, the central act of worship in the early church, should be reinstated as the principal act of morning worship, at 9.00 a.m. or thereabouts.

Sadly, Provost Waller had not enjoyed good health. In April and May 1949 he had been absent for surgery and convalescence. He died suddenly of a heart attack at the age of 59 and was buried in the cathedral churchyard on January 20th 1951. Mrs Marion Waller wrote:

"Coming to Chelmsford just two years ago—to his old Parish Church of St. Mary, the home of his beloved Canon Lake—was the most thrilling fulfilment of our dreams."[10]

A later retrospective felt that, had he lived, vestments would have been introduced and the tradition of Canon Lake's time revived and sustained.[11] In his Easter report to the Parochial Church Council the Precentor, John James, said:

"Whilst never a 'party man' our late Provost and Rector favoured that school of thought known in our Church as the 'Tractarian' movement . . . He hated 'fussiness' in worship as he hated anything which savoured of extremes. He sought always to avoid the twin evils of a 'dignified remoteness' and an 'unbecoming familiarity'. This, be it said, is a happy medium which, in the worship of a Cathedral that must also serve as a Parish Church, is not easy to find."[12]

The Provost's death had occurred during an episcopal vacancy. The appointment of his successor therefore lay with the Crown [13] even though the next bishop had already been named and his enthronement was only a month off, but once the Crown had embarked lethargically on the process, it would not hand it back, such was the bureaucratic rigidity of the system. It would be six months before the next Provost was named and nine months before he was installed.

On February 17th 1951 the fourth Bishop of Chelmsford, 44-year-old Sherard Falkner Allison, was enthroned although, in the absence of a Provost, Frederick Narborough, the Bishop of Colchester, opened the west door to his knocking. The new bishop had graduated from Jesus College, Cambridge, trained for the ministry at Ridley Hall and served a curacy in Tunbridge Wells before returning for three years as chaplain at Ridley Hall. Incumbencies at Rodbourne Cheney in Swindon and Erith in Kent were followed by a third residence at Ridley Hall, this time as its Principal, whence he came to Chelmsford.

For the Allison family installations and enthronements were not uncommon: Falkner was the son and nephew of vicars and had three brothers who were ordained as Anglican priests: one of them, Oliver, became Bishop of the Sudan and another, Gordon, had been installed in 1947 as Rector of Springfield in north Chelmsford with his rectory next door to Bishopscourt.[14]

On his arrival in Chelmsford the Bishop took against Bishopscourt, a rambling Victorian residence built to accommodate servants and half a dozen children. Bishop Wilson backed him:

"If the new bishop has £500-£1,000 a year in private resources [£12,200-£24,400 in today's money] he might be able to live there: otherwise there is no point in his living in this huge house."[15]

Bishop Allison therefore handed it over to the Church Commissioners under the Episcopal Endowments and Stipend Measure 1943 which made them responsible for see residences. A manageable part of the house would be converted into a private residence and office. The Bishop would receive a reduced income but, as the Church Commissioners would pay all the overheads, he was probably no worse off in real terms. While building work continued he would stay at his Cambridge family home and board during the week with his brother at Springfield Rectory.[16] As with all bishops his initial task was to get to know his clergy: after nine months he had driven over 10,000 miles but had visited only 93 of the 540 parishes. With 100 days reserved for confirmations and institutions of clergy he said he would have to accept fewer engagements.[17]

At his first Diocesan Conference Bishop Allison expressed the hope that the Cathedral would take an increasingly central place in diocesan life. He felt that would be helped by moving its administrative headquarters, Church House, which had already transferred from Stratford to Forest Gate in 1930,[18] to Guy Harlings in New Street, just across the road from the Cathedral. Guy Harlings had been the Rectory for St. Mary's since 1909 and had not been utilised by the first bishop in 1914 as had been anticipated: like Bishopscourt it was too vast for modern family needs. The Church Commissioners bought a property, Osborne Place in New London Road, as the new Provost's House[19], about 20 minutes walk from the Cathedral. The Cathedral now had none of its clergy resident in the vicinity: the Precentor, Curate and Organist and Choirmaster all lived in properties a similar walk south or west of the Cathedral but nowhere near each other. From July 1955 the Provost was granted an office within the new diocesan complex at Guy Harlings.[20] In 1956 he made a short move to a more suitable detached property in Southborough Road, still much the same distance south of the Cathedral, which cost £5,650 (£110,000 in today's money) with the help of a £600 loan (£11,700) from the Church Commissioners.[20] On December 13th 1956 he wrote:

> "It is not the most convenient place for the Rectory, but it is, unfortunately, the best thing that can be arranged at the moment."[22]

For Bishop Allison London-over-the-Border took on a new complexion. Bomb damage to housing had halved the docklands population of West Ham with large numbers of its residents being relocated in new overspill towns in rural Essex. Harlow New Town and Basildon were scheduled to grow to 80,000 each. Harlow would need three or four new churches, Basildon eight. In addition London County Council was building large housing estates in Essex at Hainault, Harold Hill, Debden, Aveley and Chingford and there were to be new local authority housing estates at Collier Row, Stifford, Chelmsford, Colchester and Southend. By 1961 these London and Essex County Council projects would require 20 more churches, 24 dual-purpose halls, 6 halls and 15 parsonages costing £700,000 (£12.2 million) of which £200,000 (£3.47 million) would come from war damage payments for London churches that were not being rebuilt.[23] An additional £13,500 a year (£234,000) would be needed to boost clergy stipends though the Church Commissioners would provide half.[24] The Bishop warned:

> "600 clergy cannot win for Christ and His Church the great County of Essex, with its population of over 2 million . . . The primary task of the clergy must be to instruct lay members of the Church and to inspire them." [25]

But if money-raising and evangelism were to be a joint project, the latter always a tentative matter for the laity, communications needed to be improved. Therefore the *Diocesan Chronicle*, circulation 1,200, was replaced in 1953 by the more populist *Essex Churchman*: it could be inserted into parish magazines, guaranteeing a circulation of at least 50,000.[26]

The new Provost, George Eric Gordon, was eventually installed on October 13th 1951. He came from Middleton, half-way between Rochdale and Manchester, where he was Rector and Rural Dean. He had graduated from St. Catharine's College, Cambridge, trained at Wycliffe Hall, Oxford and, after early parish experience in Leicester, trained ordinands for 11 years at the Bishop Wilson Theological College on the Isle of Man, first as Vice-Principal and then as Principal. The College was forced to close in 1942 when the supply of ordinands dried up and war made it inaccessible. His stipend at Chelmsford was still the same as William Morrow's had been in 1939. The rates on the Provost's House and that part of the rent not met by the income from the old Rectory estate, which had been sold in 1914, would be paid by the parish. On his appointment, the Assistant Curate at the Cathedral moved on, as was the custom when there was a new incumbent.[27]

Provost Eric Gordon: Chelmsford Cathedral Knightbridge Library

Eric Gordon arrived in a Cathedral whose music outshone its decorations. On July 15th 1952 Stanley Vann introduced the Cathedral Chorister's first Speech Day and a choristers' cap, tie and blazer. Morning service was broadcast on the Home Service at 9.30 a.m. on Sunday, January 25th 1953. But later that year Stanley Vann was appointed Master of Music at Peterborough Cathedral where former Chelmsford Precentor, William Dawe, had moved to the same role. As the *Cathedral Review* observed:

> "Like Dr Middleton before him there was the lure (irresistible to the born cathedral organist) of the great old building and the daily services of the normal cathedral."[28]

On Whit Sunday May 24th he was replaced as Master of the Music, as the title had now become, by Derek Cantrell B.A., B.Mus., F.R.C.O. (for which he won the Limpus Prize), Organist and Choirmaster at the Church of the Holy Rude in Stirling. In his earlier days he had spent three years in the Royal Naval Volunteer Reserve, serving as a Japanese translator and education officer, before going up to Keble College, Oxford in 1947 as Holroyd Music Scholar. After graduation he was appointed as Assistant

Organist at New College, where he played for several broadcasts of Evensong and accompanied the choir in a series of recordings of English Cathedral music, and Organist and Choirmaster of St. Giles Parish Church, Oxford. In 1950 he went to Stirling, combining his church responsibilities with a lectureship in music at the University of Glasgow and teaching at the Royal Scottish Academy of Music.

He must have been thrilled that Clive Plumb, a Chelmsford Cathedral chorister, was one of two choirboys from the Diocese of Chelmsford among the twenty chosen nationwide from affiliates of the Royal School of Church Music to sing at the Coronation of Elizabeth II; Anthony Holt of Holy Trinity, Barkingside (later a founding member of The King's Singers) was the other.[29] Equally exciting, it seemed, was the article in the *Daily Express* of January 3rd 1953:

> "At Chelmsford Cathedral the Provost, the Very Rev. Eric Gordon, is to discuss with his church officials next week the possibility of screening the televising of the Coronation Service in the Cathedral."

But it was journalistic invention.

There had been all change at the top. What might the new men accomplish?

CHAPTER 19

A Colourful Cathedral

For the first time the Cathedral had, in Eric Gordon, a Provost who, while not neglecting the parish, undertook a concerted campaign to enhance the Cathedral as a place of excellence and beauty at the core of diocesan life. He presented his ideas to the 1953 Diocesan Conference pleading that the needs of the Cathedral and those of London-over-the-Border and the new towns should not be mutually exclusive:

> "Surely in the end we can have both. This moment, I am sure, is
> not the moment for a big appeal for the Cathedral. But neither
> is it the moment for an indefinite postponement."[1]

There was universal admiration for his advocacy, save on one controversial point:

> "He did not convince a great many of the rank and file . . . that
> at great diocesan gatherings it is important to have some of the
> music which is in our parish churches congregational, performed
> by the choir in a 'cathedral' manner."[2]

Further piecemeal buildings improvements were made. The Mildmay or North Chapel was redecorated and refurbished, paid for by a gift from Hoffman's and the J.T. Ridgewell and Provost Morrow bequests.[3] In the April 1953 *Cathedral News* (as the *Cathedral Review* had been renamed) Provost Gordon, in his Rector's letter (still a confusion of titles), had a clear order in mind for the rest: re-wiring and new lights would come first to aid worshippers and enhance the building's interior; then refurbishment of the South Porch and the North and South Chapels; and finally interior re-decoration although he recognised that "many are getting impatient about the dirt." The refurbishment of the South Chapel or Chapel of the Holy Ghost (no official names had ever been agreed for the chapels) would be a memorial to Provost Waller. As a finishing touch the Friends of the Cathedral hoped to arrange for the cleaning and re-colouring of the Cathedral's memorials.

The refurbishment of the South Porch acted as a memorial to Anglo-American friendships. Essex's links with America went back to 1607: the first settlers at Jamestown, Virginia included men from Mountnessing, Castle Hedingham, West Hanningfield, Little Baddow, Tillingham and Great Easter.[4] In 1623 the *Mayflower's* pilgrims included six Essex emigrants, amongst them Christopher Jones, the ship's master from Harwich, but only three of them survived the harsh first winter.[5] A disproportionate number of Essex's ministers were Puritans who did not accept Archbishop William Laud's quest for rigid high church uniformity in worship: 18 of them sailed for America in the 1630s. In some parishes locals appointed Puritan lecturers who were not accountable to the Archbishop, relying on sympathetic clergy, who otherwise outwardly toed the line, to give them access to the pulpit: one such preacher, Thomas Hooker, lecturer at St. Mary's, Chelmsford from 1626 to 1629, moved to open a school at Little Baddow when Laud suppressed independent lectures, fled to America in 1631 and founded the town of Hartford, Connecticut where he is celebrated as the Father of American Democracy.[6] In 1630 11 ships of the Massachusetts Bay Company sailed from Southampton: over 100 of the 700 passengers were from Essex[7] hence the spawning of Massachusetts' settlements with Essex place names, from Springfield in 1636 to Chelmsford in 1655. Most famously, Lawrence Washington, great-great-grandfather of Founding Father George, was, from 1632 to 1643 Rector of Purleigh, seven miles east of Chelmsford, whence his son, also named Lawrence, emigrated to Virginia in 1656.

Even though Thomas Hooker is remembered on a tablet in the Cathedral the commemoration in this coronation year of 1953 was in recognition of the sacrifices of the 9th United States Army Air Force and the friendships made in the Second World War when eastern England had become home to so many young Americans. The great service on October 17th was attended by many who had flown from American air bases in Essex at Birch, Boreham, Boxted, Chipping Ongar, Earls Colne, Gosfield, Great Saling, Little Walden, Matching, Rivenhall, Royden, Stansted, Wethersfield and Wormingfold.

Viscount Bernard Montgomery of Alamein and Major-General F.H. Griswold, Commanding General of the 3ʳᵈ United States Air Force, attended and each unveiled one of the new porch windows. On the same day, October 18ᵗʰ 1953, the Queen unveiled the Air Forces Memorial at Runnymede and in her speech observed that "at this very hour a memorial porch is being unveiled in Chelmsford Cathedral to commemorate some of those American airmen who fought together with us against the same aggression."[8]

Viscount Bernard Montgomery of Alamein (right) and
Major-General F.H. Griswold (left), October 18th 1953:
Chelmsford Cathedral Knightbridge Library

On the west side of the cathedral porch the window contains the Great Seal of the Department of the Air Force of the United States and a shield with a heraldic thunderbolt portraying air strike power. Above the shield is the crest of the American eagle set on an ultramarine background on which are thirteen silver stars, one each for the former eastern seaboard colonies which became the United States. In another of the lights are the arms of the Washington family. On the east side of the porch the glass incorporates the Royal Arms and the arms of the Diocese and the County of Essex. In the Knightbridge Library above the porch the central light shows the emblem of the United States Army Air Forces, worn by all who served in Essex from 1942 to 1945, a blue circle edged with gold and on it a silver propeller between two gold wings. Other lights incorporate the arms of the Borough of Chelmsford and a memorial to the Reverend Philip Morant whose *History and Antiquities of the County of Essex* printed in 1768 was the first great survey of the county's history. From 1954 an annual Essex-American service was held in the Cathedral to perpetuate the transatlantic link.[9]

For a cathedral which sang from *Hymns Ancient and Modern*, it was fitting that the commemoration in 1953 of the new world coming to the rescue of the old should be followed in 1954 by the celebration of the ancient, the 1,300th anniversary of St. Cedd coming to convert the East Saxons which coincided with the Diocese's 40th anniversary. The ancient chapel of St. Peter's-on-the-Wall, standing in splendid isolation on the Essex coast, had been used as a barn for decades, but had been conveyed in 1916 by the owner, Christopher Parker, to a group of trustees comprising the Bishop, the Archdeacon of Essex, the Rector of St. Mary's and two representatives of the Parker family. Bishop John Watts-Ditchfield re-dedicated it on June 22nd 1916 and annual pilgrimages on or close to that date had started in 1921.[10] In their turn the trustees conveyed the property to the Cathedral Chapter in 1939.[11]

The 1954 commemoration was a year-long celebration, starting with a Winter Festival in February. There followed a B.B.C. broadcast service from St. Peter's-on-the Wall on May 2nd with the cathedral choir; a visit by Geoffrey Fisher, Archbishop of Canterbury, on May 8th; a rally at West Ham football stadium on June 19th attended by over 15,000 people; and a service in the Cathedral at which the Archbishop once again preached. The culmination of the celebrations came in mid-summer: 6,000 pilgrims were addressed at Bradwell on July 3rd by Noel Hudson, Bishop of Newcastle, whose diocese incorporated Lindisfarne from which St. Cedd had started his voyage south. The Bishop preached again in the Cathedral on Sunday July 4th to launch a weeklong Summer Festival which featured an exhibition of Cathedral archives; a talk on Chelmsford and its bishops; the play *I Will Arise*, first performed in the ruins of Coventry Cathedral; a concert by the Chelmsford Singers and the Essex Symphony Orchestra; and a recital by Sir William McKie, Organist of Westminster Abbey.[12] Not strictly connected with the celebrations, the first series of Keene Lectures began in the Spring.[13]

Bishop Falkner Allison, followed by Bishop's Chaplain John Barrow lead
Archbishop Geoffrey Fisher (fourth in line), May 8th 1954:
Chelmsford Cathedral Knightbridge Library

This 1954 Summer Festival inspired a repeat in 1955 at the end of May
and beginning of June[14] at which it was appropriate that John Dykes-Bower,
the Consultant Architect's brother and Organist of St. Paul's Cathedral,
should play a recital. The festival comprised a daily event, some by visiting
professional musicians and others by local musical or drama groups. The
future Poet Laureate John Betjeman and Basil Spence, who was to be
architect of the new Coventry Cathedral, also came to give talks earlier in
the year.[15]

In 1955 Provost Gordon returned to Provost Morrow's idea of
factory services. On May 1st he held the first annual Industrial Sunday
when the Cathedral was fully decorated with products of local industry:
it had been held for some years in Writtle Church but the Vicar there
had always felt its proper home was the Cathedral:[16] four years later this
service was the first to be televised from the Cathedral. On July 3rd 1955
Sunday morning service was broadcast to London and the north, the

latter as Provost Eric Gordon was well-known there: complaints were later received that the broadcast went to the wrong radio regions and missed the north entirely.[17]

From October 26th 1954 the Cathedral had a new dedication: it became the Cathedral Church of St. Mary the Virgin, St. Peter and St. Cedd.[18] The Patronal Festival continued to be on July 2nd although St. Peter would be remembered on his saint's day, June 29th, [19] and in 1956 the Bishop nominated the day of St. Cedd's death, October 26th, as the saint's day for St. Cedd and the Saints of Essex, the latter to comprise Mellitus, Erkenwald, Ethelburga, Osyth and Roger Niger as the better known and documented.[120] The triple dedication now allowed the Chapter and the Cathedral Council to end the uncertainty surrounding the names of the Cathedral's chapels on either side of the east end of the nave: from 1958 the North Chapel would become the Chapel of St. Cedd and the Saints of Essex and the South Chapel the Chapel of St. Peter.[21] In 1952 the Cathedral had also instituted a Dedication Festival on September 18th, the anniversary of the re-opening of St. Mary's in 1803 after the collapse of the nave roof.[22]

Could Chelmsford now cease to be the Cinderella amongst cathedrals and mature into something befitting its triple dedication? Sir Charles Nicholson's grand plan for a new cathedral still hung at the west end and remained a constant lure. Interest was renewed when the area just to the north of the Cathedral, bounded by Legg Street, New Street, Church Street and Cottage Place, came up for development. The Chelmsford Borough authorities were aware that the Cathedral's needs should have precedence and did not want to make a move until the Diocese was ready with its plans. Provost Gordon had hoped that 1964, the Diocese's Golden Jubilee, would have been a focus for a major new development but that would now need to be advanced.[23] In 1956 he wrote to his congregation:

"The plan is that the area concerned should be developed for office premises but that those premises should take the shape of three sides of a rectangle with the open side facing the Cathedral, the intervening space being kept open and planted with grass [a Cathedral Precinct] . . . to provide the County Town with a centre worthy of its great position in the County."[24]

To guarantee the land acquisition Sir John Ruggles-Brise and Lieutenant-Colonel John Oxley Parker organised a private appeal to raise sufficient money to enable the Cathedral to match pledges by the County and Borough Councils: this ensured that the precinct was designated in the County Development Plan.[25]

Provost Gordon waxed even more lyrical when addressing the Diocese:

> "One day the Diocese will rise in its might, determined that the present Cathedral is inadequate for its needs. A population of two million and a Diocese with five hundred parishes need a much greater Cathedral than one which can only hold eleven hundred people at its utmost . . . Of these eleven hundred only a very few hundred are in the body of the church and therefore in the heart of the worship. Sir Charles Nicholson's inspiring plans of 1920 still hang on the Cathedral walls . . . The great thing is to keep the vision clearly in our minds whilst we take steps to preserve the site and its surroundings and to make the present building as lovely and useful as we can."[26]

Making the building more lovely and useful was already under way. In 1954 all except the Chapter House and vestries were re-wired and much of it re-lighted.[27] The North Chapel or Chapel of St. Cedd and the Saints of Essex as it was about to become, was lime-washed and refurnished in memory of Provost Morrow; it was dedicated on November 15th 1955. The Chapel of St. Peter would be dedicated to Provost Waller in 1961.[28] The high altar cross incorporated the pectoral cross given by the parish to Frank Johnson in 1894 who had given it to Bishop Stevens of Barking, Mrs Waller's grandfather. Over two years the Cathedral Hall stage was enlarged and the whole Hall re-curtained and decorated:

> "We have been much ashamed of it of late years. It does not do for a Cathedral to be associated with a shabby hall."[29]

In the early summer of 1957 a new system of "voice reinforcement apparatus" was installed in the Cathedral, financed by the Keene funds[30] and the Provost received the good news that Richard Herrick, Vicar of Northampton was to be appointed as the first canon residentiary at the Cathedral. After a brief civil service career, he had graduated from the University of Leeds, trained at the College of the Resurrection, Mirfield and served curacies in Portsmouth and Northampton. The gestation period for this first canonry had been 42 years (not as tardy as St. Albans' 59 years)[31] but at last sufficient funds were available for the Diocese to afford his stipend. He would be Diocesan Director of Religious Education in addition to his cathedral duties in which he could relieve the hard-pressed Provost: it may have been his arrival that prompted the decision that Litany would be said regularly on Wednesdays and Fridays from November 6th 1957.[32]

From July 22nd 1957 the whole east end was screened off and a temporary altar placed at the front of the nave so that the roof beams of the chancel and sanctuary could be painted in richly coloured red, blue, black and gold, in imitation of East Anglian medieval church roofs, and illuminated with subdued up-lighting; it was re-opened at a thanksgiving service on December 7th. The cost was met by the L.F. Christy bequest, the Friends of the Cathedral and other legacies. Provost Gordon was delighted with the outcome:

> "The roof of the easternmost half of the sanctuary was of uncoloured oak: the remaining three bays had been painted but grown dark and dull and dim. Now, owing to the skill and imagination of Mr S.E. Dykes Bower, aided by the remarkable firm of artists [R.P. Warton Decor Ltd] who have done the painting, there is a new glory here and our roofs will be one of the great sights of Essex and one of the prides of Chelmsford . . . There are ten coats of arms [in the roof], four facing the congregation and six facing the altar. Those facing the congregation . . . are the entire coats of arms of the dioceses of London, Rochester, St. Albans and Chelmsford . . . The two middle coats of arms on the other sides of the spandrels represent the County of Essex (on the north side) and the Borough of Chelmsford (on the south side). Near the altar there is de Vere on the north side and Bourchier on the south side . . . Immediately behind the chancel arch there is Mildmay on the south side . . . and on the north side the ancient coat of arms of the Abbey of Westminster . . . the Moulsham half of Chelmsford used to belong to the deans of Westminster while the half on our side of the river [Can] belonged to the bishops of London."[33]

And, as a historical curiosity, in the cavity where the timbers join the south wall, the contractors found a clay pipe, a bottle and the names of the workmen who raised the clerestory and installed a new chancel roof in 1877;[34] that was when it was just a parish church. Now a parish church cathedral, the local element was diminishing: in April 1958 the *Cathedral*

News noted that the majority of the people on the Cathedral's electoral roll lived outside the parish boundaries. The lack of locals may explain why the ill-fated Church of England Men's Society had shrunk so much that its meetings had been suspended in 1951.[35]

In 1958 plans for a £15,000 Cathedral Appeal were announced (£273,000 in today's money) to cover pointing and flint renewal on the exterior of the tower and repairs to the decaying stonework of the porch; paying outstanding bills for the interior decoration already completed; and decorating John Johnson's 1803 perpendicular nave ceiling to "give us a carpet of colour above our heads right down the axis of the church."[36] No sooner had Provost Gordon made this announcement than serious flooding in the town on September 5th and a Mayoral Appeal for £10,000 (£182,000) to help flood victims made it necessary to delay for six months when a more ambitious £50,000 Diocesan Appeal was launched (£911,000): the additional money would finance new churches and church halls in the mushrooming urban areas.[37]

Before that happened the churchyard was re-planned to enhance the exterior view of the Cathedral and to anticipate the development of office blocks to the north. On December 18th 1958 Provost Gordon wrote:

> "The avenues of limes . . . are to come down . . . These pollarded limes grow a heavy crop of twigs and young branches and about every four years they have to be cut back to the base. All that is left is a stark ugly trunk and for the next 18 months to two years the trees look . . . utterly unworthy . . . If you want to see how ugly they were, try to see a copy of the Christmas card a few years back . . . Instead of breaking up our open space, we would leave it as one, with the building standing out clearly in the midst . . . Our aim has been to plant trees that can grow to their full stature without mutilation. They must be trees that will grow to a beautiful shape . . . which will blossom at different times of the year . . . We have felt it would be good to have rarer trees and shrubs because they would add interest . . . Some years ago the Borough authorities and the Park Superintendent took over the maintenance of the churchyard . . . as an open space of interest to the whole community."[38]

Today it still is one of Chelmsford's restful quiet spots.

In the new year of 1959 the exterior was wrapped in scaffolding. The Provost wrote:

"After thorough examination from a bos'n's chair it is clear that 300-400 squared stones need replacing or resurfacing . . . Corrosion has removed the stone to a depth of three to six inches. Many of the flints are working loose. Stonework on the south porch is also decaying rapidly with, again, inches worth of corrosion in the stones and the pinnacles."[39]

Restoration of the Tower 1959: Chelmsford Cathedral Knightbridge Library

Clipsham stone, the hardest of the Lincolnshire limestones, would be used and would be more hardwearing than the earlier 15th century Portland stone or the more recent 19th century Bath stone. Sixteen 15th century gargoyles had become unrecognisable and were to be replaced with:

". . . lively and vigorous carvings relevant to Chelmsford and its church. They should fit into a medieval surrounding but not be merely imitative of medieval work."

Thomas Huxley-Jones from Broomfield, a village just to the north of Chelmsford, designed the new carvings. The four central carvings represented the Cathedral and its dedicatees with lilies for St. Mary the Virgin and crossed keys for St. Peter, St. Cedd overlooking his Bradwell Church while a mitre symbolised the modern bishopric; the four corners comprised a harpy, representing the de Veres, a Saracen's Head the Bourchiers, a lion's head the Mildmays and a bear's head, an ancient device associated with the Provost's Gordon clan; a further four represented the traditional interests of Essex and Chelmsford with the sea represented by fishes, the land by sheep, justice by scales and the sword and industry by wheels; the last four represented Chelmsford's history with the arms of the bishops of London and the abbots of Westminster, the former lords of the manors of Chelmsford and Moulsham respectively, a man carrying a load over the 12th century bridge linking the two manors and an eagle's head and the letters SPQR to memorialise Roman Chelmsford.[40]

Thomas Huxley-Jones' gargoyle of man carrying load over the River Can bridge: Chelmsford Cathedral Knightbridge Library

In January 1961 the decoration and cleaning of the remainder of the Cathedral began, to be finished by Easter. The plaster vault, to a point just below the clerestory windows, was coloured in pastel shades and given some upward lighting so that the beautifully coloured roof could be illuminated while the remainder of the building remained dark. At the same time the sickly light from the green clerestory windows in the north aisle, which would diminish the impact of the pastel colours of the ceiling and the honey-white walls, was rectified by the insertion of clear leaded glass akin to that used in the north aisle[41] and two of the four stained glass windows on the south side were moved to the north to provide balance.[42] When that was completed the various monuments in the nave and aisles were cleaned including the glorious Mildmay Monument. But it got worse before it got better: the congregation had to worship for a good many weeks in the two north aisles (from which they could see neither the choir nor the Precentor) and then had to shift to the nave and the south aisle.[43] In 1962 it was decided to replace all heating pipes, financed by the bequests of Mr and Mrs Freedland, rather than continue with spasmodic running repairs and periods in the depths of winter with no heating at all.[44] The timing was impeccable: the winter of 1963 would be the coldest since 1740. Everything was finished for a total cost of £18,740 (£306,000 in current values) compared to the original estimate of £15,000 (£245,000). The Provost thanked the donors:

> "We have received wonderful help from the parishes of the Diocese, from generous gifts up and down the Diocese and county, from the Friends of the Cathedral, from the Friends of Essex Churches, from various charitable trusts and from many other sources. The Cathedral congregation must be proud of the part it has itself played through many individual gifts and particularly through four bazaars which raised between them over £4,000 [£65,300] and two gift days which raised between them nearly £1,500 [£24,500]."[45]

To this justified self-congratulation could be added thanks for the many gifts from faithful members of the congregation of altar frontals, cope and robe cupboards, altar ornaments, a verge and verge rests and other embellishments that appeared so frequently in the pages of the *Cathedral News*. All of these were topped in 1960 by the beautiful Cathedral Banner made by the distinguished ecclesiastical embroiderer, Beryl Dean: on a background of cloth of gold, the front depicted the Virgin Mary, in the

Byzantine style of the famous Ravenna mosaics, together with symbols of the Blessed Trinity, the Holy Spirit and the Star of Bethlehem; on the back was the badge of the donors, the Friends of Chelmsford Cathedral, based on the Cathedral's weathervane.[46] It took her 820 hours of work and had been inspired by a procession in Chartres Cathedral where the sunlight had reflected the gold on the processional banners.[47]

For Bishop Allison it was a question of constant catch-up as the Diocese's population continued to expand, though he was not alone with this problem as all the Home Counties experienced a post-war outflow from London: the Diocese of Rochester in particular saw its population increase from 600,000 to over a million between 1944 and 1954.[48] The condition of Essex's medieval churches also caused concern: the Friends of Essex Churches had already been established in 1951 as a non-denominational organisation to raise funds for their preservation. But, as Frederick Narborough, the Bishop of Colchester wrote, while Bishop Allison was visiting the U.S.A:

> "It is far too big a problem for the church people of the parishes involved . . . The people we need to reach for this purpose are the thousands of Essex people who do not belong to the Church but are proud of their county and its heritage of history and beauty . . . They are the people who . . . value the village church as an essential part of the English scene. Such are our natural allies."[49]

For this and other needs, the revenue to be raised from parishes was increased by 250% in 1954 but a rigorous new annual report on diocesan finance made available to the parishes was persuasive and worked the trick.[50]

Bishop Allison had been a low key diocesan compared to his predecessor, not a difficult accomplishment. But the Church was preoccupied with its own problems and less assertive on the national stage. Restoration and rebuilding of bombed out churches and chapels and the problem of clergy recruitment (the number of curates had halved nationally during the war) affected all dioceses. Church attendance was plummeting from an already low base in the traditional urban mission areas: in 1956 in London only 37 per 1,000 head of population made their Easter Communion (London-over-the-Border would have been no different): at the other end of the scale the figure for the Diocese of Hereford was 172. One historian observed:

"Most of the parsons were in the countryside shivering in their unheated rectories, most of the people were in the towns. But at least in the villages they were, more or less, wanted and knew what to do. If more were moved to the drearier urban areas they could find themselves simply at a loss, unless their style of ministry was altered most drastically."[51]

In addition the Church had been eclipsed by the state in the provision of social welfare and education. Where it still retained a stake as a provider it found itself having to raise even more cash to meet statutory minimum standards.

Geoffrey Fisher, Archbishop of Canterbury, aggravated this sense of inertia. One commentator described him as lacking in "charisma, ideology or theology"[52] with little or no interest in social or political issues, though he undoubtedly suffered by comparison with his extrovert predecessor, the leftward leaning William Temple who had made a huge personal impact as Archbishop of York and then of Canterbury, prompting George Bernard Shaw to admit that "to a man of my generation an archbishop of Temple's enlightenment was a realised impossibility."[53] By contrast Fisher concentrated his mind on the long overdue, but tedious, reform of canon law which had been virtually unaltered since 1603: he was to say later that this task, which took 20 years to complete, was "the most absorbing and all-embracing topic of my archiepiscopate." But one historian observed:

"Not everyone would agree with him as they saw some of the best minds in the Church of England occupied by a task whose relevance in face of the far more crucial developments in Church and State was dubious to say the least."[54]

Fisher also set up the Liturgical Commission in 1955 to revise the Prayer Book and make the Eucharist more central to Anglican worship; again some saw this as a "sign of unhealthy introversion."[55]

Another of Fisher's concerns was the divisions between the churches, though he had no olive branches for Rome:

"I grew up with an inbred opposition to anything that came from Rome. I objected to their doctrine; I objected to their methods of reasoning; I objected to their methods of operating in this country. So I grew up and saw no reason for differing from that opinion as the years went by."[56]

Pope Pius XII's 1950 proclamation of the doctrine of the Virgin Mary's Assumption into Heaven, for which there was no scriptural evidence, under the cloak of papal infallibility, would have reinforced the Archbishop's scorn for the ancient enemy. Bishop Allison gave him full support and recommended *Infallible Fallacies* published by the S.P.C.K. in response to the official attitude of the Roman Catholic Church to the Church of England:

> "Christian charity does not exclude us from the duty of standing up for our Church when it is attacked."[57]

It was in relationships with the Non-Conformist churches where Fisher sought progress:

> "It is not possible yet nor desirable that any Church should merge its identity in a newly constituted union. What I desire is that I should freely be able to enter their churches and they mine, in the sacrament of the Lord and in the full fellowship of worship."[58]

It was in this context that Bishop Allison caught Fisher's eye. His liberal evangelical outlook made him receptive to the Non-Conformist churches with whom he led discussion as Fisher's chief emissary. He was able to handle the workload. Because he was intellectually very quick and clear, writing succinct letters, his national and ecumenical responsibilities did not prevent him from being an effective pastoral bishop.[59]

Bishop Allison's relationship with the Archbishop of Canterbury had been very close. Some saw them as like minds and tipped Falkner Allison as a possible successor at Lambeth Palace.[60] That was not to be the case but in 1961, with his Cathedral now beginning to emerge from obscurity, he was elevated to the Bishopric of Winchester, an ancient and prestigious see. However, that was within a national scene where the Church in general was perceived as:

> ". . . sailing on an even keel, content with the old tried ways and the conventional orthodoxies. There was an atmosphere of

complacency . . . Bishops, deans and archdeacons dressed, as they had done for centuries, in aprons and gaiters."[61]

The bewildering sixties would soon see traditional restraints and institutions challenged as never before.

CHAPTER 20

A Beautifully Enclosed World

In January 1962 the name of the fifth Bishop of Chelmsford was announced, John Gerhard Tiarks, the Provost of Bradford Cathedral, who was already well-known nationally as a frequent religious radio broadcaster on the old B.B.C. Light Programme.[1] He had come through the familiar route of Westminster School, Trinity College, Cambridge and the evangelically-inclined Ridley Hall, before starting his ministry in Merseyside at Southport whence he moved via incumbencies in Liverpool and Widnes to become Provost of Bradford Cathedral in 1944. He was consecrated as a bishop in Westminster Abbey by Michael Ramsey, Archbishop of Canterbury, on February 24th 1962 and enthroned in Chelmsford Cathedral on March 10th just before his 59th birthday. Some assumed that he must be connected with the extraordinarily wealthy Tiarks merchant banking family, but he was at pains to point out that he was only a parson's son and that he had won his places at school and university through meritocratic scholarship:[2] indeed his personal bearing was not at all flamboyant and, as an evangelical bishop, he never wore a mitre.

His elevation had not been without controversy: Christopher Wansey, Rector of St. Mary's, Woodford, had sent a telegram to the Queen at Balmoral in August 1961 asking her to grant the Chapter and Provost the right to elect a new bishop from a short-list of names. He had also organised a petition of 4,822 signatories, including over 100 clergy, delivered to the Home Office in September, objecting to the process whereby the Cathedral Chapter was presented with just one name to rubber-stamp. The Provost and members of the Chapter wrote to the press dissociating themselves from this action[3] but Wansey had tapped into a deep well of dissatisfaction within the Church.

These farcical procedures gave as much freedom of choice as rigged elections in the Soviet Union, though with less sinister intent. Wansey, of course, was objecting to the principle, not the man. He is still remembered fondly in church circles for his parody—"I will lift up mine eyes to the Town Hall whence cometh my Bishop"—because he had seen the Prime Minister's Appointments Secretary, who dealt with ecclesiastical appointments, entering Southend Town Hall during the recent episcopal vacancy.[4] When John Tiarks retired in 1971 his successor, John Trillo, was chosen only after full consultation about the Diocese's needs with the Provost, Chapter and other interested parties.

Bishop Tiarks en route to his enthronement, not the Annual Ball,
March 10th 1962: Chelmsford Cathedral Knightbridge Library

As the new bishop contemplated his journey south the Master of the Music went north. On January 22nd 1962 Derek Cantrell, after 10 years in Chelmsford, moved to the post of Organist and Choirmaster at Manchester

Cathedral where he served until 1977. The *Cathedral News* commented that he had seen the Cathedral through the change to the *Oxford Psalter*, with its new methods of pointing that fitted the words to the rhythm of speech and, at the end of his time, to the *Hymns Ancient and Modern Revised*: above all "he has the great art of making boys enjoy their singing."[5] He had also introduced a successful series of three organ recitals each winter and contributed to amateur music making with the Chelmsford Singers, formed in 1927 and conducted from 1945 by the Cathedral's Master of Music, and the Essex Symphony Orchestra, formed in 1952.

He was replaced by 25-year-old Philip Ledger who thereby became the youngest person in such a position in England. The *Cathedral News* described him as "one of the outstanding musicians nurtured by Cambridge University in recent years."[6] At King's College he had worked alongside the legendary David Willcocks, gained first class honours in the preliminary examination parts I and II of the Music Tripos, a Mus.B. with distinction in the performing section and an F.R.C.O. with the Limpus and Read Prizes attached. He was also responsible for the musical side of Aaron Copland's opera *The Tender Land*, premiered in Europe in the presence of the composer, and shuttled between Chelmsford and Cambridge until the project was completed. There was a deeply spiritual side to Philip Ledger's music:

> "Even the simplest pieces of music have the power to evoke memories, to change and elevate our moods and to remind us of things beyond the daily worries . . . It is not always easy to be in touch with that part of God within ourselves but music, beauty and stillness help us to do so."[7]

Philip Ledger continued the Festival which, in his last year, Derek Cantrell had moved from May to October. His first venture included chamber music performed by himself, Gervase de Peyer and Cecil Aronowitz; *The Three Temptations* and *The Death of Adam* (a Cornish medieval mystery play) performed by the Royal Academy of Dramatic Art; Benjamin Britten's *Missa Brevis* sung by the cathedral choir, King Edward VI Grammar School choral society and King's College choral scholars as part of a concert of English music; an Italian Renaissance exhibition of items from the Victoria and Albert Museum; and, to the mixed feelings of the Cathedral's neighbours, another attempt by local bellringers on the Stedman Cinques Peal which they had failed to achieve the previous year. Just over a month later he introduced an Advent Carol Service which had been a tradition at

King's College, Cambridge since 1934, an innovation of the then Dean, Eric Milner-White who had also introduced King's world famous Christmas Service of Nine Lessons and Carols in 1918.

With the Bishop and Master of the Music barely in place the Cathedral received its first visit from the monarch when Elizabeth II and the Duke of Edinburgh came on Maundy Thursday, April 19th 1963, to distribute the Royal Maundy to 74 old people, a double multiple of the Queen's age. It also gave the choir a unique opportunity to sing with the Gentlemen and Choristers of the Chapel Royal. Eric Gordon seized the opportunity to point out the cramped setting for such an occasion: "Provost Plans a Dream Cathedral" screamed the *Essex Chronicle* headline on April 3rd, but a dream it remained.

The Queen and the Duke of Edinburgh with Provost Eric Gordon
carrying the Queen's bouquet, Maundy Thursday 1963:
Chelmsford Cathedral Knightbridge Library

In 1963 the new post of Assistant Master of Music was created to aid the continued development and enrichment of Cathedral music. Geoffrey Beckett had, for 16 years, played the organ when the Master of Music was away but had not been specifically a choral trainer. He would still be available for emergencies but the new Assistant Master of Music would be John Jordan B.A., F.R.C.O., B.Mus.. He had been a chorister at Birmingham Cathedral and had won the Organ Scholarship from King Edward's School, Birmingham to Emmanuel College, Cambridge when only 16, waiting a year before he went up. He would combine his organ and choral work with a full-time teaching post at Chelmsford's King Edward VI Grammar School[8] and would be an early beneficiary, at Chapter House choir rehearsals, of the new grand piano, purchased through bequests from music lovers.[9] In the June 1964 *Cathedral News* Philip Ledger wrote:

> "All who sing in the Cathedral choir have benefited since last September from the musicianship and enthusiasm that Mr John Jordan has brought to the post of Assistant Master of Music. This has been felt particularly in the performance of difficult . . . anthems and settings where his accompaniments on the organ have been of the highest order."

But the balance of his choir was not quite right:

> "The bass part has something of a baritone quality at the moment. It is a pity that the race of men with a bottom E that carries to the end of the church, seems to be dying out, at any rate in Chelmsford."

The 1963 October Festival followed its familiar pattern and included an exhibition of Victoria and Albert Museum medieval manuscripts; five performances by the Royal Academy of Dramatic Art of Samuel Beckett's *Murder in the Cathedral*; a recital by Imogen Holst and the Purcell Singers; a lecture and recital by Isobel Baillie; and, most excitingly for the locals, the newly married Philip and Mary Ledger (née Wells), principal soprano at Covent Garden, making music together. She had visited the Cathedral in January 1963 for a performance of *Amahl and the Night Visitors*, a new operatic venture in the Cathedral, and clearly liked more than just the music. Festival finances caused concern, relying on generous subscriptions and guarantees from individuals: the observation that "we approach this tenth Festival with the 'kitty' dangerously low"[10] would become a familiar refrain over the years. In the meantime the Keene funds had helped improve the organ, celebrated in the winter of 1963-4 by a formidable trio of recitalists: Philip Ledger himself, Allan Wicks (who had just moved to Canterbury Cathedral from Manchester where he had been replaced on the organ stool by Chelmsford's Derek Cantrell) and George Guest of St. John's College, Cambridge (who had been given organ lessons by Roland Middleton in the latter's stint at Chester just before he came to Chelmsford): all three of them were to be dominant figures in English church music over the next three decades.

1964 was the Diocese's Golden Jubilee year. In May and June nine great services were held as each deanery came on a pilgrimage to the mother church. The Bradwell pilgrimage Eucharist in June was presided over by Chelmsford's former diocesan, Falkner Allison, Bishop of Winchester, and, in the evening, pilgrims were addressed by Donald Coggan, Archbishop of York. The St. Edmundsbury and Chelmsford choirs visited each other for their shared celebrations providing a good swan song for Mr C.G. Herbert who retired after 62 years in the Chelmsford choir.[11] The Royal School of Church Music Summer Course came to Chelmsford for the first time in August with a broadcast on August 12th. On November 27th, Michael Ramsey, Archbishop of Canterbury, preached at the Cathedral. But the pressures ruffled some parochial feathers. The Provost wrote later that year:

> "The Cathedral, like its Provost, leads a double life! The Provost has to be Provost in relation to the Cathedral and Rector in relation to the Parish. The Cathedral itself has to be a mother church to a great Diocese, as well as a parish church to a parish and congregation. The inevitable tensions are well-known, but never so prominent as when an archbishop comes to the Cathedral. We have then to remember that he is visiting the Cathedral because it is a cathedral and therefore it is par excellence a diocesan occasion. Actually many of the congregation are there because they are ringing the bells or singing in the choir or acting as sidesmen or servers, so we do have a great share in the service. I wish we could do more but with great regrets it is impossible."[12]

In the autumn of 1965 Philip Ledger, after a short but very influential stay, moved to Norwich as the first Director of Music at the newly established University of East Anglia. Subsequently, in 1968, he became an artistic director at the Aldeburgh Festival working with Benjamin Britten and Peter Pears, in 1974 the Director of Music at King's College, Cambridge and in 1982 the Principal of the Royal Scottish Academy of Music and Drama (where he came across the young Peter Nardone who would succeed to the same Chelmsford organ stool). He was knighted in 1999.

John Jordan, at 23 years of age, became the new Master of Music and in 1966 Peter Cross a graduate of Christ Church College, Oxford and former Chapel Royal chorister, joined the music staff of King Edward VI Grammar

School and took on the responsibility of cathedral Assistant Master of Music. With his own rapid promotion within the school, he was replaced in 1968 in his dual role by David Sparrow, a graduate of Durham University and, later, a cathedral choirman. The annual pay of the Master of Music was only £600 (£8,120 in today's money) and meant that other sources of income were vital: in John Jordan's case that meant considerable examining work with the Associated Board.[13]

While cathedral music nationally was blossoming, church congregations in general were seeping away: between 1960 and 1970 there was a 19% decline. Greater affluence and choices of affordable social activities allied to the emergence of sixties satire and a strong youth culture left little room for deference to ancient institutions. They had to earn respect rather than assume it, though in a Gallup Poll in 1964 34% of respondents still nominated the priest as the person with the greatest influence for good in the community, just ahead of the doctor. But there would be fewer clergy around in the Church of England as ordinations were to plummet nationally from 636 men in 1963 to 373 in 1973.[14] In this context cathedrals always had an edge with more or less guaranteed clergy quotas, the best music and superb buildings, all subsidised to some degree from diocesan or Church Commission resources, not to mention a lingering social cachet: this could give their congregations a distorted sense of wellbeing.

The Church needed energising. In the case of Chelmsford Cathedral the congregation, no longer dominated by locals, also needed to forge its own identity otherwise its members would be as ships that passed in the night, commuting to and from church as they might do for work, praying alongside other members of the congregation but rarely interacting. Bishop Tiarks followed the earlier lead of Bishop Allison when he wrote:

> "The priesthood of the whole church is a basic concept of both the New Testament and the early fathers . . . The clergy's ministry comes to its full flower when it raises up laymen equipped to exercise the spiritual responsibility to which God has called them within the Body."[15]

Provost Eric Gordon therefore instituted monthly house meetings over the autumn and winter of 1962-3 when 14 groups of about 20 people discussed questions devised by the clergy culminating in a plenary meeting to examine the outcomes. They made a stuttering start, hampered by three months of sub-zero temperatures, but the project served a useful bonding and educational purpose. The Provost also proposed twice yearly parish meetings of the congregation to discuss whatever was of current concern: it would not usurp the roles of the clergy or the Parish Council but would improve two-way communications.[16] Annual Holy Land pilgrimages, starting in 1962 and led by the Provost, also helped. But some of the congregational sessions were rather inward looking. In 1964 they discussed whether fasting was desirable before Holy Communion which, if insisted on, inevitably meant early morning services: the Provost left it to the individual's conscience but introduced the inclusive American practice of blessing the unconfirmed. Rules were also explained: when the congregation should stand to avoid spoiling the first few lines of the hymn or canticle; the procedure for administering the bread and wine; the donning of ornate clergy stoles only for the administration of communion to emphasise the spiritual and pastoral role of administering and to preserve them from wear and tear and dragging on the ground whilst kneeling.[17] Undoubtedly all these matters had their importance but seemed limited in scope.

Embryonic signs of ecumenism were in the air. On December 19th 1963 the Provost reflected on Prime Minister Harold MacMillan's "wind of change" speech in South Africa: the same spirit seemed to be abroad within some of the Christian churches where Cathedral groups had been in earnest conversation with local Methodists. On a broader front Pope John XXIII appeared to have instigated a revolution within the Roman Catholic Church with his extraordinary reforms at the Second Vatican Council: the Provost praised "his sheer warmth and bigness of heart and refusal to be bogged down by prejudice, tradition, custom and habit."[18] Unfortunately the assumption of a radical change in relationships between the old enemies was premature. Cardinal Heenan, born locally in Ilford, was very cautious about the pace of reform and said, in 1970, that ecumenism was a little known word outside some Protestant circles,[19] though the Catholic hierarchy were to find that their congregations were prepared to be more embracing. On what seemed safer ground, there was an exchange of pulpits on January 19th 1964 between the Cathedral and the Congregationalist church in Chelmsford. Provost Gordon wrote:

> "These exchanges are not unity. They are an expression of unity
> of spirit. The vast unchurched masses of our time . . . can never
> be effectively moved by a Christian Church which is quite
> content to worship in little huddles here, there and everywhere;
> satisfied with their own ways of doing things, wanting no change,

claiming a certain sanctity for their traditions, more content with maintaining things as they are and keeping the parish pump going, than going out as one Church to serve and suffer for a crucified Christ."[20]

On May 28th 1964 Provost Gordon again challenged his readers:

"The true Christian insight is that all of us in our different branches of the Church have a compound of truth and error. Do we elevate our little mannerisms and habits of worship into matters of principle, when in fact they are simply the way we have been brought up and are things we have accepted quite uncritically from the past?"[21]

Anglicans set a 75% majority in Convocation as the hurdle to be jumped if unity with the Methodists were to be achieved: the Methodists set the same figure and just managed it in July 1969. But the two Anglican Convocations could muster only 66% with slightly lower figures at the General Synod, a black day for the Church when most outsiders who had any interest struggled to detect the significant differences that would justify such caution.

These setbacks were occurring in a somewhat febrile theological climate. John Robinson, Bishop of Woolwich, had published *Honest to God* in 1963, in which he asserted that there was no anthropomorphised God Creator out in the blue yonder to whose realms men and women passed after death: rather there was an ultimate reality and an embodiment of love that was the ground of humanity, a God within each person. He was rehashing ideas that were common currency in elite theological circles. They were to be taken to even more extreme conclusions in coming decades by theologians such as Don Cupitt. But Michael Ramsey, Archbishop of Canterbury, felt that many who read the newspaper reports "might not have had . . . the necessary brains for reading the book",[22] a patronising view that sought a simplistic literal faith for the masses while serious theology was reserved as high table talk for the episcopal cognoscenti. The *Church Times* also took John Robinson to task:

"It is not every day that a bishop goes on public record as apparently denying almost every doctrine of the Church in which he holds office."[23]

Some alleged that the faith of simple believers would be undermined, even though faith in the miraculous does not require reason as a basis. But one church historian bewailed the absence of sensible debate:

"The hysterical reaction of many was distressing because it indicated a deep insecurity. The controversy tended to polarise clergy and laity into radicals and conservatives."[24]

Hot on the heels of *Honest to God* came the 1964 Paul Report, subtitled *The Deployment and Payment of the Clergy*. It painted a dire picture:[25] half the benefices of the Church of England covered only 10% of the population and 10% of the benefices covered one third of the population; one third of the clergy were under-employed and a quarter grossly overworked; in one diocese one incumbent's stipend was £400 and another's was £4,702 (£6,320 and £74,300 in modern values). The report made 62 recommendations which included changing the parson's tenure from freehold to leasehold; regional appointment bodies and a Central Clergy Staff Board; a new form of parochial unit ("the major parish") staffed by a college of clergy to cope with high density urban parishes and widely-scattered rural parishes; a national salary structure and common stipends fund; the pooling of all endowed income; the formation of a parochial lay apostolate; and street organisation based on house communions to enhance lay ministry. Critics said that the abolition of patronage and the erosion of the freehold would create a centralised ecclesiastical bureaucracy with a civil service mentality and that time taken for implementation would divert attention from evangelism. Supporters believed it unreasonable to expect a business-like approach in parishes and dioceses but not in the overall organisation of the Church's ministry. The Church's predisposition to consensus postponed reforms for 20 years. Leslie Paul had discovered that those who are asked to think the unthinkable often end up talking to themselves.

Provost Eric Gordon had a view on both controversies. He described *Honest to God* as:

". . . a tendentious . . . and a confusing book, with much ill-digested material . . . but saying to the Church what must be said in every generation, 'Is your Gospel truly relevant? If so, and of course it is, have you made it seem so?'"

So the right question had been asked in the wrong way and, in any case, it was all a matter of presentation. Equally he did not envisage Leslie Paul's proposed reforms contributing to Gospel relevance. The Provost was a conservative, echoing others' defensive fears that an incumbent no longer protected by freehold would have his freedom of speech curtailed "through fear of powerful laymen in the congregation." He also doubted whether:

> ". . . releasing numbers of elderly men from the countryside
> [would] improve the situation of the Church in the towns . . .
> Has sufficient note been taken of the greater time it takes to do
> the same amount of work in the countryside?"

But that did not answer the pressing problem of the towns which was the very reason for the birth of the Diocese of Chelmsford and its Cathedral. He took the view that the reforms in governance of the Church since 1919 had made no effective difference:

> "Still the conversion of England eludes us . . . The quality of lives
> of Christian people are infinitely more important than the matters
> dealt with by Leslie Paul and . . . one of the temptations of our
> 20th century world is to think that if we get Leslie Paul's matters
> right then the others will follow."

In other words, the quality of a diminishing number of Christian lives would somehow permeate the unchurched masses by osmosis, the implication being that there were insufficient such exemplars.[26]

The Precentor, J.A. Bowering, standing in for the Provost while he took a group to the Holy Land, tried to pursue these themes, but seemed to lose sight of first principles. He dwelt at some length on the perceived problems of the Young People's League (Y.P.L.):

> "We have a strong nucleus who are in no way, apart from the
> Y.P.L., attached to the church. These we have to persuade and
> sometimes compel, to come to church. If we did not we would
> open our doors to any who wished to come."

But was not the established church supposed to be open to all comers without a preliminary character test? How did this fit in with the Provost's regret that conversion had proved elusive? The Precentor continued:

"As it is true of coin of the realm that bad money drives out good,
so also with youth clubs, the worse drive away the better."

But this created a dilemma. Were church-run organisations private clubs to be limited to church attendees and, if so, how did this square with the church's evangelical mission? The Precentor tried to address this:

"The Church has two main ways of going about its work in society. First, by separating itself from that society; by making a church school, by making a church club and hoping and praying that all who go to that school and club by the grace of God have that seed of faith sown within them; second, by infiltrating society and acting as the leaven in the loaf."

But not, it would seem, a third option, that of running organisations for the so-called unchurched, accepting them for who they were and allowing the leavening process time to work. Rather he took the view that provision of youth services should now be left to local authorities with whom it was "senseless to compete" but by the same logic that might also mean surrendering church schools to the state. He did not know which way to turn:

"Neither way is necessarily better or more effective: both ways are jeopardised by the mediocre Christian." [27]

So, like the Provost, he felt the inadequacy of Christians in general was at the heart of the problem, an old Pauline cry which, however, ran the risk of developing into sanctimoniousness.

The figures were stark: the confirmation rate was only 26 per 10,000 people in the Diocese of Chelmsford compared to 41 nationally and 47 Easter communicants compared to 68 nationally, with the Diocese of Hereford, on this criterion, still the most Christian of all. [28] Chelmsford's comparatively low figures for confirmations and communicants were shared with London, Southwark and some densely populated dioceses in the midlands and the north. And although the Diocese's baptisms were well above the national average the retention rate was low.

The variation between dioceses was, at least, to be diminished between cathedrals: the 1963 Cathedrals Measure would provide two residentiary canons for each parish church cathedral and their stipends, and that of the Provost, would be paid centrally by the Church Commissioners.

Chelmsford's second residentiary canon, Gordon Hewitt, arrived in September 1964, from St. Andrew's, Oxford with diocesan responsibility for post-ordination training. He had previous experience as a residentiary canon in Sheffield where he had been Diocesan Secretary for Education. He very soon penned an aspirational article that was rather more proactive than those of the Provost and Precentor. He wanted an open church without laity and clergy jockeying for position, welcoming towards Christians of other churches, a Bible translated into a modern context and a church that was openly informed and sensitive to the local community:[29] it was neatly worded and clear on the ends but not the means.

There was a further re-jigging of the Cathedral's clergy in 1966 involving a change in the Precentor's role:

> "For some time past we have regarded the Cathedral Precentorship as the equivalent of a very responsible second curacy. We have had first-class people and some of them have stayed much longer than they need have done: then they have gone on to their first living. From now onwards we are regarding the Precentorship as the equivalent of at least a first living."[30]

That would give it more status and attract more experienced men. T.G. Pughe, a former Canterbury Cathedral Head Chorister and with two Liverpool curacies behind him, would be the first of them.

Enhancement of the fabric of the Cathedral continued. The Friends of the Cathedral planned to have the building floodlit on special occasions:[31] the Borough Council chipped in on the cost.[32] A perpetual red light representing the Holy Spirit was installed, kindled from a light which Bishop Tiarks ignited at St. Peter's-on-the-Wall on the eve of Easter in 1964.[33] The Chapel of St. Peter had already been refurbished and work on the Chapel of St. Cedd and the Saints of Essex was advancing in stages to fit in with the work on the Thomas Mildmay monument which,[34] in the summer of 1966, was finally restored in full technicolour: "of course, now it looks a little brash . . . in a month or two it will mellow." Messrs Campbell Smith who did the work had undertaken similar projects at Gloucester and were scheduled to do so at Ely. On the bishops' throne they also coloured the coats of arms of the London, Rochester and St. Albans dioceses to which Chelmsford had belonged before 1914, of Bishop Frank Johnson, in whose memory the throne had been presented, and of the County of Essex. The de Vere and Bourchier arms outside the west door were also re-tinted.

The front two pews in the nave were removed and the new front pews enlarged—"the originals were so constructed that it was almost torture to our lord lieutenants, high sheriffs and mayors to sit in them"[35]—which also saved the untidy business of removing the front pews every time a stage was erected or an orchestra visited.

The old military flags had been taken down in the 1961 redecoration which left the north aisle looking much tidier, but in 1926 they had been handed by Essex County Council to the care of the Cathedral and there was a pressing obligation to restore them to view.[36] The five Essex Militia flags and the one Union Jack would be re-hung over the north door.[37] The Militia was a local civilian force raised to defend England against a Napoleonic invasion: Chelmsford was to have been the rallying point if the French penetrated north of the Thames. The banner of Field Marshal Sir Evelyn Wood was transferred to the Cathedral from Westminster Abbey and hung near the font: he was a veteran of the Crimea (where his wounds had been tended by Florence Nightingale), the Indian Mutiny (where he won the Victoria Cross) and campaigns in the Egyptian, Ashanti, Zulu and Boer Wars.[38] He was through and through an Essex man, starting his life in Cressing, spending three years in charge of Eastern Command at Colchester, retiring to Upminster and dying in Harlow. It was fitting that the cathedral town, which in 1903 had bestowed its freedom on this great soldier, should house his memorial.

In the mid 1960s plans for the modernisation of Chelmsford town centre were presented which would impinge on the vicinity of the Cathedral. A Ministry of Housing and Local Government public inquiry met to consider the positioning of a new criminal court and police station in New Street north of Guy Harlings and to the east of the Cathedral. For many years the Cathedral and Diocese had intended to build a Cathedral Close in the grounds of Guy Harlings. The Provost explained the situation:

> "Almost more than any other diocese we have been compelled to deal with new housing areas and their urgent pastoral and building problems . . . It is important that a great diocese like ours should have a centre . . . It was first proposed to plant the whole of the Court House in the Guy Harlings estate: this may have arisen from the conviction that the Church would never develop its Cathedral Close and that this important site in the middle of Chelmsford was virtually going begging. We made it clear to the public authorities that our intention was definite and practical:

we then came to an agreement to cede a small corner of Guy
Harlings estate and also land we owned in Marriages Square so
that the Court House could be built where the public authorities
wanted it. We were reluctant to do this but felt it right to agree
for the sake of peace."

The draft planning for the Cathedral Close comprised houses for the
Provost, four residentiary canons, the Precentor, the Succentor and the
Master of Music:

> "The church . . . serves the community . . . It is not being selfish
> when it says that in its desire to serve the community it needs this
> land for the precise purpose for which it has preserved it."[39]

In 1966 Provost Gordon announced that he would be leaving
Chelmsford: he would be returning to his Manx roots to become Bishop
of Sodor and Man, a tiny diocese comprising the southern islands off the
west coast of Scotland and the Isle of Man. He was consecrated as bishop
in York Minster on September 29th, paid homage to the Queen on October
18th and was enthroned in Peel Cathedral on the Isle of Man on October
28th. On June 27th the Chelmsford Cathedral bell ringers rang 5,005 changes
of a Stedman Cinques Peal as a compliment.[40] The Bishop said that Eric
Gordon had "transformed this Cathedral during the time of his Provostship
and he did much to make the Diocese more aware of the Mother Church."[41]
Happily he was to make an unexpectedly joyous return in 1971 to marry
the widowed Gwyneth Huxley-Jones who gave to the Cathedral the bronze
cast, *Christus*, on which her husband had been working at the time of his
death: it was mounted on the south wall of the sanctuary.[42]

During the Provost's last five years one could sense the emergence of a
more hesitant church. That Eric Gordon's tenure of office should end with
the Cathedral fighting for its Close was, of course, coincidental. But there
was also a deeper significance that one commentator on the modern church
has noted:

> "A cathedral close is a beautifully enclosed world. When you walk
> into it, you think, 'The world's all right after all'. This is precisely
> what some evangelicals hate about cathedrals: the world is not all
> right and cathedrals are inward-looking clusters of comfort, not
> going *out there* very much."[43]

CHAPTER 21

Time of Crisis

In 1968 Bishop Tiarks told the Diocesan Conference:

> "This was a time of crisis for the Church . . . of the same dimension as the Reformation of 400 years ago."

The welfare state, he said, had been built on the work of 18th and 19th century Christian social pioneers but had now made "the function of the Church in the world less obvious"[1] and had led to a shrinkage in the number of committed church members. This was over-simplistic. It was true that those wishing to improve society could do so through state-financed education, social or health services or through secular international peace, environmental and relief organisations. But by the 1960s falling church attendance had a great deal more to do with an educated middle-class, traditionally the backbone of Anglican congregations, declining to believe in the miracles of the Resurrection and the Ascension and no longer subject to social pressures outwardly to conform: many had not carelessly lapsed but consciously decided. The Church tended to ignore this reality and get sidetracked into peripheral issues of language and presentation.

The Bishop may also have been surprised that parish life in urban Essex was less developed than in the Lancashire and Yorkshire towns from which he had come, where there was stronger community identity and civic pride. The uniting of rural benefices, sometimes three villages to one minister, was well-advanced in Essex and the town populations, many of them newly arrived, were more socially disconnected from the Church and each other. He accepted Leslie Paul's analysis of the Church's weaknesses but argued for patient evolution, believing that the Church was earthed in the parishes to which the development of a true lay ministry could give new life.[2] For without that lay ministry the declining number of clergy would barely be able to service the needs of existing congregations, let alone reach out to new ones. And, like each of his predecessors, he bewailed church disunity as "an offence against our Lord and his will"[3] but stressed that unity must be motivated by a "burning desire to evangelise"[4] not just by a desire to huddle together for warmth.

However, the baptism argument amongst the clergy in the Diocese made it questionable whether a united ministry of laity and clergy would ever get off the ground. Some clergy were refusing baptism to non-churchgoers. The Bishop pointed out that, by canon law, they could recommend delaying baptism but were not free to refuse it;[5] if they must refuse then they should resign their living, a position that was never enforced. After interminable committee meetings, a clergy conference at Butlins at Clacton and a clergy synod at the Cathedral to examine the theology of baptism, a consensus was reached in 1968 much along the lines the exhausted Bishop wanted.[6] It was yet another demonstration of internal disunity, to be repeated many times on different issues in future decades, which made the Church resemble a political party, where one's most vehement opponents are more likely to be found inside than outside the fold: ironically, political parties, struggling to contain their dissident wings, usually describe themselves as a broad church.

Provost Hilary Connop Price:
Chelmsford Cathedral Knightbridge Library

The new Provost, Hilary Martin Connop Price, a personal friend of Bishop Tiarks from the latter's time as Provost of Bradford,[7] took up his post in 1967, aged 55, just as the baptism controversy was reaching its peak. He had graduated at the Queens' College, Cambridge and trained at Ridley Hall. He was ordained in 1938 and served a curacy at Hersham in Surrey before appointment as Chaplain of Portsmouth Cathedral in 1940 at the height of the blitz, followed in 1941 by another curacy for five years at Holy Trinity, Cambridge. He was also a chaplain in the Royal Air Force Volunteer Reserve from 1943 to 1946 and for a time was stationed in Essex at R.A.F. Hornchurch. In 1946 he became Vicar of St. Gabriel, Bishop Wearmouth and then Rector of Newcastle-under-Lyme in 1956.

In the light of Christopher Wansey's protests at the time of Bishop Tiarks' appointment it was appropriate that Hilary Connop Price should have been a member of the Howick Commission which had examined the whole process of appointing bishops: sadly, it proved to be a fruitless exercise as the Commission's 1964 report was brusquely rejected by the Church Assembly. Lord Howick, a colonial governor and high commissioner in a sequence of African colonies, treated cathedral chapters rather like local tribesmen, to be kept at a distance with decision-making remaining in the hands of the great white chiefs. The Church Assembly welcomed his recommendation that a diocese looking for a bishop should establish a vacancy-in-see committee to draw up a statement of the diocese's needs for perusal by the archbishops. But the idea that the archbishops would submit two or three recommended names from which the prime minister would choose and that the appointment would be confirmed by letters patent, by-passing the cathedral chapter, were rejected: such processes would centralise power in the hands of the archbishops, to whom all aspiring bishops would need to pay court and might even diminish diocesan bishops' influence over suffragan appointments.[8]

A second commission, chaired by Professor Owen Chadwick, was appointed in 1970. His wonderfully lucid and often wry tomes on church history were evidence of a first-class mind that was not uncritical of the Church he loved. He recommended that bishops should be appointed by an electoral college representing both the diocese and the Church at large. The General Synod, which in 1970 had replaced the Church Assembly, agreed. In 1976 they formed a Crown Appointments Commission of 12 members comprising the two archbishops, three members elected by the House of Clergy and three by the House of Laity, to whom would be added four appointees from the vacancy-in-see committee of whichever diocese was looking for a bishop. Although the Church wished the monarch, as Supreme Head of the Church of England, to continue to make the appointment, which in reality would mean the prime minister, the latter would be given a stronger steer as the Crown Appointments Commission would submit two names in order of preference.[9]

That still left the question open as to whether diocesan boundaries in England needed readjustment in the light of the redrawing of local government boundaries. In 1965 the old London County Council had been abolished and replaced by a Greater London authority to oversee strategic issues that affected the whole capital complemented by 32 boroughs, plus the City of London, to provide local services. In 1966 the Redcliffe-Maud Commission was appointed to make recommendations for reform of boundaries outside London and it was clear that the inherited 19th century labyrinth of counties, county boroughs, boroughs and rural and district councils would be abandoned.

The Archbishop's Commission on the Organisation of the Church in London and the South-East, which reported in 1967, felt that diocesan and local authority boundaries should continue, as far as possible, to be coterminous. Based on the known new structure in London, the Commission proposed that Greater London be divided into five dioceses of London, Southwark, Barking, Croydon and Kensington. The proposed Diocese of Barking, which would be extracted from the Diocese of Chelmsford, would comprise the new boroughs of Barking, Newham, Redbridge and Havering, formerly in Essex, plus Hackney and Tower Hamlets. In anticipation of the Redcliffe-Maud proposals, which were pretty much an open secret, a second option was put forward. Once again there would be a Diocese of Barking (but, this time, adding only Tower Hamlets to the four "Essex" boroughs). The Diocese of St. Albans and what remained of the Diocese of Chelmsford would then be split up to create five smaller north-east Home Counties dioceses of St. Albans, Hertford, Chelmsford, Colchester and Southend. They would fit in with the probable truncation of Essex whereby Colchester, Tendring and an area north of Braintree would merge with southern Suffolk in a new authority to be called Ipswich, Suffolk and North-East Essex; Saffron Walden would be placed in a new Cambridge-South Fens authority; and Harlow, the west of Epping Forest and western Uttlesford would be subsumed into a new East Hertfordshire authority.

Bishop Tiarks favoured the first option which amputated less of his territory[10] and was reasonably consistent with the further subdivision that

Edgar Jacob, Bishop of St. Albans, had envisaged back in 1907. But if the second option were chosen, where would the cathedrals be sited? Provost Hilary Connop Price was put in charge of a Church Assembly committee which was to examine this very question as it applied to south-east England.[10] He seemed to be fated: like the Howick Commission it would lead nowhere.

The Redcliffe-Maud Commission's final report proposed the creation of three metropolitan areas—Merseyside, South East Lancashire/North East Cheshire and the West Midlands—each with eight boroughs, akin to the London structure, and 58 new unitary authorities which would cut a swath through the old county structure. The Labour government of Harold Wilson was prepared to run with the proposals and added two more metropolitan areas, West Yorkshire and South Hampshire. Organised groups leapt to the defence of the counties: cricket-lovers, masters of the county hunts and those with military connections, where county identification was paramount, were infuriated as was anyone with even the slightest sense of history. Labour lost the 1970 General Election and the new Conservative government under Edward Heath, with its strength in the shires, rejected the Commission's proposals, though it did introduce its own reforms in 1974, creating six metropolitan counties but leaving the shire counties more or less as they were.

The Church now had no need to change and quietly backed off from tinkering with its own diocesan boundaries, though Bishop Tiarks did designate the five "Essex" London boroughs of Barking, Havering, Newham, Redbridge and Waltham Forest as a semi-autonomous episcopal area where the Bishop of Barking would carry out all institutions and confirmations and have oversight of parishes and the clergy, including the selection of ordination candidates.[11] William Chadwick, the suffragan bishop at the time, reckoned it would prepare the way for an eventual legal division into a separate diocese,[12] but that never transpired. This internal management decision did not formally affect Chelmsford Cathedral's position though it did require a renaming of London-over-the-Border, now that it was back within Greater London's borders, as East London. With the addition of a third suffragan bishopric of Bradwell, created in 1968, the Diocese possessed a stronger and more workable administrative and pastoral structure. However, it did create an inequality between suffragan jurisdictions. That was rectified on William Chadwick's retirement in 1975 when Bishop Trillo announced that a similar shared episcopacy would come into existence, as a five year experiment, whereby each of the other suffragans would have his own area corresponding to the three archdeaconries: the Diocesan Synod made the scheme permanent in 1982.[13]

Moving from parish church to cathedral roles requires some adjustment. Provost Hilary Connop Price seems to have been in the midst of thinking through the implications when in 1967, he wrote self-consciously about the generous manning levels of the Cathedral:

> "One contrast that strikes me most forcibly arises from the difference in the number of clergy on the staff—Provost, two canons and two cathedral clergy to serve one church, compared with the single handed incumbent or the incumbent with one curate serving two churches or with two curates serving three churches . . . We have at the Cathedral numbers of visiting clergy, both honorary canons and visiting preachers and it can happen not infrequently that there are four clergy present at an ordinary service which is not a diocesan occasion . . . While I entirely accept that . . . a cathedral has a special ministry to fulfil requiring a large staff, I hope I may never take it for granted and . . . forget the parochial clergy who carry on week by week single handed, preaching twice a Sunday and hard-pressed at festivals . . . They certainly deserve and need a holiday . . . It is my hope that my colleagues and myself will be available as much as is humanly possible to help parochial clergy have the holiday they need. We cannot do more than touch the fringe of the need, but what we can do we will do."[14]

One feels that he was echoing complaints commonly heard in cold and damp parish churches with their one vicar and, if lucky, a curate, which had paid their dues via the Parish Quota, or Family Purse as Bishop Tiarks renamed it, and wondered what they got out of it. Equally one can imagine a queue of people at the Cathedral telling the Provost that he did not really understand how things worked and that it was not all a bed of roses. Two months later he took, or had been persuaded to take, a broader view when he wrote:

> "Anyone, like myself, who comes from an ordinary parish church is quickly aware that at the Cathedral there is no separation between week-day and Sunday . . . Holy Communion is celebrated every day and Morning and Evening Prayer are said or sung."[15]

On that very issue of sung services, John Jordan held clear views. At the 1967 Worship and the Arts Association Conference convened at the Cathedral, the Master of Music was forthright in his condemnation of the second-rate:

> "Congregations are aware . . . of the highest professional standards of presentation and performance elsewhere. They had a right to the same standards in church. Why should a congregation whose minister has a good voice be deprived of hearing the Holy Communion sung well just because he is Low Church? Why do so many unmusical Anglo-Catholic priests *insist* on desecrating the Gospel with incompetent intonations?"[16]

If he were a judge parish clergy would need to pass a singing test in addition to having sound views on baptism. Not everyone saw it that way. One commentator on church music noted:

> "Cathedral musicians dread being polluted by evangelical choruses and evangelicals with drums and guitars dread being polluted by the lifelessness of performed anthems. The two sides scoff at each other across a chasm."[17]

They still do. The happy medium was probably Songs of Praise which was televised from the Cathedral on May 26th 1968.

Many in the cathedral congregation would have felt that the radical revision of Holy Communion with the emergence of the Series Two Alternative Communion Service was of more import to their daily lives than the great diocesan structural debates, the baptism dispute or even the vocal qualities of the clergy. Series Two had been approved by the two convocations and the houses of the Church Assembly but could be used only where a parish church council approved by a two-thirds majority: the Cathedral Council did so on September 18th 1966 and ran a successful three-week trial in November. With absolute predictability some paranoid evangelicals in the Church at large were able to read into the new wording of the administration suggestions of transubstantiation and there were others who staunchly or obdurately, depending on one's viewpoint, opposed any change. It was not until July 1967 that negotiations at the highest level produced an acceptable format that could be utilised on a permanent basis. Series Two became surprisingly popular. The Provost, aware of congregational sensitivities, took considerable care to explain the changes and their significance in the *Cathedral News*[18] while also reassuring them that the replacement of 'thee' and 'thou', the normal form of address in 16th century England, by 'you' and getting rid of the '-est' and -edst' verb endings was not irreverent but following the lead of Miles Coverdale and Thomas Cranmer in using contemporary English. The Provost suggested that:

> "Questions of faith can be more clearly expressed in modern language rather than being buried under ancient language, however beautiful."[19]

Traditionalists objected, noting that Shakespearean audiences managed well enough.

By 1968 the Provost felt able to share his thoughts with his congregation about his vision for the Cathedral though, in fact, he concentrated almost exclusively on how the Cathedral could develop and support its own congregation without which their influence as Christians would be small, suggesting that he was more comfortable at this stage with the parish than the diocesan role of the Cathedral:

> "One of the things we are charged to do and do well is to be a centre of Christian thought and instruction. People don't want to be told what to do: they want to be given the essentials of the Christian faith so that they can apply them to life."

The age of evangelical clergy as hectoring Old Testament prophets, which had been evident with some of the Cathedral's earlier bishops and provosts, seemed to have passed. The Cathedral was the mother church and the Provost observed:

> "Good mothers have a special care for their families. They protect and encourage, they love but do not spoil. They help the children be themselves and find themselves. They believe that charity does begin at home, though it should not end there."

He supported the Bishop's ideas on the ministry of the laity but was aware that churchgoers were not necessarily secure in their faith and needed nurturing:

"Our task is evangelistic . . . but a good many who worship regularly need encouragement and help. I incline to the view that our role is one of consolidating and caring for rather than [one of] pioneering: certainly our Lord himself concentrated on his chosen few, though he did not let them be a 'holy huddle'."[20]

For Mrs Dorothea Price the worship of God would be enhanced with beautiful flowers: she founded the Cathedral Flower Arrangement Group in June 1968 which became known as the Cathedral Flower Guild from 1977. The first Flower Festival was held in 1971.[21]

Michael Yorke, a product of Magdalene College, Cambridge and Cuddesdon Theological College, who had joined the Cathedral's staff in 1968 from Croydon Parish Church, pursued the theme. He wanted the congregation to be more than just passive worshippers:

"Many Christians believe the Church is active if the Archbishop says something compelling or the Vicar makes a stand on a subject of conscience . . . Outsiders are far more impressed by what they see among their own friends and acquaintances than by what they read in the national or local press . . . The impact that Christianity makes depends absolutely on the activity of each member of the Church taking his faith seriously . . . The Church, especially at the local level, is too often identified with its own organisation and not often enough with Christian work outside . . . While there are a number of Christians who do tremendous work, there are also a great many people who do not see in any way the crucial social content of the faith which they profess to follow."[22]

Gordon Hewitt added his own gloss in 1969 with an article entitled "What are clergy for?"[23] His person specification required:

" . . . a man who is prepared to seek out his fellow men and by his concern and genuine friendship gain the opportunity of presenting the case for his faith and his belief, without giving an impression that he is a better man than they. He should be able to co-operate with responsible people in other professions and earn their respect; be able to stand on his own two feet as a man and not on the fact that he is a parson; and he should have, whatever his intellectual and spiritual problems, a basic conviction about the truth and relevance of the Christian faith."

He reckoned that the layman expected a clergyman to have:

" . . . some organising and administrative skills; be a good mixer; and show a lively interest in what is going on in the world around him . . . to lead, to inspire leadership in others and to express himself intelligibly. He is a direction-finder rather than a pacemaker in holiness . . . The ones who seem happiest in the parochial ministry are those who work in a team, preferably a mixed team of clergy and laity, with some allotment of specialised tasks."

He then developed the contentious idea of clergy as backroom boys:

"Many priests see themselves, not so much as the 'provider' for the congregation as like the trainer of a football team—someone who remains obscurely in the dressing-room but who looks after the fitness of the team out there in the field. They realise that this is a very difficult idea of ministry and leadership to communicate. But they believe it is what the New Testament meant by Christian ministry and what their Lord calls them to exercise in the church and the world today."

That some clergy should see themselves as barely visible coaches was a far remove from the charismatic leadership that attracted the masses to hear John Watts-Ditchfield.

While the cathedral team sought to build up the congregation's resilience as Christian witnesses, some of the Cathedral's own organisations were in a state of flux, others in decline. In 1968 the Cathedral sought to merge its Festival activities with the town's own Festival[24] and, in any case, to spread its arts activities over the year rather than concentrate them in a Festival Week which exhausted core supporters. The Cathedral Council tried to be proactive and commissioned David Campton to write a play, *Jonah*, for performance in the Cathedral in 1971.[25] Not only was the congregation less local but the Provost was disappointed that so few Friends of Chelmsford Cathedral came from the local district.[26] In 1970 the Women's Fellowship was closed and all women's meetings were concentrated on the Mothers' Union which:

". . . has been functioning essentially as an 'in-group' and has catered for a comparatively small number of members . . . They are busy designing their future programmes . . . and meetings will be OPEN TO ALL!"

At the same time the Sunday School and Young People's League were in difficulties. The Provost was worried that "Sunday School numbers are still comparatively small"[27] and in 1970 the Y.P.L.'s activities were suspended:

"It seems unwise in the present circumstances to re-establish yet another church youth club in the town centre (there are four already) especially when we have the Y.M.C.A. doing excellent work in our parish. We have therefore decided to support and help that organisation . . . This is an experiment in an age of experiment."[28]

This rationalisation did not address the question as to why other churches' youth activities succeeded while the Cathedral's was ailing.

In this state of ebb and flow new Cathedral Statutes became law in 1968. The Bishop of Chelmsford would be Visitor of the Cathedral instead of Chairman of the Cathedral Council, thus allowing him to concentrate on his diocesan pastoral role; the chairmanship would be invested in the Provost. The Cathedral Council would assume the legal responsibilities previously vested in the Parochial Church Council which, in its turn, was to be renamed as the Parochial Church Committee.[29] The Provost also added his own small reform: the Rector's Warden would no longer be ex-officio the senior warden: that appellation would now attach itself to whichever warden had been appointed first. The Provost said that he intended to nominate his own warden for a period of only two years in office to make full use of all the talent in the congregation,[30] an initiative that had been tried 85 years before but did not last: this revival would have greater success. In the same spirit it was agreed that the *Cathedral News*, hitherto edited by the Provost and Canon Hewitt, should have a lay editor.[31]

The new statutes also gave much more freedom to the Provost to alter the titles given to assistant clergy. Since 1914 one of the assistant clergy had always been the Succentor, a grand title that meant nothing more than deputy to the Precentor. But Hilary Connop Price felt that the suggestion that one was superior to the other would "militate against that sense of partnership in the cathedral team which all of us desire." He therefore took the opportunity when a Precentor vacancy occurred to re-designate both assistant clergy as cathedral chaplains with himself as Precentor.[32]

The Provost had started his ministry at the Cathedral with an acute awareness of its generous staffing. He returned to this theme in February 1970, having re-examined the issue with his team of clergy recently augmented by Edward Finch who would be the Bishop's Advisor in Social Work, holding a leasehold canonry, a title attached to the job not the man, which would be surrendered when he left the nominated post. Hilary Connop Price wrote:

> "There are many services and events associated . . . with the Cathedral, which really do not depend on our cathedral status at all . . . Civic services, school services and parish services, for instance, are conducted in dozens of comparable town churches . . . In my last parish, a Staffordshire town rather larger than Chelmsford . . . I had one assistant curate and one part-time organist and one part-time verger. Here we have altogether five clergy, professional musicians, a secretary and two full-time vergers. By any reckoning this is a considerable concentration of resources and it would be irresponsible not to ask if we are using them fully and in the right way. The amount of time and energy we at present give to our parish church role is out of proportion to what we give to our specific tasks as a cathedral . . . There are too many points of overlap or duplication. If we assign clearly defined responsibilities to each member of the staff team, more will be achieved and more effectively . . . Many of my readers don't need me to tell them that for me personally the greatest need in these respects is . . . to have at least one of my colleagues acting as my Vicar."

So, in 1971, when Geoffrey Wrayford arrived from Cirencester Parish Church, he was made Chaplain-Vicar, Michael Yorke Chaplain-Precentor and Gordon Hewitt Director of Cathedral Services.[33] In April 1971 Geoffrey Wrayford started writing *Vicar's Notes* in the *Cathedral News* though this caused confusion, some thinking Hilary Connop Price had abdicated his parochial pastoral role: in 1975 Geoffrey Wrayford was therefore given the less confusing title of Chaplain to the Congregation and Parishioners.[34]

The Provost also sought to puncture the financial complacency of the congregation. He and the residentiary canons were financed by the

Church Commissioners for diocesan duties: parish activities needed to be financed by the Church Members' Fund to which a significant number of the congregation did not contribute.[35] The congregation would always find it difficult to appreciate that "their clergy" were often only on temporary loan from the Diocese.

Many in the congregation were still reluctant to concede to diocesan events or to have the Cathedral used for any activity that was not a formal act of worship. In 1970 Provost Hilary Connop Price wrote:

> "There is evidence to show that many are anxious to keep the church building exclusively for prayer, worship and sacrament . . . I have heard a few express anxiety about using the Cathedral for the Diocesan Synod . . . Argument is inappropriate there . . . We have already established the customs of using the Cathedral for music, drama, exhibitions and for lectures . . . It would be irresponsible of me and my colleagues here if we did not examine the way we use and do not use our Cathedral building. The one sure fact is that it is full for worship only two or three times a year."[36]

And those full occasions were usually school carol services. He claimed that, outside the peak festive period, the Cathedral was used for only three and a half hours a week on average. The next month a letter of reproof from a family of longstanding worshippers queried the figures: their mathematics may have been slightly more precise but did not invalidate the Provost's general point that a vast space was underused. The complainants had not finished:

> "We also deprecate the inference that it is a waste of lighting, heating and cleaning for the rest of the time during which it is open. The Cathedral is an oasis—a haven of peace in a noisy, busy world—and in this capacity fulfils a vital need."

That was a fair point but even oases have maintenance costs. Other letters from a layman and a down-town clergyman welcomed the whole concept of lively outreach.[37]

All would have agreed, however, that no one attempting to enter the Cathedral should be crushed by collapsing tombstones. There had been a general flattening of single grave slabs but by 1970 the weightier constructions were becoming dangerous:

"The large number of dilapidated and potentially dangerous tombstones, mostly dating from 1780-1840, tend to frustrate any efforts at landscape gardening. Tilted headstones, collapsed stone panels and the decayed brickwork bases of some monuments, give the whole churchyard an unkempt air . . . Last autumn it became clear that emergency measures would have to be taken to deal with the worst of them. 61 were identified."

Stephen Dykes-Bower, the Consultant Architect, recommended the removal of many 18th century sandstone tombs: they had weathered to an unsightly black and were falling apart as the iron clamps at the corners corroded or, lacking suitable foundations, subsided into the grave. He also suggested new flower-beds and the removal of the single tombstones that had been laid flat in 1881 as they made grass maintenance very difficult: they could be recycled as paving on the main approach paths. Finally he advocated a paved concourse outside the south porch where people tended to congregate after weddings, ordinations and other special services. The project would cost a great deal and have to be phased: the south porch concourse seemed to be the place to start. But his idea that there should be wrought iron gates in the west wall of the churchyard to enhance the ceremonial approach to the west door was not taken up.[38] Poor Dykes-Bower seemed to despair:

"Not only is it a frequent criticism that the Cathedral is hard to see—so much so that people can pass through the town and miss it altogether—but there is not one single entrance to its precincts that has any dignity whatsoever."[39]

That concern had been echoed 25 years earlier in the Chelmsford Planning Survey in 1945:

"It is regrettable that the county and local authorities should have had so little feeling for what is appropriate or for aesthetic values, as to permit the County Hall to be built to its present height in view of its proximity to St. Mary's."[40]

But the masking of the Cathedral by the 18th century Shire Hall was, in truth, the greater problem.

The Provost's earlier concerns about an inward-looking congregation were reflected at diocesan level by the Bishop who, after his experience of the newly elected Diocesan Synod which met for the first time in 1970, warned:

> "There is a possible tendency for Synod members to become so much immersed in church meetings that they become more and more inward-looking . . . Administrative reform of itself will not add one soul to the Church."[41]

But his episcopal calling would now be cut short. For some time Bishop Tiarks had been suffering from Parkinson's disease. With new synodical government as an additional challenge he decided, on medical advice, to retire in 1971 and move with his wife to be near family in Birmingham where he died in 1974.

CHAPTER 22

Finding a Role

John Trillo became Chelmsford's sixth bishop at the age of 55. He came from the Diocese of St. Albans where he had held two suffragan bishoprics, as Bishop of Bedford from 1963-8 and as the first Bishop of Hertford from 1968-71. Indeed, his education and ministry had all been in London and the northern Home Counties. Like John Watts-Ditchfield he did not emerge from the conventional public school and Oxbridge background. The son of a chauffeur and a domestic servant who knew the pain and poverty of 1930s unemployment, he won a place at The Quintin School, a state school in the City of Westminster, at a time when parents still had to pay some fees, but was unable to aspire to the expense of university and consequently worked for five years for Warner Brothers film sales department.[1] On deciding that he had a calling to the ministry he worked his way through King's College London "trying to learn Greek irregular verbs between efforts to sell *Gold-diggers of 1933* to reluctant East End cinema proprietors"[2] and achieved successive first class honours as Bachelor of Divinity, Associate of King's College and Master of Theology. After ordination he became curate at Christ Church, Fulham, where he married the vicar's daughter, and priest in charge of St. Michael's, Cricklewood. In an interesting variety of posts he then served as secretary to the Student Christian Movement, Rector of Friern Barnet, Lecturer in Divinity back at King's College and Principal of Bishop's College, Cheshunt, before his elevation to the episcopacy in Bedford.

He was uncomfortable with the pomp and ceremony of his enthronement on July 10th 1971:

"I bridled inwardly at all the splendour, the trumpets, the magnificent music and all the talk of thrones, dignities, honours, privileges and appurtenances. But . . . it was God's service: him we worshipped and the glory was his."[3]

He was, however, content to wear the full regalia of cope and mitre. The first three bishops had declined; Falkner Allison, the fourth bishop, had been reluctant and eschewed the mitre for "domestic occasions", reserving it for grand ceremonial; John Tiarks did not like the mitre at all.[4]

Chelmsford's first mitred bishop, John Trillo at his enthronement:
Chelmsford Cathedral Knightbridge Library

John Trillo would not accept Bishopscourt as an episcopal residence:

"It is monstrous that a minister of God should be required to live in a house of the size of Bishopscourt, which has not even antiquity to commend it."[5]

273

Eventually in 1982 he was able to move into the new Bishopscourt at Margaretting, just south of Chelmsford, which was less than half the size of the cavernous building in Springfield.[6] He was no longer so conveniently placed for the Cathedral and diocesan offices but, situated adjacent to the A12, he now had quick road access to all parts of his diocese even if he had to tolerate a rather noisy environment for garden parties.

He was appreciative of his clergy's hard work on stipends which were being eroded by constant double digit inflation but was critical of Christian divisions:

> "Our concern for structures and for the great burden of our inherited buildings; our introspective concern for internal affairs; the pettiness of our debates; and worst of all, our lovelessness . . . . seem often to suppress or kill our evangelical love and care for people outside our pale."[7]

He did not "contemplate a great diocesan evangelical campaign on mammoth lines" but wanted those within the Church to be a more cohesive body:

> "I do believe . . . that we can pray better together, study together, both clergy and laity, and come to understand better what God is calling us to say and do together."[8]

Reinforcing what Provost Hilary Connop Price had been striving to achieve at the Cathedral, the Bishop was therefore looking for a stronger parish base of active Christians from which some form of personal or parish evangelism would emerge.

But God answered worshippers' prayers in a bewildering manner. While 1971 saw the first joint diocesan Roman Catholic and Anglican pilgrimage to the ancient Chapel of St. Peter's-on-the-Wall at Bradwell, a sufficient minority of praying Anglicans voted in 1972 against unity with the Methodists and scuppered the whole project. The disappointed John Trillo warned the Diocesan Synod:

> "The Church does not appear to the majority of the population as credible when it speaks to them of peace, love and joy and of freedom and deliverance and reconciliation. We appear to them

all too often as a top heavy organisation concerned primarily with institutionalism."[9]

However things soon looked up. In 1976 he was to write:

"Now Roman Catholics are talking of joint evangelism with other churches and here we are at the heart of the matter. The days are past when we stole sheep from one another and called it conversion."[10]

So, perhaps that was the way forward, working together wherever possible, by-passing the legal and doctrinal problems of union. That seemed to be the view of Derek Collingwood, chairman of the London North East District of the Methodist Church:

"Who cares any longer about problems of church unity apart from a dwindling minority of clergy and church members?"

He was all for united witness but not abortive attempts to merge. In such trying times it is good for a bishop to retain a sense of humour. Bishop Trillo went bird-watching and tracked a barn owl: "I sat myself on the fence (a traditional episcopal stance in the opinion of some)."[11]

From April 9th 1972 Parish Communion in the Cathedral became the norm: it was held at 9.30 a.m. every Sunday (previously it had been on only the first Sunday in the month) followed by Matins at 11.15 a.m., so the Eucharist was now firmly at the centre of the Cathedral's worship. Provost Hilary Connop Price liked the simplicity of the Parish Communion and said that, although it was tempting to "dress up" the service a bit, the more so when the choirboys joined after Easter 1972, "a robed choir might impose a formality which we have discovered we do not need."[12]

The splendour of the great cathedral occasions or the well-established formality of Matins and Evensong would therefore sit alongside a more intimate Parish Communion though this had implications for the traditional role of the choir. John Jordan expressed regret that there were two morning services: he had hoped for a unique merged Chelmsford liturgy and doubted that the town was large enough to sustain two separate Sunday morning congregations. To avoid overtaxing the choristers at weekends, he ended the Friday evensong for boys' voices which he had introduced in 1968, having moved it at that stage from Thursdays to avoid clashes with their after-school clubs.[13]

For John Jordan the life of the Master of Music was an intense round of practices and services with little infrastructure of support. Without an endowed choral foundation or traditional choir school it had not proved possible thus far to sing daily offices. On the other hand he felt there was some compensation. The older cathedrals' choir schools were often fee-paying and choristers had to leave at 13 having passed the Common Entrance Examination to public school, though their voices may not have broken: by contrast Chelmsford boys could carry on singing, maybe as late as their 15th birthday.[14] An increasing number of choristers were now coming from outside Chelmsford, a new phenomenon, and from the Cathedral School itself where Fred Dyer, appointed as Headteacher in 1972, provided vigorous support and encouraged a greater number of recruits than hitherto.[15] John Jordan was proud of the choir's repertoire of 107 anthems of which 62 had been introduced since his appointment in 1965, 13 of them by Essex's own William Byrd.[16] The repertoire of Cliff Richard who sang at the Cathedral on January 10th 1973 to 1,000 school students, was rather different but was nicely balanced by a new series of subscription concerts, starting in 1974 with the renowned Medici Quartet.

While the Master of Music quite properly paid tribute to his choir, the extraordinary standard of his organ playing should not be underestimated. One contemporary commented on his phenomenal memory, akin to that of a concert pianist, and his capacity to produce an incomparable richness and variety of sound as though he were able to imbue the organ with some of his own swashbuckling character. Every top organist needs an element of the showman in him.[17]

In 1976 the Bishop paid tribute to John Jordan's work:

> "The Cathedral has a magnificent choir and all who worship there must be truly inspired by the music they hear. John Jordan, Master of the Music has fashioned with his men and boys a magnificent instrument to the glory of God . . . He has recently instituted a scheme of examination for young choristers in parish churches whereby they can become Bishop's Choristers."

And then with his characteristic wit: "my family motto is Cantate Domino—which might be very roughly translated Trillo to the Lord!"[18]

From 1973 Parish Communion would also be in a new format. The Series Two Communion service had been authorised for only four years and was replaced by Series Three which moved further away from traditional liturgical language to the more modern idiom that congregations had popularly requested.

One commentator wrote:

> "For all of us it will be some relief to know that the mania for trendy liturgical revision is beginning to run out of steam." [19]

He was also concerned that "the print is small and the variations confusing for the man in the pew": presumably women, who provided the majority of worshippers, did have the eyes and brains to cope. Series Three was used from May to October 1973 on the 2nd and 4th Sundays of the month at 8.00 a.m. with the 1662 Prayer Book Order at mid-morning celebrations.[20] At the end of the year Provost Hilary Connop Price concluded that there was no evidence from attendances that one order was preferred to the other. So from December 2nd Series 3 would be used at 8.00 a.m. as well as 9.30 a.m. every Sunday; the 1662 Prayer Book Order would continue to be used at 10.30 a.m. on Thursdays and midday on the second and fourth Sundays and at 7.00 a.m. on Christmas morning.[21] There should have been something there for all tastes though it is not known how worshippers reacted to the Provost's comments that "none of us can deeply understand or believe every clause of the Christian Creed"[22] and "I do not regard New Testament descriptions of what happened on Easter Day as literally true: I think it is picture language."[23] This growing tendency for clergy to move away from literal interpretations showed an honesty that was likely to confirm the continued truancy of the thinking non-churchgoer, anger the evangelical but cause others within the fold to heave a sigh of relief that everything did not have to be in uncompromising black and white.

But who were the people attending Cathedral services each Sunday? It had been evident for some time that the congregation increasingly comprised non-parishioners. According to a questionnaire distributed in 1972[24] only 24% of the congregation lived in the parish though over 80% lived in the town, so local churches were the losers; the gender imbalance continued with 40% men and 60% women; for the older members church worship was more likely to be an all day commitment with over 30% of those over 65 attending twice on Sundays; for the younger ones the day was their own after morning service as only 3% of those under 35 came to two services and overwhelmingly preferred the Parish Communion. The quality of music, the variation of preacher, dignity and tradition were all given as major factors for choosing the Cathedral, but, of course, as Provost Hilary Connop Price had observed from the moment he arrived, the odds were stacked in the Cathedral's favour. In midweek activities the Cathedral differed markedly from other town centre churches: 73% of the Cathedral's worshippers said they never supported midweek activities or services. Other town centre churches reported strong support for clubs but most of the Cathedral's had a struggle to survive. The overall conclusion seems to be that the congregation knew what they wanted and would travel to find it, although they were less interested in the community side of church life, a decline that had certainly become more marked in recent years. Of equal significance was the fact that only 2% cited warmth of welcome as an attraction: those for whom it is not a priority may not see the need to demonstrate it which might explain the perception a decade on that the Cathedral was unfriendly.

The congregation's loose attachment to the community aspects of church life inevitably affected the Cathedral's success in developing the concept of Christian Stewardship, the giving of service to the Church as well as money, though even the latter left much to be desired. The Provost was disappointed at the number supporting the Church Members' Fund. Looking back on 1971, the congregation had given only £4,426 (£48,000 in modern values):

> "Most parishes of our size would have produced £8,000 [£88,200]. Is it true that as a congregation we suffer from being a cathedral and knowing that the financial responsibility is ultimately not ours?"[25]

He returned to the subject nearly a year later:

> "I sense that some of you have felt critical because cathedral finances seemed to you to be shrouded in mystery. If you felt this way it was not because the facts were hidden from you but because the presentation was obscure. Each year copies of the cathedral accounts are available at the south porch for any who want them . . . But it is never easy to simplify accounts."[26]

He explained that trust funds and £11,400 in grants (£126,000 in today's money) from the Church Commissioners for Cathedral staff could not be used for other purposes and was not meant to cushion the Cathedral congregation from the financial commitment which faced members of every other parish in the Diocese. The 1974 budget looked as though it could be £4,000 in deficit (£32,500 in today's money) and high inflation was eroding the value of cash balances.

Taking the broader view, Bishop Trillo and the Provost were concerned about what the Cathedral could do for the Diocese. That cathedrals as "big theatre"[27] were centres of excellence in music and the presentation of worship was not in doubt. Church choirs might gain inspiration from diocesan festivals in terms of technique and repertoire or visiting clergy borrow a good theme or a telling phrase for a sermon. But such a limited vision of a cathedral's function inclined to cosy elitism. If laity and clergy were to be more equal partners in the Christian ministry and parish clergy were not to be left on their own with all the social and personal problems their parishioners presented, the Cathedral would need a stronger educational focus and provide more than pomp and splendour.

After consultation with the Tavistock Institute, Canon Richard Herrick, whose input into the discussions with Provost and Bishop had been very influential, was appointed in 1971 as Director of a new Centre for Research and Training, with Michael Yorke as his Deputy. Michael Yorke also took a lead in industrial chaplaincy, especially at the town's Marconi factories, and established a Chelmsford branch of the Samaritans.[28] At Christmas 1973 he left the Cathedral to take charge of the parishes of Ashdon and Hadstock near Saffron Walden and, though for a short while he continued to work with the Centre for a day or two a week, he was replaced as Deputy Director by Wesley Carr. His academic credentials were impeccable. He had read Greats at Jesus College, Oxford and Theology at Jesus College, Cambridge as well as studying at the Graduate School of Ecumenical Studies at the University of Geneva. He had trained for the ministry at Ridley Hall and served a curacy at Luton Parish Church before moving into higher education as a tutor and chaplain at Ridley Hall followed by a fellowship in Biblical Studies at the University of Sheffield where he had previously taken his doctorate.

From its inception the Centre for Research and Training identified three ways in which it could serve the Diocese: firstly meeting at the Cathedral with groups such as parents of older children, welfare service professionals and clergy to examine the challenges they faced; secondly helping parish clergy who were faced with new situations such as large immigrant communities of other faiths; thirdly studying the communication of religious ideas and experience through music, drama, poetry and exhibitions. In 1972 the Provost confessed that the Cathedral by and large still used long-established orders of service but promised that it would do its bit to "question and experiment on behalf of the Diocese". The establishment of synodical government meant that deanery chapters had been relieved of much administrative business so that they too could look more closely at forms of worship.[29]

In addition bespoke research into issues identified by individual parishes was on offer and a programme of in-service training for clergy was being developed covering behavioural studies as well as the more conventional theological, biblical and pastoral issues. Other areas of exploration dealt with the relationship between parish and deanery under synodical government.

Wesley Carr explained the philosophy that underpinned the research element of the Centre's work:

> "Only if a parish invited us, can we help . . . We would never go into a parish and tell them what to do—we would not know! Management consultants solve problems, we want to share experiences. If members of a parish congregation feel the need to have a clearer idea about what they should be doing, we hope we could help them clarify the questions they want to ask . . . We shouldn't have charts or stop-watches, just ourselves and the ability we hope we have to help people see where the questions lie."[30]

These ideas were good but the Centre's infrastructure was not. A year into its life a progress report noted:

> "We have no office . . . This type of enterprise cannot be run from two private homes, a briefcase in the car and a part-time typist in her own house." [31]

The boon of the Muniment Room in the 1920s vestry extension was a marginal improvement but there were no larger rooms for group work, seminars and lectures. Nonetheless, the Centre showed academic rigour: those elements of its work which involved behavioural sciences were monitored by consultants from the Tavistock Institute for Human Relations, the sociology department of Brunel University and the Grubb Institute of Behaviour Studies.[32]

John Gibbs, the Bishop of Bradwell, who was to become Bishop of Coventry in 1976, reinforced this new venture with a paper on the role of a cathedral which was published in the September 1974 *Cathedral News*. The Church had been along this path many times before and was adept at asking the big questions but not at finding big answers. This, however, was much more substantial and concentrated on the role of the Cathedral as servant and enabler rather than just as star performer.

He crystallised four ideas. Firstly ordinands, laity, clergy, teachers, lay workers and youth officers should all train together in diocesan centres linked to the Cathedral in which Christian insights would be brought to bear, not only in training for the Church's ministry, but in preparing them for a Christian understanding of their roles in the world at large: Chelmsford Cathedral had already started along that path. Secondly he had identified such an immensely diverse interpretation of ministerial roles and a confusing proliferation of terminology in describing them, that there was a need to examine those differences, identify best practice and help incumbents work out what was most suitable for them in their parish setting. Thirdly the sheer size and diversity of the Diocese—"within the Southend Archdeaconry alone we run from dockland to feudalism"—and the complexity of commuter life left him asking whether work, leisure and family should be looked at as one to enable the Church to focus its mission more effectively. Fourthly there were many small home-based study and prayer groups in the Diocese, a lot of them lacking real direction and purpose and deficient in content: they needed support and focus.

Bishop Gibbs proposed that the Cathedral should avoid duplicating work which was being done elsewhere in other educational institutions but should act as a clearing house for the Diocese to keep everyone informed of what was going on in relevant fields of research and investigation. He too identified the need for local action-research by clergy and laity to enable them to grasp new ideas, relate them to their knowledge of local situations and their own practical experience and enable others to practise them.

He stressed that theology was not the specialised possession of the clergy, though they clearly had a specialised role to fulfil. The crucial factor was:

> " . . . the education of the people in the understanding of the faith
> so that they can bring the insights of the Gospel to bear on all their
> human situations . . . This is what I mean by **doing** theology . . .
> But it requires preparation, training and articulation; it demands

knowledge of the Bible and Christian tradition; it must be related to personal prayer and to the Church's corporate worship . . . We need help and we probably need to draw on resources which are very much wider than those possessed by the average parish."

As one who had started his clerical life as a Congregational minister he longed for unity. His most exciting and possibly threatening proposals concerned ecumenism which he felt was not about structures, worship and doctrine but about mission. Was there a possibility of giving some kind of recognition to non-Anglicans with a permanent place in the Cathedral? Was it possible to set up an ecumenical group which could mount activities appropriate for a Cathedral e.g. special acts of occasional worship, experiments in worship, music and drama, dialogues about the faith with humanists, Marxists and representatives of other faiths?

> "The important thing is not just to invite people from other churches to attend but to offer the Cathedral as a place for ecumenical activity."

That the Church was moving away from a paternalist and authoritarian line of instructing its congregations on moral matters was exemplified in a *Cathedral News* article by Canon Gordon Hewitt.

> "'Many Christian scholars nowadays reject the view that theology is a matter for experts only. They think that the local worshipping community can and should, make moral judgements in the light of what it knows of Christ . . . especially, where, as in this case, experts disagree . . . Church members . . . should not simply be told what to believe and how to behave . . . Many Christian leaders now recognise that true pastoral care is not a matter of keeping the wolf out of the fold and the sheep safely penned within it."[33]

There was now a real sense of momentum. At its 40th anniversary in 1954, the Cathedral had been struggling desperately to recover from the neglect and damage of war. For the 1964 Golden Jubilee work on the Cathedral's fabric had given it colour and cohesion and its music was at an exciting stage of development but it had no other role than that of being bright and shiny. For its Diamond Jubilee in 1974 it had at last begun to have a real identity and outward-looking purpose in the Diocese with an exciting can-do philosophy, even if Provost Gordon's decorations were in urgent need of refreshment.

On June 13th 1974, because of the Cathedral's smallness, Michael Ramsey, Archbishop of Canterbury, presided over two Diamond Jubilee Services of Thanksgiving. The Bishop of Chelmsford's chaplain was 93-year-old Canon John Barrow who had been present as Precentor when the Cathedral had been hallowed in 1914, having started his ministry as a curate under Canon Lake. In November 1974 the Queen Mother attended the celebration of the Diamond Jubilee of the leprosy hospital of St. Giles at East Hanningfield when the preacher was Bishop Trevor Huddlestone:[34] monsoon rain, a flooded A12, a hole in the royal umbrella and the clerical reception party initially assembling at the wrong door, did not get in the way of a splendid occasion.[35]

Provost Hilary Connop Price greets Archbishop Michael Ramsey,
June 13th 1974: Chelmsford Cathedral Knightbridge Library

In the summer of 1977 Provost Hilary Martin Connop Price retired to Shaftesbury after 10 years at the helm. The Bishop paid tribute:

> "During his time the Cathedral has grown . . . as a centre of well-ordered worship, beautiful music, fresh cleanliness, evangelistic and social concern, sound learning and, latterly especially, as a centre of training and research."[36]

Underlying this was his caring and effective pastoral work which, as with all clergy, leaves grateful memories with those on whom it is bestowed but nothing in the written record.

The relationship between a cathedral provost and canons residentiary, who live and work in each others' pockets, can be an intense one. Hitherto Chelmsford's provosts had emerged from a parish background with responsibility for the development of a young curate or two and, if a Rural Dean, pastoral oversight of a small group of clergy. But this did not prepare a man fully for a cathedral leadership role alongside intellectually able residentiary canons with experience of wider diocesan responsibilities who were already part of the cathedral establishment. Successful leadership of such a group requires fine judgement and a willingness to accept the role of first amongst equals: the equals in this case were described by a local clergyman in his fond farewell to the Provost as "a mettlesome trio . . . all men of brilliant gifts",[37] a double-edged encomium that embraced Canons Richard Herrick and Edward Finch as well as Wesley Carr who was soon, on Hilary Connop Price's recommendation, to become a residentiary canon. The Provost's success, perhaps unappreciated by many who observed from the distant sidelines, was that he kept the team together while allowing them to develop; although the whole academic thrust of the Centre for Research and Training was not his scene, he could sense its value and allowed it to breathe.

Michael Yorke described him:

> "A gentle leader who sought to bring out the best in others; he rode with a loose rein—some misinterpreted it as weakness, but it was not, for it derived from a humility based on personal insight and recognition of his own limitations."[38]

He was also very conscious of and slightly uncomfortable with the gulf in resources between the Cathedral and the generality of parishes. That sort of perspective is much healthier than the reverse: some of the more ancient cathedrals, from time to time, have appeared rather impressed with themselves, accepting as of right their privileged position. It was therefore appropriate that Hilary Connop Price should have left Chelmsford Cathedral with a much stronger sense of being the servant of the parishes although he had found it an uphill task, as had others before him, to get its disparate congregation to pull its weight.

CHAPTER 23

Not a Closed Shop

Richard Herrick, one of the "mettlesome trio", was inducted as Rector on January 12th 1978 and installed as Provost two days later, the first internal appointment to the top job in the Cathedral's history. There was no doubt about his capacity or his experience: he had known the Cathedral from the inside for the last 21 years and he would be able to continue as Director of the Centre for Research and Training. Whether this dual function would be sustainable in future appointments without limiting bishops' field of choice would remain to be seen. The only doubt about the appointment may have been that he was 64 and not in good health.

Provost Richard Herrick:
Chelmsford Cathedral Knightbridge Library

His was the first move in the clerical equivalent of a cabinet reshuffle.[1] Wesley Carr moved up to canon residentiary but continued with his role as Deputy Director of the Centre for Research and Training. Michael Yorke, who during his four years away from Chelmsford had progressed to be national Director of the Samaritans, returned to replace the retiring canon residentiary, Gordon Hewitt. Edward Finch as a leasehold canon gathered together his own team in the new diocesan Department of Mission to be chaired by Jim Roxburgh, Bishop of Barking, though in 1985 he gave up his diocesan and cathedral roles to become Director of the InterFace Centre at Moulsham Mill in Chelmsford, an ecumenical foundation under joint Anglican, Catholic and Methodist control which would concern itself with political and social issues. Two new assistant clergy completed the line-up: John Brown arrived from Scotland as Chaplain of the Cathedral and Precentor and John Ponter from the Chaplaincy of the University of East Anglia as Industrial Chaplain.

Richard Herrick shared a number of immediate concerns with his congregation. The Cathedral Hall was unable to cope with demand and a quote of £200,000 (£895,000 in today's money) to build a new two-storey hall would be too costly;[3] Provost Gordon's cathedral refurbishments were showing signs of wear and tear; the inflexibility of the uncomfortable Victorian pews made outside organisations more reluctant to hire the Cathedral and even inhibited new patterns of worship such as the informal Parish Communion, although Richard Herrick did remove some pews at the western end of the north aisle to create a bookshop; clergy housing was still scattered throughout Chelmsford though planning permission had been obtained for building houses on the Guy Harlings' site; and new roads and retail developments in the town centre were reducing the parish's residential population. On a wider front the Provost recognised that the sheer size of old Essex meant that "the Cathedral means very little in many parts of the Diocese": the Cathedral needed to be much more outgoing though how so few staff in the Centre for Research and Training could adequately support hundreds of parishes would remain a major problem. Richard Herrick therefore concluded:

> "The resources of worship and spirituality of the Cathedral can only make their impact if people are brought to the Cathedral to experience them." [2]

That would be helped by the opening on June 30th 1979 of the restored, expanded and re-equipped Guy Harlings. Its extensions, facing onto New Street and eastwards into its tranquil garden, contained a Cathedral Office and purpose-built rooms for group meetings. The cost of £475,000 (£1.87 million in today's money) was largely met by the sale of land for the Crown Court next door[4] whose forbidding architecture was relieved by the lighter quasi-Elizabethan style of the new Guy Harlings' frontage.

The new Guy Harlings frontage: photo by Tony Tuckwell

As Richard Herrick pondered on current problems, Gordon Hewitt, who had just retired after a ministry of 42 years, a third of them at the Cathedral, reflected with equal frustration on the past. He was unhappy with the pedestrian rate of development. The Church seemed to discuss the same problems again and again without any resolution:

> "When I began my ministry in Leeds in 1936 there were four matters of church reform to which younger clergy and a fair number of laity felt themselves committed: a) an agreed deanery policy on infant baptism b) the visible unity of the Church as necessary for an effective Christian witness and to avoid waste of

resources in money and manpower c) a change in the relations of Church and State especially in the way bishops were appointed d) the fullest opportunities possible for women in the church's ministry, including ordination to the priesthood. Forty years on the Church of England has still taken no really effective action in these four areas of reform. The one significant change has been in church worship—not just in the modernisation of the forms of service, but in a new understanding of the corporate nature of Christian worship as exemplified in the Parish Communion Movement."[5]

Some would not have agreed with him about the influence of the Parish Communion Movement. Critics saw the centrality of the Eucharist as too exclusive, aimed at insiders only.[6] But worshippers had been leaching away well before the Parish Communion movement took hold: there was no evidence of queues of frustrated believers nostalgically awaiting the reinstatement of the old patterns of worship to herald their joyful return to church. Critics were as likely to be churchmen with an axe to grind (and the Church could always generate its quota on any issue) or those who had lapsed and used whatever disagreement was at hand to rationalise their position. That the Parish Communion was welcomed by so many young families at Chelmsford was surely proof of its worth. For most of the population, who never had any contact with the Church, it was a matter of no import how it worshipped on Sundays provided the big royal and state occasions were staged well on television.

On Sundays cathedrals were, relatively speaking, thriving worshipping communities and produced a visual and aural spectacle that was at least impressive and at best spiritually satisfying. But they existed at the apex of a parish pyramid whose congregational base was withering away. Rarely did people drift into Anglican churches as the socially done thing, though that could still apply at some fashionable cathedrals. The *Essex Churchman* took a rather depressing view:

"Nowadays committed church people in England are beginning to realise they are in a minority and one can detect two mistaken patterns of reaction. Some may half-consciously welcome the situation. They are those who enjoy feeling superior . . . belonging to the small band of enlightened souls whose attainments surpass those of ordinary folk. If numbers increased dramatically they would begin to wonder if they were in the right place themselves . . . Many more, again half consciously . . . finding themselves in a small congregation . . . begin to fear that Christianity cannot be true. Accordingly if they do not lapse *from* churchgoing, they lapse *into* stagnation, continuing to attend but too apathetic to attempt any evangelism."[7]

Those stereotypes were recognisable but did not allow for the honest toilers in between.

Within the Cathedral a new honour was instituted in 1978 when Sir John Ruggles-Brise and Colonel John Oxley Parker, both indefatigable supporters of the Cathedral, were made honorary churchwardens, an ecclesiastical equivalent of granting the freedom of the town. Sir John was soon to retire from the Lord-Lieutenancy of Essex; the Colonel was the oldest surviving member of the Cathedral Council and one of the Cathedral's greatest benefactors.[8]

At the same time Mrs Eileen Hance was appointed to the Standing Committee of the Cathedral Council, the first woman to be so elevated;[9] she later became the first female sidesman and, in 1984, the first female churchwarden. This was not before time in a Church whose Supreme Governor since 1952 had been a woman and in a country governed during the 1980s by a woman prime minister. But any advancement of women in the Church would guarantee a misogynist response from a vocal minority. When, in 1980, Elizabeth Shepherd wrote in the *Cathedral News* about her experiences as a server while living in the north and Richard Herrick suggested to his congregation that women might become sidesmen,[10] a few traditionalists took umbrage. Richard Herrick was constrained to reply:

"I am told that some and not only men, still take exception to my suggesting that women should be recruited as sidesmen, just as others are still not at ease with women assistants in the administration of the chalice, despite their being licensed by the Bishop for that and other ministries. Deep feelings I shall always try to treat with respect and will give them time to adjust, but in the end I have to ask everyone to be ready for decisions which can be expected to make the most sense to the larger number of

devout worshippers . . . Can anyone tell me why we should not
have women to serve at the altars? We need their help, especially
on weekdays when most of our men are on trains going to work
when services happen. And women greatly outnumber men in
their commitment to worship, do they not?"[11]

He was giving notice: it would happen. His arguments were eminently
rational but would not persuade those who felt that the words attributed
to St. Paul about women being seen and not heard in church should stand
for all time.

Meanwhile John Jordan's choir continued to perform at its highest level.
In 1979 he reviewed the choir's repertoire. At the drop of a hat they could
sing four settings of responses, six of the *Te Deum*, three of the *Benedicite*,
five of the *Jubilate*, three of the *Benedictus* and 27 of the evening canticles.
In the past year they had sung 114 anthems, eight of which were first
performances. The repertoire was also expanding to settings of the Eucharist
by Harold Darke and John Ireland and the William Byrd *Four-Part Mass*.[12]
On a broader front he was planning a series of concerts with two every other
month: he felt that concentrated festivals caused such exhaustion amongst
concert-goers and organisers that, almost inevitably, nothing happened for
the next eleven months.[13]

But Easter 1981 was to be John Jordan's final great occasion before he
left to become an overseas examiner for the Associated Board of the Royal
Schools of Music working throughout Africa and Asia. Provost Richard
Herrick commented on his enthusiasm for church music and the whole art
of Anglican liturgy and observed that the rapid turnover of previous Masters
of the Music had restricted the development of repertoire:

> "John leaves the choir with a virtually new repertoire, ranging from
> music of the 16th century, his own special love, down to that of
> today . . . Saturday Evensong has been the occasion for the choir
> to 'go its own way' while the Sunday services have music with a
> congregational appeal . . . In 1970 John was able to have a major
> say in the rebuilding of the organ at a cost of £8,000 [£96,500 in
> today's money] . . . It was fortunate that the overhaul took place
> when it did: today it would cost between £50,000 and £60,000"[14]
> [£149,000 to £179,000].

Tragically, those happy compliments in the *Cathedral News* were to be Richard Herrick's last. He died suddenly at the end of April at the age of 67. He had been an intellectual powerhouse who had been instrumental in moving the Cathedral into a much more proactive research-based and supportive role for the Diocese. But he was most loved for his pastoral work: an obituary recorded that he was first and foremost a caring parish priest and "the clergy of the Diocese knew he was their friend and staunch ally."[15] It was good that these qualities had also been acknowledged in print while he was still alive when, in January 1981, the *Cathedral News* had described his "loving and far-sighted leadership . . . there is a 'new spirit' about the place." Bishop John Trillo paid his own tribute:

> "Dick Herrick was a man of great integrity and of keen mind who last year completed 40 years as a priest. For almost a quarter of a century he spent himself for the Diocese of Chelmsford and for the Cathedral. For 16 years he was Diocesan Director of Religious Education and then Advisor for Lay Training. He was one of the early pioneers in this country using group dynamics as a means of lay training. Later he developed more sophisticated systems of behavioural studies, working as a consultant with the Grubb Institute and latterly with the Tavistock Institute. He was valued as a consultant at home and abroad and particularly in the U.S.A . . . He was the chief agent in the foundation of the Chelmsford Cathedral Centre for Research and Training . . . As well as this he contributed to the central councils of the Church, particularly in the field of education, as well as being a member of the General Synod. He was also chairman of the House of Clergy in the Diocese."[16]

After a nine month delay, during which Peter Cross held the fort, a new Master of the Music was appointed, the eminently well-qualified Graham Elliott B.Mus. (London), F.R.C.O., F.T.C.L., F.L.C.M., L.R.A.M.. Barry Rose, sub-organist of St. Paul's Cathedral, helped the Cathedral through the appointment process. For the previous ten years Graham Elliott had been the Organist and Master of Choristers at St. Asaph Cathedral. On taking up his new appointment he wrote:

> "My move takes me from a tiny cathedral city with a population of only 3,000 to a large and flourishing county town, from one of the

oldest cathedral foundations in Britain to one of the most recent . . . I think that I have been fortunate in my route to the Chelmsford organ stool. From boyhood studies at Hereford Cathedral, studentships at the Royal Academy and as organ student at St. George's Chapel in Windsor Castle and my first post as Sub-Organist at Llandaff Cathedral (and a short period as Sub-Organist at Luton Parish Church), I have had an opportunity to sample many different aspects of cathedral life . . . I am very much aware that I am in succession to very distinguished men. One of them, Dr J.R. Middleton, was, in fact, my predecessor at St. Asaph!"[17]

Graham Elliott was quickly up and running. In November Chelmsford Cathedral's choir joined with those of St. Paul's, Lichfield and Wakefield cathedrals in the Annual Festival Service for the Corporation of the Sons of the Clergy, when the Lord Mayor of London and the Archbishop of Canterbury processed in state at St. Paul's; in both 1982 and 1983 the gentlemen of the choir sang Compline in Holy Week; and the Master of the Music had ambitions for a second choir, the 9.30 Singers for Parish Communion.[18]

Provost John Moses: photo by Mervyn Marshall

293

On January 14th 1982 44-year-old John Moses, Archdeacon of Southend, was instituted as Rector of St. Mary's Parish and two days later was installed as Provost of the Cathedral. A graduate of the University of Nottingham, he had trained as a teacher at Cambridge and as a priest at Lincoln Theological College. After an assistant curacy at St. Andrew's, Bedford, where John Trillo, later his Chelmsford diocesan, was suffragan bishop, he became Rector of Coventry East Team Ministry (for most of which time he was also Examining Chaplain to the Bishop of Coventry) and Coventry East Rural Dean. He moved to the Archdeaconry of Southend in 1977. He would be the first Provost to live on site, the little close of three houses having just been built on the edge of Guy Harlings' garden to accommodate the Provost and the canons working at the Centre for Research and Training; in 1984 when the Centre closed that arrangement would be amended with the Master of the Music taking one of the canon's houses;[19] a fourth house was added much later, in 2009, for the Canon Precentor.

It seemed that the momentum built up by Richard Herrick would be sustained. For the first time a cathedral audience was addressed by a former prime minister when, on March 27th 1982, Edward Heath gave a lecture on the Brandt Report which had highlighted the huge north-south international divide in incomes and living standards. That was apt. John Moses believed difficult questions must be asked and answered: he would start on his own patch. In his installation sermon he challenged his listeners:

> "The approach that must characterise our work at the Cathedral must be living, learning, questioning, growing . . . If the Centre does its work well, it will have uncomfortable things to say to all of us—for it demands that we look critically at our work, our goals, our values . . . We know the strengths of this Cathedral. We also know . . . the inflexibility of this building . . . Our ancient churches . . . have been enlarged and adapted and re-ordered over the centuries to meet the needs of successive generations. They are not museums. They have a life and character of their own. They speak of continuity and change . . . This Cathedral is not and will not become a closed shop. It belongs to the wider community—to the town of Chelmsford; to the five London boroughs; to the county of Essex; to the whole Diocese of Chelmsford."[20]

To the extent that any of the congregation still saw the Cathedral as their church this made it clear that the needs of the Diocese, the very raison d'être for the Cathedral's existence, must be paramount.

The Provost had acknowledged the work of the Centre for Research and Training but its future was far from certain. The "uncomfortable things" it had been saying had not been to the liking of all. Its action research work into parish dynamics, a form of group psychoanalysis, required ways of working to be challenged. It can be uncomfortable if research shows that the very people who invited dissection of a problem may be part of the problem themselves. A salaried professional will swallow hard and accept the fact: it is less digestible for parochial volunteers. But no projects had been foisted on parishes: they had, in both senses of the phrase, asked for it.

Critics defined what they saw as the faults in the Centre's modus operandi. Some who liked the gentler touch thought its clinical approach appeared to be in conflict with the mother church's pastoral role: yet a loving mother will challenge as well as cosset her children. Others believed such potentially controversial work—acting as the "joker" in the pack—should have been conducted through an independent institution of higher education leaving the cathedral clergy free to perform their more traditional roles: yet the buy-in costs would probably have been unaffordable. Another line of criticism felt the mother church should concentrate on using its training arm to confirm orthodox teaching and structures: yet the Centre was not challenging belief but rather the way groups functioned, an area where the Church's contemporary history showed it had much to learn.[21]

These carefully articulated criticisms may have masked more visceral concerns. Those wedded to traditional ways do not like change. Others may take against the personalities involved. Richard Herrick, although unfailingly loyal, had been described by Hilary Connop Price as someone who "can appear angular and awkward: he is not the companion for an easy life."[22] Wesley Carr, one of the Church's outstanding intellects, was described by a contemporary as "straight as a die but not a negotiator" who would home in sharply on any weakness in others' arguments.[23]

Personalities apart, there were more serious long-term structural and jurisdictional issues surrounding the Centre.[24] An unreasonable restraint would be placed on the appointment of provosts if expertise in behavioural sciences was to be an essential attribute. Could a provost who was not so blessed work comfortably alongside an independent Centre acting in the Cathedral's name? Would he see such a body as an alternative and threatening power base? Furthermore, there seemed to be some confusion over the boundaries of the Provost's and the Bishop's authority. Normally canons residentiary performed a diocesan function, for which they were responsible to the Bishop, and a cathedral function, for which they were accountable to the Provost. The Centre seemed to have been an episcopal creation lodged in the Cathedral in which the then Provost had acquiesced and, as it grew in stature, saw itself as having a role in framing diocesan policy. This jurisdictional ambiguity, which potentially compromised the Cathedral's independence and certainly confused lines of management, had not produced conflict while Provost Hilary Connop Price had been prepared to stand back and let the Centre grow from within and Richard Herrick led both the Centre and the Cathedral, but it was fraught with potential for friction as personnel changed and roles separated. Some of these implications might have been analysed more rigorously in 1971 when the Centre had been inaugurated as a bolt-on rather than as part of a long-term strategic diocesan plan for the training of clergy and laity. There is anecdotal evidence that by the 1980s Bishop John Trillo was beginning to have second thoughts.

John Moses was not the first to be invited to take on the Provostship: another senior clergyman in the Diocese had already decided the job was too hot to handle. The appointment took the Chapter by surprise. Not only did John Moses have no enthusiasm for the behavioural sciences but the Chapter felt he had shown no great interest in the Cathedral, though with responsibility for up to 200 parishes in his archdeaconry he had had little spare time to spend on cultivating other relationships. Indeed, to the extent that there was a problem, it was much more longstanding, Richard Herrick having already acknowledged back in 1978 that there was a gulf between the Cathedral and its parishes.

Like his predecessors John Moses came to the job with no previous cathedral experience: unlike them he had no time to learn. He immediately took on the role of the Director of the Centre for Research and Training and lived in hope that he would be able to develop a working relationship with its other staff. This did not materialise and Wesley Carr resigned as Deputy Director in 1982 while retaining his diocesan training role until the internal diocesan reorganisation of 1985. One has some sympathy for his position; now in his ninth year at the Cathedral and originally recruited specifically with the Centre in mind, the jurisdictional contradictions that were inherent in the Centre's existence were not of his making. The Provost continued with other short-term Deputy Directors until 1984 at which point the Chapter decided to close the Centre.

The Cathedral Chapter of well-established clergy with strong existing relationships was now at odds with its new Provost, inadvertently drawing attention to the criticism that the Cathedral was unfriendly: ironically, they might have benefited from the intervention of behavioural scientists. Edward Finch was in his twelfth year at the Cathedral; Michael Yorke, a former Deputy Director of the Centre, had served six years at the Cathedral in two stints; Peter Marshall, Deputy Director of Diocesan Training under Wesley Carr, had joined them recently in 1981. Four of them would go on to even higher things: John Moses as Dean of St. Paul's Cathedral, Wesley Carr as Dean of Bristol Cathedral and then Dean of Westminster Abbey, Michael Yorke as Provost of Portsmouth Cathedral and then Dean of Lichfield Cathedral and Peter Marshall as Dean of Worcester Cathedral: in 1997, when they were all simultaneously in high office, they were known light-heartedly amongst their peers as the Chelmsford Mafia.[25]

Michael Yorke, calling on all the counselling skills which had made him such a force with the Samaritans, was identified as the bridge-builder: in 1984 he was appointed to the new post of Vice-Provost, through which he would give priority to the needs of the Cathedral parish and congregation, recognising the increasing demands on the Provost's time taken up by diocesan and national issues: the post has since become a permanent fixture. Outside the Chapter, the Provost and his Master of Music, Graham Elliott, had a shared vision for cathedral music and given John Moses' self-deprecation in this sphere—"I told the choirmen that the best contribution I could make to the musical life of the Cathedral would be to sing nothing"[26]—at least this alliance was able to blossom.

Whatever was happening behind the scenes, there were urgent financial issues to address. An appeal for capital funds for repair and refurbishment had started as John Moses took up office but no specific plans had been drawn up with which to enthuse potential donors. With the drive that was to characterise his Provostship he immediately appointed Robert Potter as architect: in this move he was energetically supported by Geoffrey Ireland whose oversight of the fabric personally and through committee work would be of incalculable benefit to the Cathedral over four decades. Professional fundraisers and a public relations company were also quickly brought on board. Colonel Geoffrey Morgan of Great Leighs was appointed as the Appeal Manager with an Appeals Office in the Muniment Room, as ever the initial cubby-hole for new ventures. A network of fundraising groups was formed throughout the county under the chairmanship of the Provost and Colonel George Judd of Ardleigh.[27] The appeal for £400,000 (£1.1 million in today's money) was launched at Choral Evensong on April 17th 1982. The money would make the outside of the Cathedral watertight and refurbish and refurnish the interior to create space and greater flexibility for worship, musical and drama performances and special occasions when the Cathedral interfaced with the town, county and Diocese. Congregational meetings were held in March and November 1982 to discuss the plans.

In the March 1983 *Cathedral News* the Provost advised:

> "The immediate work will consist of the installation of a new heating system, the laying of a stone floor throughout the Cathedral, the replacement of the pews by chairs and the provision of new items of furnishing appropriate to the dignity and character of the Cathedral . . . The work will take nine months and it has been necessary to take the hard decision to close the Cathedral building throughout this period."

The Chapter House and vestry, both of which could be accessed via the vestry door to the north, would, however, still be used for Saturday morning surgeries, Sunday morning celebrations of the Holy Communion at 8.00 a.m., all weekday services and Choral Evensong on Saturdays. From Sunday, May 8th all other full choral Sunday services would be held in the assembly hall of King Edward VI Grammar School, with additional provision for a crèche and the Sunday School during Parish Communion. The bells of the Cathedral would continue to be rung throughout the nine months "as a public statement that although the building is closed the work of the Cathedral continues without interruption." The Provost recognised that the Diocese as well as the congregation would be denied access to the Cathedral but was able to use other parish churches to hold a number of diocesan and cathedral services led by the cathedral staff and choir and supported by members of the cathedral congregation.

John Moses continued to keep his readers up-to-date. In the May *Cathedral News* he informed them:

> "The scheme has been commended with great enthusiasm by the Cathedrals Advisory Commission. I am aware that there will be

for many people a sense of loss . . . When the work is done we shall return to a very different cathedral. It will feel a little less like a parish church and a little more like a cathedral. And that must be."

In a reciprocal arrangement the King Edward VI Grammar School Orchestra, which had excelled itself at the Albert Hall Schools Prom the previous year, gave a fund-raising concert under the baton of the Cathedral's former Assistant Master of Music, Peter Cross. In June 1983 the *Cathedral News* reported that a large anonymous donation had taken the Appeal to its target of £400,000.

Work moved on apace and the Grammar School, founded in 1551 to teach local boys the classics and Anglican doctrine to underpin the new Protestant orthodoxy, temporarily went back to its roots as an Anglican stronghold. Indeed, the grammar school boarders and their masters had been regular church attendees since the school's foundation and, until boarding ended in 1976, had sat in the South Chapel, then called the Chapel of the Holy Spirit, at Sunday morning Matins: the cherub's head window there had been given in memory of Sarah Ellen Rogers, the Headmaster's wife who had died in 1904.[28]

In October 1983 one correspondent wrote to the *Cathedral News* to say that she had missed the Cathedral's atmosphere and silence and not being able to kneel. But there were compensations:

"Many of the sermons seem to have gained a freer and less inhibited quality—the clergy generally seem far more with us than above or apart from us . . . Also our own natural responses have become less restricted—we have been able to laugh, clap and so on without that feeling of awkwardness associated with being in a church. We have thus become closer to our real selves . . . Secondly once I'd got used to the idea of receiving the bread and wine whilst standing, I discovered that eye-to-eye contact actually becomes quite important—I felt less anonymous, more an individual and it somehow accentuates the fact that God accepts me as I am. Thirdly, you have noticed what happens after the 9.30 a.m. service? With the absence of coffee, the 'coffee cliques' have disappeared . . . We seem to have become friendlier and more united as a congregation."

In November 1983, as the work neared completion, the Provost wrote:

> "Our first impression, I am sure, will be one of openness and space. We shall see the Cathedral as it was first conceived and designed. The simple dignity of its architecture will be allowed to speak for itself, uncompromised by heavy furnishings . . . We go back into the Cathedral for Advent Sunday. The work of re-ordering will have been completed by that date, although . . . it will almost certainly be the middle of February before all the new items of furnishing are in position."

To the Diocese John Moses described the Cathedral as "large enough to be useful but small enough to retain a sense of intimacy."[29]

What more symbolic day could there have been for resuming worship than Advent Sunday, the first day of the liturgical year, the time of expectant waiting and preparation for the Nativity? What would the congregation see?[30]

In the sanctuary Beryl Dean had devised a patchwork symbolising Glory which covered the whole wall below the east window: it was described by John Moses as "a great essay in colour." A new high altar, to a design by the Cathedral's architect, Robert Potter, made of green Westmoreland slate, stood in an advanced position near the head of the nave. New congregational seating was brought into play in the open spaces on the flanks near the north and south chapels, dedicated since 1954 to St. Cedd and the Saints of Essex and to St. Peter; they now ceased to be working chapels so required less space in front of them. The choir stalls were retained but, with the altar in its new forward position, were shifted towards the east end of the chancel where Graham Elliott was confident that the sound would not be trapped by the chancel arch and would, in any case, reverberate off the new French limestone flooring. The bishop's throne continued to stand on the north side of the sanctuary, a little nearer the congregation, and was reduced in height so that it related more sensitively to the proportions of the building; however it was still an over-ornate gothic anomaly and was replaced in 1988 by a new chair designed and made by John Skelton from the same Westmoreland slate as the altar and the font and given by the family of Thomas Huxtable. The provost's stall stood opposite the throne on the south side though, again, this old stall was replaced in 1989 by a new one donated by the family of John Lindsay Scott. New chairs and prayer desks were provided for diocesan and cathedral dignitaries but these would not be permanent fixtures and would be brought in for special services as required. However, in 1993 new permanent seating was provided for the Residentiary Chapter, the area bishops and archdeacons and a section was designated in which there could be formal seating for the Greater Chapter.[31]

In the nave the timber-framed, upholstered, interlocking chairs had been designed in the first instance for Washington Cathedral; they were wider than most church chairs and could be easily removed and stacked. Designs for hassocks, each one bearing the name of a parish in the Diocese, had been provided by Beryl Dean and the Essex Handicrafts Association had accepted responsibility for making them, a project that would take 100 of them two years. John Moses explained that "it is Miss Dean's intention that the hassocks with their abstract designs shall be jewels of colour throughout the body of the Cathedral set against the discreet neutrality of the stone and the upholstered chairs."

The metal ambos, to serve as pulpit and lectern, were made of matching design by Giuseppe Lund and stood on the north and south sides of the chancel arch. John Moses wrote:

> "They have been conceived and constructed in such a way that
> they will come out of the floor and wrap themselves round the
> north and south pillars of the chancel arch."

Lund was also commissioned to design the screens to enclose the two new working chapels at the west end of the Cathedral and the cross in the western arch. The elegant slate font, designed by Robert Potter, resting on the metal tripod stand designed by Alan Evans, stood at the west end of the nave between the medieval wall cupboards. John Moses hoped to use the west door as the normal way into the Cathedral for Sunday services:

> "It will be only in this way that we can get a true perspective of
> the Cathedral . . . The font . . . has a direct relationship with the
> west door and the altar . . . It can be moved when we need to turn
> the Cathedral round for other events."

The two new working chapels at the west end of the Cathedral were to be entered through Lund's taper-like metal screens:

" . . . not merely to provide some degree of privacy to those who
are using the chapels, but also a sense to those who stand outside
that they are being drawn in and pointed upwards."

The north-western Chapel of St. Cedd (but now minus all the saints
of Essex) would be the chapel for weekday services and private prayer; the
south-western Chapel of St. Peter (formerly the Baptistery containing the
old font) was designated as a military chapel to house books of remembrance
and military memorial tablets and colours. In 1984 *The Bombed Child* or
Pieta, sculpted by Georg Ehrlich, an Austrian Jew, was added and in 1987
his bronze relief of *Christ the Healer* was bequeathed by his widow, Bettina,
in gratitude for the exhibition of both their work at the 1985 Cathedral
Festival.[32]

The re-ordered Cathedral from the altar looking east:
photo by Mervyn Marshall

The re-ordered Cathedral from the altar looking west:
photo by Mervyn Marshall

The effect delighted Bishop John Trillo:

> "The re-ordering was a very courageous step which was bound to disturb many people but the outcome is near miraculous. With the pews gone and with them much else, the Church reveals itself as a Perpendicular building with its glorious arches and the light in which it seems to float. My heart lifts always when I enter the west door in procession."[33]

On Saturday November 26th 1983 at 3.30 p.m., the eve of Advent Sunday, the doors of the Cathedral were re-opened. The refurbishment was accompanied by a reiteration by Provost John Moses of the Cathedral's responsibility to all Anglicans[34] not just a resident congregation. Therefore, it would offer the whole range of authorised liturgy, especially in celebrating Holy Communion for which different options had been included in the

303

Alternative Service Book that replaced Series Three in 1980. The old 1662 rite would be used every Sunday at 8.00 a.m. while the 9.30 a.m. Parish Communion would follow the Alternative Service Book Rite A, with its mixture of extempore prayer and eucharistic prayers linked by scholars to third century apostolic tradition. The numbers at the monthly 11.15 a.m. Sung Eucharist and Matins had not been large but the Provost felt they were worth preserving. So a Sung Eucharist according to the Alternative Service Book Rite B, with Elizabethan language and more of its roots in the 1549 Prayer Book, would be held monthly on the first and third Sundays: Matins would be retained on the second, fourth and fifth Sundays. Sunday Evensong would remain unaltered. Weekday services would stay much the same except that Thursday Communion would be a Rite B service. Festivals would have their own particular pattern and the Provost intended to extend the Cathedral's observation of Red Letter Days to incorporate a sung Eucharist at Epiphany, Ash Wednesday, Maundy Thursday, Ascension Day, St. Peter's Day and Michaelmas and a Requiem on All Souls Day. The laity would also become more involved: from September 1984 at Parish Communion the Epistle would be read and the chalice administered by members of the congregation as Lay Assistants as agreed after extensive discussions in the Cathedral Council and the Parochial Church Committee.[35] But, as this was a cathedral, diocesan or civic occasions would always take precedence where there was a clash with parish services.

The 70th anniversary of the Diocese and Cathedral was launched on March 22nd 1984 with a Service of Thanksgiving and Dedication of the re-ordered Cathedral in the presence of Princess Margaret. Other events followed: a Diocesan Eucharist presided over by Robert Runcie, Archbishop of Canterbury on Thursday May 10th; a celebratory Civic Service and Clergy Synod on Friday May 11th; the Bishop's "At Home" days for parish officers on every Saturday in June; Open Door Projects for church schools on twelve weekdays in June; and a major diocesan Bradwell Pilgrimage on July 7th. Three Keene Lectures on the theme, "Images of God", and a dramatic presentation, *Come Christianity to an Eastern Shore*, devised by Ronald Blythe, took place in the autumn.

However, the event that caught the imagination of Chelmsford's population and significantly boosted its self-image was Graham Elliott's new week-long Festival of Music and Arts in May 1984. John Jordan may have noticed festival fatigue setting in with such a concentration of events but this Festival would be of a different order with international artists displaying a wider range of musical and artistic genres which, it was hoped, would attract a range of audiences from all over the region, although in fact, over its 24 years' lifetime, two-thirds of the audience remained local to mid Essex. Taking full advantage of the capacity to turn the congregational chairs to face a specially designed stage that could be fitted snugly between the pillars at the west end, the Cathedral blossomed into a magnificent concert venue with a superb acoustic that would be complimented by many top international musicians. The Festival was born of Graham Elliott's musical inspiration, John Moses' vision of the Cathedral as an asset for the whole community, the dedication of a small army of hard-working volunteers, not all of them cathedral worshippers, who organised, staged and marketed the Festival and sufficient financial backing from Chelmsford Borough Council and Essex County Council and sponsorship from local businesses, most notably G.E.C. Marconi, to enable it to get off the ground. Over the years it would showcase top chamber orchestras and eminent international musicians from The King's Singers to Cleo Laine and Johnnie Dankworth, from Yehudi Menuhin to Georgie Fame and from the Amadeus Quartet to the Jacques Loussier Trio plus a bevy of local amateur and semi-professional talent in the activities of the Festival Fringe (or Festival in the Community as it was called in its later years). It was unlike anything that Chelmsford had seen before and moved the town out of the cultural shadow of London.

John Moses wanted the Cathedral to be open to everyone of whatever churchmanship and to be a welcoming place for the people of Essex to enjoy performing arts at the highest level. He said it would not be a closed shop. He was a man of his word.

CHAPTER 24

Tug of War

Chelmsford Cathedral was now much more open to the Diocese as a place of worship and to the community at large. But for those who attended its services or merely visited its spiritual and aesthetic ambience was paramount. The *Cathedral News* reprinted extracts from a sermon by Maurice Wood, Bishop of Norwich, which sought to capture this holistic experience:[1]

> "A cathedral is a symbol . . . on a grand scale . . . It touches men and women in a special way, through architecture, through its dimension in time and space, through its music, its liturgy, its ceremonial and its colour. Not least, it touches people powerfully through its capacity for putting them in perspective, leading them into spiritual space, investing them with a timelessness and sense of mystery, though by no means overawing them, rather lifting their hearts to heaven's door . . . A cathedral is no mere outworn symbol of an age of faith . . . A cathedral in the 1980s penetrates to the things which lie deep inside a man; the things which he finds difficult to articulate, but which are woven into the very fabric of his humanity; things which are bedrock, which won't go away and which have a habit of coming to the surface when material things wear thin and secular things begin to pall . . . A cathedral speaks to something deep within humanity."

This abandoned the elitist terms of yesteryear and was expressed in mystical, dogma-free language that was more likely to resonate with the many who were curious about the spiritual but incredulous about the miraculous.

But who should meet the costs of sustaining this beautiful and mysterious environment? John Moses identified a dilemma:

> "People come to cathedrals and town centre parish churches for many reasons. One consideration is, I believe, a desire for a greater degree of anonymity that cannot always be guaranteed in a local parish church . . . It can be a perfectly legitimate requirement but it can present peculiar problems when we as a congregation come to face the challenge of Christian Stewardship."[2]

In arguing the case for a greater commitment of money by its commuting worshippers John Moses was treading a familiar path: Provosts Eric Gordon and Hilary Connop Price had been there in the 1960s and 1970s. Yet again the cathedral congregation was told that its giving was disappointingly low:

> "We are in a very privileged position and there is hard evidence to suggest that we have avoided some of the financial responsibilities that properly belong to us within the life of the Church. It is a very sobering thought that if every member of the Church Members Fund were simply to increase his or her weekly pledge by the cost of a loaf of bread and covenant that additional item then we should meet in full all our commitments for the New Year . . . an increase that is consistent with the responsibilities that we have for the worship and witness of the church in this place."[3]

The congregation needed to double its giving. John Moses did not mince words: "a committed and guaranteed income of less than £60,000 per annum [£150,000 in today's money] would be a scandal." To consider giving 5% of net income was, he felt, "a realistic base point."[4]

However, the other half of Christian Stewardship, a more committed partnership with the clergy in spreading the gospel, seemed to some to be a euphemism for getting the laity to do more of the clergy's traditional work, an ecclesiastical equivalent of downsizing and restructuring to cope with a shrinking business. It did not sit comfortably with those who wished to attend church to commune personally with God and reflect, perhaps uncertainly, on their own faith without committing themselves to join the sales team: but even secular organisations allow only so many free goes before insisting on full paid membership. In 1984 Michael Yorke acknowledged this cynical interpretation of Christian Stewardship but put a positive spin on it, defining it as "realising our potential as individuals and as a company of Christians . . . a greater sense of togetherness, mutual trust and responsibility." The Provost added the qualification that "of course . . . the Church must never monopolise our time and our energy . . . There is also much that can be done in the life of the wider community"[5], thus allowing room for personal witness through work, friendship and voluntary activity. To this end the Schools of Prayer and a Cathedral Theological Society were established as a springboard for personal spiritual development not just for the congregation but for those from further afield.

Some of the congregation noticed that they were increasingly sharing their church with the Diocese. The re-ordering of 1983 enabled Diocesan Synod meetings to be held in the Cathedral so that there were even more days in the year when the Diocese monopolised the building. John Moses was emphatic:

> "Nothing can alter the fact . . . that we are the Cathedral Church of this enormous Diocese . . . There is bound to be a tug of war from time to time for the congregation of a parish church cathedral . . . I remain utterly convinced that Chelmsford Cathedral has no raison d'être apart from the Diocese it is called to serve."[6]

Vice-Provost Michael Yorke backed him up:

> "It is very easy for us at the Cathedral to become possessive about what we are so richly given in our congregational life. The traditions we have inherited . . . the beauty of the building . . . its physical and spiritual warmth, the quality of musicianship, the range of preaching, the beauty of the flowers . . . Some of these things have their roots in a much-loved parish church of many centuries, others are more modern and have arisen from the resources made available because we became a cathedral in 1914 . . . We are very fortunate. Let us not look on these gifts as rights to be hugged to ourselves . . . Some feel that the 'parish' side and the congregation have been overlooked in recent times while the 'cathedral' element has been enhanced. Perhaps such an adjustment has been necessary as we have sought to serve more dynamically . . . this huge Diocese."[7]

The tug of war would intensify: between 1987 and 1991 special services and events increased by 250%.[8]

The tension between parish and diocese and the growing gap between different wings of the Church as to the literal interpretation of the Bible raised questions about the Diocese of Chelmsford's preparedness for the next evangelistic thrust: it was not a new problem, just more accentuated. Given the track record of organised missions in the Diocese since 1916 many Anglicans had come to the conclusion that they could most effectively bear witness through their daily lives in interaction with others, not by preaching at them: in a sense this was a partial return to salvation by good works which had been a force for good a century earlier and was still lived out through many individual lives. But for those who supported the more old-fashioned form of missionary evangelism what exactly would one preach? With the different strands of churchmanship and numerous variations of the *Alternative Service Book* of 1980, which were to be made even more complex in the multi-volume *Common Worship* of 2000, there was no single definition of Anglican belief around which all could unite. John Moses, in his Cathedral Column in the *Essex Churchman*, explained:

> "We are at a crossroads where faith is concerned . . . There are large questions in the minds of many people about the nature of God, the meaning of Jesus, the understanding of atonement and the practice of prayer. Statements of faith that are simplistic and dogmatic and predictable are not helpful."[9]

Where did all this leave the 2,533,000[10] souls of the ever-expanding Diocese of Chelmsford? East London, which contained over 40% of that total, had been exempt from the riots which scarred some other cities in the summer of 1981 but the contributory issues of growing unemployment and feelings of vulnerability in some ethnic minority areas still pertained. The archbishops set up a commission to examine the Church's mission in Urban Priority Areas which would, in 1985, produce its report, *Faith in the City*. Jim Roxburgh, the newly appointed Bishop of Barking and diocesan Director of Mission pleaded the case:

> "'Inner City' is not just the area we speed through on the way to Liverpool Street or Fenchurch Street. It is part of our Diocese. Its people are our brothers and sisters. Christ died for Stratford as well

as for Stebbing. The Gospel is good news equally for Broxted and for Beckton . . . I would like to see the Cathedral, so central to the life of the Church in Essex, go on grappling with how equally central it can be to the life of the Church in the London boroughs. I don't just look for the re-routing of resources, though this may well have to be part of the adjustment to today's London. I do, however, look for a prayer agenda in every parish in the Diocese that shows a sense of urgency for the spiritual well-being of the 'other 42%'."[11]

A few months later another article pointed out that the Barking episcopal area was staffed at senior level by just one suffragan bishop and an archdeacon: yet two-thirds of English dioceses (excepting Sodor and Man) which had smaller populations than the Barking area all had a bishop and two archdeacons:

"None of them has the fearful social and spiritual problems of Barking . . . The real question is, are the resources in the right place? Can a rural gentlemanly diocese of the shires ever really get to grips mentally and emotionally with the needs of five London boroughs?"

That question ran the risk, which was to become endemic in education and social services, of believing that only Londoners could really understand London, a form of navel-gazing which would be more likely to alienate rather than engage the interest of the shires. The Bishop of Barking went on:

"It should not be beyond the wit of man to provide archdeacons and assistant bishops from among the beneficed clergy of the archdeaconry, preferably men who are already at work in the London boroughs . . . freed from committee work to concentrate on the pastoral and spiritual needs of the clergy and the people in their charge."[12]

Eventually in 1989 a bishop's commission, chaired by John Moses, recommended that a fourth episcopal area, with its own area bishop and archdeacon, be created for West Essex, centred on Harlow, with its barely perceptible church-going rate of under 2%, to relieve the pressure on Barking[13] though it was a fourth archdeaconry that was created. The Diocese of Chelmsford, only the twelfth largest in geographical area, remained second only to London in population: yet it was fifth in the number of parishes and seventh in the number of churches, revealing the continued discrepancy between new urban and ancient rural dioceses.[14]

Faith in the City created a furore. The Church of England identified its urban priority area parishes, according to six Department of the Environment indicators—levels of unemployment, overcrowding, households lacking basic amenities, pensioners living alone, ethnic origin and single parent households—on which basis 36 parishes in the Diocese of Chelmsford were extremely deprived and nine deprived.[15] But many, both inside and outside the Church, accused the Church of straying outside its brief. Some felt faith was an individual matter of personal belief and practice, unrelated to wider social, organisational or political matters; others felt that a middle-class church, stuck in traditional structures, would be unable to implement its recommendations; yet others believed the report was unclear about the relationship of the Kingdom of God, as perceived through the Creation and the Incarnation, to citizenship and community. Because 23 of the report's 61 recommendations were aimed at the government, incensed Thatcherite politicians saw Marxism at work in the Church. A sympathetic outsider, the Chief Rabbi, felt that the report did not lay enough stress on self-help as a way out of poverty: persecuted Jewish communities had a long history and deep understanding of looking to themselves for salvation. John Moses was one of the critics of the report, holding the more conservative view.[16] He was taken to task by Paul Brett, the Bishop of Chelmsford's Director of Social Responsibility.[17] The disagreement ended there and fairly reflected the polarity of views within the Church. But the Bishop of Barking's problems did not abate. He wrote to the Diocese to explain:

> "When a village of 2,000 was vacant recently 73 clergy enquired about it. In Newham two applied for one vacancy and both, in the end, said 'No'."[18]

It seemed easier to support the indigenous Christian population in Africa and the Caribbean than to convert the concentrated masses of East London where worship was now as likely to take place in a Jewish synagogue, Islamic mosque or Hindu temple as a Christian chapel or church. In 1980 the Diocese of Chelmsford established formal partnerships with the dioceses of Trinidad and Tobago and Mount Kenya East. John Moses had first visited Mount Kenya East in 1979[19] and had supported its drive to build a new cathedral at Embu which was consecrated on July 12th 1987 and completed in 1988; Chelmsford Cathedral raised 15% of the capital cost, the largest single contributor,[20] and established two-way exchanges. But such links were no longer in the old evangelical tradition when missionaries rode on the crest of an imperial wave as immortalised in those now unacceptable hymns, *Over the seas there are little brown children* and *From Greenland's icy mountains*: two world wars, seen as European civil wars in Africa and Asia, had shattered the myth of the superiority of Christian western civilisation and led to rapid decolonisation after 1945. As one writer observed of the Anglican Communion, the typical late 20th century communicant was:

> ". . . African, female and does not speak English as a first language . . . In many parts of Africa, Latin America and the Far East, Christianity is on a roll with booming numbers that western countries can only look at with wonder and envy."[21]

Internal governance was easier to sort out than external mission. From January 1st 1985 new statutes reformed the Cathedral Council. Hitherto it had contained representatives from the Chapter, the Diocese and the congregation though decision-making effectively lay in the hands of a smaller Standing Committee on which the Residentiary Chapter had a major influence. In its reformed state the Standing Committee would disappear and the Cathedral Council would be elevated from a nominal rubber-stamping role to that of an effective executive body. There would continue to be a balance between representatives of the Diocese, Chapter and congregation but there would also be a balance between lay and clerical members. The three churchwardens would continue to be ex-officio members and the annual parochial church meeting would elect three other lay members. The old Parochial Church Committee would now be renamed the Cathedral Congregation Committee, still under the chairmanship of the Provost; it would contain the canons residentiary, assistant clergy, accredited lay ministers who had pastoral responsibilities in the parish, the lay members elected to the Deanery Synod and the lay members elected to the Cathedral Council; and it would become a sub-committee of the Cathedral Council, thus recognising the prior rights of the Diocese and, in its new name, the fact that the congregation overwhelmingly came from outside the parish.[22] At much the same time the Friends of the Cathedral were re-launched with a new constitution under lay leadership to try to enlarge the body of members.

The Diocese was not to be left out in this restructuring mania. It produced four new councils in 1985 whose directors were all connected to the Cathedral: Peter Southwell-Sander, the Director of Ministry, and Paul Brett, the Director of Social Responsibility, became leasehold residentiary canons; Patrick Appleford as the continuing Director of Education was already an honorary canon; and Michael Proctor, the newly appointed Director of Mission, joined him in that status. By this time the number of canons' stalls in the Cathedral had been increased from 24 to 30 to allow for the permanent residentiary canons and the additional leasehold canons.

In 1985 Bishop John Trillo retired. He was described as a "man of quiet and unselfconscious holiness; a self-effacing man."[23] He had been active in the world of ecumenism as chairman of the Church of England/Roman Catholic Joint Commission and of the British Council of Churches. He was an excellent bridge builder externally but uneasy internally with the politics of the new system of synodical government which had emerged just prior to his enthronement. The smaller General Synod, which had replaced the Church Assembly in 1970, and the subsidiary diocesan and deanery synods, which replaced the old diocesan and ruridecanal conferences, had created a structure that, in the Bishop's view, attracted too many who had axes to grind: "I do not find the synodical system very easy to be in. The sad thing about synodical government is that extremes gang up."[24] The problem was not new. John Watts-Ditchfield had faced exactly the same challenge 70 years before. Those who want to gang up will always find a way of doing it. However the sheer weight of the consultative process in an age of media scrutiny, when public and politicians were less deferential to the Church's opinions, appeared to neuter bishops. While church people who personally knew a bishop would speak glowingly of his personality and goodness and the effectiveness of his pastoral work, diocesans often emerged as paler images in public. Some said that it was a result of the new vacancy-in-see committees through which the struggling parish clergy would look for:

" . . . an experienced and sympathetic Father in God who will hold their hand and the laity hope for a kindly bishop who will bring warmth to the services, not preach overlong and spend time at the party in the parish hall afterwards."[25]

If a bishop fitted this bill, did his share of committee work at national level, tried to broker disputatious synodical meetings and kept a weather eye open for unguarded statements that might be exploited by the press or zealots within his own Church, he would inevitably don the cloak of a diplomatic conflict resolver and veer in public towards the anodyne. It has been argued that these factors caused the supply of visionary and independent-minded episcopal scholars to dry up. When the Church did get one, such as David Jenkins, Bishop of Durham, who expressed his doubts about the Virgin Birth and the physicality of the Resurrection and Ascension, no great shakes within liberal theological circles, it caused a major explosion. John Trillo felt obliged to comment:

> "I take the view that the Bishop of Durham has done a service in the sense that the whole country is talking about the Christian faith. I think he has been foolish in mistaking the two roles—the one of the don and that of the bishop. The task of the don is to needle people, to make them think. The job of the bishop is more positive."

Nonetheless a poll of diocesan bishops showed that two-thirds of them felt that it was not necessary to accept the divinity of Christ to be a Christian, half had doubts about the miracles and one-third did not believe in the Virgin Birth or the physical resurection.[26] However John Trillo was absolutely clear on the role of women: "I always hoped I would be able to ordain a woman myself, but it is not going to happen for some little time."[27] Ironically, that suggestion would needle quite a few people.

John Trillo's frank views on synodical government, from which he was retiring, received a more positive gloss from Derek Bond, Bishop of Bradwell, who was still part of it. He regarded it as:

> ". . . a truer notion and a truer style of Christian assembly than the forms of Church government we have had before . . . The Church of England is itself a little ecumenical movement."

That was a clever euphemism for a church divided. He identified some of the contentious issues—embryo research, marriage in church after divorce, interpretations of the Creed, the ordination of women—but insisted that "they are not destructive differences if faith in God is working through love of the brethren." Events were to show that such love was in short supply. He echoed John Watts-Ditchfield's concerns about the Church's propensity for factionalism:

"Some of the letters I receive and some published in church newspapers ought not to have been written . . . Exclusive association with those who confirm our own viewpoint is not the way . . . We shall never learn to be members of the Anglican Church if we cling to parties within it."[28]

As a feature writer in *The Times* observed:

"Churchmen may love each other a lot, but sometimes they do not like each other very much. But the 'Oxford Union' rules apply: you can be as rude as you like as long as you are oblique, elegant and ironic in the doing of it." [29]

However, he did acknowledge that "without such civilised rules of engagement . . . the Church of England might have torn itself to pieces long ago."

It was in that climate that John Waine, Chelmsford's seventh bishop, was enthroned in the Cathedral on May 31st 1986. Educated at Manchester University, he did national service in the Royal Air Force and then trained for the ministry at Ridley Hall, Cambridge. His early curacies were in the Diocese of Liverpool at St. Mary's, West Derby and All Saints', Sutton in St. Helens followed by incumbencies at Ditton in Widnes, Holy Trinity in Southport and the Team Rectorship of Kirkby in Liverpool, then the largest parish in England with a population of 67,000 and a staff of 12, one of the priority areas mentioned in *Faith in the City*. He became suffragan Bishop of Stafford in the Diocese of Lichfield in 1975 and diocesan Bishop of St. Edmundsbury and Ipswich in 1979. He favoured the ordination of women as deacons: "I do not think there should be undue delay in action here."[30] In the wake of the David Jenkins controversy he immediately confirmed his belief in the Virgin Birth and the miracle of the empty tomb.

But the Bishop of Barking continued to be outspoken. Perhaps the area bishops were to be the thought provokers and the diocesan the shaper of solutions? Jim Roxburgh cast doubt on whether the Church was any longer a national church. He remembered a time when:

" . . . the services were for all parishioners. The organisations were for all and barriers to membership were as low as possible. Now . . . our forms of worship are seen increasingly to be for the gathered community. Whether the Parish Communion or the family service is the main act of worship it is increasingly seen to be appropriate primarily for the regulars. The charismatic forms of service are high on joy and welcome but low on enabling those who seek the timeless words of a timeless liturgy. Many clergy like to make higher and higher barriers for people to jump to become part of the worshipping family and increasingly they are resisting the pleas of the outsiders for baptism. Even funerals are regarded with suspicion and funeral directors are told 'I will bury them only if they have belonged' . . . Where are we going? What is the fundamental basis of our nationwide appeal? I do not detect a clear answer coming yet from all sides of the Church."[31]

That was a pretty unhappy analysis. Michael Vickers, the Bishop of Colchester, felt that church people were as likely to be seekers of the truth as disseminators:

"As far as the spiritual life is concerned Christians, it seems to me, are like a multitude of persons standing on a giant staircase. Some are only on the bottom step, whilst others are not far from the top and the rest are on various steps in between . . . How prone the Church is to aim all its efforts towards assisting those on the top few steps whilst almost totally disregarding all those below."[32]

If that were true there was a need for evangelism within before evangelism without.

In 1988 the archbishops set up a Church Urban Fund to support work in the priority areas identified in *Faith in the City*. They set the Diocese of Chelmsford a target of £800,000 as its share of the £18 million national figure (just over twice that amount in modern values) but Bishop John Waine, with his own inner city experience behind him and the Bishop of Barking on his right hand, increased the diocesan target to £2 million, half to be raised by parishes and half from industry and trusts: it was achieved by 1994.[33]

While there was uncertainty in the Church at large, the Cathedral's musical life continued to develop under Graham Elliott, providing the beauty and elegance of worship that many cherished. He was appointed an Associate of the Royal Academy of Music in 1984, a rare distinction for a cathedral organist,[34] and in 1985 received his doctorate from the University of Wales for his thesis on the spirituality of the music of Benjamin Britten. In July 1985 the cathedral choir undertook its first foreign tour to Flanders, singing Anglican Choral Evensong at the Benedictine Abbey at Zevenkerken and High Mass in both Bruges Cathedral and the Abbey Church of Male, the home of the Canonesses of the Holy Sepulchre whose English Order had run New Hall School in Chelmsford since 1799;[35] in July 1986 the choir sang at the cathedrals in Altenberg and Cologne in Germany, raising money for the trip through a 10 mile sponsored walk and a recital;[36] and in the same year the choristers joined in sung worship with the boys of Brentwood Roman Catholic Cathedral and the full choir made a recording with Abbey Records.[37] In September 1986 Tim Allen replaced David Sparrow[38] in his combined role as music teacher at King Edward VI Grammar School and Assistant Master of Music at the Cathedral. In 1987 the Cathedral Choir Association was formed to act as a support group for the maintenance of choir robes and facilities, provide refreshments for the choir at recitals and broadcasts and administer the travel funds which supported the annual choir tour.[39] In the same year the choir sang at Walsingham Abbey for the great pilgrimage service; performed at a televised Royal Albert Hall event in the presence of the Queen to celebrate the 60th anniversary of the founding of the Royal School of Church Music; and sang at Fécamp Abbey on the 900th anniversary of the death of William the Conqueror.[40] In late 1987 the boys began to sing Evensong on Tuesdays as well as Saturdays.[41] Ian Forrester, who had been Dean's Vicar and Succentor at St. George's Chapel, Windsor, replaced John Brown as Precentor and wrote a piece in the *Cathedral News* supporting the role of the choir:

"There will be some who find cathedral worship bewildering. 'Why' they wonder 'do the choir take over so much of the service?' The answer, of course, is that they are not taking over but are offering a particular skill to God on our behalf... The choir sings firstly to the glory of God (this is the offering of the composer and the performers and those who sustain the choir by their generosity) and secondly to help the congregation in their prayers."[42]

In July 1988 the Queen and the Duke of Edinburgh visited Chelmsford to open the new County Hall preceded by a service in the Cathedral to mark the Borough of Chelmsford's centenary. The choir followed this auspicious event with its fourth tour, this time to Caen and Bayeux.[43] In 1989 Graham Elliott reported that the choir had broadcast choral evensong more often than any other choir during the past four or five years.[44] In 1989 they returned to Belgium to sing mass at Kortrijk; led an Anglican Evensong in the Benedictine Abbey of St. Andreas attended by the Abbot and Prior with the Provost delivering the sermon; and took part once again in a service at Male.[45] At the end of that year Chelmsford was one of only three centres in the country to be chosen to teach candidates for the Archbishops' Certificate in Church Music.[46] In February 1990 John Moses wrote in the *Essex Churchman*:

> "The Cathedral seems to get more than its fair share of broadcasting these days. Our proximity to London, the intimacy and the acoustics of the building, the excellence of the choir and our willingness to share through radio or television what we are doing in our worship all count for a good deal."

The annual Cathedral Festival of Music and Arts blossomed. Sponsorship and donations in 1984 totalled £32,000 (£80,200 in modern values) and by 1990 topped £76,000 (£135,000).[47] A marquee in Guy Harlings' garden and a couple of bars and a restaurant in Guy Harlings' building gave it more of a festive flavour. In 1986 greater legal security was given when a new Festival Company was created backed by over 400 Festival Society members who registered themselves as the Friends of the Festival Charity in 1989. The Company's Annual Report for 1986-7 noted that the Festival:

> " . . . is gaining a reputation for the excellence of its standards in all its presentations: since it is dependent on a mainly local audience in a comparatively small auditorium it must continue to rely on sponsorship by industrial and commercial concerns to meet a good proportion of its expenses . . . Artists and audiences alike continue to express surprise that a festival on this scale is run entirely by volunteers."

Paid secretarial assistance, working from the Muniment Room, until an office was provided in the new Guy Harlings extension in 1987, amounted to only three mornings a week.

For the Provost the Festival was central to the Cathedral's relations with the community:

> "Artificial dividing lines between the sacred and the secular have little meaning for me . . . I have quoted before Archbishop William

Temple's famous dictum that 'the Church is the one institution that exists for the sake of those who do not belong'."[48]

There were also occasional drama productions outside the Festival; in 1985 *Waiting for Midnight*, based on the letters and papers from prison of Dietrich Bonhoeffer, was commissioned from Michael Bakewell, formerly with the B.B.C. Drama Department; the 1986 production was *One Thing More . . . Caedmon Construed* by Christopher Fry.

In 1988 John Moses had an opportunity to reshape his team of residentiary canons. Wesley Carr had been appointed Dean of Bristol Cathedral in 1987 and Michael Yorke, who had spent only one-third of his 24 years in the ministry in parish work, decided to return to a parish base as Vicar of King's Lynn in 1988, although he was subsequently to return to the cathedral environment as Provost of Portsmouth in 1994 and Dean of Lichfield in 1999.

The first canonical appointment in February 1988 was that of Timothy Thompson. He was a fourth generation New Zealander who had come to this country to study theology and subsequently trained for the ministry at Cuddesdon. After curacies in North London and Shrub End, Colchester, he had returned for three years to New Zealand and a large rural parish in the foothills of its Southern Alps, before coming back to Essex and a town centre parish at St. James' in Colchester: he was ultimately appointed Rural Dean and Chairman of the House of Clergy in the Diocesan Synod. He referred to himself as a "Sacramental Catholic."[49] He took over Michael Yorke's role as Vice-Provost, inheriting responsibility for the cathedral parish and congregation; his pastoral skills and warm personality benefited many over the years, often in private ways that of necessity are not recorded.

In October 1988 Timothy was joined by his unrelated namesake Barry Thompson in the role of Canon Theologian. This new-sounding title which at that stage existed only at Manchester, Lichfield and York Minster[50] embraced responsibilities usually associated with the Canon Chancellor in more ancient foundations. The Canon Theologian would be the link with the new Centre for Theological Study, an exciting cross-disciplinary initiative at the University of Essex in Colchester, sponsored jointly by the Cathedral Chapter and the Anglican Chaplaincy at the University where Andrew Linzey, the Chaplain in residence and an innovative theologian, had done much of the preparatory work and would provide the vision and impetus for the Centre's continued development. As an important partner in this venture, the new Canon Theologian, Barry Thompson, had an ideal cross-disciplinary academic background having originally trained as a scientist with a post-doctorate fellowship in Oxford under Nobel prize-winner Dorothy Hodgkin. He then worked as a British Council officer in Western India, strengthening scientific and technological links with the United Kingdom, before joining the British Library to develop its international services. For several years he had been considering ordination and eventually trained for the ministry, taking a Master's degree in Theology with distinction at the University of Hull during his curacy at Cottingham. After parish and industrial chaplaincy, he was appointed the Archbishop of York's Adviser on Industrial Affairs and Lecturer in Social Ethics and Director of the Unit of Applied Theology at the University of Hull. At Chelmsford Cathedral he would have responsibility for the Keene Lectures, the Theological Society, the Schools of Prayer and the Cathedral Library, which was to be developed for diocesan use, as well as his work with the Centre.

The Centre for the Study of Theology promised much but had as short a life as the Centre for Research and Training. The Provost explained that it was a brave ecumenical venture at "the most unashamedly secular university in the country"[51] and at a time when divinity faculties at many other universities were retracting. Not for him "godly learning" in which members of the church withdrew into their own huddle to talk to themselves. Rather, the Church must develop its theology in synthesis with other academic specialisms "to attempt from the standpoint of Christian faith a comprehensive and systematic understanding of the world."[52] Indeed, if liberal theological scholarship were allowed to decline he believed the Church would experience difficulty in combating resurgent fundamentalism.[53] The inaugural lecture at Colchester was given in February 1988 by Robert Runcie, Archbishop of Canterbury.[54] The Centre started with investigations into embryo research, human rights, the status of animals (a specialism of Andrew Linzey's), the use of armed force, world development and Christian/Jewish studies.[55] John Moses led this scholarly initiative by example, taking a sabbatical six months in 1987 at Wolfson College, Cambridge, to undertake research and writing on atonement theology.[56] In the end the Centre proved to be too dependent on the charisma and scholarship of Andrew Linzey who left in 1992 for an academic role at the University of Oxford. It proved difficult to sustain the impetus of the founder and in 1999 the Cathedral Chapter ended its financial sponsorship.

Only four years after the completion of the Cathedral's re-ordering it was announced that a new Cathedral Hall and Chapter House were to be built, starting in September 1988. It was scheduled to be a 12 month project[57] though it was not possible to take possession of the Chapter House until March 1990.[58] The cost would be £365,000 (just over double that amount in today's money) of which the Cathedral would have to find £85,000. The first phase of the work had, in fact, begun in 1983, with the building of Church Lane House; the second phase would provide a new Cathedral Hall and two dozen one bedroom flats; and the third phase new income-generating offices on the site where the old Cathedral Hall had stood. The Provost explained:

> "This scheme of comprehensive development—providing residential, commercial and community facilities—has been widely acclaimed. It will give a new sense of dignity at the western end of the Cathedral churchyard . . . It has been the decision of the Cathedral Council . . . that the new building should be known as the Cathedral Chapter House . . . There is no question of a public appeal or any appeal to the congregation. There must be no conflict of interest with the Bishop of Chelmsford's Church Urban Fund . . . The Cathedral will look to a handful of friends and trusts."[59]

The Chapter House was opened by the Duke of Kent on July 12th 1990 followed by a Service of Thanksgiving. The ground floor room, dedicated to St. Cedd, could be used for parish and congregational events. On the upper floors the Jacob Room, was named after Edgar Jacob, Bishop of St. Albans, who had pushed so hard for an Essex diocese; the Johnson Room, after John Johnson who had rebuilt the church following its collapse in 1800; and the Chancellor Room after Frederic Chancellor, the spearhead of Chelmsford's campaign to become see town, whose family had possibly once owned part of the site on which the Chapter House stood.[60] The large Chapter Room on the top floor would seat the Greater Chapter. The Chapter library of 3,000 volumes transferred to the new Courtyard Library in the Guy Harlings' extension with sufficient room to double its number of books.[61] The old Chapter House on the first floor of the 1920s vestry block could now be developed as a Song School, a cue for John Moses and Graham Elliott to see what else could be achieved to build on the burgeoning musical reputation of the Cathedral.

CHAPTER 25

Music, Money and Mission

"I should love to think that the next two or three years will see the commissioning of a new organ and the building of a Treasury."

Thus did Provost John Moses muse in the *Cathedral News* in January 1989. Even though he often claimed not to have a musical ear, something discordant must have registered. He warned his readers:

"The cathedral organ could collapse at any time . . . In technical terms what members of the congregation will notice from time to time are 'cyphers' . . . Notes which are not actually being played take on a life of their own and decide to play."[1]

For John Moses the wish was frequently father to the deed. There had been a successful temporary exhibition of cathedral treasures in 1989. However, the concept of a Visitor's Centre combined with a Treasury to put on permanent display Cathedral and Essex church treasures that were otherwise locked in bank vaults was soon put to one side as the plans were not approved by English Heritage.[2] In its place the idea of a new organ and Choral Foundation emerged, neither of which would require any extension of the Cathedral footprint.

Two important adjustments were made as a necessary prelude to these musical ambitions.

Firstly, in 1991 the role of Precentor was given enhanced status. Ian Forrester left to become Chaplain at Lancing College and the Bishop agreed that the next Precentor should henceforth be one of the three residentiary canons. David Knight, hitherto the Rector of Whitchurch St. Lawrence in Little Stanmore, was appointed and joined the Vice-Provost, Timothy Thompson and the Canon Theologian, Barry Thompson, as the third wise man. The Provost wrote:

> "I welcome the appointment of a Canon Precentor because it will say something about the absolute primacy of liturgy within our ministerial priorities at the Cathedral and the extent to which this must also be used as an area for development with the parishes."[3]

The Canon Precentor's role would continue to be almost completely cathedral-based. He would be responsible to the Provost for organising the regular round of services and for crafting the liturgy for the myriad of special services that the Cathedral hosted and to the Bishop for cathedral services over which he presided. The wider function of providing support for incumbents who needed to put on a service that was outside their normal experience constituted a relatively small part of the role and increasingly, in the new millennium, incumbents would be able to download templates which were made available on-line.

Secondly, at much the same time, Tim Allen, the Assistant Master of Music, left King Edward VI Grammar School to become Organist and Choirmaster at Londonderry Cathedral. Since 1963 the school had paid the assistant's salary and been flexible in allowing him time off for special weekday services. For both sides of the partnership this arrangement had clearly had its day: schools were working within an increasingly inflexible statutory framework which made the informal gentleman's agreement harder to operate and the rapid growth in the number and range of cathedral services meant that Graham Elliott needed full-time support on site. The Cathedral would have to stump up the cost. In anticipation of Tim Allen's departure, the Cathedral had, since September 1989, been employing organ scholars on an annual basis in their gap year before or after university; the first was Neil Weston, Organ Scholar elect at Worcester College, Oxford who returned after graduation as the Cathedral's Senior Organ Scholar and then became the first fully in-house Assistant Master of Music.[4]

In March 1991 the appeal for an organ and Choral Foundation was set in train. "Some newspapers suggest this might be the largest appeal for church music ever launched in the Church of England", the Provost remarked.[5] As was his wont he took the opportunity to remind his readers of its place in the big picture—on the one hand the Cathedral's theological work through the Schools of Prayer, the Theological Society, the Keene Lectures and the Centre for the Study of Theology at the University of Essex: on the other hand its work in the life of the wider community through the Cathedral Festival, the work of the Town Centre Chaplain and the links that were maintained by members of the Chapter and Cathedral staff with institutions and groups all over the county. This was also a good time to form an Old Choristers' Association which emerged in 1992.

Fund-raising troops on the ground were led by Brigadier Adam Gurdon as Appeal Director who had worked successfully on the £1.7 million St. Edmundsbury Appeal (£3 million in modern values). Chelmsford's M.P. Simon Burns chaired the Appeal Committee. Distinguished patrons lent their names including Dame Janet Baker and Sir Yehudi Menuhin, both of whom had appeared at the Cathedral Festival, Dagenham born Dudley Moore and Sir Terence Beckett, former Chief Executive and Managing Director of Ford Motor Company and Director General of the Confederation of British Industry. The organ, right on cue, gave up the ghost in February 1991 and N.P. Mander Ltd., who were eventually engaged to build its replacement, loaned a tiny extension organ.[6] By the middle of 1991 £100,000 (£167,000) had been pledged. The Provost set the congregation their own target of an additional £100,000.[7] That was reasonable; firstly the regular congregation would reap the major benefit week by week from any musical initiative; secondly, as only 10% of the 1990 electoral roll of 365 were resident in the parish,[8] and many had sought out the Cathedral for its musical excellence, this target could be considered a quid pro quo. John Moses told the Diocese that there would be no direct appeal to the parishes[9] though this still left the way open for individuals to contribute.

By the end of 1991 £300,000 (£500,000) had been raised[10] but by the autumn of 1992 the inflow of appeal funds had slowed and the total stood at only £450,000 (£726,000). The Provost was frustrated; there had been a three-year economic recession, the longest since the 1930s, which was aggravated by the Gulf War and a spike in oil prices. Fortunately, by the spring of 1993 the appeal had been boosted to £550,000 (£874,000) thanks to a grant from the Foundation for Sport and the Arts.[11] Work could therefore start on the building of the nave organ at the west end to be finished in time for the May 1994 Cathedral Festival.[12] To garner extra cash the cathedral youth organised a sponsored four day walk along the Essex Way, the canons locked themselves in the tower and were relieved that well-wishers paid for their release and an organ recital was given at St. Paul's Cathedral by

Graham Elliott and eight Anglican cathedral organists born in Essex: David Drinkell (Belfast), Adrian Lucas (Portsmouth), Michael Smith (Llandaff), Roger Fisher (Chester), Barry Rose (St. Albans), Alan Thurlow (Chichester), Marcus Huxley (Birmingham) and John Sanders (Gloucester).[13]

The completion of the organ project was delayed by six months but in mid November 1994 there was finally a Service of Thanksgiving. Critics noticed that the new organ covered the internal view of the west window: so had the first organ in 1772 with its gilded pipes and cherubim trumpeters. Others, however, loved the soaring perpendicular lines of Stephen Bicknell's organ case and pipes which fitted the architecture of the west end so perfectly. On November 30th Naji Hakim, the Organist of La Trinité, Paris, gave an inaugural recital. The smaller chancel organ was ready by mid 1995: its intrusion on the chapel in the south aisle was not crucial as it was no longer a working chapel.

At the same time the Provost wished to create a Choral Foundation. The choir schools of the ancient cathedrals had been described by Sir Sydney Nicholson as "England's oldest youth movement",[14] but they were almost all fee-paying and large endowments were needed to subsidise the choristers. By the 1990s they were struggling to maintain the value of their endowments. An ambitious parish church cathedral had the advantage of starting from scratch and, in this case, was helped by a very generous private donation.

Many of Chelmsford's choristers attended The Cathedral School (a voluntary aided primary school), St. Cedd's (an independent preparatory school), both of which took pupils up to the age of 11 and King Edward VI Grammar School (a voluntary controlled selective school) with a reputation for musical excellence: seven musicians were awarded Oxbridge Choral or Organ Scholarships in the 1990s.[15] In 1994 the three schools, all within walking distance of the Cathedral, became founder members of the Choral Foundation. This arrangement was informal as choir parents could not be required to send their child to any particular school but represented the de facto distribution of most of the choristers. The fit would never be perfect. At secondary level entry to the highly selective grammar school was controlled by the strict rank-ordering of the 11+ test though, as a self-governing grant-maintained school, it was able to arrange a slight variation, giving a place to a cathedral chorister if he was outside Chelmsford's high pass-mark but within the broader range of the Southend and Westcliff grammar schools' entry; this facility was utilised only once. Nonetheless, the schools co-ordinated activities with the Cathedral to ensure that choristers' pastoral and musical needs were looked at as a whole. There was more room for movement with Anglia Polytechnic University where the first scholarships were set up to enable some of the gentlemen of the choir to combine their musical duties with post-graduate studies. This would provide a core of contracted singers and make the membership less "fragile"[16] and vulnerable to sudden losses of personnel. The dedication of the new organs and the Choral Foundation took place in the presence of Princess Margaret on October 3rd 1995.

Provost John Moses introduces Princess Margaret to the choir, October 3rd 1995: Chelmsford Cathedral Knightbridge Library

The economic recession had not helped the appeal. But the reckless investment policy of the Church Commissioners, which imploded with the bursting of the property price bubble in 1990, now added another layer that was to have a long-term effect on congregational giving.

The Church Commissioners controlled the central funds that subsidised cathedrals, topped up clergy stipends and financed clergy pensions. The ravages of inflation, however, made it difficult to maintain the real value of this central pot; a pound in 1968 was worth only 12 pence in 1992. In

1975 Bishop John Trillo warned that inflation threatened the existence of churches of non-historic value, some of which might have to be sold off.[17]

The Church Commissioners invested 60% of their assets in the booming retail property market, way beyond the limit set by their Board of Governors. They even took out £500 million in loans[18] (£837 million in today's money) to sink into developments where none of the units had been pre-let or planning permission obtained in the hopeful expectation that all the pieces would eventually fall into place.[19] They had played fast and loose with charity law, which banned speculation with tax-free charity funds, by creating wholly-owned subsidiary companies to which they loaned church money, treating the interest received back as income rather than repayment of capital, screening the truth in their published accounts and giving a false impression of well-being.[20] The burst in the property bubble in 1990 wiped out one-third of the value of the Church of England's investments and led to a fire-sale of assets at knock down prices to finance loan repayments which were swollen by rocketing interest rates.[21] The *Financial Times* published the awful story on July 11th 1992 on the eve of the General Synod.[22]

Bishop John Waine was a member of the Board of Governors of the Church Commissioners which was supposed to set policy for and monitor the work of the Assets Committee that dealt with investments. He was ruefully reflective:

> "When there were questions about how we were financing our operations and to some extent the level of borrowings, the assurances were given that all was well and that there was no cause for anxiety . . . One worked on the assurances that others who were perhaps better qualified were able to give on these matters."[23]

Better qualified people with an eye on short-term profit maximisation do not necessarily display commensurate levels of common sense as a depressingly long sequence of banking scandals in the subsequent 20 years showed.

An internal Lambeth Palace enquiry was set up under John Waine's chairmanship. He sensibly queried whether the chairman should be independent but concluded: "'if the Church asks you to do something . . . you have to have a very good reason for saying no.' His colleagues included Peter Baring, Chairman of Barings until the Leeson derivatives scandal caused his retirement in 1995, Brian Howard, deputy chairman of the Assets

Committee which had been the guilty party in the investment scandal and accountants Coopers & Lybrand who had condoned the Commissioners' creative accounting policy.[24] This was rather like getting those who had left the front door open to advise others on security measures.

George Carey, Archbishop of Canterbury, a Dagenham lad born into the mission territory of London-over-the-Border, walked head-on into this crisis when he was enthroned in 1991 and had to endure early public scrutiny before a parliamentary select committee. He set up a further enquiry under Michael Turnbull, Bishop of Rochester when he started and Bishop of Durham by the time he finished, charged with recommending reforms in governance. The Bishop observed that "while many people participating in the Church's governance can stop things happening, few (if any) can make things happen." So the General Synod's patchwork of boards and committees was swept away, unmourned by David Hope, the Archbishop of York, who described them as "a colossal waste of time",[25] to be replaced by an Archbishop's Council supported by just four boards: mission, human resources, finance and heritage, and legal services. The Church Commissioners' staff numbers were reduced, and left their offices in Millbank to merge with the administrative staff at Church House, leaving financial and spending policy for the Council to decide and General Synod to approve. Dioceses would now pay into a separate pensions fund and clergy recruitment and training needs would be decided centrally by the Council. Parishes were warned that congregations would have to give much more to finance their clergy.

At least the recession had already put the Diocese and Cathedral in a belt-tightening mind-set well before the Turnbull Report was published. The Diocese had forecast a 15% increase in the Family Purse in 1992, the need for a smaller but highly-trained clergy, if congregational giving did not improve, and a cancellation of the annual increment to diocesan lay staff. It forecast that the cushion of central support from the Church Commissioners would be reduced to 25% in 1991 and 20% in 1992[26] though the fall-out from the bursting of the property bubble would, in fact, reduce it to 7% by 1999.[27] Bishop John Waine reminded his readers of Jesus' words: 'Freely you have received . . . freely give'":[28] they would need to if his pledge, for the Diocese to become self-sufficient by 2000,[29] was to be achieved.

In 1993 the Cathedral's triennial review of its Christian Stewardship campaign was due. Provost John Moses dispensed with subtle pastel shades:

> "I cannot disguise *the critical financial situation* in which we now
> find ourselves . . . 40% of our income as a cathedral comes in the

form of a grant from the Church Commissioners. This grant will remain unchanged in 1994 but will almost certainly be reduced in subsequent years . . . The Family Purse continues to increase at approximately the rate of 15% per annum . . . I do not believe that the Church is fighting for survival but . . . we are privileged and have been cushioned in so many ways by the historic endowments of the Church of England. Those endowments will not be able to sustain the full time parochial ministry . . . to anything like the degree that they have done hitherto . . . The external pressures are now so great that I have become nervous for the first time in my years at the Cathedral lest we have to cut back and withdraw in some areas of work."[30]

A few months later he again urged that "we embrace the ancient discipline of tithing", pledging a fixed percentage of personal income to the church.[31] It was a principle that had long been applied to congregational giving from which 10% was given to charities. Churchwarden Nick Alston, chairing the Stewardship Renewal Group, added:

"Whatever the rights and wrongs of their [Church Commissioners'] investment policies, the problems highlight how irresponsible it has been for us to rely so heavily on others (especially our predecessors) to fund our faith. The grant from the Church Commissioners is most unlikely to increase . . . The grant from the Diocese will be under pressure as the Diocese tries to balance its books and rely less heavily on the Church Commissioners. A third area under pressure is the income from our buildings. At present there is a surplus of meeting space in the town centre."

And, finally, he reiterated the time-worn complaint that there were too many non-paying worshippers:

"The Church Members' Fund has 166 members of whom many are couples so that about 250 people contribute . . . there are on average 400 people in the Cathedral each Sunday, an average of £3.50 per person per week [£5.56 in today's money], about the cost of a loaf of bread a day . . . The Church Members' Fund needs to increase by 30% each year for the next three years . . .

and each member increase giving by £5 a month [£7.94] . . . and all who pay income tax covenant their giving."[32]

By contrast football supporters were more passionate than worshippers in the annual amount pledged to their cause. The Provost then touched on a sore point:

> "I am well aware of the ambivalence that is felt by many parishes and congregations where the Diocese and Guy Harlings are concerned. I have good reasons to know that the feelings of suspicion and anger and indifference and resentment . . . are unjustified . . . Over 70% of the diocesan budget is spent on clergy, their stipends and their housing. In fact, contrary to popular belief, cathedrals nationally made a net contribution of £1.4 million [£2.22 million] to their dioceses."[33]

That may have been so but the Diocese was vast and its Cathedral geographically remote from the mass of its parochial base. Despite all the Cathedral's efforts to run a tight ship, become more open and welcoming and conduct quality outreach work, the Provost himself admitted that the Cathedral as "a living, working symbol at the heart of the Diocese . . . may not impinge greatly day by day upon the parishes of the diocese."[34] It was therefore not surprising that dwindling parochial congregations, faced with the consequences of financial irresponsibility at the top of the Church of England's power structure, should question the value for money received from their seemingly well-staffed Diocesan Offices and Cathedral.

Whatever the mixed feelings of the parishes the Provost's plain speaking had an immediate effect on the cathedral congregation. By the end of 1993 Church Members' Fund pledges had increased by 25%.[35]

In tandem with the Archbishop of Canterbury's pruning of ineffective committees, John Moses in 1994 decided to abolish the Congregational Committee, which he said "has failed repeatedly over the years . . . to serve any useful purpose." It was to be replaced by three Congregational Meetings a year. The first two would discuss the appeal and worship:

> "There is no doubt in my mind about the part that can be played by the cathedral congregations in sharing our thinking and pointing to the directions in which we must all move forward. Cathedrals are not always renowned for their open and participative style of

government. There is something here that we have yet to explore fully in Chelmsford."[36]

If the congregation were to dig deeper into their pockets it was sensible that they should be able to have their say.

If the Anglican Church had been strained by the financial pit into which it had fallen, that was as nothing compared to the fissures created by the move towards the ordination of women. From 1987 women were admitted to the Order of Deacons which permitted a woman to preside over morning and evening prayer (but not administer the Absolution) and to distribute the Holy Sacrament and read the Epistle or Gospel at Eucharist (but not to undertake any higher priestly functions). For men the equivalent deacon's role had long provided a preparatory route of additional training and experience prior to ordination a year later, but, until the General Synod had its vote on women's ordination to the priesthood, the status of deacon was a permanent holding bay for women.

John Moses was an unequivocal supporter of full ordination for women. In 1991 Jacqui Jones, after five years experience at Epsom Parish Church, joined the staff of the Cathedral as a deacon with a chaplaincy responsibility for town centre work, encompassing the Chelmsford Borough and Essex County Council offices, the law courts and the police, fire and ambulance stations. Most of Chelmsford's old industries served by the industrial chaplaincy had collapsed in the previous two decades. The Provost explained:

> "There has been a discernible shift in the last five years from a chaplaincy that was located primarily in manufacturing industries to chaplaincy that is increasingly located in those large county and town institutions . . . There is no immediate pay-off in terms of bottoms on seats."[37]

Inevitably there were uncertainties over women's ordination as priests that worried some members of the cathedral congregation but not to the extent that the issue ever became a major bone of contention. Statistics are available for the Youth Group who voted 60% for and 32% against with 8% undecided.[38] Barry Thompson, Canon Theologian, a strong supporter, wrote an article in favour but was rebuked by an older member of the congregation:

"'He has succumbed to the fashion in modern liberal society of using the equality of women as his argument for women priests . . . How can we go it alone? What authority has the Church of England in this? Deny scripture and the tradition of 2,000 years of Church life where God reveals himself as Father and not Mother?"[39]

David Knight, Canon Precentor, supported women's ministry up to but not beyond the diaconate: "that is my position until the Church as a whole and by that I mean Anglicans, Catholics and Orthodox, decides it to be different."[40] But that was conditional on leopards changing spots and was seen by many as a euphemism for never. The arcane arguments against women's ordination, illustrated by scriptural text and abstruse theological references, astonished the average person in the street and those who did not subscribe to other major monotheistic faiths that were equally unaccommodating to women. And their view had some importance as this was the established church of the land to which all had the right of access. For those within the Church it was immensely confusing. As one writer put it:

"The violence of feeling on women's ordination was remarkable. Some arguments against women priests are so euphemistic and subtle that you cannot understand them. They are about sacramentality, sacrifice and headship . . . You are left worrying you are not clever enough to understand why the priesting of women is wrong."[41]

At the Chelmsford Deanery Synod on June 4th 1991 the House of Clergy voted 31-13 for ordination as priests and the House of Laity 57-22, not hugely different from the split in the Youth Group. A year later, as the General Synod vote loomed, John Moses wrote:

"Our Lord in His incarnate life represents the whole of humanity . . . Men and women must therefore be allowed to proceed to ordination as priests if ministerial priesthood is to represent the whole of God's creation and the wholeness of our Lord himself . . . We must be sensitive to the theological stance and pastoral judgement of other Christian traditions, but the Church of England must not abandon her own integrity . . . The pain will not go away whatever the outcome of the vote at

Synod in November . . . I have made no secret over the years of my conviction that it is entirely right for women to be ordained to the priesthood and, in due course, to the episcopate. The evidence of scripture, the developing tradition of the church and the experience of women's ministry in our own church over recent generations all suggest to me that there ought to be no impediment to this development on the grounds of scripture or tradition or experience."[42]

At the General Synod all three Houses voted in favour of women's ordination to the priesthood though John Waine, Bishop of Chelmsford, voted against: he was for the principle but believed the Church needed more time. However, once the decision had been made he was entirely supportive of women priests.

On April 30th 1994 52 women deacons were ordained as priests at the Cathedral including Jacqui Jones. She was celebrant at the 9.30 Eucharist on Sunday May 1st. One writer in the *Cathedral News* was ecstatic:

"We were certainly taking part in a revolution, but one filled with the utmost joy, even moments of laughter, spontaneous applause and warm congratulations during the ceremony . . . Never again need we be embarrassed in this modern society to look our female partners in the eye . . . Never again must we rely simply on historical precedent . . . In accordance with the love we felt, we also offered opponents the hand of friendship even on the day itself."

And then, sadly, so that women priests could be avoided by those who could not stomach the idea:

"We have been careful to record the name of the celebrant at Sunday Communion, for there are some who cannot accept women priests and yet who love the Cathedral too much to move elsewhere."[43]

The Cathedral congregation was overwhelmingly accepting of this momentous step not least because Jacqui Jones, in a pioneering role she had not consciously sought, was such a unifying and widely loved personality. In 1997 she moved on to be Vicar of St. Matthew, Bridgemary in Gosport and in 2003 to be Canon Precentor at Southwell Minster. Katy Hacker-Hughes, coming from the role of assistant priest at All Saints', Maldon, replaced her at the Cathedral.

So where did this leave the evangelistic mission of the Church? George Carey had started his archiepiscopate in 1991 by declaring a Decade of Evangelism. In 1979 11.7% of the population attended church and by 1989 only 9.9%:[44] he wanted to reverse the trend. But he had not discussed strategy with the bishops' bench let alone the grassroots and the whole thing ended up as a damp squib with church attendance sinking to 7.5% by 1999 and the Archbishop admitting that "in some sections of our Western Church we are bleeding to death."[45]

That there was a need to evangelise was not contested; in 1991 in the Diocese of Chelmsford, for example, only 17 in every 1,000 of the population took communion.[46] But how? The Cathedral's Youth Group were not at all confident. Only 20% were for direct evangelism. The rest saw it as a form of "bible-bashing" associated with the charismatic movement and felt uncomfortable with the whole idea. They believed it would be off-putting unless handled well and felt that actions spoke louder than words.[47] Their elders probably held similar views. In any case within the very loose coalition of the Church of England there was no accepted version of incontrovertible doctrine to present to the few interested onlookers.

The Provost advised a gentler and humbler approach:

> "Public ministry requires patience and courtesy and great imagination and willingness to work alongside large numbers of people who may or may not share our Christian faith but who are able to cooperate gladly in the task of building a human community."

As a passionate supporter of Chelmsford he felt the Church needed to work alongside its secular friends on their community agendas:

> "The acquisition of a site for the Polytechnic, the provision of a building for a public art gallery, the extension of the museum service, the development of the cultural life of the town through the Cathedral Festival and many comparable activities and a large extension of the facilities that are provided for young people and families. But within that great mix . . . there will always be for the Christian community the prayer that all things might be sanctified

and that the private and public values of integrity and justice and mutual responsibility and accountability might be found."[48]

That made good sense; evangelism requires a respectful two-way conversation not a harangue. Placing the Cathedral at the heart of community activities was, for him, the essence of evangelism through long-term friendship with one's neighbours:

> "I am one of those who believe that we are engaged in evangelism
> the whole time—by ensuring that the Cathedral is well cared for
> and open and alive; by maintaining our pattern of services; by
> developing a congregational life which is able to receive new people
> as they come along; by the arrangements for pastoral oversight
> and care . . . by unseen work that is done by scores of people
> within the life of the congregation both within the Cathedral
> and further afield."

In addition he believed the congregation needed time to reflect: "we have made no provision for quiet days and retreats for the congregation. I think the time has come to make some changes."[49] In 1992 quiet days were held at All Saints', Stock and at the Retreat House at Pleshey.[50] In 1993 he returned to the theme with an apologia:

> "There has been an unavoidable emphasis upon capital projects . . .
> There will be no diminution of commitment where these things
> are concerned, but unless we are able to preach the gospel in such
> a way that men and women are drawn to the living Christ and
> are converted and take their place in the life of the Church there
> is no future for the Cathedral."[51]

The world of modern management-speak eventually arrived at the Cathedral, partly a sign of the times, partly a ripple effect of the management restructuring of the Church of England that followed from the creation of the Archbishop's Council and the recommendations of the 1994 Howe Commission report on cathedrals. In the January 1995 *Cathedral News* John Moses wrote:

> "It is impossible to make much progress in many walks of life
> today—and not least of all in industry and commerce—without

providing a Vision Statement and a Mission Statement. I am one of those who has sat lightly to these statements over the years. They are invariably implicit in the work undertaken, but I can see that the drafting of such statements sharpens the mind a good deal."

So the Cathedral's vision was:

"To be a place where people can find God; a place where people can pray; a place where people can make music; a place where large issues can be thought through and argued out; a place where people can meet to look again at their hopes, their goals, their values."

Its mission as the seat of the Bishop of Chelmsford was:

"To develop to the full its life and work as a centre for worship, theology, celebration and mission both for the Bishop and for the wider community."

The specific foci of the staff were summarised—policy, development and management (Provost), cathedral parish and congregation (Vice-Provost), theology (Canon Theologian), liturgy (Canon Precentor), institutions and chaplaincy (Chaplain), music and the arts (Master of the Music) and administration (Administrator and Chapter Clerk). Two months later their job descriptions were published, a useful move given the duality of some roles in Cathedral and Diocese.

And then Bishop and Provost left in tandem. In March 1996 Bishop John Waine announced his retirement and in June John Moses informed his congregation of his appointment as Dean of St. Paul's Cathedral. His farewell Eucharist was on October 15th and he was installed at St. Paul's on November 19th. Having taken a second research sabbatical in early 1994 from which his book, *A Broad and Living Way: Church and State: A Continuing Establishment*, emerged, it was apt that he should move to the grand cathedral of royal and state occasions that was at the very heart of the marriage of Church and state.

In his farewell sermon John Moses thanked his listeners: "you really have allowed me to get away with almost everything!" He had a serious message too:

"The Church of England by and large does not understand cathedrals. But I have no doubt that they stand on the boundary of Church and community life. Day by day they are in touch with large numbers of people, many of whom have only the most occasional connection with the Church. Our work is primary evangelism . . . It's getting very cold out there. There really is a kind of moral barbarism that is destroying values and I see no other institution, no other community that can hold out faith and hope and love."[52]

By chance, and at much the same time, Wesley Carr, former residentiary canon at Chelmsford, when he had been, almost literally, a sparring partner of John Moses, was appointed Dean of Westminster Abbey. In 1997 John Moses would deliver a moving televised eulogy to Diana, Princess of Wales, from the pulpit of St. Paul's and Wesley Carr would officiate at her funeral at the Abbey. Given the personnel controversies that had attracted media attention intermittently during Wesley Carr's career at Bristol, the press investigated the Chelmsford background and sought the view of John Moses who enigmatically replied: "we were colleagues and you get on better with some colleagues than others."[53] The Queen got on well with both and, in 2006, invested them as Knights Commander of the Victorian Order in recognition of their service to her. They therefore joined their former diocesan, John Waine, in these distinguished ranks: he had received the same honour in 1996, having served as Clerk to the Queen's Closet during his last seven years at Chelmsford. It is very rare for a cathedral to produce three men in the same generation who crown their careers with this ultimate accolade from their monarch.

John Moses had been a huge figure in the development of Chelmsford Cathedral. It was the classic case of the right man at the right time in a financial climate that, bar one short blip, stayed favourable. His constant reiteration of his vision for the Cathedral left none in doubt about his direction. He had brought to a conclusion the longstanding tug of war between parish and cathedral and survived the more short-lived one within the Chapter which emerged, from 1988, as a much more cohesive and happy unit. He had established the Cathedral as a focus for theological debate and research at the highest level though the Centre for the Study of Theology at Essex University was to prove unsustainable. He was very much at home in networking processes and could inspire others to buy into his vision and work with him. He enjoyed people and, with his impish sense of humour, could tailor any speech to perfection for a wide variety of audiences.

The re-ordering of the Cathedral remains as his monument. It was a great aesthetic achievement in addition to the liturgical and musical possibilities it opened up. How he allegedly did it all is hinted at in a tongue-in-cheek report, written by Canon Barry Thompson, of a football match between the clergy and the youth group in which substitute John Moses emerged on the pitch late in the game:

> "He drew on many well-known entrepreneurial and management skills . . . such as blocking, manoeuvering, bull-dozing the opposition and the creative use of rules."[54]

That caricature led one venerable churchman in the town playfully to ask, "What is he going to do now? Raise the dome of St. Paul's?"[55]

CHAPTER 26

Provost to Dean

Diocese and Cathedral had seen a double change at the top three times before, in 1928, 1949-50 and 1967-68: it was to happen again in 1996-97.

On September 14th 1996 60-year-old John Perry was enthroned as the eighth Bishop of Chelmsford. He had graduated from the London School of Divinity and trained for the ministry at St. John's College, Nottingham. In his early ministry he served a curacy in Woking, another curacy and a vicariate in Chorleywood and for 12 years was Warden of Lee Abbey, a conference and retreat centre at Lynton in Devon. Since 1989 he had been suffragan Bishop of Southampton in the Diocese of Winchester. As a marathon runner, raising money for the Southampton homeless,[1] he clearly had the stamina for the vast Diocese of Chelmsford whose varied population he described as "a microcosm of the Church of England."[2] During his episcopacy he would develop a ministry of healing in the Diocese, building on the report, *A Time to Heal* produced in 2000 by the House of Bishops whose cross-disciplinary meetings he would chair.

For eight months Timothy Thompson was Acting Provost until the installation in June 1997 of 47-year-old Peter Judd, Vicar of Iffley, near Oxford. Very usefully for a cathedral dean he had read architecture at Trinity Hall, Cambridge, returning to the University, after his initial ministry in Salford, for a five year period as Chaplain of Clare College. A subsequent position as Team Vicar in Burnham near Slough was followed by the incumbency of Iffley. His first visit to Chelmsford Cathedral fired his imagination:

"I will never forget my first glimpse . . . Nothing on the outside can prepare you for the beauty of the interior—it welcomes and it 'sings', lifting the spirit . . . I am looking forward to coming . . . (as someone who also has four letters to his name with dd) to follow as a small pilgrim in the steps of Cedd."[3]

Last Provost, first Dean, Peter Judd: photo by Mervyn Marshall

Peter Judd would have been aware that he was likely to be the last provost and first dean of Chelmsford Cathedral. English cathedrals had been under the microscope of the Archbishops' Commission on Cathedrals, chaired by Lady Elspeth Howe, which recommended significant reforms. The threat in 1988 by the Dean and Chapter of Hereford Cathedral to sell the medieval *Mappa Mundi* to finance repairs to the cathedral roof had created an uproar and highlighted the need for better strategic financial planning by cathedrals and the protection of their treasures that are part of the national heritage. But it was the horrendous problems within the chapter of Lincoln Cathedral that decided the precise timing of the Howe Commission.

Even Anthony Trollope would not have visited on Barchester such a venomous ecclesiastical civil war as the one that turned Lincoln Cathedral into an international object of ridicule. William Inge, when Dean of St. Paul's, had famously observed that a dean was "like a mouse watched by four cats."[4] No better description could be found for Lincoln where the four residentiary canons constantly used their powers under the Cathedral's ancient constitution to thwart efforts at reform. Then, in 1988, they took the Cathedral's copy of the *Magna Carta* on a trip to Australia that incurred a net loss of £56,000 (£117,000 in today's money). Dean Brandon Jackson, whom Prime Minister Margaret Thatcher subsequently appointed to sort out the mess, criticised his bishop, Robert Hardy, for failing to sack the canons and called in the Fraud Squad, who found that the profligate canons had committed no crime.[5] All of that was enough to spark off the summoning of the Commission in 1992. Unusually for the Church of England, this one reached a quick conclusion with the publication of its report, *Heritage and Renewal*, in 1994, though it took the General Synod six more years to turn its recommendations into substance.

The actors on the Lincoln stage continued their hostilities, seemingly unaware of the Howe Report and the disbelieving world outside their venerable walls. In 1995 the Bishop asked the Dean and all four canons to resign but they declined. The Bishop's knocking at the west door with his staff to seek entry for his enthronement symbolised the ancient independence of the cathedral but brotherly love and cooperation were the expected norm. Only in a case of sexual immorality, proven in a church consistory court, could a bishop dismiss a canon or dean: somewhat suspiciously, therefore, a charge of adultery was brought against the Dean in 1995 by a lady verger.[6] He regarded it as an internal conspiracy but the Bishop decided to refer the case to the consistory court, at a cost of £100,000 in lawyers' fees (£150,000 in modern values), earning further verbal retribution from the Dean on his acquittal. The Cathedral Chapter could not function in such a poisoned atmosphere, The Archbishop of Canterbury, George Carey, was desperate to excise this "cancer in the body of Lincoln" and "scandal dishonouring the name of Our Lord."[7] He and the Bishop unsuccessfully called upon the Dean and Sub-Dean to resign. The Bishop consequently declined to preach his 1996 Christmas sermon in the Cathedral. Eventually the Dean left his post in 1997.

Outdated methods of governance were therefore clearly becoming unfit for purpose. With an air of timeless lassitude, the ancient cathedrals had, well into the 20th century, relied on their impressive looks and gravitas, content to be nothing more than "self-explanatory monuments of the historical continuity of English Christianity"[8]: rather like the soldiers in the trenches they might have sung "we're here because we're here." Reforming Victorian governments had been concerned only with rationalising endowments not spiritual function or governance: in 1840 non-residential canonries and prebendaries had been abolished and their endowments diverted to poorer parish livings, but that was all; the Cathedrals Commission of 1852 had recommended attention to educational work and theological training but nothing happened; another commission meeting from 1879-85 had urged the creation of a standing parliamentary committee empowered to alter ancient cathedral statutes but that was delayed for nearly a century. So modernisation of function, which was applied by the Victorians to parliamentary and local government, the civil service, the army, schools and universities, by-passed the Church. Even in 1950, when it was decided to launch a competition for the architectural design of the new cathedral at Coventry, Bishop Neville Gordon and Provost Richard Howard were still asking: "in terms of function what should such a cathedral express?"[9]

At least the ancient cathedrals were a tourist attraction. With that partly in mind, the 1976 Cathedrals Statutes Commission had given greater priority to preserving them as national cultural assets with English Heritage taking on responsibility for approving work on their fabric, though not, as the Hereford case showed, their treasures. The 1990 Care of Cathedrals Measure brought into being the Cathedrals Fabric Commission which was charged with approving significant building works proposed by chapters and required each cathedral's architect to report at least every five years, in conjunction with the cathedral archaeologist, on work required to the fabric. Peter Judd, an architect by training, was to become one of the two cathedral deans sitting on that Commission.[10]

Members of the Archbishops' Commission came to Chelmsford from February 26th-28th 1993 to see how things were done in Essex.[11] They were followed in the summer by the annual meeting of provosts and deans which had for some years been urging the archbishops for a review of cathedral constitutions and in 1990 had set up a working party to that effect.[12] They made good ecumenical use of the occasion, boarding at New Hall Catholic School just north of Chelmsford where they were able to use the Chapel and share in the worship of the Canonesses of the Holy Sepulchre.[13]

Chelmsford was not on the tourist circuit. The commissioners found that its 42,000 visitors in 1992 placed it in the middle of the 13 parish church cathedrals at the bottom of the tourist pile with visitor numbers at or under 75,000: it lay below Manchester, St. Edmundsbury, Wakefield, Southwark and Sheffield though above Newcastle, Bristol, Birmingham, Leicester, Bradford and, somewhat surprisingly, Portsmouth which did not appear to benefit significantly from the city's other heritage attractions.[14] Most of Chelmsford's visitors came in for the "quiet and prayerful" atmosphere rather than for photo opportunities.[15] But given that nearly one-third of its visitors were children, the Cathedral's educational outreach was picked out as good practice: "Chelmsford has experienced a marked increase in school visits in recent years despite not being a natural place of pilgrimage or tourism."[16] The research and teaching work based on the Centre for the Study of Theology also received special mention.[17]

Some parish church cathedrals did not live up to their dual identity. In relative terms Chelmsford Cathedral had a reasonable parish link: 15% of the 3,500 residents attended as regular worshippers. However, Portsmouth, an example quite close to Chelmsford in parish size, took 31% of its congregation from its 4,000 parochial residents. Two found it very difficult to attract locals: St. Albans and Wakefield had well over 2,000 parish residents but only 3% of them worshipped in their local cathedral. Several parish church cathedrals—Birmingham, Coventry, Derby, Leicester, Newcastle, Sheffield, Southwark and even St. Edmundsbury—had negligible parish populations so attracted their congregations from elsewhere. The most parochially based were two relatively isolated cathedrals, Southwell, where 95% of the congregation came from its parish, and Ripon which attracted 75%.[18]

Although no new cathedral seats had been created since 1927, the Commission was concerned that the process would now be prohibitively costly compared to a century before. In 1978 it was decided that any newly established cathedral would be required to have, from the outset, the full package of residentiary canons and free housing. The Commission compared this with the flexible development of parish cathedrals: Chelmsford was taken as "a typical example . . . where it was not until 1935 that the Rector and Sub-Dean became the Provost and the Cathedral Council was actually established as a governing body. The first residentiary canon was not appointed until 1957."[19] It omitted to state that this slow rate of progress was because the Diocese was strapped for cash: even so it gave a warm glow to be included amongst the virtuous poor.

However, the main meat of the Commission's recommendations lay in its proposals on governance and finance. In the light of Lincoln's troubles processes were established for the dismissal of canons and deans. Furthermore, all cathedrals would be governed by the same regulations thus ending the distinction between parish church cathedrals and those of the Old and New Foundations. All would have new Great Chapters that would be more broadly representative and salaried lay Cathedral Administrators who would sit in the new Administrative Chapters which would oversee day-to-day operational management. Both bodies would be expected to do something about the "dangerously low level of forward thinking and planning in too many cathedrals."[20] Chelmsford could reflect with some satisfaction that it had appointed its first Administrator in 1983, Lieutenant-Colonel Mike Davies, who had been replaced by Terry Mobbs in 1993 and that forward planning had been evident since Provost Gordon's time.

The Cathedral Measure of 1999 that sought to implement many of the Howe Commission's 81 recommendations received only three dissenting voices in the General Synod, a rare sign of church unity. Chelmsford, on February 6th 2000, was the first cathedral to receive its new statutes.

Provost Peter Judd now became Dean of Chelmsford Cathedral, thus ensuring an end to the division between the so-called first-class medieval cathedrals with their deans and the apparently second-class parish church cathedrals with their provosts. All would now, simply, be cathedrals without any other qualification, just as all institutions of higher education had been dubbed as universities in 1992: contemporary function rather than historical origin would determine one's title.

The new Administrative Chapter would comprise the Dean, the three residentiary canons, the Cathedral Administrator, three lay members (one appointed by the Dean, one elected by the cathedral congregation, one appointed by the Bishop's Council) and one member of the diocesan clergy appointed by the Bishop's Council: that would prevent the canons ganging up on a dean as at Lincoln. It would be responsible to the slightly more ecumenical Cathedral Council, which would review strategy, meet twice a year and comprise the Dean, three members of Chapter, two members of the College of Canons, four lay representatives of the Cathedral elected by the cathedral congregation, one area or rural dean, one person elected by Churches Together in Chelmsford, one representative of the universities in the Diocese, one representative from each of the four diocesan areas and four appointed by the Bishop's Council: they would be the long-stop to resolve any impasse in the Administrative Chapter. The former Great Chapter, renamed the College of Canons, would include the Dean, every area bishop and archdeacon and provision for up to six residentiary lay canons in addition to the honorary clerical canons: it would meet annually and was the more decorative part of this trinity of governance.[21] The Bishop would act as Visitor and could attend any meeting but without voting rights. The Cathedral Finance Committee was enlarged, required to make five-year plans and forecasts to ensure that the budget balanced and, through the Association of English Cathedrals, encouraged to share good practice, especially on income generation.

It was appropriate that, while the Howe Commission recommendations were under deliberation, Chelmsford should be considering yet another development project as evidence of its good practice in forward-planning. But the concept of a Visitors' Centre incorporating a refectory, shop and Song School, made no further progress than the previous one for a Treasury and Visitor's Centre and was scotched on Provost John Moses' last day in office. Those responsible for Heritage Lottery grants said it would be too big and out of scale:[22] one glance at the architect's drawings suggests that they were right. In the summer of 1998 Peter Judd explained that there would be no significant extensions: rather, he wanted to see "the existing qualities of the building, its sense of space and calm, preserved and enhanced along with its intimacy of scale, while developing its jewel-like qualities."[23] And maybe, he mused, the old school building, just beyond the northern edge of the churchyard, could be acquired for the Song School, releasing the current Song School for an Education Resources Centre.

A year later new plans were finalised as property acquisition proved impractical. With a fresh architect's imaginative planning everything would be cleverly achieved within the existing floor area. A Millennium Appeal aimed to raise £1 million (£1.35 million in today's money).[24] The first phase would deal with the Cathedral's lighting and sound; the second would see a revamp of the 1920s vestry block to include new toilets, vestries and vergers' offices, with a permissible extension on the first floor to infill a space. The Song School would be left in situ in the old Chapter House on the first floor of the vestry extension, but with more room created by the insertion of a mezzanine gallery for the musicians' offices. "Everything we are trying to do is ordinary bread and butter stuff", Peter Judd explained, "there isn't a piece of self-indulgence or extravagance in it."[25] The Cathedral Centre offices in the Guy Harling's extension would also be re-shaped, with an open plan office space on the first floor and an Education Resources room on the ground floor.

The Cathedral was closed from June to October 2000 for the installation of new lighting and sound systems, the restoration of the east window and the re-roofing of the north transept. The Queen's Building of Anglia Polytechnic University was used for the 9.30 Sunday Eucharist and St. Cedd's Hall in the Chapter House for other Sunday services. Three evensongs were held in local parish churches.[26]

Once the Cathedral was back in use the Dean's first art commission, Peter Ball's *Christ in Glory*, was installed above the chancel arch:[27] its weathered and twisted woods and the varied and distressed patina of its metal components convey a sense of age yet, in the Dean's words, "the outstretched arms reinforce the welcome and the soaring figure inspires faith."[28] The artist's *Mother and Child* was already in St. Cedd's Chapel and he was soon to present a Christmas crib set of 13 figures. On November 1st 2000 Bishop John Perry re-dedicated the Cathedral and commissioned the new Cathedral Chapter and Council.

By 2003 £708,000 (£873,000 in today's money) had been raised towards an increased target of £1.3 million (£1.6 million). The work already completed within the Cathedral had cost £408,000 (£503,000); the re-ordering of the vestry block and the Cathedral Centre remained and would be financed by £413,000 (£509,000) from the Heritage Lottery Fund, £138,000 (£170,000) over and above the £50,000 (£61,700) that had already been raised by the Freemasons' Grand Provincial Lodge of Essex and £35,000 (£43,200) from other fund-raising events.[29] There had always been unease within the Church about the secrecy and unique theology of Freemasonry, despite the fact that many churchmen were members (former Provost, William Morrow, had held high office)[30] and the Grand Master was the Duke of Kent, the Queen's cousin: there was a predictable outburst of opposition to the Lodge's gift, but the storm soon passed.

Dean Peter Judd's judgement had been vindicated:

> "Our original fund-raising advisors warned me that my shopping list of wiring, lighting, sound system and toilets was too boring . . . What we would need to do would be to have a prestige project like a new tower or a new chapel. So against advice we've tried to do this without building a white elephant."[31]

The vestry block was finished by Christmas 2003 and the Cathedral Centre adaptations in 2004.

To complement the developments Mark Cazalet was commissioned to paint a Tree of Life in the north-east corner of the Cathedral to mark the 1,350th anniversary of St. Cedd. It would be placed in the window of the north transept that had been blocked by the 1920s vestry extension. The artist began the work in a disused church near St. Paul's Cathedral and finished it on location during the last two weeks of January 2004: it was financed by a millennium grant from Chelmsford Borough Council and by the Friends of Chelmsford Cathedral. The Dean explained:

> "When St. Augustine came to England he was told by the Pope not to cut down the sacred groves but to Christianise them. The groves were usually yew trees. It was only later that churches were built by these yews with a preaching cross. In Essex the sacred groves were oak trees and St. Cedd would have preached under these, hence the name Gospel Oak."

And there is St. Cedd sitting under a huge Essex oak in high summer to receive the Christian pilgrims. Judas hangs by the neck from one of the branches though at a higher level he is sitting on a bough, redeemed and striving upwards. Adam and Eve as children run in and out of a wheat field. An extinct Essex butterfly, the Purple Emperor, and birds adorn the scene. A corn field and a landfill site illustrate contrasting use and abuse of the land. The tree is dying away on one side: the Dean hoped that "would communicate something in a poem by Philip Larkin where he says of trees that renew themselves each year: 'they seem to say, begin afresh, afresh, afresh.'"[32] The use of subtle spotlighting illumined it as did internal lighting for the hidden west window, blocked by the organ, to give life to the stained glass when viewed at night from the churchyard.[33] At the same time a new altar frontal was designed and woven by Philip Sanderson of West Dean College in West Sussex which depicted the journey of Cedd to the shores of Essex and the county's distinctive long low coastline.[34] All were dedicated in a special service on March 18th in the presence of the Duke of Kent.

Six years later, in 2010, further art works were added. Four blank windows in the chancel were filled with icons of Christ, the Virgin Mary, St. Peter and St. Cedd and a further icon of Christ was added to the north transept wall, opposite the Tree of Life, looking down on the choir and clergy as they processed into services from the vestry. The icons were the work of painters from the Orthodox Monastery at Tolleshunt Knights in Essex.[35] In 2011 Helen McIldowie-Jenkins painted a figure of Christ, encased in a perpendicular frame to match the doorways on either side and placed under the Tree of Life.

And music in the Cathedral continued to flourish. It was probable that Master of the Music, Graham Elliott, was not inspired by the Archbishops' Commission Report on Church Music which devoted only one of its 29 chapters to cathedrals and sought to please all-comers, celebrating the fact that the musical "remoteness of the past is being dispelled" while at the same time delighting that "the cathedral tradition is an absolute gem." He single-mindedly continued to press on with his own mission to make Chelmsford synonymous with excellence in the world of cathedral music. The choir undertook a summer tour in every year bar 1993. In 1997 he took pride in the fact that "this young cathedral now has a pattern of weekly choral evensong which matches that taken for granted by many ancient cathedral foundations."[36] In 1998 he noted that Chelmsford Cathedral had featured in 16 B.B.C. choral evensongs in 12 years. In 1999, eight years after Salisbury Cathedral breached the all-male singing bastion, female choral scholars were appointed to sing one of the weekly services and lighten the load on choristers:[37] the lack of cathedral opportunities for women's voices had been one of the issues raised in the Howe Commission report.

But in the summer of 1999 Graham Elliott announced he would be leaving to be Director of Music at St. Paul's Episcopal Church in Washington D.C: his final service was on October 22nd. His work in the Diocese as Organs Adviser and his support for parish musicians through the training and support programmes set up by the Essex and East London Music Committee, which he chaired from its inception in 1997, were being copied by other dioceses.[38] He was a man of immense determination and uncompromising tenacity but with a clear vision of what he wanted to achieve and had formed a formidable partnership with Provost John Moses with whom he had worked closely for most of his time in Chelmsford. A nationally admired choir and an acclaimed Festival, albeit always struggling to keep afloat financially, were huge achievements, the latter acknowledged in 1998 by Great Eastern Railway who named one of their trains *Chelmsford Cathedral Festival*.[39] Nor should his skills as an organist be forgotten, especially in the complex art of improvisation. Appropriately he was to found a festival in Washington and was on loan to Washington National Cathedral as Acting Director of Music in 2001 when he directed the choirs at the National Prayer Service which was broadcast worldwide following the terrorist attacks of September 11th on the World Trade Centre. In 2008 he became Executive Director of North Highland Connections, an organization founded under the auspices of the Prince of Wales, to promote a wide-ranging year-round programme of Arts and educational activities throughout the North Highlands of Scotland.

So after that the Dean must have thought it was time for something completely different. Peter Nardone, with the new title of Director of Music, was appointed from March 2000. As an F.R.C.O., a most sensitive piano accompanist of international singers and a vocalist himself at the highest level, his experience was richly varied. He had been a chorister at Paisley Abbey and graduated at the Royal Scottish Academy of Music and Drama, where he trained as an organist with piano as second study. In 1986 he won the Countess of Munster Scholarship to study as a countertenor at the London Royal Academy of Music. He was Assistant Organist at Croydon Parish Church and the Chapel of St. Peter ad Vincula in the Tower of London where he often appeared as a soloist in the City of London Festival and for many B.B.C. broadcasts. In 1992 he was appointed Organist at Croydon Parish Church and in 1998 Musical Director of the Croydon Bach Choir. He sang professionally with the Taverner Consort, the Tallis Scholars and the Monteverdi Choir as also with the King's Consort[40] for whom he occasionally acted as conductor. With considerable prescience Graham Elliott had already booked the King's Consort for the Festival of 2000, so, within two months of his arrival, Peter Nardone found himself both compering and performing.

The Dean wrote that Peter Nardone would bring "zest, musical panache and humanity to all he does."[41] The Festival, as expected, showed him to have a superb singing voice and a mischievous line in stand-up comedy and mimicry. He proved to be a first-class teacher of singing whether of the finely trained voices in the cathedral choir or the amateurs of the Chelmsford Singers which he took over in 2004, thus sustaining that body's almost unbroken link with the Cathedral. He also ensured that the Cathedral Consort for girls of 11-18 continued to blossom, under the tutelage of the Assistant Director of Music: since 2004 they have led Tuesday Evensong as well as singing at Christmas Midnight Mass, some Sunday Eucharists and Choral Matins and on special occasions such as Ash Wednesday, Ascension Day and Epiphany. He trained his singers with a unique mix of musical insight and amusing anecdote. His inimitable style also made him an effective recruiter of choristers in primary schools and his willingness to take the choir out and about secured a £30,000 award in 2008 from the Chorister Outreach Programme (£35,900 in today's money) to finance continuing work by the Cathedral's musicians in the community and by the Chelmsford Children's Choir, jointly led by choirman Simon Warne.[42]

In tandem with Peter Nardone's arrival, Edward Wellman was appointed as Assistant Director of Music, coming from the post of Assistant Organist at Chester Cathedral:[43] one of his first tasks was to start a voluntary choir in 2001 to lead services when the cathedral choir was on holiday:[44] he moved on to become Director of Music at St. Peter's, Hammersmith in 2003.

Robert Poyser, Sub-Organist at York Minster, replaced him: he started the Epiphany Carol Service and left in 2008 to be Director of Music at St. Mary's, Portsea. Tom Wilkinson, former Organ Scholar of Queen's College, Oxford and top-flying academic took over for a year but was soon head-hunted to be Organist and Director of Chapel Choir at St. Andrew's University. Oliver Waterer, Assistant Organist at Peterborough Cathedral, replaced him in 2009.

Maybe the Cathedral would find a Canon Theologian to match the Director of Music's wit. A vacancy arose in 1998 when Barry Thompson moved to a prestigious canonry at St. George's Chapel, Windsor and a key role in St. George's House, co-founded in 1966 by the Duke of Edinburgh[45] as an international conference centre, where Barry would serve until his retirement in 2002 when the Queen appointed him Canon Emeritus, not always an automatic honour at this Royal Peculiar. The Bishop chose Andrew Knowles who, for some years, had written scripts for the satirist and comedian Willy Rushton,[46] though his roles in the Diocese of Guildford, as Adviser in Continuing Education and Development and Vicar of St. Mark's, Wyke, proved to be the more immediately attractive aspects of his experience; however, a preacher who can raise a smile as well as make theology relevant is always a bonus. He had graduated from St. Catharine's College, Cambridge and prepared for ordination at St. John's College, Nottingham. He served curacies in Leicester and Cambridge before moving to Woking to plant a church on a new housing estate. He was author of three of the popular *Lion Manuals*—one of them, *Finding Faith*, published in 16 languages—and the *Fount Children's Bible*. His *Bible Guide*, published in 2001, was to be equally successful. Given his publications it was not surprising that he did a great deal to support and encourage younger families but he also continued to develop adult theological education through the Emmaus groups, the Keene Lectures (whose scripts were put on-line) and work at diocesan level with ordinands through St. Mellitus College founded in 2007 to serve the mission needs of the dioceses of London and Chelmsford.

In 2001 two new canons residentiary, Genny Tunbridge and Walter King, joined Peter Judd and Andrew Knowles in the cathedral team.

Genny Tunbridge, the first woman residentiary canon, replaced Canon Precentor David Knight who was installed as Vicar of Ranmoor in Sheffield. Fluent in four languages, she graduated at Clare College, Cambridge, took a doctorate at Oxford, and trained for the ministry at the Ecumenical Centre at Queen's College, Birmingham. She was a curate in Boston and then priest in charge of a daughter church on a council estate in the same town.[47] On the retirement of the genial Timothy Thompson, Walter King was appointed as Vice-Provost and Canon Pastor. A graduate of New College, Oxford, he had trained for the ministry at Cuddesdon followed by curacies in Wisbech and Barrow and the Rectorship of St. Nicholas', Hereford in which diocese he was also Director of Ordinands. He was Team Rector and Rural Dean of Huntingdon immediately prior to his arrival in Chelmsford.[48]

Back on the musical front, Peter Nardone inherited serious financial difficulties with the Cathedral Festival of Music and Arts. Sponsorship income had remained flat at about £30,000 annually from 1994 to 1998 (in modern values £46,500 reducing to £41,200) while artists' fees steadily inflated. The decision to appoint a professional fund-raiser in 1998 did not work out and the cost of his fees depleted reserves by over one-third. But the bursting of the dot-com bubble in 2000 was the critical disaster. G.E.C. Marconi, having switched its emphasis from defence to telecoms in 1997, saw its share price tumble. In the 1990s its establishments in Chelmsford had often sponsored the Festival with £10,000 or more a year (over £17,000 in today's money): that harvest of plenty was now over. Marconi's implosion, the globalisation of banks and other businesses whose local discretion in sponsorship was removed and the ripple effects of the stock market crash halved sponsorship income over two years. Relatively few independent local firms remained who were able to sponsor and most of them were small organisations of more modest means. An exception was M&G Investments which stayed true to the Festival to the end and has sustained long-term support over more than a quarter of a century for a variety of other local arts events. Chelmsford Borough Council and Essex County Council cash grants and help in kind also diminished: they had a myriad of local organisations with competing claims to satisfy though the Borough Council's box office facilities remained a constant boon.[49]

The Festival Board was reorganised from 2001. Every member now held a major hands-on portfolio in the Festival; team work on the ground would be reflected in the Board. It was resolved that box office takings must cover artists' fees: that was precisely achieved over the next six years, whereas in previous years there had been a 25% shortfall covered by sponsorship and financial reserves. Peter Nardone's experience as a performer enabled him to call in favours from friends. He reduced the emphasis on expensive big names to concentrate on musically exciting young artists near the start of their careers, cutting good deals by not committing the Festival to contracts too early. Loss-making professional lunch-time concerts were abandoned. But nothing could counteract commuters' lengthening working hours which caused a dip in ticket sales for most mid-week evening concerts. And, as had been observed in 1968, festival fatigue can set in over a week's events: festival veterans were getting older, although they were often revived by the excellent food and real ales in the marquee. A scheme to persuade private patrons to make a gift-aided £400 annual donation boosted income by about £20,000 annually from 2004 (£23,900 in modern values) when business sponsorship was bottoming out at only £17,500 (£21,000): that had been the level of sponsorship income in 1987 but then the pound had been worth over twice as much. In 2006 ticket sales fell for just one Festival to only 55% of capacity. Cash balances were insufficient to guarantee a Festival beyond 2007, especially as marketing costs, office rental and salaries of the part-time staff had to be found for eight months prior to fresh income coming on tap. So 2007 was the celebratory 24th and final Festival, complete with a fireworks farewell. The Festival had been living on the edge for some years and did well to last that long.

The remaining Festival cash has been used since to support other events such as the Nativity mystery plays in 2009 which harked back to the first recorded mystery plays in 1563* performed on an adjacent field with the Tudor theatrical props stored in the unique medieval cupboards at the west end of the church.[50] After 2007 Peter Nardone moved back to a limited number of concerts spread throughout the year to support the Choral Foundation which would receive good support from the cathedral congregation and former Friends of the Festival and required limited marketing costs. And alongside all these ventures the Friday lunch-time concerts, started in 1993, featuring local musicians, attracted large audiences.

Beautiful buildings and music are important but one can be too house-proud. The Diocese's and Cathedral's Christian mission to the world outside would remain central to its purpose. The nature of the mission within the Diocese had changed: the full quota of churches had been built in East London and the post-war new towns but potential Christian souls had been replaced in many areas by practising Muslims and Hindus. Dialogue and mutual respect between faiths would now be very significant in a world where religious conflicts, not least the violent rifts within Islam, were a matter of international concern. To this end it was important that

---

* Mystery Plays continued in Chelmsford long after they had disappeared elsewhere but became boisterously secularised. In 1574 ten of St. Mary's windows were damaged and in 1576 the props and costumes were sold off.[51]

the Christian churches acted as one. Churches Together in Chelmsford and the Christian Festival that emerged in 2008 manifested their spirit of fellowship. For historic reasons, and very relevant to the divisions within the Church of England, the friendship with local Roman Catholic communities was crucial. Bishop Thomas McMahon, the Catholic Bishop of Brentwood was a sincere supporter of ecumenical endeavours. In 1983 he had given Holy Week addresses in Chelmsford Cathedral.[52] In 1993 Bishop John Waine had attended a service at Brentwood Cathedral to celebrate the 350th anniversary of the English House of the Canonesses of the Holy Sepulchre in Liège: fleeing French revolutionary armies they had emigrated to England and founded a school for Catholic girls at New Hall in 1799.[53] Continued dialogue and cooperation, including musical projects, led to the Brentwood-Chelmsford Covenant signed on November 30th 2008 whereby the two cathedrals pledged "to do apart nothing we can do together and to do together what we cannot do apart."[54] But Pope Benedict XVI's creation in 2010 of the Anglican Ordinariate as a reception area for Anglo-Catholic parishes who wished to secede from the Church of England has attracted interest from six parishes in the Diocese of Chelmsford and, in the minds of many local Anglicans and Catholics, added a complication to their growing friendship which they had not anticipated.

Looking beyond these shores, links between the dioceses of Chelmsford and Karlstad in Sweden had been developing since 1988[55] and formal links and exchanges were set in train following the 1997 agreement that brought the Lutheran Church in Scandinavia and the Baltic States into full communion with the Church of England.[56] In 2003 an agreement was signed at the Cathedral between the Diocese of Chelmsford and the Orthodox Diocese of Iasi in Moldavia in north-east Romania.[57] In Africa the links with the Kenyan Dioceses of Kirinyaga, Embu, Mbeere and Meru (into which the former Diocese of Mount Kenya East had been divided) were the most long-standing, going back to 1980. The Cathedral also wished to support an AIDS ridden area of southern Africa: a link with the parish of Khayelitsha in Cape Town, where Peter Judd spent his sabbatical leave in 2006,[58] was replaced later that year by one with Swaziland in support of the work of mission partners Andrew and Rosemary Symonds:[59] in 2007 it was decided that the principle focus of the Cathedral would be on the work in Swaziland and the Diocese of Embu. Aware of the challenges facing the developing world, the Cathedral has been a strong advocate of a fair trade policy and in 2009 became the first cathedral congregation to be awarded eco-congregation status.[60]

A long-serving Dean will see his cathedral staff come and go. In 2007 Genny Tunbridge was installed as Vicar of All Saints', Gosforth in Newcastle-on-Tyne and was replaced as Precentor by Simon Pothen, Vicar of Pinner in Middlesex: he had graduated from Westminster College, Oxford, trained at Cuddesdon, served two curacies in north London, and been a Team Vicar in Great Grimsby before returning to north London for two incumbencies in Friern Barnet and Pinner. On Walter King's retirement in 2010 Ivor Moody took over as Vice-Provost and Canon Pastor: a graduate of King's College London, he had trained at Mirfield and knew the Diocese well, having ministered in Stratford, Leigh-on-Sea and Tilbury before taking on the chaplaincy of Anglia Ruskin University (as Anglia Polytechnic University had been renamed in 2005):[61] he was awarded an Honorary Fellowship by the University in 2010 in recognition of the quality of his work in the area. In 2012 Peter Nardone, to whom the University had awarded an Honorary Doctorate in 2010, moved on to become Organist and Director of Music at Worcester Cathedral with a major role in the Three Choirs Festival, and Andrew Knowles retired as Canon Theologian. James Davy, Assistant Organist at Blackburn Cathedral, was appointed as Director of Music: he had graduated at the University of Durham and trained at the Royal Northern College of Music in Manchester. Edward Carter was chosen as Canon Theologian: he had trained at Cuddesdon, served a curacy in Norwich, moved to St. George's Chapel, Windsor as a Minor Canon and Dean's Vicar and then to St. Peter's, Didcot as Vicar whence he came to Chelmsford.

Bishops too move on. John Perry, honoured in 2001 with a doctorate by Anglia Ruskin University, retired in 2003. John Gladwin, Bishop of Guildford, was enthroned as the ninth Bishop of Chelmsford on January 10th 2004 complete, at this epiphanal time, with gifts of gold, frankincense and myrrh and, after the service, a jazz band.[62] A product of Churchill College, Cambridge and St. John's College, Durham, he had returned to Durham as a tutor after a curacy in Huddersfield. He believed strongly in Christian engagement in public affairs: in 1977 he became Director of the Shaftesbury Project on Christian Involvement in Society and in 1982 Secretary to the General Synod's Board of Social Responsibility. In 1988 he was appointed Provost of Sheffield Cathedral and in 1994 was enthroned as Bishop of Guildford. On taking up his diocesan role in Chelmsford he knew he had inherited a well-run cathedral and was able to concentrate his energies on the strategic issues of his massive diocese as well as travelling the world as Chairman of Christian Aid, a post which he held from 1998 to 2008. He handled all his responsibilities with characteristic good humour and, on his retirement in 2009, continued his engagement with public affairs as Chairman of the Citizens Advice Bureau. That he was called on in 2011 by Rowan Williams, the Archbishop of Canterbury, to lead the enquiry into child sex abuse by some clergy in the Diocese of Chichester, could not have been in his plans, but was a testament to his reputation for wise judgement.

The tenth bishop, Stephen Cottrell, was enthroned on November 27th 2010. As a Leigh-on-Sea lad, he was coming home. He had trained at St. Stephen's House in Oxford and served in parishes in London and Chichester and on the staff of Chichester Theological College before moving into cathedral work as Canon Pastor and Vice-Dean at Peterborough whence he also acted as missioner in the Diocese of Wakefield and as part of Springboard, the Archbishop of Canterbury's evangelism team. In 2004 he was consecrated suffragan Bishop of Reading in the Diocese of Oxford. He has written widely about evangelism and was one of the team who wrote the *Emmaus* programme, used by about 3,000 churches in Britain including Chelmsford Cathedral. At his enthronement he reminded the congregation of Luke chapter 1, verse 63: "His name shall be John"; he would be the first Bishop of Chelmsford for 48 years where that was not the case.[63]

A cathedral dean lives in a half-way house, sometimes serving his bishop in a diocesan role, but week by week caring for his own worshippers. For Peter Judd the pastoral care and spiritual development of his congregations was central. It had been thus ever since the early church nurtured the faith of its communities scattered round the Mediterranean. He sought clarity of language and a move away from theology-speak:

> "We and our doctrines and our services and liturgies speak of the language of Adam and Eve, of Cain and Abel and the fall from perfection into sin . . . and then the long slow road to redemption and atonement. But this has become 'in-house' language . . . The Church can sometimes go on speaking its private language like the proverbial Englishman abroad . . . If you speak loud enough the natives will understand eventually—but, of course, it doesn't happen."[64]

He took the directness of Jesus' teachings as his inspiration:

> "You all, I hope, have gathered from my preaching that Christianity needs pruning and simplifying . . . Christ was a simplifier . . . Love God and love they neighbour."[65]

He wanted to nurture his congregations and recognise their strengths as they negotiated the twists and turns in their faith journeys rather than moan about the ones that got away:

"The Church would look more attractive if it was not continually yearning, like a neglected lover, over those who stay away. It could try celebrating the clientele it has got . . . a general lightening up."[66]

Indeed, the change of title from *Cathedral News* to *Cathedral Life* in 2007 encapsulated that idea, incorporating interviews with cathedral worshippers about how they try to live out their beliefs in their daily lives.

For Peter Judd, the role of the laity is crucial, as a matter of personal conviction, not just as a reaction to insufficient ordinands:

"Although the proclaiming of the message is crucial . . . the living out of the faith needs to be done together in a community and fellowship, which is mutually supportive and healing . . . More and more the Church's ministry is being led by non-stipendiary clergy and lay people and it won't be long before the majority of ministry will be like this . . . And if we get it right it will be church without power or wealth, but rich in service and love."[67]

That thought genuinely fires his imagination and is reflected in the volunteer force that runs over 30 organisations, including the Ministry of Welcome established in 2000[68] to ensure that there is always a friendly face in the Cathedral to greet visitors and listen to those in turmoil: in 2011 the replacement of the heavy and forbidding wooden south door by automatically opening glass doors added to the welcome. The much broader concept of Christian Stewardship, giving one's talents as well as one's money, seems to have taken root. For those whose stewardship has been faithful and long, Peter Judd instituted the Order of St. Cedd: its first recipient was Harry Goodman in 2003.[69]

In a Keene Lecture in 1998, Will Hutton, then editor of *The Observer*, called the Church of England "one of this country's great moral communities."[71] And it certainly is the case that one recognises this within Chelmsford Cathedral. However, this thriving cathedral community exists in a context where church attendance at parish level generally continues to dwindle and the Church at large has inflicted so many wounds on itself that its moral leadership is now in question. The poisonous response in some quarters to homosexuality and women's ordination to the priesthood, and most recently advancement to the episcopacy, has left secular society aghast at such a lack of charity. Even more sinisterly, the cover up of paedophilia in the Catholic Church, with some evidence of it in the Anglican Church, has inflicted awful damage on public perceptions of organised Christianity. Many who would formerly have been indifferent to the Church now question its right to retain the trappings of establishment.

Yet in the midst of all this mayhem the peaceably tolerant men and women in the pew (or indeed, in the temple, mosque and synagogue) are lost to view. One writer concludes:

> "While . . . fanatical clergy exist at both ends of the spectrum . . .
> in the middle, calm and diligent people are trying to get on with
> their jobs . . . The average churchgoer is a good sort, trying hard
> to become a better sort."[70]

One has glimpsed them in this history. They remain the sensible, pragmatic core of the Church who are genuinely inclusive, find theological hair-splitting irrelevant and, with quiet determination, try to live out their lives in accordance with Gospel values.

When the Cathedral emerged Britain ruled a quarter of the globe, war was an adventure, women did not have the vote and the local newspaper, which assiduously reported church affairs, was peppered with advertisements for domestic servants. The past truly did seem to be a foreign country. For half a century the Cathedral struggled with the effects of devastating world wars and their impoverishing financial consequences which destroyed social, imperial and economic certainties. Its congregation also struggled with the notion that cathedral status brought obligations as well as honour. However, when it began to find its feet as servant as well as ornament of the Diocese, this Cinderella, as Bishop Henry Wilson described it, began to throw off its rags and showed more adventure than many of its medieval counterparts. When it was granted equality of status with the more ancient cathedrals Peter Judd, preaching as the first Dean, could rightly claim that Chelmsford Cathedral was "coming of age."[72]

BIBLIOGRAPHY

Anon, *The Diocese of Chelmsford and its First Bishop*, London Robert Scott, 1914

D.W. Barrett, *Sketches of Church Life in the Counties of Essex and Hertfordshire forming the Diocese of St. Albans*, London Skeffington and Son, 1902

J.V. Beckett, *City Status in the British Isles 1830-2002*, Athenaum Press, 2005

Trevor Beeson, *The Bishops*, S.C.M., 2002

Trevor Beeson, *The Deans*, S.C.M., 2004

Trevor Beeson, *The Canons*, S.C.M., 2006

A.J. Begent, *Chelmsford at War*, Ian Henry, 1999

James Bettley and Nikolaus Pevsner, *The Buildings of England, Essex*, Yale University Press, 2007

Peter Brierley, *The Tide is Running Out; what the English church attendance reveals*, Christian Research, 2000

Nancy Briggs, *John Johnson 1732-1814: Georgian Architect and County Surveyor of Essex*, Essex Record Office, 1991

Tom Buchanan, *Britain and the Spanish Civil War*, Cambridge University Press, 1997

Owen Chadwick, *The Victorian Church, Part 1 1829-1859*, S.C.M., 1987

Owen Chadwick, *The Victorian Church, Part 2 1860-1901*, Black, 1970

Owen Chadwick, "The Victorian Diocese of St. Albans" in *Cathedral City, St. Albans Ancient and Modern*, Robert Runcie (editor), Martyn Associates, 1977

Chelmsford Cathedral and The Chapel of St.-Peter-on-the Wall, Bradwell-on-Sea, Heritage House Group, 2002

Andrew Clark (editor James Munson), *Echoes of the Great War; The Diary of the Reverend Andrew Clark 1914-19*, Oxford University Press, 1985

B.I. Coleman, *The Church of England in the Mid-Nineteenth Century*, The Historical Association, 1980

Jeffrey Cox, *The English Churches in a Secular Society*, Oxford University Press, 1982

G.J. Cuming, *A History of Anglican Liturgy*, MacMillan, 1982

Don Cupitt, *Sea of Faith*, S.C.M., 1984

R.C.K. Ensor, *England 1870-1914*, Oxford University Press, 1936

ESOTEC Research and Consulting Ltd, *The Economic and Social Impacts of Cathedrals in England*, Final Report, 2004

Stewart M. Foster, *A History of the Diocese of Brentwood 1917-1992*, The Diocese of Brentwood, 1994

Monica Furlong, *C. of E: The State It's In*, Hodder & Stoughton, 2000

Alan D. Gilbert, *Religion and Society in Industrial England: Church, Chapel and Social Change 1740-1914*, Longman, 1976

Robin Gill, *The Empty Church Revisited*, Ashgate Publishing, 2003

D.I. Gordon, *A Regional History of the Railways of Great Britain, Volume 5, The Eastern Counties*, David & Charles, 1990

Ellis N. Gowing, *John Edwin Watts-Ditchfield, First Bishop of Chelmsford*, Hodder & Stoughton, 1926

Ysende Maxton Graham, *The Church Hesitant, A Portrait of the Church of England Today*, Hodder & Stoughton, 1993

Hilda Grieve, *The Sleepers and the Shadows, Chelmsford: a town, its people and its past, Volume 1, The Medieval and Tudor Story*, Essex County Record Office, 1988

Hilda Grieve, *The Sleepers and the Shadows, Chelmsford: a town, its people and its past, Volume 2, From Market Town to Chartered Borough 1608-1888*, Essex County Record Office, 1994

S.J. Gunn, "Henry Bourchier, Earl of Essex, 1472-1540", in *The Tudor Nobility*, (editor G.W. Bernard), Manchester University Press, 1992

Adrian Hastings, *A History of English Christianity 1920-2000*, S.C.M., 2001

Gordon Hewitt, *A History of the Diocese of Chelmsford*, Chelmsford Diocesan Board of Finance, 1984

Ann Holden, "A brief description of the life and work of Frederic Chancellor 1825-1918" in *Essex Archaeology and History 26*, 1995

Richard Holmes, *Tommy, The British Soldier on the Western Front 1914-1918*, HarperCollins, 2004

Kenneth Hylson-Smith, *Evangelicals in the Church of England 1734-1984*, T. & T. Clark Edinburgh, 1988

Ludovic Kennedy, *All in the Mind*, Hodder & Stoughton, 1999

Stanford Lehmberg, *English Cathedrals*, Hambledon and London, 2005

Terry Lovell, *Number One Millbank; the financial downfall of the Church of England*, HarperCollins, 1997

Diarmaid MacCulloch, *A History of Christianity; The First Three Thousand Years*, Penguin, 2010

Iain Mackenzie (editor), *Cathedrals Now*, Canterbury Press, 1996

Kenneth Medhurst and George Moyser, *Church and Politics in a Secular Age*, Clarendon Press Oxford, 1988

Philip Morant, *The History and Antiquities of the County of Essex*, T. Osborne, 1768

John Moses, "Chelmsford Cathedral, 'A great county should have a cathedral at its heart'" in *Essex 'full of profitable things': Essays presented to Sir John Ruggles-Brise*, Kenneth Neale (editor), Leopard's Head Press, 1996

Alan Mould, *The English Chorister: a history*, Hambledon Continuum, 2007

E.R. Norman, *Church and Society in England 1770-1970*, Clarendon Press, Oxford, 1976

Edward Norman, *Anglican Difficulties: A New Syllabus of Errors*, Morehouse, 2004

Alan Palmer, *The East End: four centuries of London life*, John Murray, 2000

Stephen Platten and Christopher Lewis (editors), *Dreaming Spires? Cathedrals in a New Age*, S.P.C.K., 2006

Doreen Rosman, *The Evolution of the English Churches 1500-2000*, Cambridge University Press, 2003

James Ross, *John de Vere 1442-1513, Thirteenth Earl of Oxford, 'The Foremost Man of the Kingdom'*, The Boydell Press, 2011

Paul Rusiecki, *The Impact of Catastrophe; the people of Essex and the First World War (1914-1920)*, Essex Record Office, 2008

J.R. Smith, *Pilgrims and Adventurers: Essex (England) and the Making of the United States of America*, Essex Record Office, 1992

K.D.M. Snell and Paul S. Ell, *Rival Jerusalems: The Geography of Victorian Religion*, Cambridge University Press, 2000

A.J.P. Taylor, *English History 1914-1945*, Oxford Clarendon Press, 1963

The Report of the Archbishops' Commission on Cathedrals, *Heritage and Renewal*, Church House Publishing, 1994

The Report of the Archbishops' Commission on Church Music, *In Tune with Heaven*, Hodder & Stoughton, 1992

Tony Tuckwell, *New Hall and its School*, Free Range Publishing, 2006

Tony Tuckwell, *That Honourable and Gentlemanlike House; a History of King Edward VI Grammar School, Chelmsford 1551-2008*, Free Range Publishing, 2008

Victoria County History of Essex, Volume 2, 1907

Paul A. Welsby, *A History of the Church of England 1945-1980*, Oxford University Press, 1984

Alan Wilkinson, *The Church of England and the First World War*, S.P.C.K., 1978

Henry A. Wilson, *Reflections of a Back-Bench Bishop*, Latimer House, 1948

SOURCES

The main narrative of events surrounding St. Mary's as parish church and cathedral derives from the *Parish Magazine* which started in 1879 and morphed into the *Cathedral Review* (1949), *Cathedral News* (1953) and *Cathedral Life* (2007). These are to be found in the cathedral archive in the Knightbridge Library. Other documentary sources from that archive are as detailed below in the references.

The diocesan narrative is to be found in the *Chelmsford Diocesan Chronicle* which is deposited in the Essex Record Office, though the Second World War years are incomplete. It was replaced by the less informative *Essex Churchman* (1952), *East Window* (1987) and, more recently, *The Month* available online. Some copies of *Essex Churchman* are bound with the relevant copies of the *Parish Magazine* in the Cathedral's Knightbridge Library. Others, together with *East Window*, were kindly made available to me by the Diocesan Office but have not yet been formally archived.

Contemporary newspapers are a rich source. Knowing where to look can be a problem unless a specific event points to an obvious date. Combing randomly through microfiche copies of local newspapers for other pertinent information is bad for the eyes and resembles the search for the proverbial needle in a haystack. Discovery of the online British Newspaper Archive, containing over 200 local newspapers (including four from Essex), which can be interrogated using standard electronic search mechanisms, has proved a boon. So has the Essex County Council Online Reference Library which gives access to *The Guardian, The Observer* and *The Times* historic archive as well as the *Oxford Dictionary of National Biography*. However, I am also indebted to past archivists of the Knightbridge Library who had the presence of mind to take cuttings from local and national newspapers, especially in the 1880s and the Cathedral's early days. Several of these publications are now defunct and their archives, if they survive, are not yet digitalised.

I have tried to talk with as many people as I can who I think can throw further light on events. They have been acknowledged at the start of this book but I was particularly grateful for access to some of the private papers of John Moses and Hilary Connop Price.

As for the pictures I must thank Mervyn Marshall for providing me with the photographic portraits of John Moses and Peter Judd, the two internal east and west views of the post-1983 Cathedral and the two photographs of the Nicholson plans for a new Cathedral which David Lloyd kindly digitalised for publication. The picture of Bishop Guy Warman at The Gun is from a *Daily Sketch* cutting found in the Knightbridge Library. I took the photos of St. Peter's-on-the-Wall at Bradwell, Guy Harlings frontage and the Vestry Extension. The photograph of the Cathedral on the front cover was taken by Chris Reeve. All the other pictures are from the Knightbridge Library picture archive.

With regard to secondary sources, the bibliography gives a clear indication of some of the reading that provided detail and context for this history. The Local Studies section of Chelmsford Library provided several out-of-print gems on the early history of the Diocese and Cathedral.

At various places in the text there are references to sums of money. In each case I have given, in brackets, their estimated worth in the money of 2010 to give some idea of real values as measured by increases in the retail price index. I have used the work of Lawrence H. Officer and Samuel H. Williamson, *Purchasing Power of British Pounds from 1245 to the Present,* and the accompanying calculator found on www.measuringworth.com

REFERENCES

Chapter 1 The Parish Church

1. *Essex Archaeological News*, Spring 1984
2. Moses, *Essex 'full of profitable things'*, 91: Grieve, *The Sleepers and the Shadows Vol. 1*, 68-9
3. English Life Publications 1983, *Hedingham Castle*
4. Ross, *John de Vere*, 16-18
5. Ibid., 19
6. Details of manorial holdings can be found by index search in Morant, *The History and Antiquities of the County of Essex* and the *Victoria County History of Essex*
7. Mortimer, *The Fears of Henry IV*, 91-4 and 138
8. Ross, *op.cit.*, 33-4
9. Details of family genealogy in this chapter can be found under relevant names in the *Oxford Dictionary of National Biography* and the online *Luminarium Encyclopaedia Project*
10. Ross, *op.cit.*, 38
11. Ibid., 25-6
12. Ibid., 39-47
13. *Parish Magazine* September—November 1906; Grieve, *op. cit., Vol. 1*, 72; Morant *op.cit.*
14. Moses, *op.cit.*, 99
15. Grieve, *op.cit., Vol. 1*, 72
16. Grieve, *The Sleepers and the Shadows, Vol. 2*, 170 and 274
17. Grieve, *op.cit., Vol. 1*, 108
18. Knightbridge Library CHEp 726.6 "Oddities of Chelmsford Cathedral" by Dick Swann reprinted from *The Polytechnic Magazine*
19. Grieve, *op.cit.*, Vol. 1, 64
20. Ibid., 30

21. *Chelmsford Chronicle,* May 13th 1881 and *Daily Telegraph,* November 11th 2001

22. Letters to Thomas Beard, January 11th 1835 *in The Letters of Charles Dickens, Vol. 1 1820-39*

Chapter 2 The Pew Rent War

1. *Essex Standard,* July 15th 1842

2. *Chelmsford Chronicle,* December 31st 1858 and February 4th 1859

3. *Bury and Norwich Post,* February 8th 1859

4. *Essex Standard,* May 8th 1867

5. *Essex Standard,* March 12th 1869

6. *Chelmsford Chronicle,* September 26th 1873

7. *Chelmsford Chronicle,* April 25th 1873

8. *Chelmsford Chronicle,* July 5th 1895; Clarke rev. Mathew, Oxford Dictionary of National Biography, *Robert William Hanbury*

9. *Chelmsford Chronicle,* April 2nd 1875

10. *Chelmsford Chronicle,* April 19th 1878

11. *Chelmsford Chronicle,* December 28th 1877

12. *Chelmsford Chronicle,* November 15th 1850

13. *Chelmsford Chronicle,* December 6th 1850

14. *Essex Independent,* December 20th 1876

15. Grieve, *The Sleepers and the Shadows, Vol. 2,* 383

16. Norman, *Church and Society in England 1770-1970,* 59

17. Marsh, Oxford Dictionary of National Biography, *Archibald Campbell Tait*

18. Norman, *op.cit.,* 175-7

19. Ibid., 178

20. *Parish Magazine,* January 1909

21. Snell and Ell, *Rival Jerusalems,* 346

22. *The Times,* February 5th 1925

23. *Chelmsford Chronicle,* June 29th 1866

24. Knightbridge Library W1/242

25. Romans chapter 25 verse 3

26. William H. Morley, *The Church and Parish of St. Saviour, St. Albans, More Such Days 1910-1952,* found online at www.ssaviours.org/TheStory/Morley.htm

27. *Parish Magazine,* March 1883

28. *York Herald,* May 9th 1885

29. Snell and Ell, *op.cit.,* 354

30. Knightbridge Library W1/242

31. Chadwick, *The Victorian Church, Vol. 1,* 333

32. *Parish Magazine,* October 1886

33. *Essex Review*, Vol. XLVII, October 1938, "The Churchwardens' Book of St Mary's"
34. *Chelmsford Diocese Year Book and Clergy List*, 1915
35. Knightbridge Library W1/395
36. *Parish Magazine*, September 1882
37. *Parish Magazine*, January 1888
38. Grieve, *op.cit.*, 348, 371
39. *Parish Magazine*, September 1882
40. *Parish Magazine*, January 1910

Chapter 3 The Charitable Church

1. Gordon, *A Regional History of the Railways of Great Britain, Volume 5 The Eastern Counties*, 23
2. *Parish Magazine*, August 1879, October 1912 and November 1912
3. *Parish Magazine*, May 1894
4. *Parish Magazine*, September 1912
5. *Parish Magazine*, April 1887
6. *Parish Magazine*, September 1881
7. *Parish Magazine*, November 1883
8. *Parish Magazine*, December 1883
9. Grieve, *The Sleepers and the Shadows*, Vol. 2, 269
10. Ibid., 322-3
11. Ibid., 114
12. Ibid., 368
13. *Parish Magazine*, January 1888 and April 1892
14. *Parish Magazine*, February 1893
15. *Parish Magazine*, August 1914
16. *Parish Magazine*, June 1901
17. *Parish Magazine*, January 1895
18. *Parish Magazine*, April 1895
19. *Parish Magazine*, April 1905 and October 1907
20. *Parish Magazine*, April 1889
21. *Parish Magazine*, June 1900
22. *Essex County Standard*, April 28th 1900
23. *Parish Magazine*, January 1911
24. *Parish Magazine*, January 1912
25. *Chelmsford Chronicle*, April 10th 1874
26. Parish *Magazine*, May 1904
27. *Parish Magazine*, June 1896

Chapter 4 The Poor Relation
1. Chadwick, *The Victorian Church Part 1*, 4
2. Beeson, *The Bishops*, 154
3. Barrett, *Sketches of Church Life*, 320
4. Chadwick, "The Victorian Diocese of St. Albans" in *Cathedral City, St. Albans Ancient and Modern*, 79
5. Beeson, *op.cit.*, 145
6. Chadwick, "The Victorian Diocese of St. Albans", 75
7. Barrett, *op.cit.*, 321
8. Sanders and Pease-Watkin, Oxford Dictionary of National Biography, *Edmund Beckett*
9. Chadwick "The Victorian Diocese", 84
10. Ibid., 85
11. *Essex Church News*, January 1938 in Knightbridge Library AAAp 262.3
12. *Household Words*, Issue 390, September 12th 1857
13. Chadwick, "The Victorian Diocese", 96

Chapter 5 The East Anglian Plan
1. *Essex Church News*, January 1938 in Knightbridge Library AAAp 262.3
2. Gibbs, Oxford Dictionary of National Biography, *Bishop Edgar Jacob*
3. *Hansard*, May 4th 1905
4. Snell and Ell, *Rival Jerusalems*, 64
5. Knightbridge Library, W1/41 AAA

Chapter 6 Is Braintree the Hub of the Universe?
1. *Hansard*, March 3rd 1909
2. Knightbridge Library, W1/52
3. Knightbridge Library, W1/48
4. Holden, *Essex Archaeology and History 26 (1995)*, 205-221
5. Taylor, *English History 1914-1945*, 249
6. Coleman, *The Church of England in the Mid-Nineteenth Century*, 27
7. Gordon, *A Regional History of the Railways of Great Britain, Volume 5, The Eastern Counties*, 121
8. Ibid., 120-1
9. *Victoria County History of Essex, Volume 16*

Chapter 7 A mess of Chelmsford pottage
1. Knightbridge Library, W1/42 AAA P270
2. Knightbridge Library, W1/45

3. Knightbridge Library, W1/44 for invitation and subsequent replies
4. Hewitt, *A History of the Diocese of Chelmsford*, 45
5. Knightbridge Library, W1/49

Chapter 8 A Parliamentary Marathon
1. Norman, *Church and Society in England 1770-1970*, 273
2. Hastings, *A History of Christianity 1920-2000*, 51
3. Ibid., 53
4. Hewitt, *A History of the Diocese of Chelmsford*, 59
5. The Sheffield Bishopric http://youle.info/history/fh_material/Making_of_Sheffield/8-BISH.TXT
6. *The Times*, September 4th 1913
7. Hewitt, *op.cit.*, 50
8. Ibid., 46
9. Moses, *Essex, 'full of profitable things'*, 106
10. *Essex Churchman*, July 1977
11. Gowing, *John Edwin Watts-Ditchfield, First Bishop of Chelmsford*, passim
12. Bearman, *John Watts-Ditchfield*, Oxford Dictionary of National Biography
13. Knightbridge Library W1/62 AAAp 276, *Some Reminiscences*
14. *Essex Weekly News*, April 24th 1914
15. Knightbridge Library W1/62 AAAp 276, *Some Reminiscences*

Chapter 9 Town or City
1. Beckett, *City Status in the British Isles 1830-2002*, 25-6
2. Ibid., 30-1
3. Ibid., 36-7
4. Ibid., 39-40
5. Ibid., 86

Chapter 10 Willingly to War
1. *Daily Graphic*, April 20[th]1911
2. *Parish Magazine*, June 1913
3. *Parish Magazine*, October 1913
4. *Parish Magazine,* July 1913
5. *Parish Magazine*, November 1917
6. *Parish Magazine,* January 1915
7. *Parish Magazine,* March 1915
8. Knightbridge Library CHEp 726.6 Wykeham Chancellor, *A Short History of the Church of St Mary*, 1938

9. Wilkinson, *The Church of England and the First World War*, 7
10. *Parish Magazine*, December 1914
11. Knightbridge Library W1/21
12. Wilkinson, *op.cit.*, 30
13. Ibid., 32
14. Ibid., 39
15. Quoted in Rusiecki, *The Impact of Catastrophe; the people of Essex and the First World War*, 98
16. *Chelmsford Diocesan Chronicle*, February 1916
17. Holmes, *Tommy, The British Soldier on the Western Front 1914-1918*, 514
18. Wilkinson, *op.cit.*, 217
19. Beeson, *The Deans*, 141
20. Quoted from the *Harwich Daily Standard* in Rusiecki, *op.cit.*, 98
21. *Chelmsford Diocesan Chronicle*, January 1915
22. *Chelmsford Diocesan Chronicle*, September 1915
23. *Chelmsford Diocesan Chronicle*, April 1915
24. *Essex County Chronicle*, March 26th 1915
25. *Essex County Chronicle*, September 11th 1914
26. Witham War Memorial and Commonwealth War Graves Commission www.cwgc.org
27. Rusiecki, *op.cit.*, 129
28. *Parish Magazine*, May 1916
29. *Chelmsford Diocese Year Book and Clergy List*, 1915
30. *Chelmsford Diocesan Chronicle*, February 1915
31. *Chelmsford Diocesan Chronicle*, April 1915
32. *Chelmsford Diocesan Chronicle*, February 1916
33. *Parish Magazine*, March 1915
34. *Chelmsford Diocesan Chronicle*, April 1915
35. Rusiecki, *op.cit.*, 25, 63-64
36. *Parish Magazine*, January 1916
37. *Parish Magazine*, May 1916
38. *Parish Magazine*, May 1901
39. *Parish Magazine*, February 1915
40. *Parish Magazine*, November 1916
41. *Parish Magazine*, September 1915
42. *Chelmsford Diocesan Chronicle*, November 1916
43. *Parish Magazine*, November 1916
44. *Chelmsford Diocesan Chronicle*, November 1917

45. Rusiecki, *op.cit.*, 302 and *Chelmsford Diocesan Chronicle*, November 1916
46. *The Times* April 18th 1916; Wilkinson, *op.cit.*, 248

Chapter 11 The National Mission
1. Wilkinson, *The Church of England and the First World War*, 76
2. Wilkinson *op.cit.*, 248; *The Times*, April 18th 1916
3. *Parish Magazine*, January 1917
4. Grimley, Oxford Dictionary of National Biography, *Herbert Hensley Henson*
5. Wilkinson, *op.cit.*, 77
6. Rusiecki, op.cit., 66 quoting the *Essex County Chronicle*, October 1916
7. Clark, *Echoes of the Great War*, 115
8. Ibid., 150
9. *Chelmsford Diocesan Chronicle*, September 1916
10. Rusiecki, *op.cit.*, 224 and *Essex County Chronicle* August 11th 1916
11. *Chelmsford Diocesan Chronicle*, November 1916
12. *Parish Magazine*, January 1917
13. *Chelmsford Diocesan Chronicle*, November 1918
14. *Chelmsford Diocesan Chronicle*, November 1917
15. *Parish Magazine*, November 1916
16. *Parish Magazine*, January 1917
17. *Chelmsford Diocesan Chronicle*, January 1917
18. *Chelmsford Diocesan Chronicle*, May 1917
19. *Chelmsford Diocesan Chronicle*, March 1917
20. Ibid.
21. *Chelmsford Diocesan Chronicle*, February 1917
22. *Chelmsford Diocesan Chronicle*, May 1918
23. *Chelmsford Diocesan Chronicle*, October 1931
24. *Chelmsford Diocesan Chronicle*, February 1918
25. *Chelmsford Diocesan Chronicle*, December 1918
26. Essex Record Office DB/7 quoted in Rusiecki, *op.cit.*, 147
27. *Parish Magazine*, July 1917
28. *Parish Magazine*, August 1917
29. *Parish Magazine*, November 1916; Psalm 46 verse 11

Chapter 12 The Crusading Bishop
1. *Chelmsford Diocesan Chronicle*, July 1919
2. *Chelmsford Diocesan Chronicle*, August 1919
3. *Parish Magazine*, December 1918

4. *Parish Magazine,* May 1920
5. *Parish Magazine,* January 1919
6. *Chelmsford Diocesan Chronicle,* March 1919
7. *Chelmsford Diocesan Chronicle,* January 1919
8. *Chelmsford Diocesan Chronicle,* February 1919
9. Ibid.
10. *Chelmsford Diocesan Chronicle,* May 1923
11. *Chelmsford Diocesan Chronicle,* April 1919
12. *Chelmsford Diocesan Chronicle,* February 1923
13. *Chelmsford Diocesan Chronicle,* August and September 1919
14. *Chelmsford Diocesan Chronicle,* January 1922
15. *Parish Magazine,* September 1919
16. Norman, *Church and Society in England 1770-1970,* 231
17. *Chelmsford Diocesan Chronicle,* September 1919
18. *Chelmsford Diocesan Chronicle,* February 1919
19. *Parish Magazine,* February 1920
20. *Chelmsford Diocesan Chronicle,* December 1922
21. *Parish Magazine,* January 1923
22. Nicholson's original plans are in the Knightbridge Library: see also *The Cathedral Church of St Mary the Virgin Chelmsford,* a pamphlet issued by the Cathedral Committee 1920, Essex Record Office C9(B)
23. *Chelmsford Diocesan Chronicle,* June 1920
24. *Chelmsford Diocesan Chronicle,* December 1920
25. Sadgrove in *Dreaming Spires,* 85-7
26. *Parish Magazine,* October 1919
27. *Parish Magazine,* January 1922
28. *Parish Magazine,* June 1921
29. *Parish Magazine,* August 1922
30. *Chelmsford Diocesan Chronicle,* September 1922
31. *Parish Magazine,* February 1921
32. *Parish Magazine,* June 1921
33. *Parish Magazine,* January 1923
34. *Parish Magazine,* December 1923
35. *Chelmsford Diocesan Chronicle,* June 1923
36. *Parish Magazine,* August 1923
37. Hastings, *A History of English Christianity 1920-2000,* 56
38. *Chelmsford Diocesan Chronicle,* August 1923
39. Bearman, Oxford Dictionary of National Biography, *Bishop John Watts-Ditchfield*

COMING OF AGE

Chapter 13 Exhaustion, extension and excursions

1. Hylson-Smith, *Evangelicals in the Church of England 1734-1984*, 247
2. Knightbridge Library, CHEp270, Gerard Hockley, *Early Reminiscences of a Cathedral Server*
3. *The Times*, October 4th 1923
4. *The Times*, January 14th 1925
5. *Parish Magazine*, November 1923
6. *Parish Magazine*, December 1923
7. *Parish Magazine*, February 1924
8. *Parish Magazine*, August 1925
9. *Parish Magazine*, June 1926
10. Knightbridge Library, CHE 783.8, Choir Minute Book 1874-1954
11. *Parish Magazine*, March 1926
12. Knightbridge Library, W1/261 CHEp 262.3, Response to 1926 Commission Report of Enquiry questionnaire
13. *Parish Magazine*, July 1924
14. *Chelmsford Diocesan Chronicle*, July 1925
15. *Parish Magazine*, July 1924
16. *Chelmsford Diocesan Chronicle*, December 1925
17. *Chelmsford Diocesan Chronicle*, February 1925
18. *Chelmsford Diocesan Chronicle*, June 1925
19. Knightbridge Library, W1/258, 1914 Stalls in the Cathedral Church
20. *Chelmsford Diocesan Chronicle*, December 1927
21. *Parish Magazine*, June 1926
22. *Chelmsford Diocesan Chronicle*, November 1926
23. *Parish Magazine*, December 1927
24. *Parish Magazine*, January 1928
25. *Chelmsford Diocesan Chronicle*, May 1928
26. *Chelmsford Diocesan Chronicle*, November 1927
27. *Chelmsford Diocesan Chronicle*, December 1927
28. Knightbridge Library, W1/405
29. *Parish Magazine*, November 1928
30. *Parish Magazine*, January 1925
31. *Parish Magazine*, December 1925
32. *Parish Magazine*, February 1925
33. *Parish Magazine*, August 1925
34. *Parish Magazine*, December 1925
35. *Cathedral News*, November 1989
36. *Parish Magazine*, August 1924

373

37. *Parish Magazine,* June 1925

38. Ibid.

39. *Parish Magazine,* August 1925

40. *Parish Magazine,* December 1925

41. *Parish Magazine,* August 1926

42. *Chelmsford Diocesan Chronicle,* January 1926

43. Knightbridge Library W1.125A, letter to Terry Mobbs

44. *Essex Churchman,* April 1953

45. Hastings, *A History of English Christianity 1920-2000,* 206

Chapter 14 Rector to Provost

1. Wilson, *Reflections of a Back-Bench Bishop,* 8

2. *Chelmsford Diocesan Chronicle,* February 1929

3. *Chelmsford Diocesan Chronicle,* March 1929

4. Wilson, *op.cit.,* 26

5. Ibid., 27

6. Ibid., 28

7. Ibid., 30-31

8. Essex Record Office, D/CN 6/3

9. Knightbridge Library, CHEp270, Gerard Hockley, *Reminiscences of a Cathedral Server*

10. Hewitt, *A History of the Diocese of Chelmsford,* 104

11. *Chelmsford Diocesan Chronicle,* March 1950

12. Knightbridge Library, W1/515, letter from the Bishop, February 9th 1929 and *Essex Chronicle,* February 22nd 1929.

13. *Chelmsford Diocesan Chronicle,* January 1997

14. *Essex Weekly News,* November 22nd 1929

15. Knightbridge Library, W1/405

16. Ibid.

17. *Chelmsford Diocesan Chronicle,* December 1929

18. *Parish Magazine,* November and December 1931

19. *Parish Magazine,* January 1932

20. Knightbridge Library CHEp270 Gerard Hockley *op.cit.*

21. *Parish Magazine,* April 1932

22. *Parish Magazine,* June 1932

23. *Parish Magazine,* August 1932

24. *Parish Magazine,* May 1934

25. *Parish Magazine,* May 1933

26. Knightbridge Library, W1/405

27. *Parish Magazine,* April 1933
28. *Essex Chronicle,* letter, September 26th 1952
29. *Parish Magazine,* July and October 1932
30. *Essex Chronicle,* April 10th 1874
31. *Essex Chronicle,* April 17th 1874
32. Bettley and Pevsner, *The Buildings of England*
33. *Parish Magazine,* August 1930
34. Essex Record Office, D/P 607: D/P 138/28/11,12; *Chelmsford Diocesan Chronicle,* January 1929
35. *Parish Magazine,* May 1931
36. *Parish Magazine,* August 1930
37. *Parish Magazine,* October 1930
38. *Parish Magazine,* May 1929
39. *Parish Magazine,* November 1930
40. *Parish Magazine,* August 1930
41. *Chelmsford Diocesan Chronicle,* January 1931
42. *Chelmsford Diocesan Chronicle,* May 1931
43. *Chelmsford Diocesan Chronicle,* May 1933
44. *Chelmsford Diocesan Chronicle,* June 1931
45. Ibid.
46. *Chelmsford Diocesan Chronicle,* March 1931
47. *Chelmsford Diocesan Chronicle,* June 1931
48. *Chelmsford Diocesan Chronicle,* March 1933
49. *Chelmsford Diocesan Chronicle,* March 1931
50. *Parish Magazine,* July 1932
51. *Parish Magazine,* August 1930
52. *Essex Chronicle,* September 26th 1930
53. *Chelmsford Diocesan Chronicle,* January 1933
54. *Essex Chronicle,* April 17th 1931
55. *Chelmsford Diocesan Chronicle,* August 1932
56. *Cheltenham Chronicle,* October 15th 1932
57. *Chelmsford Diocesan Chronicle,* May 1934
58. *Chelmsford Diocesan Chronicle,* January 1934
59. *Parish Magazine,* November 1931
60. *Parish Magazine,* January 1932
61. *Parish Magazine,* January 1935
62. *Parish Magazine,* October 1934
63. *Parish Magazine,* January 1935

Chapter 15 The Bolshie Bishop

1. Wilson, *Reflections of a Backbench Bishop*, 21
2. *Parish Magazine*, December 1936
3. Hastings, *A History of Christianity 1920-2000*, 221
4. *Parish Magazine*, August 1935
5. *Parish Magazine*, January 1936
6. *Parish Magazine*, March 1936
7. *Parish Magazine*, May 1936
8. *Parish Magazine*, December 1936
9. *Parish Magazine*, July 1936
10. *Parish Magazine*, August 1936
11. *Parish Magazine*, April 1936
12. *Parish Magazine*, October 1938
13. Medhurst and Moyser, *Church and Politics in a Secular Age*, 95
14. Wilkinson, Oxford Dictionary of National Biography, *Cosmo Lang*
15. Hastings, *op.cit.*, 253
16. Wilson, *op.cit.*, 8-9
17. *Chelmsford Diocesan Chronicle*, February 1934
18. Wilson, *op.cit.*, 22
19. Essex Record Office C9B, *The Church in Essex: 1952 Commission to examine the financial needs and resources of the diocese*
20. *The Times*, July 17th 1961
21. *Parish Magazine*, July 1951
22. *The Times*, January 23rd 1932
23. *The Times*, August 14th 1936
24. *The Times*, August 24th 1936
25. *Hull Daily Mail*, July 20th 1948
26. *Hull Daily Mail*, December 23rd 1936
27. *Chelmsford Diocesan Chronicle*, April 1934
28. Buchanan, *Britain and the Spanish Civil War*, 171
29. *The Daily Telegraph*, May 16th 2007
30. *The Times*, May 20th 1938
31. McCulloch, *A History of Christianity*, 940
32. *The Times*, May 23rd 1938
33. *The Times*, May 27th 1938
34. *The Times*, January 30th 1939
35. Wilson, *op.cit.*, 12
36. Ibid., 13-14

37. *Chelmsford Diocesan Chronicle*, July 1943

38. *Chelmsford Diocesan Chronicle*, May 1944

39. *Chelmsford Diocesan Chronicle*, September 1944

40. *Essex Newsman*, November 7th 1944

41. Wilson, *op.cit.*, 19

42. *Parish Magazine*, January 1935

43. *Parish Magazine*, May 1935

44. *Parish Magazine*, June 1935

45. *Parish Magazine*, July 1935

46. *Parish Magazine*, October 1936

47. *Parish Magazine*, January 1938

48. *Parish Magazine*, June 1937

49. *Parish Magazine*, February 1938

50. *Parish Magazine*, November 1938

51. *Parish Magazine*, September 1939

52. Wilson, *op.cit.*, 13

53. *Parish Magazine*, August 1939

54. Begent, *Chelmsford at War*, 1

55. *Parish Magazine*, October 1939

Chapter 16 Wearily to War

1. *Parish Magazine*, October 1939

2. *Parish Magazine*, November 1939

3. *Parish Magazine*, October 1939

4. Ibid.

5. *Parish Magazine*, November 1939

6. *Parish Magazine*, September 1940

7. *Parish Magazine*, October 1939

8. Begent, *Chelmsford at War*, 60

9. *Parish Magazine*, December 1939

10. *Parish Magazine*, May 1947

11. *Cathedral News*, November 1989

12. *Parish Magazine*, April 1940

13. *Cathedral News*, November 1989

14. *Parish Magazine*, April 1940

15. *Parish Magazine*, June 1940

16. Begent, *op.cit.*, 2

17. *Parish Magazine*, August 1940

18. *Parish Magazine*, October 1937
19. *Derby Daily Telegraph*, February 20ᵗʰ 1939
20. *Parish Magazine*, November 1939
21. *Parish Magazine*, December 1939
22. *Parish Magazine*, July 1940
23. Ibid.
24. Begent, *op.cit.*, 4
25. Ibid., 10
26. *Parish Magazine*, November 1940
27. *Parish Magazine*, December 1941
28. Commonwealth War Graves Commission website www.cwgc.org
29. Begent, *op.cit.*, 18
30. Ibid., 30
31. Knightbridge Library, CHEp 726.6 "Oddities of Chelmsford Cathedral" by Dick Swan reprinted from *The Polytechnic Magazine*
32. *Daily Telegraph*, March 21ˢᵗ 2011
33. *Chelmsford Diocesan Chronicle*, April 1944
34. *Chelmsford Diocesan Chronicle*, February 1943
35. *Chelmsford Diocesan Chronicle*, March 1943
36. *Chelmsford Diocesan Chronicle*, August 1943
37. *Chelmsford Diocesan Chronicle*, September 1943
38. *Chelmsford Diocesan Chronicle*, August 1944
39. *Chelmsford Diocesan Chronicle*, September 1943
40. *Parish Magazine*, February 1944
41. Begent, *op.cit.*, 53
42. Ibid., 58
43. *Parish Magazine*, September 1944
44. *Essex Chronicle*, January 12ᵗʰ 1945
45. *Chelmsford Diocesan Chronicle*, October 1944
46. Ibid.
47. *The Times*, September 8ᵗʰ 1944
48. *Chelmsford Diocesan Chronicle*, October 1944
49. *Chelmsford Diocesan Chronicle*, March 1945
50. *Parish Magazine*, June 1945
51. *Parish Magazine*, July 1945
52. *Parish Magazine*, May 1945
53. *Parish Magazine*, June 1945

Chapter 17 Dirt, damage and departures

1. *Parish Magazine,* June 1950
2. *Parish Magazine,* September 1947
3. *Parish Magazine,* April 1947
4. *Chelmsford Diocesan Chronicle,* October 1947
5. *Parish Magazine,* May 1946
6. *Parish Magazine,* September 1947
7. *Parish Magazine,* April 1947
8. *The Times,* June 27th 1946
9. *Parish Magazine,* September 1947
10. Knightbridge Library, Improvement Committee 29/2/58
11. *Cathedral News,* December 1971
12. *Parish Magazine,* May 1946
13. *Parish Magazine,* September 1946
14. *Parish Magazine,* May 1946
15. *Cathedral News,* March 1999
16. Chadwick, *The Victorian Church, Part 2,* 383
17. *Chelmsford Diocesan Chronicle,* August 1946
18. *Chelmsford Diocesan Chronicle,* September 1945
19. *Chelmsford Diocesan Chronicle,* June 1945
20. *Chelmsford Diocesan Chronicle,* July 1945
21. *Chelmsford Diocesan Chronicle,* March 1950
22. Welsby, *The History of the Church of England 1945-1980,* 45
23. Ibid., 46
24. *Chelmsford Diocesan Chronicle,* December 1945
25. *Chelmsford Diocesan Chronicle,* November 1947
26. *Chelmsford Diocesan Chronicle,* April 1949
27. *Chelmsford Diocesan Chronicle,* June 1949
28. *Chelmsford Diocesan Chronicle,* December 1949
29. *Chelmsford Diocesan Chronicle,* July 1949
30. *Chelmsford Diocesan Chronicle,* January 1946
31. *Hull Daily Mail,* December 20th 1947.
32. Foster, *A History of the Diocese of Brentwood 1917-1992,* 3
33. On-line *Catholic Encyclopaedia* www.newadvent.org/cathen
34. *Chelmsford Diocesan Chronicle,* April 1946
35. Foster, *op.cit.,* 85
36. Ibid., 75-6
37. *Chelmsford Diocesan Chronicle,* April 1946

38. *The Times,* November 19th 1949
39. *Chelmsford Diocesan Chronicle,* December 1946
40. *Chelmsford Diocesan Chronicle,* March 1948
41. *Chelmsford Diocesan Chronicle,* September 1946
42. *Chelmsford Diocesan Chronicle,* October 1946
43. *Chelmsford Diocesan Chronicle,* December 1948
44. *Parish Magazine,* October 1948
45. *Parish Magazine,* November 1948
46. *Parish Magazine,* October 1946
47. *Parish Magazine,* February 1947
48. *Parish Magazine,* June 1947
49. Ibid.
50. *Chelmsford Diocesan Chronicle,* December 1948
51. *Parish Magazine,* January 1949
52. Hewitt, *A History of the Diocese of Chelmsford,* 104
53. *Chelmsford Diocesan Chronicle,* July 1950
54. Hewitt, *op.cit.,* 137
55. *Essex Chronicle,* September 29th 1950
56. *Essex Chronicle,* November 3rd 1950
57. Ibid.
58. *Chelmsford Diocesan Chronicle,* October 1946
59. *Chelmsford Diocesan Chronicle,* December 1950

Chapter 18 All change

1. *Essex Chronicle,* June 3rd 1949
2. *Parish Magazine,* December 1948
3. *Parish Magazine,* September 1949
4. *Cathedral Review,* November 1949
5. *Parish Magazine,* March 1949
6. *Daily Telegraph,* April 1st 2010
7. *Cathedral Review,* August and September 1950
8. *Cathedral News,* Summer 1978
9. Ibid. and *Cathedral Review,* December 1950
10. *Cathedral Review,* January 1951
11. *Cathedral News,* Summer 1978
12. *Cathedral Review,* May 1951
13. Hewitt, *A History of the Diocese of Chelmsford,* 139
14. Ibid., 137-8
15. Ibid., 139

16. *Chelmsford Diocesan Chronicle,* February 1951
17. *Chelmsford Diocesan Chronicle,* November 1951
18. Hewitt, *op.cit.,* 127
19. *Cathedral Review,* October 1951
20. *Cathedral Review,* October 1951; *Cathedral News,* July 1955
21. Knightbridge Library W1/429
22. *Cathedral News,* January 1957
23. *Chelmsford Diocesan Chronicle,* November 1951
24. Hewitt, *op.cit.,* 143
25. *Chelmsford Diocesan Chronicle,* November 1951
26. Hewitt, *op.cit.,* 142
27. *Cathedral Review,* August 1951
28. *Cathedral Review,* February 1953
29. *Cathedral News,* April 1953: www.rscm.com/info_ resources /news/Coronation. php

Chapter 19 A Colourful Cathedral

1. Hewitt, *A History of the Diocese of Chelmsford,* 153
2. *Essex Churchman,* December 1953
3. *Cathedral News,* July 1956
4. Details taken from information boards at the Jamestown site
5. Smith, *Pilgrims and Adventurers,* 24-5
6. Ibid., 42-3
7. Ibid., 29
8. *The Times,* October 19th 1953
9. *Cathedral News,* November 1953
10. Hewitt, *op.cit.,* 69-70
11. Knightbridge Library, Cathedral Chapter Minutes April 23rd 1971
12. *Essex Churchman,* October 1954
13. *Cathedral News,* April 1954
14. *Cathedral News,* May 1955
15. *Cathedral News,* April 1953
16. *Cathedral News,* April 1955
17. *Cathedral News,* September 1955
18. *Cathedral News,* August 1954
19. *Cathedral News,* September 1955
20. *Essex Churchman,* July 1956
21. *Cathedral News,* May 1958
22. *Cathedral News,* September 1955

23. *Cathedral News,* July 1956
24. *Cathedral News,* June 1956
25. Hewitt, *op.cit.*, 154
26. *Essex Churchman,* July 1956
27. *Cathedral News,* June 1954
28. Hewitt, *op.cit.*, 154
29. *Cathedral News,* September 1958
30. *Cathedral News,* July 1957
31. Chadwick, "The Victorian Diocese of St. Albans", 94
32. *Cathedral News,* September 1957
33. *Cathedral News,* July and September 1957
34. *Cathedral News,* December 1957
35. *Cathedral News,* November 1958
36. *Cathedral News,* September 1958
37. *Cathedral News,* October 1958
38. *Cathedral News,* January 1959
39. *Cathedral News,* February 1959
40. *Cathedral News,* August 1959
41. *Cathedral News,* March 1961
42. *Cathedral News,* December 1960
43. Ibid.
44. *Cathedral News,* June 1962
45. *Cathedral News,* January 1964
46. *Cathedral News,* July 1941
47. *Cathedral News,* October 1986
48. Welsby, *The Church of England 1945-1980*, 29
49. *Essex Churchman,* October 1954
50. Hewitt, *op.cit.*, 155
51. Hastings, *A History of English Christianity 1920-2000*, 438
52. Ibid., 437
53. Ibid., 255
54. Welsby, *op.cit.*, 42
55. Ibid., 72
56. Hastings, *op.cit.*, 522
57. *Essex Churchman,* December 1953
58. Hastings, *op.cit.*, 467
59. *Independent*, June 4th 1993
60. Hewitt, *op,cit.*, 141
61. Welsby, *op.cit.*, 94

Chapter 20 A Beautifully Enclosed World

1. Hewitt, *A History of the Diocese of Chelmsford*, 166
2. Ibid., 165
3. Ibid., 167
4. Quoted by John Buchanan, Bishop of Woolwich, Keene Lecture, November 8th 2000
5. *Cathedral News*, January 1962
6. Ibid.
7. *Cathedral News*, July 1994
8. Conversation with John Jordan; *Cathedral News* June and September 1963
9. *Cathedral News*, August 1963
10. *Cathedral News*, October 1963
11. *Cathedral News*, January 1965
12. *Cathedral News*, November 1964
13. Conversation with John Jordan
14. Welsby, *The Church of England 1945-1980*, 104
15. *Essex Churchman*, March 1963
16. *Cathedral News*, September 1962
17. *Cathedral News*, March 1964
18. *Cathedral News*, January 1964
19. Foster, *A History of the Diocese of Brentwood 1917-1992*, 85
20. *Cathedral News*, January 1964
21. *Cathedral Life*, October 2009
22. *Cathedral News*, June 1964
23. http://homepages.which.net/~radical.faith/reviews/robinson.htm
24. *Church Times*, January 22nd 1963 quoted in Welsby, *op.cit.*, 113
25. Welsby, *op.cit.*, 113
26. Ibid., 131-5
27. *Cathedral News*, February 1964
28. *Cathedral News*, May 1964
29. *Essex Churchman*, March 1962
30. *Cathedral News*, December 1964
31. *Cathedral News*, December 1965
32. *Cathedral News*, June 1963
33. *Cathedral News*, September 1963
34. *Cathedral News*, April 1964
35. *Cathedral News*, June 1964
36. *Cathedral News*, August 1966
37. Knightbridge Library, W1/429

38. *Cathedral News,* October 1965 and Knightbridge Library, Cathedral Gift Book 1958-63
39. *Cathedral News,* February 1991
40. *Cathedral News,* January 1966
41. *Cathedral News,* July 1966
42. *Cathedral News,* April 1967
43. *Cathedral News,* March 1971
44. Graham,*The Church Hesitant, A Portrait of the Church of England Today,* 117

Chapter 21 Time of Crisis
1. *Chelmsford Diocesan Gazette,* June 1968
2. Hewitt, *A History of the Diocese of Chelmsford,* 169-70
3. *Essex Churchman,* April 1963
4. *Essex Churchman,* July 1964
5. *Essex Churchman,* June 1965
6. Hewitt, *op.cit.,* 181-2
7. *Essex Chronicle,* November 4th 1968
8. Welsby, *The Church of England 1945-1980,* 219
9. Ibid., 220
10. *Essex Churchman,* August 1969
11. *Cathedral News,* April 1969
12. Hewitt, *op.cit.,* 184
13. *Chelmsford Diocesan Gazette,* December 1970
14. Hewitt, *op.cit.,* 212-3
15. *Cathedral News,* May 1967
16. *Cathedral News,* July 1967
17. *Cathedral News,* June 1967
18. Graham, *The Church Hesitant, A Portrait of the Church of England Today,* 214
19. *Cathedral News,* August 1967
20. *Cathedral News,* October 1968
21. *Cathedral News,* April 1968
22. *Cathedral News,* August 1968
23. *Cathedral News,* May 1969
24. *Cathedral News,* October 1968
25. *Cathedral News,* November 1969
26. *Cathedral News,* February 1969
27. *Cathedral News,* July 1969
28. *Cathedral News,* September 1970
29. *Cathedral News,* September 1968

30. *Cathedral News,* April 1968
31. *Cathedral News,* January 1969
32. *Cathedral News,* June 1969
33. *Cathedral News,* February 1971
34. *Cathedral News,* February 1970
35. *Cathedral News,* May 1974
36. *Cathedral News,* October 1970
37. *Cathedral News,* November 1970
38. *Cathedral News,* February 1970
39. *Cathedral News,* February 1970: Knightbridge Library W1/372, Dykes-Bower Churchyard Report
40. Knightbridge Library, Chelmsford Planning Survey 1945, 26-7
41. *Chelmsford Diocesan Gazette,* 1971

Chapter 22 Finding a Role

1. Hewitt, *A History of the Diocese of Chelmsford,* 199-200
2. *Essex Churchman,* December 1979
3. *Essex Churchman,* September 1971
4. Knightbridge Library CHEp 270, Gerard Hockley, *Early Reminiscences of a Cathedral Server,*
5. *Essex Churchman,* March 1975
6. Hewitt, *op.cit.,* 202
7. Ibid.
8. Ibid., 204
9. *Chelmsford Diocesan Gazette,* June 1972
10. *Essex Churchman,* March 1976
11. *Essex Churchman,* March 1977
12. *Cathedral News,* February 1973
13. *Cathedral News,* January 1973
14. Ibid.
15. *Cathedral News,* Summer 1974
16. *Cathedral News,* July 1973
17. Conversation with Peter Cross
18. *Essex Churchman,* May 1976
19. *Essex Churchman,* April 1977
20. *Cathedral News,* April 1973
21. *Cathedral News,* December 1973
22. *Cathedral News,* January 1974
23. *Cathedral News,* April 1977

24. *Cathedral News,* September 1972 and Knightbridge Library W1/240 CHEp 262.15
25. *Cathedral News,* January 1973
26. *Cathedral News,* November 1973
27. Jeffery in *Cathedrals Now,* 4
28. *Cathedral News,* October 1973
29. *Cathedral News,* October 1972
30. *Essex Churchman,* May 1977
31. *Cathedral News,* November 1974
32. Hewitt, *op.cit.,* 227
33. *Cathedral News,* February 1974
34. *Cathedral News,* May 2002
35. *Chelmsford Weekly News,* November 28th 1974
36. *Essex Churchman,* July 1977
37. *The Tower,* Ingatestone and Fryerning Parish Magazaine, September 1977 (courtesy of Martin Connop Price)
38. Text of Michael Yorke's funeral eulogy, July 7th 1998 (courtesy of Martin Connop Price)

Chapter 23 Not a Closed Shop
1. *Essex Churchman,* February 1978
2. *Cathedral News,* Easter 1978
3. *Cathedral News,* April 1979
4. Hewitt, *A History of the Diocese of Chelmsford,* 228
5. *Cathedral News,* Easter 1978
6. Brian Green in *CrossWay* Winter 2003 No 87 and David Self in *Church Times* Issue 7560 February 8th 2008
7. *Essex Churchman,* November 1978
8. *Cathedral News,* June 1978
9. Ibid.
10. *Cathedral News,* October 1980
11. *Cathedral News,* November 1980
12. *Cathedral News,* March 1979
13. *Cathedral News,* September 1979
14. *Cathedral News,* Easter 1981
15. *Chelmsford Weekly News,* May 14th 1981
16. *Cathedral News,* July 1981
17. *Cathedral News,* May 1981
18. *Cathedral News,* November 1982

19. *Cathedral News,* January 1982 and conversation with John Moses
20. *Cathedral News,* March 1982
21. Private correspondence to John Moses (courtesy of John Moses)
22. Hilary Connop Price private papers (courtesy of Martin Connop Price)
23. Conversation with Michael Yorke
24. For understanding more fully the micropolitics of the Centre for Research and Training I am indebted to conversations with John Waine, John Moses, Wesley Carr and Michael Yorke
25. Conversation with Michael Yorke
26. Chapter Day address 1982, courtesy of John Moses
27. *Cathedral News,* January 1982
28. Tuckwell, *That Honourable and Gentlemanlike House, a History of King Edward VI Grammar School, Chelmsford, 1551-2008,* 21-4
29. *East Window,* February 1988
30. *Cathedral News,* March 1983
31. *Cathedral News,* January 1993
32. *Cathedral News,* December 1987
33. *Cathedral News,* September 1985
34. *Cathedral News,* November 1983
35. *Cathedral News,* July/August 1984

Chapter 24 Tug of War

1. *Cathedral News,* January 1984
2. *Essex Churchman,* November 1984
3. *Cathedral News,* December 1983
4. *Cathedral News,* October 1984
5. Ibid.
6. *Cathedral News,* January 1987
7. *Cathedral News,* April 1987
8. *East Window,* February 1991
9. *Essex Churchman,* December 1984
10. *Essex Churchman,* June 1985
11. Ibid.
12. *Essex Churchman,* November 1985
13. *East Window,* May 1989
14. *East Window,* March 1989
15. *East Window,* July 1987
16. *Cathedral News,* January 1986
17. *Cathedral News,* March 1986

18. *Essex Churchman,* February 1986
19. *Cathedral News,* June 1984
20. *Cathedral News,* January 1986
21. Furlong, *C of E: The State It's In,* 139
22. *Cathedral News,* Christmas 1984
23. *Cathedral News,* September 1992
24. *Essex Churchman,* September 1985
25. Beeson, *The Bishops,* 45
26. Kennedy, *All in the Mind,* 258
27. *Essex Churchman,* September 1985
28. *Essex Churchman,* October 1985
29. *The Times,* December 11th 1985
30. *Essex Churchman,* February 1986
31. *East Window,* November 1986
32. *East Window,* January 1987
33. *East Window,* October 1994
34. *Cathedral News,* May 1984
35. *Cathedral News,* August 1985
36. *Cathedral News,* August 1986
37. *Cathedral News,* Christmas 1986
38. *Cathedral News,* August 1986
39. *Cathedral News,* December 1987
40. *Cathedral News,* June 1987
41. *Cathedral News,* November 1987
42. Ibid.
43. *Cathedral News,* Summer 1988
44. *Cathedral News,* June 1989
45. *Cathedral News,* July 1989
46. *East Window,* November 1989
47. Essex Record Office A12736 for deposited documents concerning the Cathedral Festival
48. *Cathedral News,* May 1991
49. *Cathedral News,* July 1988
50. *Cathedral News,* June 1989
51. Knightbridge Library, Chapter Minutes, March 13th 1991
52. Moses in *Cathedrals Now,* 66-7
53. Ibid., 71
54. *Cathedral News,* January 1988
55. *East Window,* January 1988

56. *Cathedral News,* May 1989
57. *Cathedral News,* May 1988
58. *Cathedral News,* March 1990
59. *Cathedral News,* November 1988
60. *Cathedral News,* June 1990
61. *East Window,* June 1989

Chapter 25 Music, Money and Mission
1. *Cathedral News,* May 1990
2. Knightbridge Library, Cathedral Chapter Minutes March 20th 1990 and March 13th 1991
3. *Cathedral News,* April 1991
4. *Cathedral News,* December 1999
5. *Cathedral News,* April 1991
6. *Cathedral News,* August 1991
7. *Cathedral News,* May 1991
8. *Cathedral News,* May 1990
9. *East Window,* April 1991
10. *Cathedral News,* January 1992
11. *Cathedral News,* March 1993
12. *Cathedral News,* May 1993
13. *Cathedral News,* August 1993
14. www.ofchoristers.net
15. Tuckwell, *That Honourable and Gentlemanlike House, a History of King Edward VI Grammar School, Chelmsford, 1551-2008,* p 255
16. Knightbridge Library, Chapter Minutes March 20th 1990
17. Lovell, *Number One Millbank; the financial downfall of the Church of England,* 39
18. Ibid., 51
19. Ibid., 63
20. Ibid., 147
21. Ibid., 172-3
22. Ibid., 162
23. Ibid., 160
24. Ibid., 171-2
25. Ibid., 207
26. *East Window,* Aug 1991
27. *East Window,* Aug 1992
28. *East Window,* November 1991
29. *East Window,* August 1991

30. *Cathedral News*, April 1993
31. *Cathedral News*, September 1993
32. Ibid.
33. *Heritage and Renewal*, 172
34. Moses, *Essex, 'full of profitable things'*, 119
35. *Cathedral News*, December 1993
36. *Cathedral News*, June 1994
37. *Cathedral News*, September 1991
38. *Cathedral News*, November 1991
39. *Cathedral News*, June 1989
40. *Cathedral News*, February 1992
41. Graham, *The Church Hesitant, A Portrait of the Church of England Today*, 236
42. *Cathedral News*, November 1992
43. *Cathedral News*, June 1994
44. Brierley, *The Tide is Running Out*, 27
45. Ibid.
46. *Cathedral News*, June 1994
47. *Cathedral News*, November 1991
48. *Cathedral News*, October 1991
49. Ibid.
50. *Cathedral News*, January 1992
51. *Cathedral News*, August 1993
52. *Cathedral News*, November 1996
53. *Mail Online*, May 13th 2004
54. *Cathedral News*, August 1992
55. As told to the author

Chapter 26 Provost to Dean

1. *East Window*, March 1996
2. Interview with John Perry
3. *Cathedral News*, June 1997
4. Quoted in Beeson, *The Deans*, 136
5. *Independent*, December 26th 1995
6. *Independent*, July 17th 1995
7. *Independent*, July 5th 1996
8. *Heritage and Renewal*, 4
9. Ibid., 194
10. *Cathedral Life*, November 2009
11. *Cathedral News*, February 2003

12. *Heritage and Renewal*, 2
13. *Cathedral News*, June 1993
14. *Heritage and Renewal*, 223
15. ESOTEC Research and Consulting, *The Economic and Social Impacts of Cathedrals in England*, 36
16. *Heritage and Renewal*, 43
17. Ibid., 46
18. Ibid., 59
19. Ibid., 72
20. *Independent*, October 12th 1994
21. *Cathedral News*, November 1999
22. *Cathedral News*, January 1998
23. *Cathedral News*, June 1998
24. *Cathedral News*, June 1999
25. *Cathedral News*, March 2000
26. *Cathedral News*, November/December 2000
27. Ibid.
28. *Chelmsford Cathedral*, Heritage House, 1
29. *Cathedral News*, January 2003
30. *Essex Chronicle*, February 17th 1950
31. *Cathedral News*, July 2003
32. *Cathedral Mews*, December 2002: Philip Larkin *The Trees*
33. *Cathedral News*, February 2004
34. *Cathedral News*, April 2004
35. *Cathedral Life*, March 2010
36. *Cathedral News*, February 1997
37. *Cathedral News*, February 1999
38. *East Window*, August 1999
39. *Cathedral News*, May 1998
40. *Cathedral News*, February 2000
41. *Cathedral News*, January 2000
42. *Cathedral Life*, October 2008
43. *Cathedral News*, February 2000
44. *Cathedral News*, February 2001
45. *Cathedral News*, February 1998
46. *Cathedral News*, May 1998
47. *Cathedral News*, October 2001
48. *Cathedral News*, May 2001
49. Essex Record Office A 12736, Cathedral Festival archives

50. *Cathedral Life,* September 2009

51. *Essex Review Vol XLVII,* July 1938, "The Churchwardens' Book of St Mary's"

52. *Cathedral News,* March 1983

53. Tuckwell, *New Hall and its School,* 193

54. *Cathedral Life,* February 2009

55. *Essex Window,* December 1994

56. *Cathedral News,* November 1997

57. *East Window,* January 2003

58. *Cathedral Life,* August/September 2006 and October/November 2006

59. *Cathedral Life,* December 2006/January 2007

60. *Cathedral Life,* June 2009

61. *Cathedral Life,* December 2009

62. Knightbridge Library W/216 CHEp 254.8, Annual Report to the Cathedral Chapter 2004

63. *The Month,* January 2011

64. *Cathedral News,* January 1999

65. *Cathedral News,* June 1999

66. *Cathedral News,* May 2000

67. *Cathedral News,* September 2002

68. *Cathedral News,* January 2001

69. *Cathedral News,* November 2003

70. Graham, *The Church Hesitant,* pp 240-1

71. *Cathedral News,* January 1999

72. *Cathedral News,* March 2000

INDEX

I

N

9011294R00246

Printed in Great Britain
by Amazon.co.uk, Ltd.,
Marston Gate.